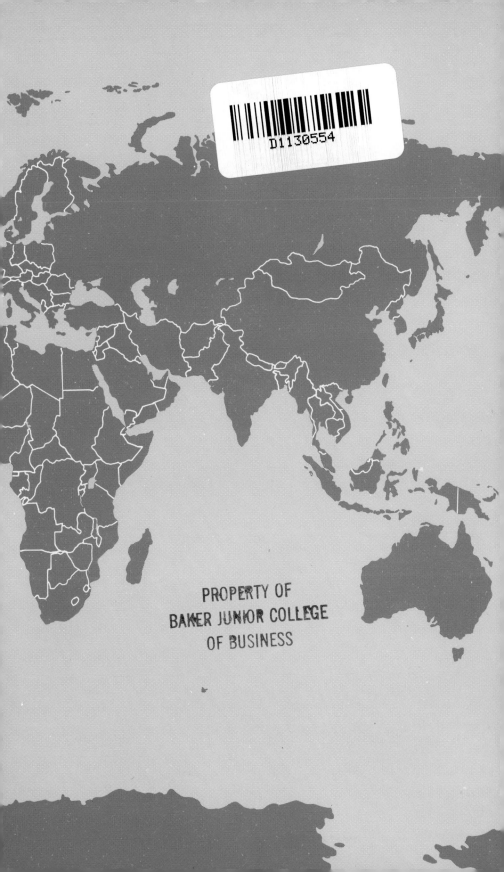

PROPERTY OF
BAKER JUNIOR COLLEGE
OF BUSINESS

Romania
a country study

Foreign Area Studies
The American University
Coauthors
Eugene K. Keefe, Donald W. Bernier,
Lyle E. Brenneman, William Giloane,
James M. Moore, Jr., Neda A. Walpole
Research Completed February 1972

Detail on cover is taken from the state

emblem as depicted on the national
colors. It was prepared by
Julia Stacey under direction of
Michael T. Graham, The American
University, Department of Art.

First Edition, Second Printing: 1979

Library of Congress Catalog Card Number: 72–600095

Headquarters, Department of Army
DA Pam 550-160

For sale by the Superintendent of Documents, U.S. Government Printing Office
Washington, D.C. 20402

Stock No. 008–020–00433–2/Catalog No. D101.22 :550–160

FOREWORD

This volume is one of a continuing series of books written by Foreign Area Studies, The American University, under the Area Handbook Program. The last page of this book provides a listing of other country studies published. Each book in the series deals with a particular foreign country, describing and analyzing the economic, military, political, and social systems and institutions and examining the interrelationships of those systems and institutions and the ways that they are shaped by cultural factors. Each study is written by a multidisciplinary team of social scientists. The authors seek to provide a basic insight and understanding of the society under observation, striving for a dynamic rather than a static portrayal of it. The study focuses on historical antecedents and on the cultural, political, and socioeconomic characteristics that contribute to cohesion and cleavage within the society. Particular attention is given to the origins and traditions of the people who make up the society, their dominant beliefs and values, their community of interests and the issues on which they are divided, the nature and extent of their involvement with the national institutions, and their attitudes toward each other and toward the social system and political order within which they live.

The contents of the book represent the work of Foreign Area Studies and are not set forth as the official view of the United States government. The authors have sought to adhere to accepted standards of scholarly objectivity. Such corrections, additions, and suggestions for factual or other change that readers may have will be welcomed for use in future revisions.

William Evans-Smith
Director, Foreign Area Studies
The American University
Washington, D.C. 20016

PREFACE

The former Kingdom of Romania emerged from the post-World War II chaos as the Romanian People's Republic, a communist satellite so closely aligned to the policies of the Soviet Union that it often appeared to be ruled from Moscow. During the 1950s, however, Romania cautiously began seeking to loosen its ties to Moscow and to assert some measure of autonomy. The widening Sino-Soviet rift of the early 1960s provided an atmosphere of tension among communist states that the Romanians used to their own advantage by remaining neutral in the communist struggle and by seeking greater contacts with noncommunist states. In internal affairs, the Romanian regime maintained a rigid hold on all elements of the society. In 1965 the regime changed the name of the country to the Socialist Republic of Romania and proclaimed that it was well on the way toward communism. In the early 1970s Romania remains a member of the Soviet-led military and economic alliances but has become known as the most independent member.

The changes wrought by the Communists during a quarter century in power are numerous and far reaching. Despite the desires of the Soviet leaders that Romania remain predominantly agricultural, the new Romanian leadership was determined to industrialize. Enforced socialization and concurrent industrialization brought a host of problems in the political, social, and economic life of the country. Reorientation of the society and the political structure was brought about by force when necessary, but the restructuring of the economy within the framework of the avowed Marxist-Leninist ideology proved to be more difficult and led to problems that had still not been overcome by early 1972.

This handbook attempts to describe the social, political, and economic bases of Romanian society and, more particularly, how these bases have been affected by Romania's independent stance within the alliances of Eastern European communist countries. The authors of the handbook have tried to be objective in order to provide a comprehensive exposition of the dominant aspects of Romanian life in the early 1970s. Often hampered by a lack of credible statistical information as well as an overabundance of biased propaganda, the authors have attempted to piece together sufficient factual material to present an accurate appraisal and an indication of observable trends.

English usage follows *Webster's Seventh New Collegiate Dic-*

tionary. Place names used in the text are those approved by the United States Board on Geographic Names. Tonnages are given in the metric system, but for other measurements standard United States terminology has been used. The use of Romanian words has been held to a minimum and, where used, they have been explained in the text and in the Glossary, which is appended for the reader's convenience. The acronym PCR, derived from Partidul Comunist Roman (Romanian Communist Party), is used throughout the book and is fully explained in the Glossary.

COUNTRY SUMMARY

1. COUNTRY: Officially redesignated the Socialist Republic of Romania under Constitution of 1965. Established originally as the Kingdom of Romania in 1881, was converted into the Romanian People's Republic in 1948 by communist party with Soviet backing.

2. GOVERNMENT: Constitution of 1965 provides for a unicameral legislature and a collegial executive known as the Council of State. Romanian Communist Party controls elections and runs the government at all levels. Top party officials concurrently occupy top governmental offices. Ultimate political power rests in the party hierarchy, particularly in the person of the party general secretary who, since 1967, has also been head of state.

3. SIZE AND LOCATION: Area of over 91,700 square miles. In southeastern Europe, shares 1,975 miles of demarcated and undisputed land borders with Bulgaria, Yugoslavia, Hungary, and the Soviet Union. With 150 miles of shoreline, shares riparian rights on Black Sea with Turkey, Bulgaria, and the Soviet Union.

4. TOPOGRAPHY: Terrain is generally irregular. The Transylvania basin in the northwest occupies about one-third of the country and is separated from the plains and lowlands of Walachia, Dobruja, and Moldavia to the south and east by the curving course of the Carpathian Mountains and the Transylvanian Alps, which cut across the central portion of the country.

5. CLIMATE: Generally Eastern European Continental, dominated by high pressure systems from European Soviet Union and north-central Asia. Little variation or moderation experienced in the prevailing long cold winters and short hot summers.

6. POPULATION: Almost 20.6 million in 1971; annual growth rate of 1.3 percent, among the highest in Eastern Europe. Density more than 224 persons per square mile. Largest minority is Hungarian, comprising 8 percent of population, followed by German, with 2 percent.

7. LANGUAGE: Romanian, the official language, spoken by virtually all elements of the population. Hungarian and German also recognized and utilized in areas of large minority concentrations.

8. LABOR: Working population employed by the state in 1969 numbered about 5 million. About 40 percent were employed in in-

dustry; about 51 percent, in agriculture. Women constituted about 43 percent of the industrial and 57.5 percent of the collective farm labor forces.

9. RELIGION: Freedom of worship is guaranteed by Constitution, but state controls all church activities. About two-thirds of population belong to Romanian Orthodox Church. Importance of Roman Catholic and Protestant minorities enhanced because of their identity with Hungarian and German ethnic groups.

10. EDUCATION: Restructured in 1948 into a highly centralized system with a broad base, standardized curricula, mandatory attendance through tenth grade, and heavy emphasis on vocational and technical subjects above the elementary level. Political indoctrination permeates entire system.

11. JUSTICE: Theoretically independent, the three-level court system (local, district, and Supreme Court) functions as part of executive branch. Military tribunals operate as part of system under Supreme Court.

12. ADMINISTRATIVE DIVISIONS: Thirty-nine counties, each subdivided into varying numbers of communes, villages, and municipalities. Bucharest administered as an independent political entity. Governmental functioning ostensibly decentralized, but policy and control exercised by higher state and party organs.

13. ECONOMY: Government controlled, with basic five-year plans patterned on Soviet model. Development hampered by scarcity of raw materials and manufacturing equipment and by insufficient number of experienced workers and managers.

14. AGRICULTURE: About 63 percent of land is agricultural; of this, 65 percent under cultivation. Food production adequate for domestic needs, but exports limited because of insufficient investment and lack of labor incentives.

15. INDUSTRY: Rapid growth since 1950 stimulated by massive inputs of capital, labor, and imports of modern machinery and technology. Labor productivity and quality of manufactured products have improved but remain low.

16. FOREIGN ECONOMIC RELATIONS: Foreign trade is state monopoly and is conducted primarily with Soviet Union and East European communist countries. Balance of trade generally negative, reflecting imports of high-quality machinery from West necessary for industrial advancement. Exports limited to light machinery, foodstuffs, and some consumer goods.

17. FINANCE: Monetary unit is the nonconvertible leu. The

1972 exchange rates varied between the official 5.53 lei per US$1 to tourist rates of about 16 lei per US$1. Currency and foreign exchange are state controlled, administered through the National Bank.

18. COMMUNICATIONS: All information media party or state owned and controlled. Press and radio more extensively developed than television, but all function as parts of ideological and political indoctrination system.

19. RAILROADS: Important freight and passenger carrier. About 6,900 miles of trunkline in operation, almost all standard gauge. About 100 miles electrified, and rest of system converting to use of diesel locomotives.

20. HIGHWAYS: Of 47,800 total road mileage, about 6,600 miles nationally maintained as principal operating network. System supplanting railroads as major short-haul carrier of freight and passengers.

21. INLAND WATERWAYS: About 1,500 miles of principal rivers and canals are navigable. Water transport has minor role as a cargo carrier.

22. AIRWAYS: Romanian Air Transport, the state-owned airline, operates domestic service to twelve principal cities and to about twenty national capitals in Europe and the Middle East.

23. PIPELINES: Largest network serves oilfields and moves most liquid petroleum and refined products to refineries and ports. Natural gas lines exist, but mountainous terrain limits general distribution.

24. MERCHANT MARINE: Small in number but operates modern ships and equipment. Transport limited principally to truck cargo and freight.

25. ARMED FORCES: In 1972 consisted of about 200,000 men organized into ground, naval, air, air defense, and frontier forces, all administered by a single ministry. All elements operate as part of army, which is largest single component.

26. SECURITY: Security forces, nationally organized and centrally controlled by Ministry of Internal Affairs, consist of ordinary police (militia) and security troops, which perform counterespionage and countersubversive functions.

27. INTERNATIONAL ORGANIZATIONS: Member of the United Nations and a number of its specialized agencies. Member of the Warsaw Treaty Organization (Warsaw Pact) and the Council for Mutual Economic Assistance (COMECON).

ROMANIA

TABLE OF CONTENTS

LIST OF ILLUSTRATIONS

LIST OF TABLES

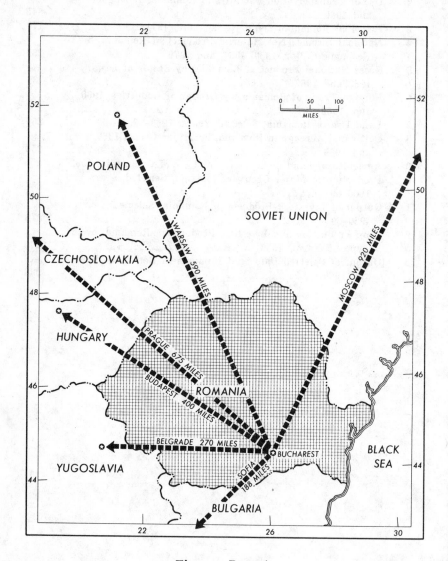

Figure 1. Romania.

SECTION I. SOCIAL

CHAPTER 1

GENERAL CHARACTER OF THE SOCIETY

The Romanian Communist Party (Partidul Comunist Roman—PCR) is the leading force in the political, economic, and social life of Romania. The party general secretary, Nicolae Ceausescu, in early 1972 celebrated his seventh anniversary in power, displaying complete confidence in the stability of his regime. Ceausescu serves concurrently as the president of his country, which is known officially as the Socialist Republic of Romania. Although tied militarily and economically to the Soviet Union through membership in the Warsaw Treaty Organization (Warsaw Pact) and the Council for Mutual Economic Assistance (COMECON), Romania since the mid-1950s has pursued an independent course in both its internal development and its foreign relations.

In April 1964, in furtherance of its independent stance, the PCR Central Committee issued a statement concerning the rights of all communist parties and socialist states to choose their own methods of development according to "the concrete historic conditions prevailing in their own countries." This statement, which has been referred to as Romania's declaration of independence, was directed primarily to the leaders of the Soviet Union and, in effect, was a warning to them to cease their interference in the domestic and foreign affairs of Romania. It was a declaration of sovereign rights and self-determination by which the Romanian Communists asserted that they were the masters of their country's destiny rather than a puppet state to be manipulated by and for outside interests.

The reasons that the Soviet Union did not crack down on its former subservient satellite are both obscure and complex. One factor operating in favor of the Romanians was the rift that had developed between the two communist giants—the Soviet Union and the People's Republic of China. This rift had become very deep, and the Soviets were striving to gain adherents to their position in the struggle and probably were reluctant to use force against Romania because of the danger of alienating other communist parties. It is probable that dissension within the Moscow

1

leadership, which shortly ended the career of Premier Nikita Khrushchev, also inhibited action against Romania.

In their drive to establish rights of autonomy and free choice for their country, Romania's leaders have not tried to withdraw from the Soviet alliances, nor have they changed the basic nature of their communist government. Their actions have demonstrated that their goals have been to lessen the influence of the Soviet Union in Romania's domestic and foreign affairs, at the same time they themselves maintained an absolute, single-party monopoly of power.

After issuing their declaration of independence, the Romanians in subsequent years earned a reputation for opposition to the Soviet Union within the Warsaw Pact and COMECON as well as in the conduct of their relations with noncommunist states. Pursuit of these goals has sometimes led the Romanians into situations that have been considered dangerous by outside observers, and the leadership has often expressed fears of Soviet retaliation against Romania's independent line.

One obvious result of the independent status has been the resurgence of Romanian nationalism. Ceausescu, when he talks about "Romania for the Romanians," even though he may be speaking in the context of building a communist society, receives wide popular support and, at times, appears to have genuine appeal among the people he rules. In contrast to the new nationalism, during the early years of the Romanian communist era it was generally accepted (at least by party members) that the Soviet Union deserved to be emulated in every aspect of national life. Not only were the party and government patterned on Soviet models, but the entire social and economic life of the country was altered to the point of almost losing its Romanian uniqueness.

Russian became a required language in the schools, and the history books were rewritten to play down the traditional orientation toward Western Europe and to highlight Russian influence in the country, which had been considerable since the time of Tsar Peter the Great but which had not always been beneficial from the Romanian point of view. Pseudoscholars intent on the Russification of their country were publishing papers in the late 1940s "proving" that the ancient Dacians, to whom modern Romanians trace their ancestry, were actually Slavic tribes—a thesis that had never before been suggested. Other spurious scholarship attempted to show that the Romanian language was Slavic-based rather than Latin-based as linguists had clearly shown.

While Josef Stalin, Soviet dictator and generally acknowledged leader of world communism, was still alive, Romania was an obedient satellite, and Stalinism was the hallmark of communist

2

rule. Even before Stalin's death in March 1953, however, there was dissension in the Romanian communist ranks as a Moscow-oriented group vied for power with indigenous Communists. The latter group was eventually victorious and, after a series of purges, Gheorghe Gheorghiu-Dej emerged as a party strong man; the first glimmerings of a distinctive brand of Romanian communism can be traced to this period in the early 1950s.

The blending of nationalism and communism did not, however, ameliorate the conditions that existed in the country. Gheorghiu-Dej was a totalitarian ruler, the party brooked no opposition, few basic freedoms for the people existed except in the constitution, and the secret police was an effective instrument of control over the people. Gheorghiu-Dej did, however, establish a foundation, albeit a very shaky one, for a structure of national communism. He and his successor, Ceausescu, strengthened this structure through the years to the point that Romania became known as the most independent of the former Soviet satellites with the exception of Yugoslavia, which has been traveling its own path since 1948.

The Socialist Republic of Romania, ruled in early 1972 by Ceausescu and the PCR, comprised over 91,700 square miles and contained a population of more than 20.6 million. The size and shape of modern Romania is remarkably similar to the ancient country of Dacia, which was conquered by the Romans in the early second century A.D. and became a province of the Roman Empire. Although Roman occupation lasted only about 165 years, it is to the mixture of Roman legionnaires and colonists with indigenous Dacians that modern Romanians trace their origin. These Daco–Romans are almost absent from history's pages for several centuries, but Romanian historians state that they existed in the mountains, tending their flocks and fending off the vast migrations and avoiding absorption by invaders who used the territory as a crossroads into the Balkans or into Europe. After they did achieve some semblance of autonomy during the Middle Ages, primarily in the historic provinces of Moldavia and Walachia, they were always pressured by powerful empires that existed during various historic epochs, and a great portion of former Dacia, the province of Transylvania, was occupied by Magyars (Hungarians) and was not joined to Romania until after World War I.

The great majority of the people are ethnic Romanians, although two sizable minority groups, Hungarian and German, still resided within Romania's borders in 1972. Other, much smaller, minority groups include Jews, Ukrainians, Serbs, Russians, Bulgarians, Czechs and Slovaks, Tatars, Turks, and Gypsies. Most of the lesser minorities have been assimilated to some degree, particularly in the use of the Romanian language in the conduct of their daily affairs. The Hungarians and the Germans, however, have resisted assimilation, and their education, business, and social lives are carried on in their native tongues. Their cultural traditions also reflect their Hungarian or German background rather than that of the country in which they live.

The religious affiliations of the people follow very closely their ethnic differentiations. The vast majority of ethnic Romanians are members of the Romanian Orthodox Church, which is one of the autocephalous branches of the Eastern Orthodox church. The Romanian Orthodox Church was traditionally considered the state or national church, which, with its great size, gave it a favored position. Although its near-monopoly position was contested by Roman Catholics, Uniates, and several Protestant denominations, particularly after the post-World War I inclusion of Transylvania within Romania's borders, it still remained the predominant religion and was able to retain this position even after the communist takeover.

The Hungarians of Romania are Roman Catholics, Calvinists, and Unitarians; similarly, the Germans are divided between Roman Catholicism and Lutheranism. These religions suffered a period of repression under the Communists, some of their clergy being imprisoned and some of their churches falling into disrepair because of lack of funds. Nevertheless, their adherents still numbered in the hundreds of thousands in the early 1970s, and the former vigorous effort by the government to discourage the practice of religion seems to have softened as the regime concentrates on dissuading young people from the acceptance of religious beliefs rather than trying to eliminate such beliefs in older generations.

The post-World War II Romanian Jewish community has shrunk considerably through emigration to Israel, which has been allowed by the government and encouraged by Jewish leaders. There continue to be many Jewish enclaves, particularly in urban areas, but because Jews have not been listed separately in official statistics since the mid-1950s, it is difficult to estimate how many remain in the country. There are several operating synagogues, but most Jewish services are led by laymen because emigration has drained away almost all rabbis and none are being trained in the country; the last rabbinical school was closed during the late 1950s because of lack of faculty and students.

Most of the small Slavic minorities belong to the Orthodox faith, and the few remaining Muslims—Turks and Tatars—retain their adherence to Islam and have their principal mosque in the port city of Constanta. Relatively small numbers of Romanians are Baptists, Seventh-Day Adventists, and Unitarians. Officially, the communist-ruled country advocates atheism, but the Constitution allows for freedom of religion or freedom to profess no religion. Atheism does not seem to have made any great inroads into the established religions during the first quarter century of communist rule.

The activities of all religions are supervised by the government through its Department of Cults. The separation of church and state is constitutionally guaranteed, but in practice this guarantee serves to impose limitations on the churches and clergy but does not in any manner restrict government interference in religious activities.

Though the Communists were unsuccessful in eradicating religion in the country, they have been successful in transforming the politics, society, and economy. With the promulgation of the 1948 Constitution, based on the Soviet Constitution of 1936, and the establishment of the Romanian People's Republic, the new rulers were ready to construct a socialist state. Out of this transformation, the leaders were confident that a "new socialist man" would ultimately evolve, just as Marx and Lenin had prophesied.

In more pragmatic areas the Communists altered the form of government, the social structure, and the economy. The 1948 Constitution established a form of government much like that of the Soviet Union and other communist-ruled states in that the government is structured to be the instrument through which the party runs the country. There is an interlocking of party and government positions that ensures party control over every facet of Romanian life. There are no competing political parties, but there are several mass organizations, thoroughly PCR dominated, in which the people are urged to participate. These include labor unions, youth leagues, women's organizations, and sports societies, which serve to involve the people in national and local affairs while the party hierarchy retains absolute authority in all areas.

The 1948 Constitution was superseded by another in 1952 that brought no significant changes and did not greatly alter the structure that had been established earlier. The Constitution of 1965, however, changed the name of the country to the Socialist Republic of Romania, and, in communist jargon, this change was of particular importance because it signified that the transition from bourgeois capitalism to socialism had been achieved and that Romania could now proceed on its path toward communism. Significant also in the 1965 Constitution was the absence of any mention of the Soviet Union, which had been featured prominently in the previous documents as a model to be copied and as the liberator of Romania.

The most prominent feature of the Romanian political system

is its extreme centralization in both the party structure and the government organization. The people vote for their representatives at all levels of government from a single list of party-approved candidates. Local governments always look for direction from a higher level or from the center. The PCR has a similar pyramidal structure, the topmost organs being self-selecting and self-perpetuating. The concentration of power in the hands of the party hierarchy has prevented the rise of any overt opposition groups, and there has been no observable coalition of dissenters within the party ranks.

In the transformation of the social structure, the Communists brought down the former aristocracy and anyone else who they considered might be opposed to the new order. They then attempted to elevate the status of the former lower classes—that is, the workers and peasants—but because of the elitist structure of the party the great leveling process faltered, and new classes were created despite the prescribed ideology of a classless society. The party elite became the new upper class, and immediately below them was a growing group of lesser party functionaries, technocrats, managers, scientists, teachers, and other professionals. The privileges, life-styles, and aspirations of these groups ran far ahead of those of the workers and peasants who once again found themselves at the bottom of the social pyramid.

Upward mobility is possible, and the key to it is education; the key to educational opportunity, however, is most often political influence, which also plays a large role in the accessibility to jobs that lead to higher social status. A stabilizing of the social structure that became apprent toward the end of the 1960s, although it did not block upward mobility, would seem to indicate that such social movement will be more difficult in the future. Children of workers and peasants will not be denied opportunity for higher education, but it would appear that the path to opportunity will be easier for children of the party elite and the professional classes.

To the people, education is important as a means of social advancement; to the regime, however, the educational system is the prime means through which it inculcates socialist ideals and trains the professionals, technicians, and skilled workers needed to run the country. The first great goal under the Communists was the eradication of illiteracy, which, according to the government, had been achieved by 1958. A concurrent and continuing goal was the training of skilled technicians, foremen, and middle-level managers. The country's rapid industrialization and economic growth caused severe shortages in these categories and, in the early 1970s, the educational and training programs still had not met the demands for the upgrading of unskilled workers.

Modifications of the educational system have been concentrated on the extension of basic primary education from the four-year program that existed after World War II to a compulsory ten-year program that is expected to be fully operative by 1973. Along with the expansion of curricula and the extension of the time spent in primary grades, the regime has also reemphasized the importance of ideological and political indoctrination for the nation's youth. Adult education has also been stressed by the government in its efforts to raise the overall educational and skill levels of the entire population.

In the cultural area there has been a shifting of attitudes by the party overseers that has seemingly left artists and intellectuals confused and wary about the limits of creativity. In the early communist period there was slavish imitation of the Soviet doctrine known as Socialist Realism, which required that all expression reflect the struggle for social justice and the positive aspects of communist achievements. After the death of Stalin and particularly after the initiation of de-Stalinization in the Soviet Union, there was a relaxation of the dogmatic controls forced upon Romanian artists and intellectuals, and more emphasis was placed on historical themes and nationalism. Restrictions continued, however, and "art for art's sake" was not tolerated; even the mild liberalization permitted during the 1960s was curtailed to some degree in 1971 as the regime tightened controls on artistic and intellectual expression. The new hard-line approach of 1971 did not signal a return to the extreme dogmatism of the early 1950s but was a stern reminder to artists, writers, and journalists of their duties to the socialist society.

Militarily, Romania in 1972 maintained about 200,000 men in its armed forces, the great majority serving in the army and much smaller numbers serving in the navy, air force, and frontier troops. All armed services are administered by the Ministry of the Armed Forces, but policymaking is a top-level function of the PCR. Manpower needs are filled through universal conscription, and serving a term in the military seems to be accepted as a normal way of life by young Romanian males.

Romania is a signatory to the Warsaw Pact, but Ceausescu's refusal to participate in the Soviet-led invasion of Czechoslovakia in 1968 and his subsequent condemnation of that action placed the country in the position of being a rather reluctant ally within the pact. Ceausescu has also refused to allow Warsaw Pact maneuvers to be held in his country, and during the Czechoslovak invasion he refused to allow Bulgarian troops to cross Romanian territory. These actions, plus Ceausescu's repeated reference in public speeches to the desirability of the dissolution of both the North Atlantic Treaty Organization (NATO) and the Warsaw Pact, caused publication of anti-Romanian propaganda in the Soviet Union and the omission of an invitation to Ceausescu to attend a meeting of Eastern European leaders in the summer of 1971. The Romanian people were reportedly concerned about possible Soviet intervention in their internal affairs, as they had been often since 1968, but the situation seemed to stabilize in late 1971, at least in outward appearance.

Despite the military and political uncertainties brought about by Romania's independent stance in the Warsaw Pact and COMECON, the country has enjoyed a rapid economic growth rate. Direction of the country's economy is highly centralized and rigidly controlled by the PCR. A variety of economic ministries within the governmental structure are responsible for the administering of specific sectors of the economy, but policymaking is a function of the Standing Presidium of the party. The economy operates in accordance with five-year and annual plans that are all-encompassing and binding on all economic enterprises. Some attempts at decentralization have been made since 1968 in an effort to increase initiative on the part of lower level managers, but intransigence on the part of the hierarchy in releasing its hold has all but nullified the lukewarm reform efforts.

In 1972 Romania was into the second year of its Five-Year Plan (1971–75) and was beset by a host of economic problems. The planners had set high goals for growth during the period, but past overemphasis on heavy industrialization had left a residue of problems in all other areas. Agriculture had been neglected, production of consumer goods had never reached planned goals, and balance of payment deficits with Western nations threatened the foreign trade base. In seeking political and economic independence from the Soviet Union, the regime had placed itself in a precarious position, which forced it to find ways of becoming more competitive in world markets and fulfilling the basic needs of its people at the same time it sought to mollify the resentments of its COMECON partners and retain its ideological commitments to socialism and ultimate communism. Despite its maverick approach and its growing relations with the West, Romania was still tied by treaty, ideology, and geography to the Soviet Union and to its Eastern European communist neighbors.

8

CHAPTER 2

HISTORICAL SETTING

Romania's history as an independent state dates from about the middle of the nineteenth century; as a communist state, from about the end of World War II. The history of the Romanian people, however, is long, complex, and important when considered in the context of the overall history of the Balkan region. The origin and development of the Romanians remain controversial subjects among Romanian and Hungarian historians, whose arguments serve to support or deny claims to rightful ownership of large areas within Romania's borders (see fig. 1).

Until the end of World War II Romania's history as a state was one of gains and losses of territory and shifting borders. As the Ottoman Empire in Europe receded, the Romanians found themselves pressured by the Russian and Austro-Hungarian empires. Borders arranged by the victorious powers after World War I increased Romania's territory but also increased its minority population, particularly the Hungarian. Between the two world wars the country experienced a period of fascist dictatorship and aligned itself with Nazi Germany early in World War II, but it eventually overthrew the fascists and finished the war on the side of the Allies.

The borders arranged after World War II formalized the loss of territory to the Soviet Union but have remained stable since the end of the war. In the postwar chaos of the late 1940s, with Soviet troops occupying the country, Romania deposed its king and emerged as a communist state under the close scrutiny and supervision of its powerful northern neighbor, the Soviet Union. After the death of Josef Stalin the Romanian leadership began a slow pursuit of nationalist goals, which continued in the early 1970s. Although the Moscow-Bucharest ties have often been strained, the Romanians have carefully avoided a break that would provoke a reaction such as the Soviet-led invasion of Czechoslovakia in 1968.

The Romanian people see themselves as a Latin island surrounded by Slavs and Magyars (Hungarians). They are proud of their long, distinctly different historical development and consider that their history is important to them as proof of their ethnic uniqueness in the area and as proof that Romania belongs to the Romanians.

9

EARLY ORIGIN

The earliest recorded inhabitants of the area included in present-day Romania were Thracian tribes, known as Dacians, who settled in the area well before the Christian Era and established a major center in Transylvania (see fig. 2). These people practiced a primitive form of agriculture and engaged in limited trade with Greek settlements along the western coast of the Black Sea. By the middle of the first century A.D. the Dacians had grouped themselves into a loosely formed state ruled by a series of kings who attempted to expand their power to the north and west and, most aggressively, to the south into the area below the lower Danube River.

In their advance southward the Dacians came into conflict with the Romans who, during the same period, were attempting to extend their control over the Balkan region and to push the northern border of their empire up to the natural barrier formed

Note. Internal boundaries have not been shown because of the long history of expansion, contraction, and shifting borders and because the provinces are no longer political entities.

Figure 2. Romania, Historic Provinces.

by the Danube River. In a series of campaigns between A.D. 101 and 106, the Roman emperor Trajan succeeded in conquering the areas known as Banat, Oltenia, and Walachia and in finally reducing the Dacian stronghold in Transylvania. After consolidating and unifying his control over the people, Trajan fortified the area, stationed Roman legions in garrisons at strategic points, and organized the region to serve as a province of the Roman Empire.

As a border province, Dacia developed rapidly and became one of the most prosperous in the empire. Colonists were brought in from other parts of the empire, cities were built, agriculture and mineral resources were developed, and profitable commercial relations were established with other regions under Roman control. The province proved vulnerable to periodic barbarian incursions, however, and toward the end of the third century the Roman emperor Aurelian was forced to abandon Dacia and withdraw the Roman troops to defend similarly threatened areas farther to the south.

Aside from the romanization of the native population, little evidence of the occupation survived the Roman evacuation of Dacia. Among the traces of the Roman presence remaining were the vestiges of Christianity introduced in the second century and the legacy of the name of the future state of Romania as well as the Latin basis for its language.

Lacking natural geographical barriers to invasion from the east and south, the greater part of the Dacian territory was overrun by successive waves of barbarian invaders for ten centuries after the withdrawal of the Romans. Little is known of the fate of the Daco-Roman population during this long, turbulent period until new settlements inhabited by a Latin-speaking people known as Vlachs emerged on the Romanian plains in the eleventh century. Although historic records are lacking, these Vlachs were believed to be descendants of the earlier Daco-Roman colonists, many of whom either sought refuge in the Carpathian Mountains of Transylvania or migrated south of the Danube River to escape the invaders. Having survived, they returned to reestablish themselves in their historic homeland.

The succession of barbaric invasions exploited and devastated the country. The Germanic Goths were followed by Slavs and Avars, and not until the Bulgars overran the area in the seventh century was a semblance of civic order established. The region developed a rudimentary form of cultural life, and Christianity in the Eastern Orthodox form was introduced after the conversion of the Bulgar Tsar Boris in 864. The Bulgars were eventually displaced by Hungarians who, in turn, gave way to Asiatic Tatars, all of whom left limited, but lasting, influences on the land and its inhabitants.

FORMATION OF THE PRINCIPALITIES

Walachia and Moldavia

As the threats of invasion diminished, the Vlachs gradually moved farther into the foothills and plains of the Danube basin and fused with a population that, while retaining a small Vlach element, had by then acquired a heavy mixture of Slavs and Tatars. Two distinct groups eventually emerged, one settling in the area now known as Walachia and the other settling farther to the east and north in Moldavia. The earliest events surrounding the development of these areas are not known, but after a period of colonization the two regions emerged, in the thirteenth and fourteenth centuries, respectively, as the semi-independent principalities of Walachia and Moldavia.

When the Ottoman Empire overran southeastern Europe in the fifteenth century, these Danubian principalities were forced to accept Turkish suzerainty and remained Turkish dependencies until the middle of the nineteenth century. Unlike other areas under Turkish rule, the Romanian principalities were controlled by native princes, who maintained their position through concessions to the nobles, from among whom they had gained preeminence, and through the concurrence of the Turks, to whom a substantial annual tribute was paid. This system of political control led to intrigues and a long succession of rulers who, assisted by the nobles, systematically exploited the peasantry, from whom the heavy annual tribute was collected.

Continued misrule and long-term economic exploitation of the regions seriously affected the social structure within the principalities. The lesser nobility, including the landed gentry, was reduced to the level of free peasants; the peasantry itself was placed in virtually complete serfdom; and cultural activity became almost nonexistent. Even the appearance of outstanding political and military leaders, such as Michael the Brave of Walachia (1593–1601) and Stephen the Great, prince of Moldavia (1457–1504), could not reverse the general trend of deterioration, although the harshness of the fuedal system was somewhat lessened during their tenure in office.

At the beginning of the eighteenth century the Ottoman Empire began to decline, and the Turks instituted a system of direct control over Walachia and Moldavia, in order to ensure the continued receipt of maximum revenue from the countries. Greek merchants known as Phanariots, named for the Phanar district of Constantinople, which was their center, were invested as rulers in the principalities upon direct payment of large sums of money. Since their period in office was indefinite and generally lasted only until outbid by a successor, an even more intensive system of exploitation within the countries was introduced to extract greater tribute in shorter periods of time. This period of oppressive rule lasted until 1821 and proved to be the most disastrous experienced by the inhabitants. Conditions under this corrupt system became almost intolerable and led to massive resistance and eventually to the heavy migration of the peasantry into neighboring areas, particularly Transylvania.

Transylvania

The historic development of Transylvania was substantially different and more complex than that experienced by the principalities of Walachia and Moldavia. Overrun by Asiatic Magyars as early as the ninth century, the region was organized originally as a province in the eleventh century. In order to strengthen this eastern outpost, the Hungarians encouraged two groups of people—Szeklers, or Szekelys, an ethnic group of people akin to the Hungarians, and Germans—to emigrate from the west into the area. Although these colonists eventually reached substantial numbers, the native Romanian speakers remained in the majority (see ch. 4).

With the expansion of Turkish power, Transylvania became the battleground for opposing Turkish and Hungarian forces. Under Turkish pressure Hungarian control declined in the fifteenth and sixteenth centuries, and by 1526 the region had become a semiautonomous principality ruled by Hungarian princes but still subject to Turkish authority. At the end of the sixteenth century Michael the Brave, the ruler of Walachia and Moldavia, succeeded in revolting against Turkish rule and united Transylvania with the other Romanian territories. This union, however, was short lived, and all three principalities subsequently reverted to Turkish control. Toward the end of the seventeenth century Austria conquered Hungary, and Transylvania as part of Hungary then was included in the Austro-Hungarian Empire.

From the earliest times the position of the Romanians in Transylvania was inferior to that of the other nationalities, and accounts of the long-term measures practiced against them have been perpetuated among their descendants. The Romanians were mostly serfs, and their social and economic status was the lowest in the province. Their Orthodox Christianity was not recognized, in contrast to the Lutheran, Calvinist, Unitarian, and Roman Catholic faiths practiced by the various other nationalities (see ch. 5). To gain religious equality and to win a larger measure of economic and social recognition, many of the Romanians gradually abandoned their Eastern Orthodox creed and became Uniates by accepting papal authority in 1698.

Although the Romanians were slow to benefit from the relatively high cultural and political level reached in Transylvania under the Austro-Hungarians, an appreciable number of concessions had been made to them by the middle of the nineteenth century. They began to share in the political life after political parties were established, schools were opened for Romanian children, and education became more widespread among the general population. Progress in these and associated fields stimulated the Romanian desire for full equality and the hope for eventual unification of all Romanians in their own national state.

WESTERN INFLUENCES

Although Romania was late in achieving national recognition, many of the factors that were to influence its Western orientation after independence began to evolve as early as the seventeenth century. In Transylvania the Uniate church became an important medium by which Romanian national identity was fostered in the struggle against foreign assimilation. The Habsburg rulers favored the expansion of the church and permitted the opening of seminaries for the training of young Romanian clergy. Many of these young clerics were sent to Rome to complete their studies and, while there, became aware of their Roman ancestry. They saw the famous column of Trajan, which recorded, in stone, the early conquest of their Dacian ancestors by the Romans, and they also discovered that Romanian was an essentially Latin language (see ch. 4).

The contacts established with Rome encouraged the scholarly development of a "Latinist" movement in the homeland in the late eighteenth century, which produced many adherents among the Transylvanian Romanians. It was the efforts of this group that led to the replacement of the Cyrillic alphabet, then in common use, with the Latin, the writing of the first latinized Romanian grammar and, later, the introduction of the first dictionary that traced the full historical development of the Romanian language. These reforms helped to create a uniform literary language as an essential basis for the broad development of Romanian culture (see ch. 7).

During their long experience under the Habsburgs and Hungarians, the Transylvanian Romanians also became intimately associated with the events of central and western Europe. Opportunities for travel and cultural contacts that later developed were also predominantly within Western areas and intensified the political consciousness of the Romanians along Western lines.

Meanwhile, in Walachia and Moldavia interest in Western ideas and affairs was provided by French influences introduced initially by the Greek Phanariot princes, who were in power during most of the eighteenth century. These rulers established French as the court language, and many of the Greek merchants, clergymen, and teachers who followed them into the areas helped spread the use of French among the urban population in Bucharest and Iasi, the respective capital cities. Gradually, French was introduced into Romanian schools, and eventually Romanian students from the principalities were sent abroad in considerable numbers to study at French universities.

In addition to Romanian students, many of the young sons of Romanian nobles traveled in France. These two groups gradually formed the nucleus of an intellectual class, which favored French philosophy and thought and which became receptive to the liberal ideas of the French Revolution and later periods.

NATIONAL INDEPENDENCE

A phase of major significance and a turning point in Romanian history began in 1821 with a revolt led by Tudor Vladimirescu, a Romanian and former officer in the Russian army. This uprising against the harsh Phanariot rule was the first with a national character, and it attempted to give expression to the revolutionary ideas of emancipation and independence. Although the outbreak was suppressed by the Turks, it did achieve the objective of bringing about the early abolition of the Phanariot regime and the restoration of Romanian princes as rulers in the Danubian principalities.

After the Russo-Turkish war from 1826 to 1828 Russian forces occupied both Walachia and Moldavia to ensure the payment of a large war indemnity by the Turks. Under the ensuing six-year enlightened and competent rule of the Russian governor Count Pavel Kiselev, the foundations were laid for a new Romanian state. The first constitutional assemblies were organized along identical lines in each province; a rudimentary governmental administration was established and modeled on that of the French; an educational system was begun; commerce and a modest industry were encouraged; and provisions were made for the creation of a national militia. The intentional similarity in the fundamental laws that were also enacted in each area further encouraged the two principalities to develop side by side.

During the two decades after the departure of Russian occupying forces, the national movement within the two principalities continued to grow under the rule of native princes who had been restored to power. Considerable stimulation was provided by the 1848 revolutionary events in France, the basic ideas of which were imported by the French-educated Romanians. Dissension arose, and street demonstrations took place during which demands were made for freedom of speech, assembly, and the press, as well as for the unification of all Romanians in one independent state. Similar emancipation efforts were also organized in Transylvania, but they, too, were forcibly repressed, as were those in Walachia and Moldavia.

Despite the setbacks suffered by the intellectuals and other leaders of the revolutionary movement, the modern ideas of liberal government took firm root and continued to flourish. The dispute between Russia and Turkey that culminated in the Crimean War, however, provided the actual opportunity for the first step toward ultimate independence. French and Russian collaboration at the Congress of Paris, which concluded the war in 1858, succeeded in producing agreements that finally led to the establishment of the autonomous United Principalities of Walachia and Moldavia in 1859.

Although still subject to Ottoman authority, the United Principalities moved rapidly under their newly elected leader, Alexander Cuza, to further unify and modernize themselves. Cuza fused the administration of the two principalities into a single government, established a single capital at Bucharest, and changed the name from United Principalities to Romania. Domestic reforms were also undertaken, among which were the emancipation of the serfs in 1864, the institution of a broad land distribution program, the introduction of free and compulsory education, and the adoption of the French civil and penal codes as the basis for a revised legal system. Political parties on the Western pattern began to take form as well, the conservatives representing the large landowners and the liberals representing the new urban class.

The reforms instituted by Cuza were bold and progressive, but his methods proved to be harsh and unpopular. Forced to abdicate in 1866, he was succeeded by a German prince, Charles of Hohenzollern-Sigmaringen. Charles, who reigned from 1866 to 1914, extended the reforms initiated by Cuza. He gave the country its first formal constitution modeled after that of the Belgians, built the country's first railroad, and modernized and enlarged the small army. In 1878 the country's full independence was recognized by the Treaty of Berlin, which ended the two-year Russo-Turkish war in which Romania participated as an ally of Russia. The Kingdom of Romania was proclaimed formally in 1881 with the crowning of Prince Charles in Bucharest as Carol I.

The period from 1878 to 1918 brought significant advances in Romania, largely in the economic and political fields. Under the initiative of King Carol I and with considerable backing from German capital, new industries were started, and others were expanded; railroad and port construction was emphasized; and the considerable petroleum resources of the country were developed and exploited. The goals of political parties and leaders became more clearly defined, and modern government institutions, including a bicameral parliament, were organized.

Economic and formal political progress, however, was not matched by similar advancement of democratic processes in the social field. The liberal provisions of the 1866 Constitution were circumvented under the authoritarian governmental system, leaving much actual power in the hands of the landed aristocracy. The slowly rising middle class and small number of industrial entrepreneuers were granted some rights, but the increasing number of industrial workers and the great peasant majority shared very little in the political life of the country.

A major peasant revolt in 1907 attempted unsuccessfully to rectify the serious social imbalance. The uprising was forcefully suppressed with extensive loss of life and, although some corrective measures were later instituted that improved working conditions and resulted in the division of more large landholdings, the general political strength and living standards of the peasants and workers were not materially improved. Related also to this social unrest was another problem that grew more intense during the latter half of the nineteenth century—that of the increasing size and economic importance of a large Jewish minority.

Forbidden to own land and subject to many other restrictions, the Jews had settled in urban areas, engaged successfully in commercial activities and, as a class, gained economic influence and position generally out of proportion to their overall numerical strength in the population. To an unusual degree, they formed the prosperous urban middle class, overshadowing the far smaller number of native Romanians in that category. In rural centers, as moneylenders, they also became the middlemen between landlords and peasants; as such, the Jew became a symbol of oppression, which over the years was transferred into intense anti-Semitism. Consequently, the Jews were included as a target in the 1907 uprising, and the animosity shown then remained a feature of later Romanian society.

WORLD WAR I

At the outbreak of World War I in 1914 Romania's leaders were indecisive and proclaimed an armed neutrality, which lasted for nearly two years. Much of the pro-Russian and pro-French political orientation of the 1840s and 1850s still existed in the country, but this was offset in large measure by the strong ties of King Carol I with Bismarck's Germany and by the rapprochement with Germany that had resulted from the large investment of German capital in the country. In addition, territorial inducements, which were attractive to Romania, were made by each side to influence its entry into the conflict. The Central Powers offered Bessarabia to be taken from Russia, and the Allies promised the cession of Transylvania from Austro-Hungary.

After the death of King Carol I and the accession of his nephew, King Ferdinand, to the throne, Romania entered the war on the Allied side in 1916. By December 1917, however, Romania was forced to conclude an armistice when the Russian forces disintegrated on the Balkan front after the Bolshevik revolution of that year. Before the armistice was ratified, however, and as the defeat of the Central Powers was becoming apparent, the Romanian army, which had not been demobilized, reentered the war, liberated Bucharest from the Germans, and occupied much of Bessarabia and Transylvania. After the war, in response to the expressed will of the popular assemblies in Transylvania, Bessarabia, and Bukovina, those provinces were united with the Kingdom of Romania—often called the Old Kingdom. Formal treaties in 1919 and 1920 confirmed these decisions, and virtually all Romanians were finally reunited within the historic homeland.

INTERWAR YEARS, 1918–40

With the annexation of Transylvania, Bessarabia, and Bukovina, postwar Romania, sometimes referred to as Greater Romania, doubled in size, as well as in population. Included among the newly acquired population were large ethnic minorities—principally Hungarians, Germans, and Jews—whose diverse backgrounds and development presented complex social, political, economic, and administrative problems for the Romanian government. The various traditions of the people within the acquired lands could not easily be transformed into new patterns, largely because of the government's reluctance to share power with any political leaders except those representing the Transylvanian Romanians. As a result, minority elements were largely excluded from national affairs, and discriminatory policies developed that bred resentment and increased political instability (see ch. 4).

The immediate postwar years were dominated by the Liberal Party of the Old Kingdom. The party instituted a series of land reforms, fostered increased industrialization, and sponsored a broadly democratic constitution in 1923, which made the new state a centralized constitutional monarchy. The Transylvanian Romanians, long accustomed to considerable autonomy and self-government under Hungarian rule, resented the imposition of central control, especially under the administration of officials from Bucharest. In protest, a new party, the National Peasant Party, was formed in 1926 by a fusion of the Transylvanian National Party with the Peasant Party in the Old Kingdom.

Other parties were active during this early period, but all were overshadowed by the Liberal Party and the National Peasant Party. The Social Democratic Party had been organized at the beginning of the twentieth century but, lacking any sizable number of industrial workers, the socialist movement remained weak. After the Russian revolution, however, the radical left-wing elements of the Social Democratic Party seceded and formed the Romanian Communist Party in 1921. The Communists went underground after being banned in 1924 and were largely ineffective until after World War II.

The death of King Ferdinand in 1927 and the elections of the following year brought significant changes in the Romanian government. Ferdinand's son, Carol II, was excluded from the succession because of his earlier renunciation of all claims to the throne to accept exile with his mistress, Magda Lupescu. A regency was therefore appointed to rule in the name of Carol's young son, Michael, and a new government led by Iuliu Maniu and the National Peasant Party was elected, thus ending the six-year tenure of the Liberals.

Although Maniu's government instituted a series of reforms intended to improve general economic and social conditions, its efforts were largely offset by the adverse effects of the worldwide depression of the early 1930s. Also, early dissatisfaction with the regency resulted in the return of Carol II from exile and his assumption of the crown in late 1930. His agreement to sever relations with Magda Lupescu was not kept, however, and in protest Maniu resigned the premiership. In the unstable conditions that followed, King Carol II emerged as the chief political figure in the country, and his rule evolved into a royal dictatorship.

King Carol's assumption of power was aided initially by the rise of a fanatical fascist and anti-Semitic group known as the Iron Guard. This group was strongly pro-German and employed tactics similar to those of the Nazi party, which was then emerging as the dominant political force in Germany. The fascist movement, with financial and indirect support from Germany, increased the influence of the Iron Guard, which was reflected in the 1937 elections. The coalition government that resulted supported King Carol but was later overthrown, bringing to power a new coalition of right-wing extremists.

In order to halt the increasing threat to his power, Carol proclaimed a personal dictatorship in 1938 and promulgated a new constitution that abolished all political parties and instituted censorship and other control measures. This action was followed by the suppression of the Iron Guard, whose leader, Corneliu Codreanu, was shot. Absolute authority was maintained by the king, who was supported by the army and by the National Renaissance Front, a monopoly party that he founded later in the same year.

Internal instability and uncertainty were aggravated by rapidly developing international events that threatened the security of the state. The swift rise of Germany under Adolf Hitler resulted in the annexation of Austria in 1938 and the subsequent dismemberment and absorption of Czechoslovakia. These actions, unopposed by the Western powers, were early warnings of weakness in the Western-oriented collective security system on which Romania had depended since World War I. The lessening of confidence in the West led Romania in 1939 to conclude a treaty of economic collaboration with Germany. This agreement greatly increased German influence in the country and placed the extensive Romanian oil and other resources at Germany's disposal for later wartime use.

Although Romania's territorial integrity had been guaranteed by both Great Britain and France after the fall of Czechoslovakia, these assurances were nullified by the early German military successes achieved following the outbreak of World War II. After the conclusion of a nonaggression pact with the Soviet Union in August 1939, Germany invaded and occupied Poland and, by mid-1940, had defeated France and forced the evacuation of the European mainland by British forces. Faced with the loss of its two strongest partners in the alliance system and with the aggressive ambitions of the two strongest totalitarian powers on the European continent—Germany and the Soviet Union—Romania had little chance of continued independent survival.

WORLD WAR II

The first claims against Romania were made by the Soviet Union, which in June 1940 demanded the immediate cession of Bessarabia and northern Bukovina. Under German pressure Romania acceded to these demands, as well as to the later loss of northern Transylvania, which Germany and Italy transferred to Hungary at a joint conference held in Vienna on August 30, 1940. A third loss of territory, also under German pressure, followed one week later with the return of southern Dobruja to Bulgaria, which had already entered the war on the side of Germany.

The crisis caused by these territorial losses had a serious impact within the country. King Carol was forced to appoint a pro-German cabinet, and the government was heavily infiltrated with members of the Iron Guard, most of whom were released from custody under German pressure. A national protest against the king in early September culminated in his abdication in favor of his son, Michael. A new government under General Ion Antonescu was formed, composed almost entirely of members of the Iron Guard, whose leader was made vice premier. German troops entered the country under the pretext of protecting the oilfields, and on November 23, 1940, Romania joined Germany, Italy, and Japan in the Anti-Comintern Pact.

In January 1941 members of the Iron Guard, attempting to seize full control of the government, initiated a terroristic campaign that was suppressed with much bloodshed by the Romanian army, which had remained loyal to the government. With the continued support of the Germans, Antonescu dissolved the Iron Guard and formed an almost exclusively military dictatorship. After stabilization of the government, Romania entered the war against the Soviet Union and incurred heavy losses in the prolonged fighting on the eastern front.

After the defeat of the German and Romanian forces at Stalingrad in early 1943, the Soviets mounted a counteroffensive, which by mid-1944 had liberated the southwestern portions of the Soviet Union and had advanced deep into Romania and threatened Bucharest. On August 23, 1944, King Michael, with the support of the major political and military leaders, overthrew the regime of Antonescu, halted all fighting, and installed a new, moderate, coalition government. Under the terms of the armistice that followed, Romania reentered the war on the side of the Allies, agreed to reparation payments, and accepted the military occupation of the country until the conclusion of a final peace settlement.

Romanian forces that continued the war were committed in support of the Soviet army in Transylvania, Hungary, and Czechoslovakia. Those engaged on the Moldavian front were disarmed, and control over the greater part of the country was maintained by the Soviets. Among the occupation troops stationed in Romania was the communist-indoctrinated "Tudor Vladimirescu" division, a force composed of captured Romanian prisoners that had been organized after the German-Romanian defeat at Stalingrad. In addition, the Soviets were given the chairmanship of the Allied Control Commission, the joint body that was established to administer the occupied country.

COMMUNIST SEIZURE OF POWER

The several conferences held by the Allied powers concerning postwar arrangements and the understandings that resulted from bilateral discussion among individual leaders indicated that the Soviet Union was to become the dominant military and political power in the Balkans. As a result, the Soviets, from the outset of their period of occupation, acted determinedly to consolidate their position within Romania and to influence the development of a permanent postwar governmental system designed along communist lines.

Although Romania had surrendered in August 1944, it took several months to create a government stable enough to carry out essential programs. The first postwar coalition regimes included relatively few Communists who ostensibly cooperated with the revived traditional political parties. Despite their small numbers, however, they vigorously engaged in disruptive antigovernment tactics to prevent the stabilization of political authority along democratic lines. This course of action was dictated by the general weakness of the Communists who had surfaced after the war and was handicapped by the absence of partisan or resistance organizations, which could have been used as a basis for expanding political control.

Lacking popular support, the Communist Party set about creating mass organizations, labor unions, and front organizations through which they could increase their power. Among the leaders in these activities were Gheorghe Gheorghiu-Dej, an early Communist who had been imprisoned during the war, and Ana Pauker, who had spent the war years in Moscow before returning to Romania after the entry of Soviet forces. By the fall of 1944 the Communists had been successful in grouping a leftist-oriented agrarian party called the Plowman's Front, splinter elements of the Social Democratic Party, various labor unions, and several social welfare organizations into the National Democratic Front. The front became the principal instrument through which the party worked to achieve political dominance.

The National Democratic Front received recognition in the December 1944 government of General Nicolae Radescu and, although given a number of important posts, was generally held to a role subordinate to that of the National Peasant, the Liberal, and the Social Democratic parties. In late January 1945 after a visit to Moscow by Pauker and Gheorghiu-Dej, the leftist leadership within the government initiated a virulent campaign of disorder, agitation, and denunciation against Radescu and called for the replacement of his regime with one to be formed by the National Democratic Front.

The anti-Radescu campaign was prolonged and intensified by the Communists who, through their control of the printer's union, were able to silence the opposition press and thus enhance their own propaganda. In February 1945, during a staged demonstration, the Communists provoked an incident in which several participants were killed. Demands were made for Radescu's arrest, and he was forced to seek asylum within a foreign mission. Using this latest incident as a pretext, Soviet Deputy Commissar for Foreign Affairs Andrei Vyshinsky, who arrived from Moscow within two days of the event, forced King Michael to accept a National Democratic Front government to be headed by Petru Groza, the leader of the Plowman's Front and longtime communist sympathizer.

The government installed by Groza on March 6, 1945, was dominated by Communists and fellow travelers and represented an effective seizure of power by relatively peaceful means. Although a few dissident former members of the Liberal and National Peasant parties were given posts to maintain the facade of representative government, no leaders or representative members of the historic political parties were included.

After recognition by the Soviet Union in August 1945 and by the United States and Great Britain in February 1946, the Groza government held rigged elections for the Grand National Assembly and emerged with 379 of the 414 seats. Having thus achieved legislative as well as executive control, the Communists proceeded methodically during the following year to eliminate all political opposition. National Peasant and Liberal leaders were arrested and tried, and these two major parties were outlawed in June 1947. This action was followed in the spring of 1948 by the fusion of the Social Democrats with the Communists into a new party called the Romanian Workers' Party, which the Communists controlled. As a final step the National Democratic Front was reorganized into the People's Democratic Front, which then included the Romanian Workers' Party, the Plowman's Front, and two new puppet organizations—the National Popular Party and the Hungarian People's Union.

By the end of 1947 the only remaining link with the prewar system was the monarchy. King Michael, in addition to being a popular ruler, represented a national symbol around whom anticommunist opposition could rally and, as such, was an unacceptable threat to the embryonic communist dictatorship. Accordingly, in a meeting in December requested by Groza and Gheorghiu-Dej, King Michael was forced to abdicate under the threat of civil war. On the same day the government announced the creation of the Romanian People's Republic. This action represented the last step in the seizure of power and placed Romania under complete communist control.

THE COMMUNIST STATE

Having seized effective control of the government, the Communists embarked on a program of organizing the state along totalitarian lines. As the first step toward consolidating their position, the Communists initiated extensive purges and liquidation of anticommunist elements in preparation for the holding of new parliamentary elections. The carefully controlled elections held in March 1948 overwhelmingly favored the single list of candidates put forward by the People's Democratic Front, which received 405 of the 414 seats. The new National Assembly met the following month, adopted a constitution modeled after that of the Soviet Union, and formalized the establishment of the Romanian People's Republic.

Over the next five years the country rapidly assumed the characteristics of a satellite state of the Soviet Union. The Allied Control Commission was withdrawn by mutual consent, and the Soviets were given the right to retain occupation troops in the country beyond the 1947 peace treaty date on the basis of an alleged need to protect the lines of communication with other Soviet forces being maintained in Austria. Under these favorable conditions and with close party supervision, locally appointed people's councils had little difficulty in administratively organizing the local governments in accordance with the Soviet system.

Soviet-style instruments of control also appeared in a broad pattern in all major fields and included the collectivization of agriculture, the nationalization of industry, the centralization of control of the national economy on a planned basis, and the creation of militia and police forces whose function was to maintain the authority of the communist regime and to eliminate all actual or potential opposition to its policies.

The 1951–53 show trials and political purges within the communist ranks, which were spearheaded from Moscow, served more to strengthen than to weaken Romanian leadership in the party. Although Gheorghiu-Dej, a native leader, had headed the party as its general secretary since 1945, his influence and that of other Romanian Communists in government affairs was limited. The Moscow-trained element led by Pauker, which followed the Soviet forces into Romania, had become dominant in the party organization, largely because it enjoyed both the support and confidence of the Soviets. This group, considered essentially foreign within the Romanian communist movement, firmly controlled the party apparatus, including the secret police, the key posts that dealt with foreign affairs, and the domestic economy.

This maldistribution of power within the ruling group led to factional disputes and internal bickerings, which were brought to the surface and finally solved by the purging of Pauker and the remainder of the Muscovite group in 1952. After the purges Gheorghiu-Dej and his close collaborators assumed full and undivided authority within the party. The party was successful in maintaining a high degree of homogeneity in its leadership, and the resultant stability within its ranks enabled it to adopt, and later carry out, policies that favored Romanian over international interests in communist affairs.

After the purges Gheorghiu-Dej assumed the premiership and, as the government and party machinery were now in Romanian hands, the nationalistic character of the communist government began to appear. In the early stages emphasis was placed on disengaging the country from many of the tight Soviet controls that still existed. As an initial move the Romanians in 1954 successfully negotiated the dissolution of the onerous joint Soviet-Romanian industrial concerns that had been used by the Soviets to drain the Romanian economy during the postwar years. This was followed in 1958 by obtaining Soviet agreement to the withdrawal of all occupation forces from Romanian territory. At the same time efforts to stimulate and improve the economy led to the establishment of limited economic relations with several Western and noncommunist bloc countries (see ch. 14).

Despite the nationalistic shift in Romanian external policy during this period, the Romanians were careful to indicate to Moscow that, although they wished to conduct their affairs with a minimum of Soviet interference, they had no intention either of abandoning their adherence to the Soviet bloc or of diminishing their efforts toward the achievement of all basic communist aims in the country. The manner and form of internal control in Romania remained repressive and essentially Stalinist; only minor liberalizing changes took place over the next several years.

After the death of Stalin in 1953 Gheorghiu-Dej supported the new form of collective leadership, which separated government and party functions. Following the Soviet pattern he gave up his party post but reclaimed it two years later, coincidentally with the emergence of Nikita Khrushchev as the leading figure in the Soviet hierarchy. Also, Romania further demonstrated its allegiance to the communist cause by formally endorsing the drastic action taken by the Soviets in suppressing the Hungarian revolt against the communist regime in 1956.

The next step in the pursuit of national goals was taken in the economic field and consisted of measures that sought to lessen Romania's economic dependence on the Soviet Union and the more developed East European countries. These goals were embodied in the country's Five-Year Plan (1960–65), which called for the accelerated creation of an expanded industrial base supported by its own natural resources and technical assistance from the more advanced noncommunist countries. This ambitious program was vigorously pursued beginning in 1960 and, by 1962, had come into sharp conflict with Premier Khrushchev's announced plans of revitalizing the Council for Mutual Economic Assistance (COMECON) and transforming it into a unified system that would integrate the economies of all Eastern European member nations (see ch. 14).

COMECON, set up by the Soviets in 1949 as a counterpoise to the European Recovery Program (Marshall Plan), was basically an economic commission designed to assist the economic development of the communist Eastern European nations during the post-World War II period. Within this organization Romania had acted largely as a supplier of agricultural products, petroleum, and other raw materials and depended on the more industrialized member states for most manufactured goods. Under the Khrushchev plan, Romania's role in this organization would remain unchanged, and all domestic plans that had been developed to produce a balanced economy through increased industrialization would be effectively nullified.

Khrushchev, in pushing his revised plans for COMECON, publicly called for the creation of a supranational planning agency within the organization that would be empowered to select investment projects, allocate regional resources, and prescribe economic tasks to be undertaken by the individual member states on the basis of a majority vote. Romanian leaders reacted firmly and resolutely to this suggestion by publishing a statement of the party Central Committee that definitely rejected the policy of supranational economic integration and the utilization of majority decisions as a means of forcing economic cooperation. The committee's resolution further pointed out that economic collaboration should be based on respect for national independence, sovereignty, and the equality inherent in the rights of nations.

Pressure was exerted to bring the Romanian leadership into line. To counter this, the Romanians took steps to demonstrate their determination to hold to their independent views. A program of desovietization was begun throughout the country, during which Soviet bookshops were closed, the compulsory study of the Russian language in schools was ended, and those street names that had been changed to honor Soviet persons or events reverted to their original Romanian designations. Also, in the field of foreign policy Romania adopted an attitude of nonalignment in the Sino-Soviet dispute, resumed relations with Albania (which had been severed after that country left the Soviet bloc in 1961), and conducted negotiations for increased trade with the People's Republic of China as well as with several Western nations.

By the end of 1963 it was apparent that Soviet plans for revising COMECON could not be implemented and, with Romania retaining its membership, it remained an organization of national economies cooperating with one another along both bilateral and multilateral lines. The Soviets, however, retained leadership of the organization and continued to be a major benefactor from its operation.

The surfacing of the policy conflict with Moscow and the subsequent activities of the Romanians in defiance of general Soviet interests and leadership were followed in April 1964 by a formal statement published by the party Central Committee that proclaimed Romania's inalienable right to national autonomy and full equality in the communist world. This so-called declaration of independence made it abundantly clear that the national and independent character of Romanian policy had been extended to all fields and would be applied in both domestic and foreign relations.

The policy of greater national autonomy and political independence from the Soviet Union was continued by Nicolae Ceausescu, who succeeded Gheorghiu-Dej as party chief after the latter's sudden death in March 1965. A militant nationalist in the Gheorghiu-Dej pattern, Ceausescu acted quickly after assuming power not only to maintain the political momentum generated by the new national line but also to more closely identify the communist leadership and policies with this expression of traditional national aspiration (see ch. 9).

In April the name of the Romanian Workers' Party was changed to the Romanian Communist Party, and new organizational measures were adopted that were intended to broaden the party's popular base. This action was followed by the adoption of a new constitution, which changed the name of the country to the Socialist Republic of Romania, a step that elevated the country to an advanced status in the communist system by self-proclamation.

In 1967 Ceausescu's position was further strengthened when he assumed the presidency of the Council of State to become the head of the country in title as well as in fact. Since that time Romania has maintained a firm, orthodox communist control pattern in its domestic affairs but has continued to pursue an independent foreign policy, which has diverged remarkably, from time to time, from those of the Soviet Union and its Warsaw Treaty Organization (Warsaw Pact) allies.

Differences have included opposition to the full integration of the Warsaw Pact military alliance, refusal to joint the Soviet bloc in condemning Israel after the 1967 Six-Day Arab-Israeli War, and unilateral establishment of diplomatic relations with the Federal Republic of Germany (West Germany). Perhaps the strongest position vis-à-vis the Soviet Union was taken in 1968, when Ceausescu denounced the so-called Brezhnev Doctrine of limited sovereignty among socialist nations, which was used by the Soviets to justify the invasion of Czechoslovakia (see ch. 10).

CHAPTER 3

PHYSICAL ENVIRONMENT AND POPULATION

Jacolin

Romania, located in southeastern Europe and usually referred to as one of the Balkan states, shares land borders with Bulgaria, Yugoslavia, Hungary, and the Soviet Union and has a shoreline on the Black Sea (see fig. 1). The interior of the country is a broad plateau almost surrounded by mountains, which, in turn, are surrounded, except in the north, by plains. The mountains are not unduly rugged, and their gentle slopes plus the rolling interior plateau and the arc of lowlands on the country's periphery provide an unusually large percentage of arable land.

Romanian historians have remarked that their country's history might have been different had its mountains been located on its borders rather than in the interior. Romania's mountains provided a refuge for indigenous populations but did not constitute barriers against invaders who sought to dominate the area or use it as a crossroad for deeper invasions of the Balkan region (see ch. 2).

The prevailing weather is eastern European continental, with hot, clear summers and cold winters. Rainfall is adequate in all sections, and in normal seasons the greater share falls during the summer months when it is of most benefit to vegetation and crops. Soils on the average are fertile. Forests occupy about 27 percent of the land surface.

All of the major streams drain eventually into the Danube River and to the Black Sea. The entire length of the Danube in or bordering the country is navigable. There are few canals, and the Prut River is the only other waterway that is navigable for any considerable distance. Several of the rivers originating in the Carpathians have a good potential for hydroelectric power but, because oil and natural gas are abundant, their development has not had high priority.

In 1971 railroads carried by far the greatest volume of long-distance freight and passenger traffic, but highway transport was supplanting them in short-haul traffic of both types. Commercial aviation had multiplied its capacities since 1950 but still carried only a minute percentage of total traffic. Pipelines were the principal carriers of liquid petroleum and natural gas. The merchant marine had developed relatively rapidly after 1960 and, although still small, consisted almost entirely of modern ships and equipment.

The population, estimated at more than 20.6 million in 1971, was growing at the second highest rate in Europe. The country's officials, however, did not expect the 1971 rate to be maintained throughout the remainder of the century.

The standard of living was among the lowest in Europe. Living conditions improved markedly after 1950, but emphasis on heavy capital investment held down production of consumer goods. The land has been more than self-sufficient in the agricultural sector, but food products have been exported in quantities that have made some of them scarce locally.

NATURAL FEATURES AND RESOURCES

Topographical and Regional Description

All of the mountains and uplands of the country are part of the Carpathian system. The Carpathian Mountains originate in Czechoslovakia, enter Romania in the north from the Soviet Union, and proceed to curl around the country in a semicircle (see fig. 3). The ranges in the east are referred to as the Moldavian Carpathians; the slightly higher southern ranges are called the Transylvanian Alps; and the more scattered but generally lower ranges in the west are known as the Bihor Massif. A few peaks in the Moldavian Carpathians rise to nearly 7,500 feet, and several in the Transylvanian Alps reach 8,000 feet, but only a few points in the Bihor Massif approach 6,000 feet.

Lowland areas are generally on the periphery of the country— east, south, and west of the mountains. A plateau, higher than the other lowlands but having elevations averaging only about 1,200 feet, occupies an area enclosed by the Carpathian ranges.

Moldavia, in the northeast, constitutes about one-fourth of the country's area. It contains the easternmost ranges of the Carpathians and, between the Siretul and Prut rivers, an area of lower hills and plains. The Moldavian Carpathians have maximum elevations of about 7,500 feet and are the most extensively forested part of the country. The western portion of the mountains contains a range of volcanic origin—the longest of its type in Europe—that is famous for its some 2,000 mineral water springs. Small sections of the hilly country to the northeast also have forests, but most of the lower lands are rolling country, which becomes increasingly flatter in the south. Almost all of the nonforested portions are cultivated.

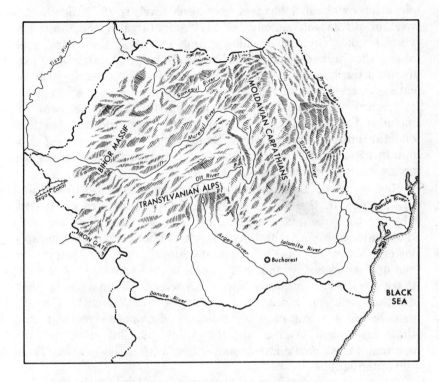

Figure 3. Topography of Romania.

Walachia, in the south, contains the southern part of the Transylvanian Alps—called the Southern Carpathians by Romanian geographers—and the lowlands that extend between them and the Danube River. West to east it extends from the Iron Gate to Dobruja, which is east of the Danube in the area where the river flows northward for about 100 miles before it again turns to the east for its final passage to the sea. Walachia is divided by the Olt River into Oltenia (Lesser Walachia) in the west and Muntenia (Greater Walachia), of which Bucharest is the approximate center, in the east. Nearly all of the Walachian lowlands, except for the marshes along the Danube River, and the seriously eroded foothills of the mountains are cultivated. Grain, sugar beets, and potatoes are grown in all parts of the flatland; the area around Bucharest produces much of the country's garden vegetables; and southern exposures along the mountains are ideally suited for orchards and vineyards.

The Transylvanian Alps have the highest peaks and the steepest slopes in the country; the highest point, with an elevation of about 8,340 feet above sea level, is 100 miles north-west of Bucharest. Among the alpine features of the range are glacial lakes, upland meadows and pastures, and bare rock along the higher ridges. Portions of the mountains are pre-dominantly limestone with characteristic phenomena, such as caves, waterfalls, and underground streams.

Transylvania, the northwestern one-third of the country, includes the historic Transylvanian province and the portions of Maramures, Crisana, and Banat that became part of Ro-mania after World War I. The last three borderland areas are occasionally identified individually.

Nearly all of the lowlands in the west and northwest and the plateau in the central part of the province are cultivated. The western mountain regions are not as rugged as those to the south and east, and average elevations run considerably lower. Many of the intermediate slopes are put to use as pasture or meadowland but, because the climate is colder, there are fewer orchards and vineyards in Transylvania than on the southern sides of the ranges in Walachia. Forests usually have more of the broadleaf deciduous tree varieties than is typical of the higher mountains, but much of the original forest cover has been removed from the gentler Tran-sylvanian slopes.

Dobruja provides Romania's access to the Black Sea. The Danube River forms the region's western border, and its north-ern side is determined by the northernmost of the three main channels in the Danube delta. The line in the south at which the region has been divided between Romania and Bulgaria is artificial and has been changed several times.

For nearly 500 years preceding 1878, Dobruja was under Turkish rule. When the Turks were forced to relinquish their control, the largest elements of its population were Romanian and Bulgarian, and it was divided between the two countries. Romania received the larger, but more sparsely populated, northern portion. Between the two world wars Romania held the entire area, but in 1940 Bulgaria regained the southern portion. The 1940 boundaries were reconfirmed after World War II, and since then the Romanian portion has had an area of approximately 6,000 square miles; Bulgaria's has been approximately one-half as large.

Dobruja contains most of the Danube River delta marsh-land, much of which is not easily exploited for agricultural purposes, although some of the reeds and natural vegetation have limited commercial value. The delta is a natural wildlife preserve, particularly for waterfowl and is large enough so that many species can be protected.

Fishing contributes to the local economy, and 90 percent of the country's catch is taken from the lower Danube and its delta, from Dobruja's lakes, or off the coast. Willows flourish in parts of the delta, and there are a few deciduous forests in the north-central section. To the west and south, the elevations are higher. The land drains satisfactorily and, although the rainfall average is the lowest in the country, it is adequate for dependable grain crops and vineyards.

Along the southern one-half of the coastline there are pleasant beaches. In summer the dry sunny weather and low humidity make them attractive tourist resorts.

Bukovina, more isolated than other parts of the country, has a part-Romanian and part-Ukrainian population. Romanian Bukovina is small, totaling only about 3,400 square miles. It was part of Moldavia from the fourteenth century until annexed by Austria in 1775. Romania acquired it from Austria-Hungary in 1918, but after World War II the Soviet Union annexed the 2,100-square-mile northern portion with its largely Ukrainian population.

The approximately 1,300 square miles of the former province remaining in Romania is picturesque and mountainous. Less than one-third is arable, but domestic animals are kept on hillside pastures and meadows. Steeper slopes are forested.

Drainage

All of Romania's rivers and streams drain to the Black Sea. Except for the minor streams that rise on the eastern slopes of the hills near the sea and flow directly into it, all join the Danube River. Those flowing southward and southeastward from the Transylvanian Alps drain to the Danube directly. Those flowing northward and eastward from Moldavia and Bukovina reach the Danube by way of the Prut River. Most of the Transylvanian streams draining to the north and west flow to the Tisza River, which joins the Danube in Yugoslavia, north of Belgrade.

Romanian tourist literature states that the country has 2,500 lakes, but most are small, and lakes occupy only about 1 perecnt of the surface area. The largest lakes are along the Danube River and the Black Sea coast. Some of those along the coast are open to the sea and contain salt sea water. These and a few of the fresh water lakes are commercially important for their fish. The many smaller ones scattered throughout the mountains are usually glacial in origin and add much to the beauty of the resort areas.

The Danube drains a basin of 315,000 square miles that extends eastward from the Black Forest in the Federal Republic of Germany (West Germany) and includes a portion of the southwestern Soviet Union. It is about 1,775 miles long, including the 900 miles in or adjacent to Romania, and is fed by more than 300 tributaries, from which it collects an average of about 285,000 cubic feet per minute to discharge into the Black Sea. Much of the Danube delta and a band of up to twenty miles wide along most of the length of the river from the delta to the so-called Iron Gate—where it has cut a deep gorge through the mountains along the Yugoslav border—is marshland.

For descriptive purposes the river is customarily divided into three sections; most of the portion in Romania—from the Iron Gate to the Black Sea—is its lower course. The northern bank of this course, on the Romanian side, is low, flat marshland and, as it approaches its delta, it divides into a number of channels. It also forms several lakes, some of them quite large. At its delta it divides into three major and several minor branches. The delta has an area of about 1,000 square miles and grows steadily as the river deposits some 2 billion cubic feet of sediment into the sea annually.

Climate

The climate is continental and is characterized by hot summers and cold winters. Typical weather and precipitation result from the high pressure systems that predominate over European Soviet Union and north-central Asia. Southern Europe's Mediterranean weather and western European maritime systems occasionally extend into the area but not frequently, and they prevail only for short periods. Winters are long, and the months from November through March tend to be cold and cloudy, with frequent fog and snow. Although summers may be hot, they are sunny, and the humidity is usually at comfortable levels.

Precipitation ranges from fifteen to fifty inches; the countrywide average is about twenty-eight inches. Dobruja, along the lower Danube River and adjacent to the Black Sea coast, averages the least, followed by the lowlands of Moldavia and southernmost Walachia, which usually receive less than twenty inches. The remaining lowlands of the country and the Transylvanian plateau average between about twenty and thirty-two inches. Bucharest receives about twenty-three inches. In all of the agricultural regions the heaviest precipitation, most of it from thunderstorms and showers, occurs during the summer growing season when it is of maximum benefit to crops and vegetation.

Scattered areas in the Transylvanian Alps and in the other mountains of the northern and western parts of the country receive more than fifty inches annually. Foothills on all exposures also get more than the country average. Western exposures benefit from the generally eastward movement of weather systems; southern and eastern slopes benefit from the clockwise circulation around the high-pressure systems that are characteristic of the continental climate.

January is the coldest month; July, the warmest. Bucharest, located inland on the southern lowland, is one of the warmest points in summer and has one of the widest variations between average temperatures of the extreme hot and cold months. Its average January temperature is about 27° F, and in July it is 73° F. Summer averages are about the same at other places in the eastern lowlands and along the Black Sea, but the moderating effect of winds off the sea makes for slightly warmer winters in those areas. Hilly and mountainous sections of the country are cooler but have less variation between winter and summer extremes.

Nowhere in the country is the climate the deciding factor on the distribution of population. There are no points where summer temperatures are oppressively high or winter temperatures are intolerably low. Rainfall is adequate in all regions and, in the lower Danube River area where it might be considered the most nearly marginal, marshes and poorly drained terrain are more of a problem than is lack of rainfall.

Soils

The most fertile soils of the country occur generally on the plains of Moldavia and parts of Walachia. This is the black earth known as chernozem, which is rich in humus. Most of the black earth and some of the brown forest soils also have a high loess content, which tends to make them light, fine, and workable. These rich varieties also occur on the lowlands of the west and northwest and on the Transylvanian plateau. Lighter brown soils are more prevalent in rolling lands and in foothills throughout the country.

Soils become progressively poorer at higher elevations and as the slopes become steeper. Layered soils, which take over as elevations increase, vary widely and tend to become thinner and poorer at higher elevations until bare rock is exposed. In some lower areas, where there are areas of brown forest soils, erosion is a serious problem. Although the sandy and alluvial soils along the Danube River are of excellent quality and are valuable where drainage is good, those in a fairly wide belt along the river are too moist for cultivation of most crops.

Vegetation

Before the land was cleared, lowland Romania was a wooded steppe area, but the natural vegetation has largely been removed and replaced by cultivated crops. Forests still predominate on the highlands. Of the country's total area, about 63 percent is agricultural land; 27 percent is forest; and 10 percent is bare mountain or water surface or is used in some way that makes it unsuitable for forest or cultivation. Of the agricultural land, 65 percent is under cultivation, 30 percent is pasture and meadow, and 5 percent is orchard and vineyard (see ch. 15).

Forests remain on most of the slopes that are too steep for easy cultivation. Most of the larger forests are in Transylvania and western Moldavia in a roughly doughnut-shaped area that surrounds the Transylvanian plateau. Broadleaf deciduous and mixed forests occur at lower elevations; forests at higher levels are coniferous with needle-leaf evergreens. There are alpine sheep pastures at 5,000- and 6,000-foot elevations, and tundra vegetation occurs at some of the highest locations.

Orchards are found in all sections of the country. Peaches can be grown in Walachia, but only those fruits that can tolerate colder winters are raised in Moldavia and Transylvania. Vineyards, especially on the Walachian mountain slopes, have become more important since World War II, and wine, although it is not of a quality that receives international acclaim, is exported.

Natural Resources

The most important natural resources are the expanses of rich arable land, the rivers, and the forests. The land is agriculturally self-sufficient and, when fertilizers become more readily available, crop yields will be appreciably larger. The rivers have a high potential for the generation of hydroelectric power. Most of them rise in the mountains and fall to the plains quite rapidly and could be profitably harnessed. Rainfall distribution is good throughout the year and would provide more than an ordinarily dependable source of waterpower. The potential was only beginning to be tapped in 1971 (see ch. 15).

Large fields of oil and natural gas are the most important subsurface assets. Both are of the best quality in Europe, with the possible exception of those near Baku in the Soviet Union. Liquid petroleum is pumped from large fields in the Ploiesti area and also from an area in central Moldavia. Natural gas is available under a large part of the Transylvanian plateau.

A few minerals, such as lead, zinc, sulfur, and salt, are available in quantities needed domestically, but iron and coal are not plentiful. Deposits of lignite, gold, and several other minerals occur in concentrations having sufficient value to be mined.

BOUNDARIES AND POLITICAL SUBDIVISIONS

Boundaries

When it gained full independence in 1878, Romania contained the historic provinces of Moldavia and Walachia, some of Bessarabia, and a portion of Dobruja. Substantial numbers of Romanians remained outside the original state's boundaries in Transylvania and in the Russian portion of Bessarabia. The first boundaries remained little changed until after World War I, although the strip of Dobruja was enlarged somewhat in 1913, after the Second Balkan War (see ch. 2).

In the 1918 settlement after World War I about 38,500 square miles were ceded to Romania from the dismantled Austro-Hungarian Empire. In addition to historic Transylvania, with its area of about 21,300 square miles, a strip along its western side, with a substantially Magyar population, and Bukovina, part of which is now the most north-central section of the country, were included. Also in the aftermath of World War I and the Russian revolution, Romania acquired Bessarabia from the new Bolshevik regime and enlarged its holdings in Dobruja at Bulgaria's expense.

During the brief period of accord between the Soviet Union and Nazi Germany immediately before World War II, portions of Romania were sliced away and divided among Hungary, Bulgaria, and the Soviet Union. The post-World War II settlement, arrived at in 1947, again transferred Transylvania from Hungary to Romania, and Dobruja—with a somewhat modified southern border—was transferred from Bulgaria. The Soviet Union retained all of Bessarabia and the northern portion of Bukovina. In 1971 none of Romania's borders were disputed, and all of them were satisfactorily demarcated.

The total circumference of the country is about 1,975 miles. The northern and eastern border with the Soviet Union extends for about 830 miles; the southern border with Bulgaria, for 375 miles; the southwestern border with Yugoslavia, for 345 miles;

and the northwestern border with Hungary, for 275 miles. The Black Sea coast is about 150 miles long. The eastern boundary generally follows the Prut River, and most of the southern boundary is formed by the Danube; in the west and north the border follows no distinctive terrain features, often having been drawn according to ethnic, rather than geographic, considerations.

Political Subdivisions

Until 1968 the communist regime had divided the country into seventeen regions—including one consisting of the Bucharest metropolitan area only—and 152 districts. In an extensive reorganization of local governments at that time, the regions were done away with and replaced by the prewar system of counties (*judete*). In 1971 there were thirty-nine counties, plus Bucharest and its suburban areas, which were still administered separately. Bucharest was one of forty-six municipalities, but it was the only one not subordinate to the district in which it was located. Each county is named for the town that is its administrative center. The newer organization has served to increase public participation in local government but has also increased the authority of the central government.

Bucharest, with a population of nearly 1.5 million in 1969, was about six times larger than Brasov, the next largest city. The Bucharest district was smallest in area and greatest in population. Other districts had roughly similar areas and populations. They averaged about 2,350 square miles in area and, although their populations varied between fewer than 200,000 and about 750,000, two-thirds of them had between 350,000 and 650,000 persons.

The 1968 reorganization also made extensive changes in the lower portion of the local administrative structure, reducing the number of communes by about 40 percent and villages by nearly 15 percent. Typical counties had about fifty communes of about 4,000 to 5,000 persons each. The smaller local units were created, dissolved, or combined as population and local requirements changed but, as of January 1970, there were 236 towns, 2,706 communes, and 13,149 villages. Of the towns, the forty-seven most important were classified as municipalities, and the communes included 145 that were suburban areas of the larger towns (see ch. 8).

POPULATION

The area approximating that defined by the 1971 boundaries of the country had a population estimated at about 8.2 million in 1860. Thirty years later it had increased to about 10 million.

Growth began to accelerate slightly after 1890, with periods of greatest increases between 1930 and 1941 and between 1948 and 1956, until it reached an estimated 20.6 million in 1971.

The 1971 estimate was derived from the 1966 census and projected from vital statistics compiled locally through 1970. On this basis the estimated annual rate of growth was 1.3 percent, exceeded in Europe only by that of Albania. Density of the population was 224 persons per square mile. Projected at the 1971 growth rate, the population in 1985 would be 23.3 million, and it would take fifty-four years for the population of the country to double.

The 1971 growth rate, however, may not be maintained. Legislation enacted in 1966 stringently restricted abortions and discouraged birth control practices, resulting in an increased birth rate for the next few years, but by 1971 there were indications that the rate was again declining. Unofficially, it is expected that the population will reach only 25.75 million by the year 2000, or about 27 percent more than in 1970. The projection is based on a growth rate of less than that of the 1970–71 period. It is expected to average about 1.1 percent for the 1971–75 five-year period and to decrease thereafter, resulting in an average of between 0.7 and 0.8 percent over the entire period. Moreover, the increase is expected to be far greater in the over-sixty age group and to provide only about 14 percent more workers in the productive age brackets between fifteen and fifty-nine.

In 1970 the birth rate, at 23.3 births per 1,000 of the population, was also exceeded only by Albania's in all of Europe. The rate of infant mortality, at 54.9 deaths during the first year of life for each 1,000 live births, was slightly lower than those of Yugoslavia and Portugal and was exceeded significantly only by that of Albania. The death rate, at 10.1 per 1,000 was very close to the overall European rate of ten per 1,000.

According to the 1971 official estimate there were 10.1 million males and 10.4 million females, or 102.8 females for every 100 males in the population. Males outnumber females slightly in the childhood years and are the majority sex in each five-year segment of the population to about the age of thirty. Females outnumber males in the thirty to thirty-four age group, after which there is near numerical equality between ages thirty-five and forty-four. Females attain a clear majority beyond age forty-five. Female life expectancy, at 70.5 years, is approximately four years greater than that of males.

The population group with ages from fifty to fifty-four had both a low overall figure and an abnormally low percentage of males (see table 1). The low total reflected a low birth rate during World War I years; the abnormal sex distribution reflected World War II combat losses. The low total in the twenty-five to twenty-nine group resulted from the low birth rate during World War II, and the low figure for the five-to-nine age group reflected the fewer number of parents in the group twenty years its senior and their disinclination to have children because of low incomes and inadequate housing.

The size of the five-to-nine age group was of concern to the country's economists because it will provide a smaller than desirable augmentation to the labor force at the end of the 1970 decade and for the early 1980s. The seemingly much larger group that was under five years of age in 1971, on the other hand, would appear on the surface to more than compensate for the smaller one preceding it. The country's economists, however, did not believe that an alleviation of the chronic shortage of people in the most productive working ages would occur during the twentieth century.

Aside from natural growth and additions and subtractions of territories and their occupants, the country's population has been comparatively stable. It has been affected to a lesser degree than others in eastern Europe by migrations during and after World

Table 1. *Romania, Population Structure, by Age and Sex, 1971 Estimate*
(in thousands)

Age Group	Total	Percentage of Total Population	Male	Female	Number of Females for Each 100 Males
Under 5	2,255	11.0	1,149	1,106	96.4
5–9	1,392	6.7	713	679	95.3
10–14	1,743	8.5	892	851	95.3
15–19	1,787	8.7	911	876	95.6
20–24	1,588	7.7	806	782	97.2
25–29	1,316	6.5	666	650	97.6
30–34	1,533	7.4	757	776	102.4
35–39	1,542	7.5	773	769	99.2
40–44	1,502	7.3	752	750	99.6
45–49	1,303	6.3	623	680	109.2
50–54	806	3.9	363	443	121.7
55–59	1,020	5.0	468	552	117.8
60–64	950	4.6	452	498	110.0
65–69	737	3.6	351	386	109.6
70–74	540	2.6	235	305	129.8
75 and over	551	2.7	227	324	142.1
Total population	20,565	100.0	10,138	10,427	102.8

Source: Adapted from Godfrey Baldwin (ed.), *International Population Reports* (U.S. Department of Commerce, Series P-91, No. 18), Washington, 1969, pp. 32–33.

War II, probably losing between 300,000 and 400,000 persons in various resettlement and population exchange movements. The largest emigration involved Jews to Israel. Israeli data show an average of about 30,000 immigrants from Romania during the three immediate postwar years, and Jewish people accounted for a major share of all emigration between then and the late 1960s.

Within the country the greatest shift of people has been from rural to urban areas. The rural population grew by about 0.5 million, from 11.9 million to 12.4 million, between 1945 and 1971. During the same period urban population increased by about 3.5 million, from 4.7 million to about 8.24 million, and has become about 40 percent of the total. Officials anticipate that the rural population will stabilize and that most future increases will be to the towns and cities.

Of the 60 percent of the people who still live in small villages and settlements, most depend upon agriculture for their livelihood. Isolated farms and dwellings prevail in the more remote hills and mountains, and life in those areas has been little affected by industrialization of the country or by the collectivization of agricultural land, which has been accomplished in most of the better farming areas.

Older villages most typically have individual family houses, with farm buildings adjacent and with considerable separation between houses. In areas that have been collectivized there has been some effort to remove buildings from productive land and to nucleate the villages.

Population is most dense in the central portion of Walachia, centering on, and west of, Bucharest and Ploiesti and along the Siretul River in Moldavia. Southwestern Walachia and central and northwestern Transylvania are also more densely settled than the average for the country. The area around Dobruja, lands of high elevation, and marshlands along the lower Danube River are the most sparsely settled areas.

LIVING CONDITIONS

According to semiofficial Romanian sources, the national income increased by six times during the twenty-year period between 1950 and 1970, and real wages, by 2.7 times. Between 1966 and 1970 improved economic conditions and a broader based industry had created about 800,000 new jobs, most of them in the industrial sector.

Increases in national income have been accompanied by increased outlays for social and cultural programs. The 1970 allocations for such programs were ten times greater than in 1950 and amounted to 27.5 percent of the total national budget.

Housing, production of consumer items, and changes in food consumption had also improved. Between 1966 and 1970 about 345,000 state-funded apartments and about 315,000 privately built dwellings became available. New facilities for production of automobiles, furniture, wearing apparel, television sets, and other domestic electrical appliances increased output in these areas by about seven times that of 1950. Foods with high nutritive value were consumed in larger quantitites. Consumption of milk, garden vegetables, fruit, eggs, and fish nearly doubled between 1966 and 1970. More meat and cheese were also eaten, but the increase in their consumption was less spectacular.

Efforts on behalf of public health were reflected in increasing the life expectancy from forty-two years in 1932 to a figure that was more than 60 percent greater in 1970. Additional and better equipped hospitals and other medical facilities contributed to this, as did more emphasis on public sanitation and increased numbers of doctors and medical assistants. In 1970 there was a ratio of one physician for every 700 inhabitants, which was near the overall European average.

Despite an impressive record of achievements in the production of industrial goods, the standard of living—with the exception of Albania's and Portugal's—was probably the lowest in Europe in 1971. During the preceding twenty years production of consumer goods was held down, while heavy capital investment was encouraged. This was deliberate economic practice calculated to be of maximum benefit to the country in time but not intended to produce the greatest immediate results.

The rent for an ordinary three-room apartment in 1971 was about one-third of the average worker's monthly wages; the cost of a new automobile was about forty times his monthly income. Housing area was small, the countrywide average being about eighty-two square feet of living space per person. Although about 140,000 urban apartment units became available in 1969 and similar numbers were programmed for succeeding years, the housing situation was worse in cities than in small towns and rural areas.

Commentary on the lot of the consumer varies widely, frequently to the point of direct contradiction. Visitors that have had a less than totally favorable impression of the country report that food items—even the common staples, such as eggs, cheese, and sausage—are not always available and that, when they are, purchasers wait in long lines. Because food items are often available only in small shops individually specializing in milk, cheese and sausage, or vegetables and eggs, for example, the mere task of buying food is a time-consuming undertaking. Persons disenchanted with the situation also complain that, although poor harvests in 1968 and 1969 and floods in 1970 contributed further to food shortages, much was still exported during those years. In 1971 the government reiterated its plans to devote primary attention to the development of its heavy industrial base. Plans at that time, they alleged, would discourage increased production of consumer goods through 1975 at the least.

TRANSPORTATION

Railroads

Romania's early rail lines were developed largely in relation to external points rather than to serve local needs. Until World War I the one major trunk line ran south and east of the Carpathians from western Walachia to northern Moldavia. Feeder lines and branches connected to it, but there was little early construction in the marshy areas near the Danube River, and only one bridge, at Cernavoda, crossed it. Transylvania, not yet part of the country, was linked to the old provinces by only one line across the Carpathians. Total route mileage was about 2,200 miles.

Hungary had developed lines connecting Budapest with Transylvania and branch lines within that province. When the area was annexed in 1918, Romania inherited the existing railroads and set about linking them more advantageously with the rest of the country. Most of the modern system was completed by 1938, but route mileage was increased by about another 10 percent after World War II. Late construction included another bridge over the Danube River, this time at Giurgiu, south of Bucharest (see fig. 4).

The system probably attained its maximum mileage in 1967, when it totaled almost 6,900 route-miles, all but about 400 of them standard gauge. About ten miles of line were retired during 1968 and 1969, and other little-used feeder lines will probably be abandoned as it becomes more practical to carry small loads over short distances by truck.

Railroads transported nearly ten times as much freight in 1969, measured in ton-miles, as did the highways. Their average load was carried a greater distance, however, and motor transport actually handled a larger volume of cargo (see table 2). During 1969 the railroads also carried over 300 million passengers, for an average trip distance of thirty-two miles.

The Romanian State Railroads, directed by the Ministry of Transportation, operates all but a few minor lines and, in 1969, had about 147,000 employees. As steam locomotives are retired, they are being replaced by diesels. Only a little more than 100 route-miles have been electrified. Officials expect that roads and motor vehicles will take increasing percentages of short-haul

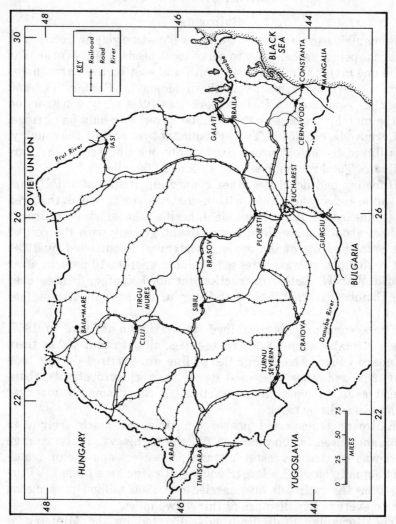

Figure 4. Romanian Transportation System.

44

Table 2. Use of Transportation Facilities in Romania, 1950, 1960, and 1969

Cargo Traffic	Total Freight (in million tons)			Ton-Miles (in millions)		
	1950	1960	1969	1950	1960	1969
Railroads	35.1	77.5	155.4	4,740	12,380	27,500
Motor transport	1.0	56.7	215.6	26	583	2,830
Inland waterways	1.1	1.9	3.1	418	540	728
Sea	0.2	0.2	5.0	382	663	24,400
Air	0.003	0.003	0.02	1	1	21
Pipeline	1.0	5.6	9.2	118	637	790

Passenger Traffic	Total Passengers (in millions)			Passenger-Miles (in millions)		
	1950	1960	1969	1950	1960	1969
Railroads	116.6	214.8	305.9	5,080	6,710	10,450
Motor transport	11.3	71.8	306.9	242	887	4,220
Inland waterways	0.6	1.2	1.4	10	25	43
Sea	0.05	0.08	0.02	59	17	14
Air	0.04	0.2	0.8	9	54	550

cargo and short-trip passenger traffic. Airlines may cut somewhat into the long-distance passenger traffic, but the railroads are expected to remain important for both their freight and passenger services.

Roads

Of the 47,800 miles of road, in 1969 about 6,000 miles—or 14 percent—were considered modernized. A little more than one-third had gravel or crushed stone to harden them, and almost exactly one-half had unimproved dirt surfaces.

About 7,600 miles were nationally maintained and included the greater portion—5,200 miles—of those in the modernized, improved category. Only about 1,400 miles of the local roads were modernized, and less than one-half of them had hardened surfaces. According to government planning reports, the road network is considered adequate in size, and all that can be allocated to it will be applied to its modernization. Motor transport was nearly neglible until after World War II, but between 1950 and 1969 it assumed importance that rivaled the railroads in both cargo and passenger traffic.

Waterways

Nearly 1,500 miles of the rivers are considered navigable. All of the Danube—over 900 miles—that is within or along the southern border of the country is navigable and, in fact, connects the Black Sea and Romania with all points upstream—through Yugoslavia, Hungary, Czechoslovakia, and Austria to Ulm in West Germany. The Prut, flowing along much of the eastern border with the Soviet Union, accounts for most of the remaining navigable mileage. Other streams are useful in some degree for timber rafting and for floating agricultural products downstream. Rapid currents in hilly sections, silting and meandering stream-beds in the lowlands, and fog and ice in winter months, however, limit the commercial usefulness of the rivers. Ice stops traffic on the Danube River for an average of more than one month per year and on the other streams from two to three months.

The country's topography does not lend itself to the development of an extensive system of canals. There are short canals in the western lowlands. Two of them connect to the Tisza River in Yugoslavia but, as with this pair, further development of the waterways in this portion of the country would be economically advantageous only when they connected to points in Hungary or Yugoslavia. Most of the northern and central regions are hilly or mountainous.

Cargo shipped on rivers and canals in 1969 was less than 1 percent of that carried by the other transport systems, but most of it was transported for relatively long distances along the Danube River. Passengers carried constituted an even more minute percentage of the total and, because the largest numbers of them rode river ferries, the relative passenger mileage percentage was even lower.

Airlines

Commercial aviation is altogether state owned and is operated by an office in the Department of Automotive, Maritime, and Air Transportation that, with the Department of Railroads, is part of the Ministry of Transportation. Romanian Air Transport—always referred to in common and in most official usage as TA-ROM, derived from Transporturi Aeriene Romane—serves a dozen or more cities in the country and contacts about twenty national capitals outside the country. These include Moscow, all of the capitals of the Warsaw Treaty Organization (Warsaw Pact) member nations, and about a dozen capitals in Western Europe and the Middle East. Service to nearly all of the external points consists of no more than one round trip flight weekly to each. Domestic service has expanded steadily since 1950 but varies throughout the year to provide more frequent trips during the holiday and tourist seasons.

The line carries some cargo but an insignificant amount when compared with other modes of transportation. It has, however, begun to carry a more significant number of passengers. This traffic increased from less than 40,000 in 1950 to about 780,000 in 1969. Each year since 1965 it has carried approximately 100,000 more passengers than in the year preceding.

Pipelines

Most liquid petroleum products and natural gas are moved via pipeline. The largest network of liquid lines serves the large oilfield in the Ploiesti area and the smaller one in west-central Walachia. They connect the fields with refineries and transport the refined products to Danube River ports and to Constanta on the Black Sea coast. Lines also transfer crude oil from the Moldavian oilfield to its refineries, but there were no lines in 1970 to transport finished products from those refineries.

Natural gas is piped to all parts of Transylvania from sources in the center of the province, but the Carpathians are an obstacle to its distribution to other parts of the country. One major line crosses the Transylvanian Alps to serve the Bucharest area, and another crosses the Moldavian Carpathians through Gheorghe Gheorghiu-Dej. It serves areas to the southeast as far as Galati, on the Danube River.

Merchant Marine

The country has a small, but growing, merchant marine. Although most of its ships are new, the more than 100 percent increase—to nearly 0.5 million deadweight tons—claimed to have been achieved between 1967 and 1969 was accounted for by less than a dozen ships, consisting of two tankers and some bulk cargo carriers that were built in Japan. The government releases no official statistics on its merchant fleet, but fragmentary information indicates that before 1967 it consisted of about thirty-five ships. One of them was a 2,000-deadweight-ton passenger-cargo vessel, and there were a few tankers totaling something over 100,000 deadweight tons. The remainder were freighters, averaging about 5,000 deadweight tons each.

Statistics on goods transported by sea substantiate the size and growth of the merchant marine fleet. Until about 1960 it had relatively little importance, but by 1966 cargo carried was almost ten times that of 1960, and by 1969 it had again tripled. The impressive growth statistics notwithstanding, sea transport in 1969 accounted for only about 1.5 percent of the total cargo transported.

Constanta is the major port on the Black Sea, but some smaller seagoing vessels go up the Danube River to Galati and Braila. All of the larger river towns, and all of those on rail lines that cross it or terminate at the river, are considered river ports. Mangalia, on the Black Sea coast south of Constanta and about five miles from the Bulgarian border, is a secondary seaport but has the country's largest naval installation (see ch. 13).

CHAPTER 4

SOCIAL SYSTEM AND VALUES

Since the end of World War II Romanian society and its values have been in a state of flux. The aim of communist social and economic policies has been to destroy the old order and replace it with a new one that will reflect communist ideaology. The resulting changes have been fundamental and far reaching, particularly in the structure of the society and the place occupied in it by particular individuals. The effect on values has been less easy to determine.

The extent and the pace of change have been slowing down since the early 1960s, and some aspects of the old social order were beginning to reemerge, although in different forms. The changes that were continuing to affect the society in the 1970s were more the result of economic growth than of conscious efforts to bring them about. This was particularly true of the changing role of the family, which has come about as a consequence of increased industrialization and urbanization as much as by government design.

Least affected by the social upheaval since 1945 have been the ethnic composition of the country and the relations between the various ethnic groups. Although the population has always been predominantly Romanian, Hungarians and Germans constitute a majority in some areas of the country and remain a source of potential political and social problems. The Hungarian minority in particular, making up more than 8 percent of the population in 1966, has always been very sensitive to what it considers Romanian domination and has at times harbored irredentist feelings.

ETHNIC COMPOSITION

The population of Romania is basically homogeneous, although it includes elements of almost every ethnic group in Central and Eastern Europe. At the time of the 1966 census, Romanians constituted 88 percent of the population. The largest single minority group were the Magyars, or Hungarians, constituting 8.4 percent of the population. They were followed by the Germans with 2 percent of the population. All other ethnic groups—Serbs, Croats, Slovenes, Ukrainians, Russians, Czechs, Slovaks, Turks,

Tatars, Bulgarians, Jews and Gypsies—were simply listed as "other" and together made up only 1.6 percent of the population.

The Constitution of 1965 guarantees equal rights to all citizens regardless of nationality or race and stipulates legal sanctions against both discrimination and instigation of national or racial animosities. National minorities are guaranteed the free use of their mother tongue in education, the communications media, and their dealings with government authorities and unrestricted perpetuation of their cultural traditions.

Romanians

The origins of the Romanians and their language have been the subject of differing interpretations and controversy. Romanians are related to the Vlachs, a pastoral people speaking a Latin-derived language who are found in the mountainous regions of northern Greece and southern Yugoslavia.

According to Romanian tradition, Romanians are the direct descendants of the Dacians, who inhabited the territory of modern Romania before the Christian Era. The Dacians were conquered by Roman legions under Emperor Trajan in A.D. 106 and became romanized during 165 years of Roman control. When Emperor Aurelian abandoned control of Dacia in 271, in the face of Gothic invasions, the romanized Dacians sought refuge in the rugged Carpathian Mountains, where they preserved their Latin language and culture until more settled conditions allowed them to return to the plains in the tenth century (see ch. 2).

The period of Roman rule of Dacia is well documented, but the absence of any firm indication of the presence of a Latin-speaking population in the territory of contemporary Romania until the tenth century has given rise to another theory of the origin of Romanians, developed mostly by Hungarian historians. This theory maintains that the Dacians withdrew with the Roman legions south of the Danube. There they absorbed elements of Thracian and Slavic culture, in addition to that of their Roman rulers. Starting in the tenth century, a people speaking a Romance language moved northward across the Danube as far as Slovakia and settled in the area that later became Romania.

The Romanian theory of their origin stresses that a people speaking a Romance language continuously occupied the territory claimed by the Romanian state, thus rendering legitimacy to the claim. The other theory stresses the absence of a Romance-language-speaking people in Transylvania at the time of the Magyar immigrations into that region, thus giving legitimacy to the Hungarian claim to Transylvania.

Whatever their origin, Romanians have occupied the territory of their present state since the Middle Ages. In 1966 they numbered 16.8 million and formed the majority population in most of the country (see fig. 5).

Romanian, a Romance language, differs sharply from the languages of neighboring countries which, with the exception of Hungarian, are all Slavic tongues. The basis for Romanian seems to be the Vulgar Latin of ancient Rome. Long contact with Slavic-speaking peoples has left its mark on the vocabulary but has not affected grammar or syntax, which remain similar to those of other Romance languages. The vocabulary of literary Romanian is more purely of Latin origin than that of the spoken dialects. Frequently, parallel words of Latin and Slavic derivation exist for an object or concept and are used interchangeably. Turkish, Albanian, Hungarian, and German have also influenced the vocabulary of the spoken language in various parts of the country.

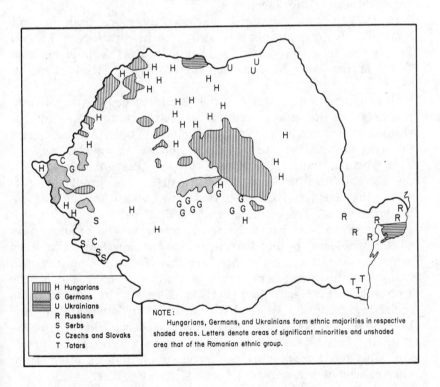

Source: Adapted from Ian M. Matley, *Romania: A Profile*, New York, 1970, p. 276.

Figure 5. Romania, Distribution of Ethnic Groups, 1966.

Hungarians

In the 1966 census Hungarians numbered 1.6 million, constituting 8.4 percent of the total population. Since 1947, when Romania acquired its present borders, the number of Hungarians within its borders has remained relatively stable, although their percentage in the total population has been declining.

Hungarians form the majority population in parts of Transylvania and in pockets along the Hungarian border. They form a significant minority of the population in the rest of Transylvania and in the Banat region. In 1952 the area of greatest Hungarian concentration in eastern Transylvania was designated the Hungarian Autonomous Region (Mures-Magyar) and was given considerable degree of self-government to deal with complaints of political and cultural oppression by Romanians. The region was eliminated in the administrative reorganization of 1968 (see ch. 9).

In 1971 it was estimated that slightly more than half of Romania's Hungarian minority still lived in rural areas. Several Transylvanian cities—including Cluj, Oradea, Baia-Mare, and Tirgu Mures—also have a high percentage of Hungarian inhabitants.

Hungarians first moved into the territory occupied by modern Romania in the ninth century as part of the Magyar invasion of the central European plain. Their number grew through colonization during the period of Hungarian rule of Transylvania, which began with the conquest of the area in the eleventh century and ended in 1918. One group of colonists—the Szeklers, or Szekelys—were settled in the eastern borderlands of Transylvania in the first part of the twelfth century to protect the plains from invaders. The ethnic origin of the Szeklers is in dispute. Some authorities claim they are Magyars; others claim they are non-Magyars who absorbed Magyar culture over long years of contact. During the Middle Ages, Szeklers were distinct from Magyars in political and social organization. Although the distinction between them and the Hungarians has disappeared in modern times and Romanian official statistics do not differentiate, Szekler culture is still considered more purely Magyar than that of other Hungarians who have absorbed influences from the West.

With the exception of some Szekler characteristics, the culture and language of the Hungarian minority in Romania are indistinguishable from those of their kinsmen in Hungary. They are, however, quite distinguishable from the Romanians. This distinction is accentuated by religious differences. Romanians are predominantly Orthodox, whereas more than half of the Hungarians in the country are Roman Catholic, most of the remainder are Calvinists, and some are Unitarians.

The culture and language of the Hungarian minority are being preserved and promoted through schools, newspapers, periodicals, books, theater, and other cultural activities. Members of the Hungarian minority, however, frequently complain that the number of schools, books, and other cultural material available to them in their own language is far short of the demand and not nearly proportionate to their numbers.

Germans

Approximately 380,000 Germans lived in Romania in 1966. The size of the German minority was greatly reduced through voluntary repatriation since the 1930s, when it numbered over 600,000. It has continued to decrease since 1966 through emigration to the Federal Republic of Germany (West Germany) supported by the West German government and permitted in varying volume by the Romanian authorities.

The German population is divided into two groups—the Saxons and the Swabians. Although more or less equal in size, the groups differ in origin and, partly, in culture. The origin of the group usually identified as Saxons is not quite clear, but it was settled by the Hungarian rulers in the Transylvanian borderlands in the twelfth century for the same purpose as the Szeklers. The Saxons live mainly in the cities, such as Sibiu, Brasov, and Sighisoara, which they themselves founded and which have distinctly German characteristics. Some live in rural areas surrounding these cities.

Forming the majority population in a small area, the Saxons have lived in relative isolation until modern times. Their dialect and culture have retained medieval characteristics long abandoned by Germans elsewhere. All Saxons have been Lutheran since that denomination was introduced into Transylvania in the sixteenth century.

The Swabians are Roman Catholics and live in the Banat region. As with the Saxons, their designation as Swabians does not truly reflect their origin. They were settled in the Banat during the eighteenth century to work the land recently vacated by the Turks. Before their arrival there, the language and culture of the Swabians had undergone various modifications to which the Saxons had not been exposed. Most Swabians are peasants farming the rich plain around Timisoara.

Like the Hungarians, the German minority in Romania has

resisted assimilation and maintains its cultural identity through German-language schools, books and newspapers, radio and television programs, and theatrical performances and through the perpetuation of their characteristic dress, dances, and folk art.

Jews

In those censuses in which they are identified (but not in-including that of 1966), Jews are listed as an ethnic group or nationality rather than as members of a religious denomination. In the 1956 census they represented the third largest minority in the country with a membership of 146,000. In early 1972 Western observers roughly estimated the number of Jews still residing in Romania at slightly under 100,000.

The influx of Jews into Romania took place during the first half of the nineteenth century when large numbers left the unsettled conditions of Poland and Russia to seek new opportunities in prospering Moldavia and, later, Walachia. A small number of Jews from various parts of Austria-Hungary settled in Transylvania at the same time and earlier. By 1900 Jews constituted more than one-half of the urban population of Romania, most of them engaged in commerce, banking, or industry. Not allowed to assimilate by various restrictions on their movement and activities, the Jews remained apart from the rest of the population. This apartness and their role in the economy engendered distrust and resentment, which periodically erupted into persecution by some elements of the population (see ch. 2).

The loss of Bessarabia to the Soviet Union and the deportations and exterminations during World War II by the Nazis reduced the Jewish population in Romania to its 1956 size. It has been further reduced since then through emigration to Israel.

Despite their historic separateness from the rest of the society, most Jews in the mid-twentieth century tend to think of themselves as Romanians of the Jewish faith rather than an ethnic minority. All speak Romanian, and only one-fourth claimed Yiddish as their mother tongue in the 1950s. They continue to be urban oriented, and one-fourth of them lived in Bucharest in 1956.

Other Minorities

Eight other ethnic groups were counted in the 1956 census. The largest was Ukrainian, numbering 60,000. Ukrainians formed the majority population in the southern part of the

Danube delta and in pockets along the Soviet border. Some 45,000 Yugoslavs, mostly Serbs, lived in the southern Banat around the Iron Gate. Other Slav minorities included 39,000 Russians in northern Dobruja, near the Bessarabian border; 12,000 Bulgarians, mostly in southern Dobruja; and between 18,000 and 35,000 Czechs and Slovaks in the Banat.

Other ethnic groups of significance were 20,000 Tatars and 12,000 to 14,000 Turks in Dobruja, remnants of the period of Turkish rule. Gypsies, variously estimated between 50,000 to 100,000, are not recognized officially as an ethnic minority and not counted separately in censuses. This, combined with their still largely nomadic life, makes any reasonably accurate enumeration difficult.

Interethnic Relations

Relations between Romanians and Hungarians, the two largest ethnic groups, have been less than smooth. During the eight centuries of Hungarian rule of Transylvania, Romanians, who constituted the poorest rural elements of the population, occupied a subservient position to the wealthier, more urbanized, and better educated Hungarians and Germans. With the joining of Transylvania to Romania in 1918, the Hungarian and German populations of the region lost much of their favored position and, through land reform and nationalization since World War II, they lost their source of wealth. These factors have engendered ill feeling between the groups and have made Transylvania a continuing source of potential problems (see ch. 2; ch. 10). Other factors dividing Romanians and Hungarians have been religious and cultural differences.

Sensitive to the respective nationalist feelings of the Romanians and Hungarians and to the historical dissensions between them, government policy since 1947 has been one of promoting unity and cooperation among all groups for the good of the country as a whole. The theme of equality of all members of different ethnic groups and their close cooperation permeates all official documents, reports, and statements. The Romanian Communist Party, which before World War II had a high percentage from ethnic minorities, represents itself as the historic protector of minority populations and their rights. In the late 1960s the party claimed that over 11 percent of its membership were non-Romanians, in line with the proportional strength of minorities in the population.

During the first decade of communist rule, the government and the people were so preoccupied with efforts to restructure society and foster communist internationalism that ethnic chauvinism and problems of interethnic relations receded into the background. The 1960s, however, saw the development of Romanian independence vis-à-vis Soviet domination and a resurgence of Romanian nationalism, which again raised the potential for minority problems. As the government and party stressed Romanian national independence and gave new emphasis to the historic and cultural heritage of the Romanians, they also emphasized the unity, equality, and fraternal cooperation between Romanians and minority groups. National unity became a vital factor in August 1968, and people's councils were established in the Hungarian, German, and other minority communities to act as spokesmen for the ethnic minorities in the Socialist Unity Front (see ch. 9).

The German minority, while anxious to preserve its cultural identity and rights, seems to have good relations with the Romanians and with other ethnic groups. Although their historic experience and their religion give them a cultural affinity with the Hungarians, they have remained aloof from the Hungarian-Romanian issue in Transylvania. As a whole, Germans have remained to themselves in their own communities and have made little effort to integrate into the national society. This has engendered some resentment on the part of Romanians but no real hostility.

Historically, the relations between Jews and other Romanians have been fraught with suspicion and resentment, which found expression in occasional outbursts of anti-Semitism (see ch. 2). Although the same emotions undoubtedly still color the attitudes and reactions of some of the people, they have been less evident since World War II, possibly because those Jews who survived and remained in the country have integrated themselves into society and identify with the Romanian majority.

SOCIAL STRUCTURE

Family

Traditionally, the family had been the basic social unit that gave identity and security to the individual and furthered the values of society. Family cohesion was great, and close relations were maintained with parents, brothers and sisters, uncles and aunts, and first cousins. Increased mobility and changing life-styles have somewhat loosened this cohesion, particularly among urban families. A growing number of women work outside the home; many men combine work and study, or they work at more than one job in order to improve the family standard of living; and children spend most of their time in school or youth organization activities. Thus, members of the family spend less time together, and the emphasis in daily life is to some degree shifting from the family to the outside world.

In official writing the family is hailed as the cornerstone of socialist society; and family cohesion, loyalty, and responsibility, as socialist virtues. Exemplary family life, particularly exemplary motherhood, is honored with citations and prizes. At the same time, however, all the factors that tend to undermine traditional family life, such as the employment of a greater number of women, are encouraged and promoted.

Since World War II families have tended to be small, having one or two children. Among the German and Hungarian minorities, families have always tended to be small, but Romanian families in the past were larger, particularly in rural areas where children were an important source of labor. The government became so alarmed by the dropping birth rate that it passed strict new laws in the 1966–67 period to limit divorce, abortions, and the sale of contraceptives. The following years showed a sharp upsurge in the birth rate and a dramatic drop in the divorce rate, but in 1970 the birth rate again began to decline.

The main reasons for the drop in the birth rate and reduction in family size have been low wages and a shortage of housing. Many wives must work to help support the family, but published interviews with working wives indicate that they want few, if any, children because they lack the time and energy to care for them as they would like. In addition, the continuing housing shortage in urban areas forces families to live in crowded and inadequate quarters, which mitigates against having children.

In the eyes of the state, marriage is a secular matter. Religious ceremonies are permitted but must be preceded by a civil marriage. The minimum age for marriage without parental consent is eighteen for men and sixteen for women. People generally marry young—43 percent of the men married in 1968 were aged twenty to twenty-four, and another 30 percent were twenty-five to twenty-nine; 46 percent of the women married that year were aged fifteen to nineteen, and another 32 percent were twenty to twenty-four. The urban marriage rate was dropping considerably in the late 1960s, probably owing to the housing shortage, but the rural marriage rate remained fairly stable during the decade.

57

The law assigns equal rights and obligations to both marriage partners. In case of divorce the father is obliged to provide financial support for his children. After the passage of a stringent new divorce law in 1967, the divorce rate dropped from 1.94 per 1,000 population in 1965 to 0.35 per 1,000 population in 1969, making it the lowest rate in Eastern Europe.

In most families the husband and wife are partners whose relationship is based on cooperation and mutual respect. The husband is the titular head of the family who represents it to the outside world, but within the family he customarily consults with his wife on almost all matters. Patriarchal families where the father is the undisputed head are encountered among some peasants. Ideally, the husband provides for the family and protects it from the outside world, and the wife concerns herself with keeping house and raising children.

The diminution of the family's significance in rearing children has, however, fundamentally affected the role of the family in the second half of the twentieth century. As a result of the growing number of working women the roles of the husband and wife are no longer as clearly differentiated. Almost two-thirds of women aged over fifteen in 1966 were employed. Approximately three-fourths of these were married women who had assumed some of the husband's role of provider for the family. At the same time they had relinquished some of their former functions in the household and with respect to children, some of which have been taken over by husbands or by outside institutions.

Social Stratification

Patterns of social stratification have undergone a complete change since World War II. First, land reform immediately after the war eliminated the agricultural aristocracy and increased the number of small peasants who owned their own land. Then nationalization of industry and commerce in the late 1940s eliminated the urban propertied class. Finally, collectivization of agriculture eliminated most of the newly enlarged small peasant class. By the early 1950s the old system had been destroyed, and a new one was in the process of formation.

The period of so-called socialist reconstruction of the 1950s resulted in a general leveling of social strata through the demotion of formerly privileged groups and the promotion of formerly underprivileged groups. Persons of peasant or worker origin received preferential treatment in the allocation of housing and other necessities of life that were in short supply, in the appointment to jobs, and in access to higher education. At the same time persons of middle or upper class background were deprived of their housing, removed from key jobs, and denied educational opportunities for their children through a discriminatory quota system at secondary and higher schools. A policy of equalizing incomes made little distinction between differing levels of education or skill, thus eliminating material rewards as a basis for social stratification. At the same time, however, a small group of party stalwarts, most of them of lower or middle class background, rose rapidly into the top positions of administrative and political power and became the new ruling elite.

As viewed by its own ideologists and sociologists, Romania in 1971 was in the socialist stage of development heading toward a classless communist society. This meant that there were distinctions in income, standard of living, and prestige among different groups in the society; the distinctions, however, were based on occupation rather than ownership of property. Members of all groups were employees; the only employer was society as a whole through its organ, the state. The main basis for the distinction of classes was the difference between manual labor and intellectual work. This difference was gradually being eliminated through the continuous upgrading of the prestige of manual labor.

Most Romanian writing on social strata or differentiation based on occupation separates society into three classes: workers, intelligentsia, and peasants. By most definitions, workers are all those engaged in productive occupations, including both the unskilled laborer and the highly skilled technician. Intelligentsia are all those engaged in nonproductive occupations, such as office work or service jobs, including both the unqualified clerk and the enterprise manager or university professor. Sometimes, however, the intelligentsia is defined as all those with a secondary or higher education without regard to their occupations. Members of agricultural cooperatives are classified as peasants, whereas employees of state farms are considered workers. The small number of peasants still working private agricultural holdings are considered to be a disappearing remnant of the past and, therefore, are not included in any segment of the socialist society.

In 1969 workers were reported as constituting 40 percent of the population; intelligentsia, 12.3 percent; and peasants, 47.7 percent. Comparable statistics for 1960 divided the population into 28.6 percent worker, 9.5 percent intellectual, and 61.9 percent peasant. Thus, the peasant class was growing smaller while the worker and intellectual classes were expanding. A continuation of this trend was forecast for the 1970s.

Cutting across this division was one based on skill and education. Thus the unskilled worker, the unskilled peasant, and the unqualified clerk were all members of the same stratum but of different classes. It was not clear whether or not a division into strata would continue after class distinctions were eliminated.

This view of the social structure seems to be more a statement of ideology than an analysis of the actual structure. On the basis of material rewards, social prestige, and political power, the highest stratum is the ruling communist elite, followed in turn by the intelligentsia—professional, managerial, and administrative personnel with a higher education—skilled manual workers, lower level white-collar personnel, and unskilled workers and peasants.

The ruling elite is composed of the top communist leadership in the party, government, mass organizations, and various branches of the economy. The main criterion for membership in that elite is power derived from approved ideological orientation and political activism. Most members of the ruling elite in 1971 were of lower class background and were veterans of the communist movement in the interwar period. The lifestyle and privileges enjoyed by the ruling elite do not differ much from those of the intelligentsia, the next level in the social scale, but the elite holds a monopoly of power.

The intelligentsia consists of those professionals, managers, technicians, and middle-level party functionaries whose skill and talent are needed to run the society. Education and competence are usual criteria for membership in the group as is ideological orthodoxy. In 1970 the intelligentsia numbered somewhat over 1 million persons, approximately 22 percent of the working population. The size of the group has been growing rapidly in line with the manpower demands of the expanding economy. Most members were relatively young, had advanced educations, and were loyal to communist principles. Their social origins represented the entire spectrum of precommunist society, but a high percentage were of peasant or worker background reflecting the educational advantages afforded to the former lower classes.

The life-style and aspirations of the intelligentsia are those of an industrial middle class. Because of their key position in the economy, they command incomes and special benefits that afford them a standard of living considerably higher than that of the lower levels of the social scale. Among the benefits that individual members of the intelligentsia may enjoy are high-quality housing; the use of official cars; access to special facilities, such as clubs, restaurants, shops, and vacation resorts; and travel opportunities at home and abroad. The growing identification of the intelligentsia with the Romanian Communist Party has also enhanced its privileged status as a group. On an individual basis, party membership provides access to a network of informal contacts within the power and control structure, which can open many doors and win many favors.

Skilled manual workers constitute the top level of the lower social strata. A considerable gap exists in the income, prestige, and commensurate standard of living between the skilled worker and the intelligentsia. The gap can be breached only by acquiring higher education. The skilled worker, however, enjoys considerable material advantages over the lowest levels of society by virtue of his important position in the economy. His prestige, although higher than that of unskilled workers, differs little from that of the lower level white-collar personnel because of the low esteem in which manual work continues to be held.

The level of gradation in material rewards of peasants, unskilled workers, and lower level white-collar personnel is very slight. The difference among these groups is mainly one of prestige and opportunity for advancement. The first step up the social ladder is to leave agriculture and join the industrial labor force. Then, through education and training, one can advance to the various levels of skill and their respective income levels and benefits. Despite their lack of skill, lower level white-collar personnel hold a higher position on the social scale than other unskilled persons, principally because of the prestige attached to nonmanual work.

The main avenue for upward mobility is education. Political considerations, however, influence both accessibility to education and accessibility to jobs that confer higher social status. Admission to educational facilities beyond the required minimum is strictly controlled and manipulated to achieve desired political, social, and economic goals (see ch. 6). The emphasis on educational credentials for upper level jobs limits the possibility of upward mobility through skill or competence alone. On-the-job training, however, does provide a means for mobility within the industrial labor force.

Partly as a result of conscious government effort and partly as a natural consequence of rapid economic expansion, upward mobility has been considerable since the end of World War II. In the early years of communist rule, this upward mobility was accompanied by a significant downward mobility of members of the former middle and upper classes who lost their property and their jobs and were forced to take up occupations at the lower end of the social scale. By the end of the 1960s the social structure seemed to be stabilizing. The restructuring desired by the communist rulers had been accomplished, and the intelligentsia had grown to the point where it could satisfy from its own ranks most of the demand for professional and managerial personnel. This reduction of openings in the upper strata of society for recruits from the lower levels was beginning to solidify the social structure into self-perpetuating groups whose status and privileges, or their lack, are passed down from one generation to the next. The avenues of education and skill, however, remained open and, together with political loyalty, provided the means for social advancement.

SOCIAL VALUES

The differing life-styles of the rural and urban populations are reflected in somewhat differing values. Rural values are rooted in the land and in deep religious faith. Individualism, self-reliance, strength of character, and love of land and God are admired attributes of the rural population. For the mountain shepherd and the small farmer, self-reliance and resourcefulness are essential for survival. These qualities are praised in song and legend and are widely held responsible for the survival of the Romanian people and their culture during centuries of foreign domination. Loyalty is also a highly admired peasant quality—loyalty to the land, to the family, to God, to country, and even to one's animals.

The strong religious convictions that pervade the life of most peasants in the form of carefully observed rules of conduct and rituals are viewed by some sophisticated urbanites and peasant youths as superstition and as a sign of backwardness (see ch. 5).

The values of urban Romanians are more complex than those of peasants. They have been influenced by ideas and values from abroad, particularly by those emanating from France. Educated Romanians have long felt a kinship with the French emotionally and intellectually and have looked to French culture as a model to emulate. As a result, Bucharest was often referred to as the "Paris of the Balkans."

Among the values shared by both urban and rural Romanians are self-reliance, resourcefulness, and patriotism or loyalty to country. Having been ruled by Turks and Hungarians for centuries and being almost surrounded by Slavic peoples, the Romanians are very proud of their Latin heritage and their connection with ancient Rome. It is the shared Latin heritage that probably makes Romanians look to France as their cultural contact in the West.

The emphasis on self-reliance, resourcefulness, and making the best of a situation has given Romanians the reputation of being shrewd businessmen and hard bargainers.

The extent to which communist efforts to change the traditional values of the people have been successful is difficult to determine. Such values as independence, resourcefulness, and patriotism continue to be reflected in the international relations of the country, particularly in its relations with the Soviet Union.

CHAPTER 5

RELIGION

Romanians have traditionally been a very devout people. The vast majority belong to the Romanian Orthodox Church, and regular church atttendance and participation in church functions have been a normal part of daily life. In rural areas the clergy are heavily depended upon as counselors and confidants. As in most peasant societies, the religious beliefs and practices fostered and approved by the churches are often intermingled with folklore. Belief in the evil eye, werewolves, and vampires is common among peasants, although younger ones are less likely to take such beliefs seriously.

Aware of the deep-seated religious beliefs of the people, the communist government has done little to restrict their free expression, and officially religion is viewed as a private and personal matter. Religious persecution has been limited to clergymen who have openly opposed the government and its policies. Government efforts, however, have been aimed at controlling the churches and using their influence with the people to further official policies and programs. At the same time, public information media and schools have been attempting to undermine the hold of religion on younger people by equating religious faith with superstition and backwardness and stressing scientific and empirical knowledge as the basis for a modern world view. Many religious values are attacked as lacking a basis in true knowledge and reality. Those values that the government wants to preserve and promote are given a scientific-intellectual justification and are stripped of any religious meaning.

In line with its view of religion as a private and personal matter, the government has not published any statistical or other information pertaining to the various religious communities since 1950. Research on the role of religion in the daily life of the people has been discouraged; therefore, up-to-date information is restricted to observations by foreign visitors to the country. According to reports from such observers, more than twenty years of communist effort to undermine religion as a force in the life of people has been unsuccessful. Some of the clergy have lost their former influence by openly working on behalf of the government, and some young people question the relevance of some beliefs and practices. The fundamental faith of the people, however, has been little changed. Even longstanding members of the party have been publicly criticized for subscribing to religious views and practices.

CHURCH-STATE RELATIONS

The Constitution of 1965 guarantees freedom of conscience and freedom of religion to all citizens. It also specifically guarantees the right not to profess any religion. The organization and activities of any church are regulated by state law, and religious organizations are prohibited from operating any educational institutions other than those for the training of clergy and members of religious orders.

Within these broad guarantees and prohibitions, the state exercises strict control over the organization and activities of religious denominations through its Department of Cults, which functions in accordance with the General Regulations for Religious Cults passed by the Grand National Assembly in 1948. Under these regulations the state must approve the statute of organization and administration and the statement of beliefs of any church before it can be recognized as a legal body. Clerical appointments are subject to state approval, and all clergy must take an oath of allegiance to the Socialist Republic of Romania.

All legally recognized churches receive state subsidies for salaries of clergy and other operating expenses; churches are not allowed to receive any income or financial assistance directly. Budgets are subject to approval by the Department of Cults, which may withhold funds for individual parishes or for salaries of individual clergymen if their activities are found to be in violation of the policies or laws of the state. The Department of Cults may also suspend any policy decision, regulation, or other measure passed by the governing body of a church if it is deemed contrary to the provisions of law either directly or indirectly.

State supervision and control of administrative and financial affairs of religious denominations had existed in Romania before the communists took power. The terms of the General Regulations for Religious Cults followed in many ways the Law on Cults of 1928; however, several differences in the degree of control point out the fundamental difference in church-state relations in these two periods. Before 1948, for instance, the churches could receive income from property and donations in addition to the state subsidy. More important, however, the earlier law gave the state no right to interfere in matters of belief except in the case of minor sects whose specific beliefs were subject to approval. The 1948 law makes the state the ultimate authority on matters of faith as well as administration. Thus the intent of the earlier law appeared to be the regulation of the activities of essentially independent bodies, but the intent of the present law is to give complete authority and control to the state.

In practice, state control of religious bodies has been carried out through its control over finances and through its confirmation of clerical appointments. No changes have been made in the traditional methods of selecting and appointing clergy and laymen for the various positions in the church. By using its power to confirm these selections, however, the state has managed to fill all the important positions and decisionmaking bodies with persons willing to cooperate and carry out state policy. The state has refused to grant recognition to the Roman Catholic Church because of the church's belief in the supremacy of the pope in all matters of faith and morals and in church administration; however, the church does function with the tacit agreement of the regime.

THE ROMANIAN ORTHODOX CHURCH

The Romanian Orthodox Church is the most important church in the country and the one into which the vast majority of Romanians are born. It is an independent Eastern Orthodox church headed by a patriarch in Bucharest. Its membership in the 1950s, after the incorporation of the Uniate church, was estimated at more than 15 million.

Romanians were introduced to Christianity during the period of Roman rule of Dacia. By the tenth century they were known to be following the Slavonic liturgy of the Eastern Christian Church. Old Church Slavonic remained the liturgical language until the late sixteenth century, when it began to be replaced by Romanian.

During the period of Turkish rule in Walachia and Moldavia and of Hungarian rule in Transylvania, the Romanian Orthodox Church helped to maintain the national consciousness of the Romanian people and was active in their struggle to achieve national unity and independence (see ch. 2). The Turkish policy of religious tolerance enabled the church to thrive in Walachia and Moldavia; in Transylvania, however, a post-Reformation settlement between the Hungarian rulers and the various churches did not recognize the Romanian Orthodox Church as a legal denomination.

In order to gain legal status and its accompanying freedoms and benefits, a major portion of Romanian Orthodox clergy and laymen in Transylvania agreed, in 1698, to accept the jurisdiction of the pope while retaining Orthodox liturgy and ritual. The resulting Uniate church was an important religious and political force in Transylvania until the communist government forced it to reunite with the Romanian Orthodox Church in 1948. As the church of the Romanian people in Transylvania, the Uniate church played a major role in their emancipation and eventual integration into a greater Romania.

With over 1.6 million adherents in 1948, the Uniate church in Romania was the second largest and second most influential church in the country. Fearing and resenting the influence of the Roman Catholic pope with such a large number of its people, the communist regime decreed that the Uniates be merged with the Romanian Orthodox Church and disavow allegiance to the pope. Some Uniate clergy and laymen resisted and were persecuted and imprisoned. The pattern for the dissolution of the Uniate church was the same everywhere in Eastern Europe, and from 1946 to 1950 the Uniate congregations were absorbed into the various national Orthodox churches.

Until the Romanian state was enlarged in 1918, the Orthodox faith was, with minor exceptions, the exclusive religion of the country. The Romanian Orthodox Church was legally accepted as the national church and was supported by the state. Its hierarchy generally supported the policies of the government both as individuals and as officials of the church. The close relationship between church and state was of particular significance in rural areas, where the church was often called on to carry out local government functions. As the only literate person in the area, the parish priest was often not only the spiritual mentor of the population but also the teacher, judge, and government official. The power of the church in relation to the population, therefore, was based on both spiritual and governmental authority. In the eyes of the devout peasant, the local priest was an important authority on a variety of matters as well as a confidant and adviser.

The role of the Romanian Orthodox Church in the life of the country changed considerably after World War I with the addition of substantial populations of other faiths. Efforts to secure a favored position in its legal relationship to the state and to other denominations were defeated when pressure from the Roman Catholic and Uniate churches forced the government to guarantee religious freedom and the complete equality of all churches. At the same time, the Orthodox church's former role in the administration of governmental affairs at the local level was being lost to a growing secular civil service and educational system. The position of the church in the life of the average communicant, however, continued to be one of considerable power and influence. As the largest Orthodox church outside of the Soviet Union, the Romanian Orthodox Church also exercised a degree of leadership among other Orthodox churches.

The revised statutes of the Romanian Orthodox Church issued in 1949 differ little from those in effect before that date. Authority was somewhat more centralized, and the prerogatives of the patriarch were more clearly defined, but the structure of the church remained essentially the same. The patriarchate is divided into five metropolitanates, which in turn are divided into twelve dioceses. Each diocese is composed of parishes encompassing 1,500 to 2,500 communicants each. The clerical head at each level is assisted in his religious and administrative duties by a council composed of one-third clergymen and two-thirds laymen. The administration of monasteries falls under the jurisdiction of the head of the diocese. Since a 1952 reorganization of institutions for religious training, the Romanian Orthodox Church has had two theological institutes for the training of clergy and six schools for chanters and for monastic priests.

THE ROMAN CATHOLIC CHURCH

The Roman Catholic Church is second in size of membership to the Romanian Orthodox Church and, since the absorption of the Uniates by the Orthodox church, the most important minority religion. Its estimated membership of between 1.2 million and 1.5 million in the 1960s was composed mostly of Hungarians and German Swabians (see ch. 4).

As the principal denomination of the Hungarian minority, the Roman Catholic Church has played a cultural and political role in the life of the country as well as a religious one. The well-organized body of the church and its related institutions have been a natural vehicle for the promotion of Hungarian group interests and the preservation of Hungarian cultural traditions. Catholic schools, which were independent of government control until 1948, most often used Hungarian or German as the language of instruction.

The Concordat of 1927 between the Holy See and the Romanian state defined the legal position of the Roman Catholic Church in Romania until the communist takeover. It gave the church full equality with the dominant Romanian Orthodox Church and other denominations and granted it sole control over its educational institutions, hospitals, and charitable organizations. In contrast to all other denominations, the Roman Catholic Church was free from state administrative control and did not receive any financial support from the state. The concordat was abrogated by the Romanian government in 1948, and since that time the position of the Roman Catholic Church has been unclear.

The Catholic bishops have refused to recognize the supremacy of the state over church affairs as expressed in the General Regulations for Religious Cults of 1948, and consequently the state has not granted the church legal recognition as a religious denomination. Between 1948 and 1967 the government tried to force the church into submission by systematically weakening its position. Uncooperative clergy were either imprisoned or otherwise prevented from exercising their clerical and administrative duties; all church schools, hospitals, and charitable institutions were taken over by the government, and all other church assets were confiscated. All but two monasteries and three convents were disbanded, and even these were not permitted to accept new novices. In addition, the organization of the church was reduced from six to two dioceses, Alba-Iulia and Bucharest. Since the church has not been receiving a state subsidy and has been forbidden to seek contributions, most clergy have been supporting themselves by working at lay jobs. Church buildings have been deteriorating because of lack of maintenance, and many travelers have commented on the marked difference in appearance between the decaying Catholic churches and the well-maintained Orthodox churches.

As part of a general political liberalization in 1967 the archbishop of Alba-Iulia, head of the Roman Catholic Church in Romania, and other clergy were released from imprisonment. The action marked the reopening of contacts between the Roman Catholic Church and the Romanian government in an effort to reach a satisfactory agreement that would normalize the position of the church in the country. Additional government effort to reach an accommodation with the church has been demonstrated by the appropriation of funds for the restoration of the historic cathedral of Alba-Iulia. Other denominations had been receiving regular funds for the maintenance and restoration of religious buildings of historic or artistic significance, but the Roman Catholic Church had been denied such funds until 1967. In 1972 contacts between Romania and the Holy See, which had begun in 1967, were continuing. Several meetings had taken place between the Romanian Orthodox patriarch, Justinian, and Cardinal Koenig, who heads the Vatican secretariat for nonbelievers. No agreement legalizing the position of the Roman Catholic Church in Romania has been reached, however.

The government promoted the creation of the Catholic Church of Romania, which was formed in 1951. It is administratively independent of the pope and recognizes the supremacy of the state over church affairs. Legal justification for the move was found in a statute passed in Transylvania in the seventeenth century that placed the conduct of Catholic church affairs in the hands of clergy and laymen directly subordinate to the pope in order to preserve the church from engulfment by the Reformation. In early 1972 the Catholic Church of Romania was headed by a council composed of both lay and clerical members. It recognized the pope as supreme authority on matters of faith, morals, and dogma but rejected any organizational connection with the Holy See.

PROTESTANT CHURCHES

Protestantism is closely identified with the Hungarian and German minorities of Transylvania. Although the churches themselves have refrained from any political activity on behalf of the minorities, their ethnic composition has made them politically significant at times. The Protestant population, estimated at about 1.2 million in 1950, was divided into Calvinist, Lutheran, Baptist, Seventh-Day Adventist, Evangelical, and Pentecostal churches.

The largest Protestant denomination is the Reformed (Calvinist) Church, with a membership estimated at 780,000 in 1950. The membership of this church is almost entirely Hungarian, and its center is at Cluj, a Calvinist stronghold since the Reformation. Most of the Hungarian aristocracy in Transylvania adopted Calvinism during the Reformation, a period when the Roman Catholic Church was weak in that region. This weakness of the Roman Catholic Church and the political and economic independence of the Transylvanian nobles prevented an effective counterreformation and allowed Protestantism to remain strong in Transylvania while the rest of Hungary was Roman Catholic.

Next in size are the Lutherans, with an estimated membership of 250,000 in 1950. Lutheranism is represented by the Evangelical Church of the Augsburg Confession, headed by a bishop at Sibiu, and the Evangelical Synodal Presbyteral Church of the Augsburg Confession, headed by a bishop in Cluj. Membership of both churches is predominantly German. Lutheranism was adopted by the Transylvanian Saxons at the same time that Calvinism was adopted by the Hungarians. In 1938 there were 400,000 Lutherans in Romania; their number was reduced through the loss of northern Bukovina and through the emigration of Saxons to Germany during the 1940s. Continued emigration is further reducing the Lutheran population.

The Baptist, Seventh-Day Adventist, and Pentecostal churches were united by government decree in 1950 into the Federation of Protestant Cults. The estimates of the membership at the time of the merger vary greatly, but it probably included between 50,000 and 100,000 Baptists, 15,000 to 70,000 Adventists, and about 5,000 Pentecostals. Before their merger none of these churches had a central organization in Romania, as their congregations were directed from abroad.

In the reorganization of theological education in 1948, the Department of Cults assigned one school for church singers and one theological institute for the training of clergy to each Protestant denomination. There was some indication that all denominations had difficulty recruiting young men for the ministry after World War II. After more than a decade of complete isolation from their fellows in other countries, all the Protestant churches resumed an active association with the World Council of Churches in 1961.

OTHER RELIGIONS AND CHURCHES

Government statistics on the ethnic composition of the population in 1956 listed 146,000 Jews. Jewish sources outside the country estimated the size of the community in 1968 at between 80,000 and 110,000. Once an important ethnic and religious minority, the Jewish community has shrunk as a result of territorial losses, extermination during World War II, and emigration. Between 1958 and 1969 large numbers of Jews emigrated to Israel with the encouragement of the chief rabbi and the Romanian government. Many of the rabbis have emigrated with their congregations, leaving only nine rabbis to care for some seventy congregations. Most of the congregations were directed by laymen but received regular visits from one of the rabbis. The only rabbinical school in the country was closed in the 1950s. The congregations are supervised by the Federation of Jewish Communities, which is the legally recognized representative body of the Jews in Romania and is headed by the chief rabbi.

Islam is the religion of the Tatars and Turks in Dobruja. Moslems were estimated to number between 30,000 and 35,000 in the mid-1950s. Mosques, most of them built during the Turkish occupation of the area, are found throughout the region. The seat of the grand mufti, religious head of the Moslems in Romania, is at the Central Mosque in Constanta.

Unitarianism was introduced into Transylvania in the mid-sixteenth century, when a group of former Calvinists founded a Unitarian church in Cluj. The church has always been closely connected with the Hungarian minority, from which it draws most of its members. The number of adherents in the mid-1950s was estimated at 70,000. The seat of the Unitarian Church is in Cluj, which is also the location of its seminary.

Two other legally recognized churches are the Armenian-Gregorian Church and the Christians of the Old Rite. The Armenian-Gregorian Church is headed by a bishop in Bucharest, and the Christians of the Old Rite, also known as Old Catholics, by a bishop in Bukovina. Each had an estimated membership of 25,000 in the 1950s.

CHAPTER 6

EDUCATION

The Romanian educational system has been transformed to fit the communist pattern of total subordination to the needs of the state. Since 1948 the educational system has developed as a major force for increasing the general educational level of the population, for inculcating members of society with socialist ideals in support of the regime and its policies, and for providing technical specialists and skilled workers for the nation's labor force. Modifications and adjustments in the system have taken place periodically, but such changes have largely reflected a shift in emphasis among these major objectives rather than any change in basic educational principles.

Considerable progress has been made in the educational field since the end of World War II. An intensive campaign to eradicate illiteracy was undertaken and, according to the government, was successfully concluded by 1958. The number of schools was significantly increased, as were student enrollments throughout the system, although in 1972 the number of students continuing their education beyond the primary level was still proportionately low. The growth of the school structure was further indicated by the successive extension of the period of compulsory education from four years in 1948 to ten in 1968. Full enrollment under the ten-year program, however, was not expected to be achieved before 1973.

To meet the demands for skilled and semiskilled industrial and agricultural workers, the educational system was gradually transformed, heavy emphasis being placed on scientific and technical programs and on vocational training. The most recent reforms, promulgated in 1968, not only reinforced education to meet national economic requirements but also placed renewed stress on the need for increased ideological and political training of the country's youth as a prime element in the successful development of the Romanian socialist state.

Despite the progress achieved in producing a disciplined work force, which benefits the country's economic development, the educational system continued to show basic limitations and shortcomings. Overspecialization and excessive student workloads served to limit the effectiveness and efficiency of secondary and higher schools. Furthermore, the constant effort to expand the mass base of the system, although achieving uniform and satisfactory results by communist standards, lowered the quality of education and sacrificed individual creativity.

BACKGROUND

The educational history of Romania has followed closely the political development of the country. The earliest educational institutions were established in the principalities of Walachia and Moldavia during the sixteenth century and served as the basis of the first system of public education, which became operative in 1832. The unification of the principalities in 1859 led to the adoption of the Educational Act of 1864, which established the principle of free and compulsory education, "where schools were available," under state supervision. Despite the legal provisions for an adequate school system, however, administrative and financial limitations kept the number of schools small and pupil enrollment low.

Little progress was made in improving the scope and substance of public education until the latter half of the nineteenth century and the early part of the twentieth. Beginning in 1893, the country's educational process underwent extensive reorganization: the structure and functions of elementary and normal schools were revised, the curricula of secondary schools and institutions of higher education were revamped, and the position of vocational training in the system was strengthened. Although these advances served to improve the quality of education then available, the number of state-supported schools continued to be low.

Romania's territorial acquisitions after World War I almost tripled its population and added greatly to the problems of public education. Educators considered the system deficient in many respects through the 1930s and the mid-1940s, but they succeeded in achieving considerable uniformity among the school programs at the various educational levels and, in the main, imparted a basic general education to the majority of pupils who completed courses through the secondary school level.

Precommunist Education

The educational system that had evolved in precommunist Romania was operated largely, but not exclusively, by the state and reflected the traditional European order of the times, in which the socially and economically privileged classes were the chief recipients of the benefits of education. Only a limited number of children of the peasantry received more than the four years of elementary education required by the state, and both they and the children of the urban lower classes were discouraged from going on to secondary schools either by the lack of sufficient institutions or by the inability of their parents to pay tuition fees beyond the compulsory level. The public, state-supported system administered by the Ministry of Education consisted of kindergartens, elementary schools, secondary schools, vocational schools, and institutions of higher learning. Academic standards were generally high, and advancement was based primarily on scholastic merit.

Kindergartens were open to children between the ages of five and seven in both state and private schools. No specific subjects were taught and, although theoretically compulsory, attendance was seldom enforced. Attendance records for the 1929–38 period indicated that only approximately 13 percent of all eligible children attended public kindergartens and that fewer than 1.5 percent were enrolled in private ones.

The seven-year elementary school system, four years of which were theoretically compulsory, comprised two types of institutions for children between the ages of seven and fourteen: four-year schools for pupils preparing for secondary schools and seven-year schools for students terminating their education at the elementary level. Elementary education was free except in private schools and, although attendance was supposedly mandatory, enrollments before 1940 averaged less than 75 percent of all children of elementary school age.

Curricular requirements were demanding at this level, particularly in the four-year primary schools. All students studied the Romanian language, literature, history, geography, and natural sciences, in addition to participating in physical education classes and handicraft programs. In the seven-year schools the curriculum during the last three years also included a variety of vocational subjects.

Four types of educational institutions made up the secondary school system: lyceums, primarily preparatory schools for universities; teacher training schools; theological schools; and trade schools. Most of these institutions were public, and each type offered an eight-year course with varying degrees of specialization. Attendance was generally limited to children of the landed aristocracy and the urban upper class. All subjects, even those of a vocational nature, were taught on a theoretical basis. The general curricula in the lyceums included the Romanian language, history, literature, the physical sciences, mathematics, and music. Before being accepted in a university, all graduates of lyceums were required to have passed the baccalaureate, a special comprehensive examination given after all graduation requirements had been met.

The theological schools, also state supported, trained priests in the different faiths; the teacher training schools trained kindergarten and elementary school teachers; and the trade schools prepared students for work in business and commercial concerns. No qualifying examinations were given to graduates of theological, teacher training, or trade schools, since none were eligible for admission to higher level schools. Enrollment throughout the secondary schools was also low; statistics show that over the 1928–39 period less than 6 percent of the total number of students enrolled in elementary schools entered a secondary school after completing four years of compulsory elementary education.

Higher education in precommunist Romania was centered in four universities; two polytechnical institutes; and a limited number of academies specializing in architecture, the arts, physical education, agronomy, and higher commercial and industrial studies. All academic disciplines could be pursued at one or another of these various institutions, and three to seven years were required to obtain the basic university degree. An additional two to four years of study and research were required for the awarding of an advanced degree. The number of students attending higher institutions was proportionately small, and the number receiving the basic degree was even smaller.

Communist Educational Policies

After communist seizure of the government in 1948, the educational system was reoriented away from basic French educational concepts toward those based on the communist philosophy as developed in the Soviet Union. The ultimate objective of the reformed system was to make education available to as large a segment of the population as possible, with a view to transforming the citizenry into a cohesive and effective element for the building of a socialist society along Marxist-Leninist lines. The new system was specifically designed to be tightly controlled, uniform in operation and administration, exclusively secular and public, and fully coordinated with the labor needs of the planned economy.

The August 1948 decree revamping education spelled out in detail the specific policies and methods that would be employed in meeting the new educational goals. Foremost among the basic aims were the eradication of illiteracy and the broadening of the educational base to include all children of school age. Other specific goals of the educational process included: inculcating all youth with the ideological spirit of so-called popular democracy;

guiding the use of leisure time by organizing outside activities for students; educating, on a "scientific" basis, the higher and lower cadres of specialists needed for the construction of all aspects of a socialist society; and training the teachers necessary for the proper functioning of the educational system.

Although these policies have been adjusted and modified and certain aspects have received additional emphasis at particular times, they have been retained as the basic guidelines for Romanian public education. The implementation of these policies since 1948 has resulted in the restructuring of the school system, the expansion of educational facilities, the recasting of the content of curricula and courses, and a major reorganization of the teaching profession, heavy stress being placed on teachers as indoctrinators as well as educators.

EDUCATIONAL REFORMS SINCE 1948

Although the educational reform law of August 1948 has been amended many times, most of the changes that have taken place have not materially altered the basic pattern of communist education that the law established but rather have reflected the vicissitudes of Romanian political life and the country's economic needs. Almost all changes in the educational process have served to implement the original concept that the role of public education is primarily to serve as a vital instrument in the creation of an industrialized society subservient to the interests of the state.

The initial changes introduced by the Communists immediately after coming to power in 1948 affected the content more than the form of education. The public school structure was left virtually unchanged except for the addition of those religious and private educational facilities that had been expropriated by the government. An extensive purge of all categories of teachers was undertaken, and a number of special schools were set up for the political indoctrination of those retained in the system. In addition, the student bodies, particularly in the schools of higher learning, were carefully sifted, and adjustments were made in the availability of courses and in the size of classes in order to redirect students into selected fields of study.

As a further means of control the regime organized students into associations comparable to communist labor unions. The groups included the Union of Student Associations, the Union of Communist Youth, and the Pioneers Organization. The activities of these organizations affected students at all levels and consisted of planned and supervised extracurricular programs. Among the activities scheduled were special exhibitions, sports events, meetings, lectures, and competitions based on ideological themes.

By the late 1950s the reorganization of the educational process along communist lines was virtually completed, and some expansion of facilities had taken place. Curricular requirements had been codified; new textbooks had been written, printed, and introduced throughout the system; new teaching methods were in general use; and the revised teacher training program had produced adequate numbers of "reliable" teachers at all school levels. Additional schools for minority groups had been built, and overall progress throughout the system was sufficient to permit the extension of the compulsory system of education from four to seven years beginning with the 1958/59 school year.

In the early 1960s demands for skilled and semiskilled agricultural and industrial workers brought further changes in the educational system. A renewed general emphasis was placed on polytechnical education, and a period of practical on-the-job training before entering permanent employment was instituted for all secondary technical school graduates. The achievement of this new objective required a further extension of the compulsory education period to eight years and a relative deemphasis of the amount of class time allocated to the humanities and other purely academic subjects.

In 1968 a new educational law was enacted that had far-reaching consequences, but by late 1971 it had not yet been fully implemented. Changes provided for under this law were intended to improve the general quality of education at all levels and to relate education more closely to expanding technological and industrial needs. In addition, the law instituted new measures that gave stronger impetus to the political indoctrination of youth in order to counteract student unrest and dissatisfaction as well as the spread of Western liberalism (see ch. 9).

Specific modifications to be made in the system under the 1968 law included the extension of compulsory education to ten years, the establishment of additional specialized secondary schools, the introduction of more practical classroom work on vocational and technical subjects, closer coordination and supervision of extracurricular projects by the Union of Communist Youth, and the requirement that teachers include a greater number of political and ideological themes in all social science courses. The importance attached to the political aspects of the new program by the regime was indicated by the creation, in July 1971, of the new post of first deputy minister of education with the specific function of expanding and supervising all ideological indoctrination throughout the school system.

LITERACY

Before World War II the literacy rate in Romania ranked among the lowest in Europe. In 1930, at the time of the first official census, more than 38 percent of the population over seven years of age were considered illiterate—50 percent of the women and over 25 percent of the men in the entire population of about 18 million were unable to read or write. In rural areas, where most of the population lived, it was generally considered that the illiteracy rate was even higher. Much of the lack of literacy could be attributed to the fact that children of school age either were not enrolled in school or, if they were enrolled, did not attend classes regularly. There was also a fairly large percentage of children who left school without completing their studies or, having completed only the mandatory first four grades, relapsed into illiteracy in adult life.

Although the proportion of literacy had been increased somewhat by the time the Communists came to power, it was still low. The emphasis given to expanded educational opportunities by the party and government between 1948 and 1956 brought a substantial decline in the number of illiterates. Classes were organized throughout the country by the various people's councils, and a determined campaign was undertaken to increase enrollment. Most of these courses lasted two years and were conducted on a weekly basis by both regular teachers and literate volunteers; successful completion was officially considered equivalent to graduation from a four-year elementary school.

As a result of these increased efforts, the 1956 census showed an overall increase in the literacy rate to about 90 percent. According to this census the greatest proportion of illiterates was still to be found in the rural areas and among women. Literacy courses were continued until late 1958, when the government officially declared that illiteracy had been eliminated. Despite this authoritative statement, Western demographers consider that, although illiteracy has been significantly reduced, it probably still exists among older segments of the population, particularly in remote areas of the country.

THE EDUCATIONAL SYSTEM

In early 1972 the public education system included all levels of instruction from preschool or kindergarten through elementary, secondary, and higher polytechnical schools and universities (see fig. 6). At the beginning of the 1971/72 academic year approximately 4.5 million students were enrolled in the more than 16,000 schools operated throughout the system. Kindergartens and nurseries were organized on a voluntary basis, but attendance at elementary school and through the first two years of secondary school was compulsory for students between the ages of six and sixteen. Attendance at higher level institutions was voluntary, but admission was subject to selective procedures that included heavy emphasis on political reliability as well as scholastic achievement.

All schools were state owned, and tuition, textbooks, and other classroom materials were free at all levels. An extensive system of scholarships existed, sponsored by government agencies, labor unions, state enterprises, and mass organizations. These scholarships were awarded on a selective basis to students in both secondary and higher schools to help defray transportation costs, living costs, and recreational expenses. The state also operated hostels, low-cost boardinghouses, child care centers, dining halls, and canteens for students above the elementary level. A planned increase in the number of these facilities, however, had not been achieved, and the authorities were under pressure to both improve and expand them.

The educational system, in general, stressed technical, political, and economic subjects; and the classroom work in the elementary and secondary schools was underscored by the Pioneers Organization, whose extracurricular activities were considered an integral part of the educational program. The Union of Communist Youth and the Union of Student Associations performed similar functions in the higher schools. The academic year ran from October to September, and elementary and secondary classes ended at the end of May. At the university level all instruction was divided into two semesters, running respectively from October 1 to January 14 and from February 15 to June 30. The grading system at all levels utilized numbers from a high of ten to a low of one, five being the minimal passing grade.

Administration and Finance

The Ministry of Education exercised overall control and direction of the educational system and implemented all party policies and directives concerning its management. In carrying

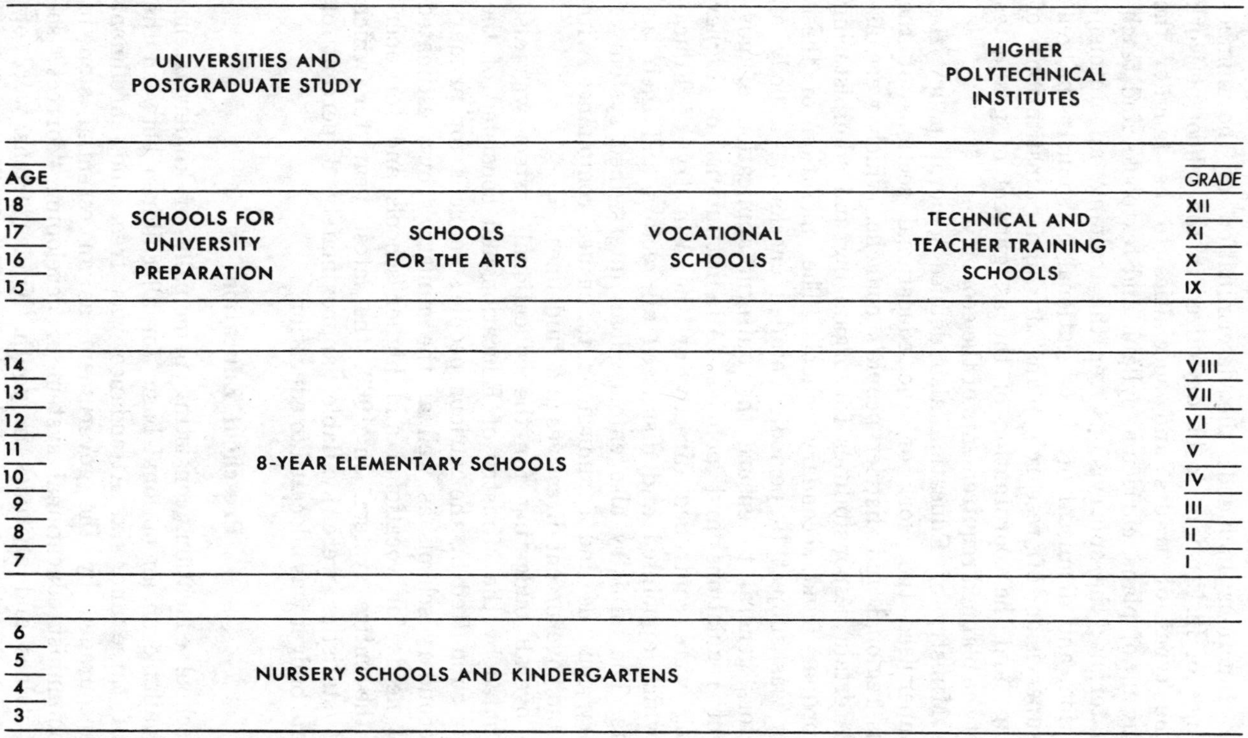

Figure 6. Romania, Structure of Education, 1972.

AGE			GRADE
	UNIVERSITIES AND POSTGRADUATE STUDY	HIGHER POLYTECHNICAL INSTITUTES	
18	SCHOOLS FOR UNIVERSITY PREPARATION	TECHNICAL AND TEACHER TRAINING SCHOOLS	XII
17			XI
16			X
15	SCHOOLS FOR THE ARTS	VOCATIONAL SCHOOLS	IX
14	8-YEAR ELEMENTARY SCHOOLS		VIII
13			VII
12			VI
11			V
10			IV
9			III
8			II
7			I
6	NURSERY SCHOOLS AND KINDERGARTENS		
5			
4			
3			

Note--Attendance is compulsory through grade X.

81

out this broad mission, the ministry cooperated with other central organs of state administration and principally with the Romanian Academy of Social and Political Sciences. Under the country's highly centralized control system, the ministry's specific functions included: the determination of the number and kinds of institutions to be organized in the school network and the types of trades and specialties to be taught; the drawing up of plans, curricula, syllabi, and textbooks and teaching materials; the supervision over the training, appointment, promotion, and dismissal of all educational personnel; the general supervision of research plans at higher institutions of learning; and the coordination of the assignment of graduates to meet the planned requirements of the economy.

The Ministry of Education also defined general policy for, and supervised the work of, the educational sections of the various regional and district people's councils, which were assigned certain responsibilities for organizing and administering local primary and secondary schools. The operation of these schools was subject to periodic detailed checks by a body of inspectors general to ensure the uniform application of government regulations and policies. All institutions of higher learning were controlled directly by the Ministry of Education, which appointed and dismissed all rectors and their assistants. The ministry also employed an intertwined system of advisory councils and commissions to ensure compliance with party and government directives and guidelines.

The overall budgeting for the educational system was also coordinated by the Ministry of Education and consisted of the budgets submitted by the various people's councils for primary and secondary schools as well as the ministry's own estimated budget needs for vocational and higher schools and for operating the entire system. In 1969, the latest year for which official statistics were available, approximately 6 percent of the state budget was allocated to education.

Preschool Education

Preschool education, consisting principally of kindergartens, was available on an optional basis for all children between the ages of three and six. Attendance was free, and enrollment was encouraged by the government as an essential step in the communist educational system of developing "correct" socialist values and attitudes in youth. Kindergartens were organized by districts and were located at the facilities of local enterprises, state organizations, and cooperative agencies. In certain areas, day nurseries attached to kindergartens provided care for the children of working mothers, for which a fee, generally in proportion to the parents' wages, was charged.

If the school was large enough, classes were generally organized on an age-group basis, each with a teacher or supervisor. The number of children attending kindergartens has steadily increased since 1960. During the 1969/70 school year more than 428,000 children, approximately 40 percent of all those eligible, were enrolled in about 10,000 kindergartens and nurseries. Official estimates anticipated that this attendance figure would increase appreciably in future years as more working mothers were added to the labor force.

Primary Education

Primary education was provided, in early 1972, to all children between the ages of six and sixteen in eight-year elementary schools as part of the compulsory education program. During the 1969/70 school year enrollment was about 3.3 million students in about 15,000 schools throughout the country. Instruction was conducted principally in the Romanian language, but in those areas with large minority populations Hungarian- or German-speaking teachers were employed, and special texts were also available in those languages.

Courses taught throughout the first four years, in addition to stressing the Romanian language, included history, geography, arithmetic, elementary biology, art, music, and physical education. Classes usually met six days a week for periods ranging from four to five hours, depending on the type of subject matter to be covered. Grades five through eight emphasized the development of the pupils' ability to express themselves orally and in writing through the intensified teaching of many of the subjects presented in the first four grades. In addition, foreign-language instruction was introduced in the fifth grade, offering a choice of French, German, Russian, or English. In all grades the foundation of political education was laid within the scope of Marxist-Leninist tenets concerning the materialistic development of society, usually presented as part of other general subjects.

Examinations were held in each area of study at the end of the school year. Promotion to the next higher class required a passing grade of five (on the one-to-ten scale) in the substantive work covered, as well as a minimum grade of six for general conduct. A student was permitted to repeat an examination before being failed in a course but, if he failed that too, the entire course had to be repeated.

At the end of the eight-year program all graduates were

required to pass written examinations in history, geography, and literature as well as oral tests in other selected subjects. Those successfully completing both examinations were awarded diplomas and became eligible to take the competitive entrance examinations for secondary school. It was at this point that students were grouped into general categories according to their aptitudes for advanced education: ultimate university-level study, teaching and technical training, the professional arts, and vocational training.

Secondary Education

In late 1971 the necessary adjustments in the secondary school structure to accommodate the changeover from eight to ten years of compulsory education, as provided in the 1968 educational law, had not yet been completed. Although the extension of the program through the tenth grade began with the 1969/70 school year, shortages in funds, educational personnel, and facilities needed for higher student enrollment still existed and were not expected to be overcome until 1973. Secondary schools of all types numbered about 800 in 1970 and had an enrollment of about 370,000 students, roughly one-quarter of those of secondary school age.

General education secondary schools were of the college preparatory type, offered a four-year program, and had the most rigid entrance requirements. Students could select a course either in the humanities or in the natural sciences. The humanities course included such subjects as the Romanian language, a modern language, Latin, history, psychology and logic, and the history of literature. The science course covered mathematics through advanced algebra and probability theory, astronomy, physics, chemistry, biology, and economic and political geography. Physical education and art were included in both courses, as was a subject called sociopolitical science, which covered elements of political economy, "scientific" socialism, and the history of the Communist Party and the labor movement in Romania.

After satisfactory completion of either course of study, all students were required to take the state baccalaureate examination, which qualified them for admission to higher schools or for district employment in middle-level positions in government or in industry. The number of entrants to schools of higher education was determined by the Ministry of Education each year in the light of the needs of the various sectors of the economy and of cultural life. Since the number of applicants usually exceeded the number of spaces allocated to

84

each higher institution, competitive examinations were held, and candidates were selected on the basis of marks received and their general political attitude. Those who either failed the entrance examination—that is, did not receive marks sufficiently high to qualify for a university or polytechnical institute—or were considered politically apathetic were usually placed in short-term vocational courses to qualify them for employment as technicians.

Specialized secondary education was conducted in schools for the professional arts and in technical and teacher training schools. Studies in art schools lasted one or two years and consisted of combined courses of general subjects and specialized training in cultural activities, including various forms of art and drama. Technical schools specialized in industrial fields, agriculture and its associated subfields, forestry, socialist economics, and public health. Courses offered covered four or five years, the time depending on the area of specialization, and included basic courses in general education. Graduates in these technical fields were designated for employment in intermediate-level positions. Teacher training schools, also of four or five years' duration, trained students exclusively for teaching positions at the preschool and elementary levels.

Vocational secondary education encompassed the largest number of schools and was reported to enroll almost 50 percent of all secondary school students. These schools provided a one- or two-year program of combined general education and vocational training in all the trades necessary for the national economy. Vocational schools were usually organized at the locations of industrial enterprises and socialist cooperatives, and students were trained as skilled workers. Additional vocational training was also provided in the form of apprentice or on-the-job training to workers already employed in industrial installations. The bulk of these trainees had either completed the compulsory level of education and then dropped out of school or had failed to be selected in the competitive examination for entrance into secondary school. Vocational training had not kept pace with increasing industrialization, and in 1972 the demand for trained workers continued to surpass the supply (see ch. 16).

Higher Education

The system of higher education was comprised primarily of universities and polytechnical and specialized institutes, which in 1971 had a total enrollment of approximately 150,000 students. All institutions were under the direct supervision of the

Ministry of Education and were geared to produce specialists in the humanities, in the social, natural, physical, and engineering sciences, and in education as needed to fill positions in government and all sectors of the economy. The schools of higher learning were generally headed by a rector (university) or a director (technical institute), who was appointed by the Ministry of Education for a period of four years.

Schools were divided into faculties, headed by deans; faculties, in turn, were divided into departments, each headed by a chairman. Collectively the rector, deans, chairmen, and certain other selected faculty members were grouped into an advisory council, which had broad authority in carrying out the government's educational policies, approving the faculty work programs, supervising the instruction carried out by the departments, and granting degrees at the graduate level.

Students were admitted to all higher schools on the basis of competitive examination and assigned to particular faculties according to government-directed areas of study. Most degree courses at universities required three to six years to complete, and those at polytechnical institutes, from two to three years. Medical and dental degrees were granted at institutes attached to universities and required six years of study.

After completing all course requirements and passing a comprehensive state examination, graduates of the various institutions were assigned to positions in the government or industry as dictated by their specialized work. Students who graduated with distinction were given preference in assignment to positions and in the selection of candidates for postgraduate study. Two higher degrees were available: the Candidate of Science, which required an additional three years of study, the passing of several examinations, and the successful defense of a thesis that made an original contribution to the student's field of specialization; and the Doctor of Science, which also required extensive study, the passing of oral and written examinations, and the successful defense of a thesis based on original and extensive research work in the student's selected field.

Adult Education

Adult education as a supplementary form of instruction was considered an integral part of the educational process. Initiated in the early 1950s, the program was intended to give the workers and peasants the opportunity to improve their level of education and skill and, at the same time, to provide the government with the means of intensifying the ideological and political indoctrination of the general population.

A variety of schools was established throughout the country that offered evening and correspondence courses to volunteer enrollees, mostly between the ages of forty and sixty. The courses consisted of lectures given by volunteer instructors in the social, natural, and political sciences; although no degree or diploma was offered, those who successfully completed courses were eligible, after passing a state examination, for certificates as elementary or higher school graduates.

In 1958 the program was revised and expanded. In that year people's and workers' "universities" were established under the guidance of labor unions, local committees on art and culture, and committees of the Union of Communist Youth. These universities were established at cultural centers, in libraries, in museums, and at collective farms and industrial enterprises. The enrollment age was lowered to twenty to attract youthful school dropouts, and a greater variety of basic general educational and technical courses was introduced. Despite these changes, in 1967 the press reported a general lack of public support for the program. Deficiencies in the system included a lack of adequate classrooms and equipment, the low quality of instruction, and the absence of a vigorous recruitment program.

After the enactment of the new law on education in 1968, the system was again revised; extensive modifications were made in the curricula, and closer supervision of the program was undertaken. In rural areas the school year was shortened to four or six months during the winter, and additional general cultural courses were offered, as well as special courses in foreign languages and modern agricultural techniques. In urban schools the program was reduced to eight or nine months, and modern courses in stenography, television repair, and automatic data processing were made available. As a result of these efforts, official reports in 1970 claimed that the number of schools providing adult education had increased to 171 and that student enrollment totaled almost 100,000.

Teacher Training

Teachers and educators were considered important elements in the ideological and political conditioning process directed toward the country's youth. In addition to their primary task of teaching, they were relied upon to supplement the educational program by acting as disseminators and interpreters of the communist line and by encouraging and influencing young students to participate in state-sponsored activities. In 1971 there were approximately 200,000 teachers assigned to the 16,000 schools throughout the country, and this number was expected to increase with the continued emphasis on mass education.

Teacher training was accomplished at three main levels: pedagogical schools for training preschool and elementary teachers; pedagogical faculties or departments at universities and teachers' institutes for training secondary teachers; and a postgraduate studies program to prepare lecturers and professors for higher educational institutions. There were also refresher training courses conducted at various centers, which all teachers were required to attend once every five years until they had accumulated twenty-five years of experience in the profession. These courses varied in length and generally stressed advances in pedagogical science, counseling techniques, and utilization of modern teaching aids.

As evidence of the importance it placed on the teaching profession, the government, since 1967, has instituted many practices intended to improve the social position of teachers in the community as well as to increase their personal benefits. Among these innovations was the creation of the titles of professor emeritus, educator emeritus, outstanding professor, and outstanding educator in order to honor individuals for exceptional work. The government also authorized several orders and medals to be awarded to teachers for outstanding service and accomplishments.

Teachers were also nominated for places on local people's councils, and increasing numbers were declared eligible for election to the Grand National Assembly. To raise the standard of living for the teaching corps, a new wage system was introduced in 1969, which granted pay increases at all teaching levels, improved promotions, and raised retirement benefits. Government assistance was made available to all teachers for the construction of individual homes in either urban or rural areas in which they were assigned.

EDUCATION OF MINORITIES

Although the government has recognized in principle the right of the national minorities to use their native languages in education, the implementation of official educational policies has reflected a strong preference for the incorporation or integration of all minority groups into the general population. The dissatisfaction of the large Hungarian and German minorities with the inadequacies of minority education eventually surfaced in early 1969 at the national congress of educational workers, and since that time the regime has taken steps to reduce inequalities in the system by providing additional facilities, trained personnel, and teaching materials for the improvement of minority instruction.

As a result of this increased government support, groups as small as six were made eligible to be instructed by a full-time teacher in any non-Romanian native language. High schools with instruction in Hungarian or German were set up in a number of the larger cities and towns that had sizable populations in those nationalities. In addition, sections or classes were organized in certain vocational and industrial schools for the teaching of selected subjects in minority languages, and candidates for admission to higher schools were permitted to take competitive examinations in either Romanian or their native language. By the opening of the 1971/72 school year the government reported that more than 280,000 minority students in 3,162 schools and sections were receiving instruction in their native languages from approximately 14,000 teachers.

CHAPTER 7

ARTISTIC AND INTELLECTUAL EXPRESSION

The arts and intellectual activity reflect Romania's position as a crossroads of Eastern and Western cultures. Elements of ancient Roman culture from the second and third centuries mingle with Byzantine elements (dating from the Middle Ages) and with Islamic elements (brought by the Turkish conquest of the fifteenth century) (see ch. 2). In more recent times, these were joined by elements of Western European culture. Underlying all these influences from abroad are elements of a native peasant culture that can be traced back to the Neolithic settlement found on the territory of the Romanian state. The mixing of all the elements has produced a cultural mosaic that, although it has much in common with the cultures of neighboring countries, is purely Romanian.

The Romanian people are very proud of their cultural heritage and of the artistic and intellectual expression that it has inspired. Artists and intellectuals have always occupied a favored position in society as transmitters of the aspirations of the people. They continue to feel an identity as the social class that is responsible for the spiritual well-being of the nation.

The communist government has promoted this pride in the cultural heritage by devoting considerable funds and effort to the restoration and preservation of antiquities. It has also fostered the preservation of folk art and folk traditions through the establishment of the Village Museums in Bucharest and Cluj and through the continued urging of contemporary artists to produce a national art based on folk traditions.

The various ethnic minorities have preserved their own cultural traditions and forms of expression. Although these forms reflect the same modern influences of foreign origins that have affected Romanian forms, they show relatively little direct borrowing from each other or from the Romanian majority.

Because artistic and intellectual activity is a very effective means of protest and social criticism and, therefore, opposition to the established order, the communist leadership has tried to keep such expression under control and to use it for its own purposes. The degree of cultural freedom and the content of cultural output have been indicators of the political situation in the country.

Despite controls, artists and intellectuals continue to create. Not all of their effort becomes public, and that which does is not necessarily sincere or direct. Symbolism and allusion have been developed to a high degree and are well understood by both the creator and his audience.

THE ROLE OF THE ARTS UNDER COMMUNISM

Since the communists took control of the government in 1947, artistic and intellectual expression has been dominated by the cultural policy of the Romanian Communist Party (Partidul Communist Roman—PCR), which follows the model developed by the Soviet Union. The policy is based on the concept known as Socialist Realism, whereby an artist must strive to grasp the essence of human and social relations and depict them truthfully in the light of socialist ideals. Art must be directed toward the working man; therefore its style must be simple and straightforward.

Adherence to this concept in the formulation and execution of cultural policy has varied, however, and generally reflects the political climate of the time and the particular outlook of the men in power. During the 1950s, which has come to be known as the Dogmatic Period of cultural life in post-World War II Romania, the content of the arts and of intellectual expression was strictly controlled and restricted. Socialist Realism was interpreted to mean the presentation of the glories of communist ideals through the various forms of art and the use of such forms to further these ideals. All cultural effort, therefore, had to be directed to these goals, and no deviation was tolerated. The merits of a book, painting, or play were judged only by how well they fulfilled the propaganda function. Most individuals entrusted with passing judgment on what was or was not acceptable had no professional qualifications. As a result of all these factors, artistic production that was made public during this period was, with few exceptions, dull and mediocre.

With the discrediting of Stalin and his policies in the mid-1950s, dogmatism in artistic expression gave way to a more liberal interpretation of what was considered appropriate. Emphasis on Socialist Realism was replaced with emphasis on nationalistic and historical themes, as Romania strove to gain greater political and economic independence from the Soviet Union. In order to be acceptable to the administrators of cultural policy, artistic expression no longer had to confine itself to the presentation of communist ideals in traditional styles, but it could address itself to a variety of themes and could experiment in innovative styles. Although artists were criticized for submitting to so-called decadent bourgeois culture if they moved too far away from the standards of Socialist Realism, they were not punished or enjoined from further creative activity unless their work could be interpreted as an attack on the regime or its policies.

At the same time, expanding relations between Romania and the noncommunist world brought artists and intellectuals into contact with cultural developments elsewhere and stimulated Romanian creative expression. Cultural exchanges with Western countries were often used by the government to allow artists more freedom of expression than could be politically justified at home. Artists were allowed to exhibit or perform abroad works that had been highly criticized at home. The critical praise received abroad was proudly publicized at home as an example of Romanian genius, at the same time that these very works were being criticized for not meeting the desired standards of artistic expression.

The apparent inconsistency in the application of cultural policy in the late 1960s was indicative of a widespread effort to determine what the role of art and literature should be in a socialist society. By 1971 this had become a much debated topic. Party ideologists, communist and noncommunist artists and critics, and other members of the intellectual elite, including students, aired their views through roundtable discussions, through polemics in the press, and through other means. The debates appeared to be unrestricted and lively, and the views expressed ranged from strict adherence to the concept of Socialist Realism to a plea for "art for art's sake." The opinion of the majority, however, seemed to be that art and literature in a socialist society, as in any other society, have both an aesthetic and a social role. Neither of these functions should overshadow the other; social and political elements in a work of art or literature should be implicit and artistically presented rather than the sole justification for the existence of the work.

In July 1971 President Nicolae Ceausescu announced a tightening of cultural reins in order to bring cultural and educational activity back toward its socialist purpose. The statement was followed by the removal of some books from publication schedules, the cancellation of some theatrical productions, and the resignation or removal of several editors of literary and cultural periodicals. Most observers, however, agreed that, despite some tightening of controls, artistic and intellectual expression in Romania at the end of 1971 was far from returning to the restrictions of the Dogmatic Period of the 1950s.

Cultural policy was administered in 1971 by the Council on Socialist Culture and Education, which had replaced the State Committee for Culture and Art. The council had the status of a ministry in the government, as had the committee that preceded it (see ch. 8). The main overseers of cultural policy and the principal organs of control on artistic and intellectual expression, however, have been the various professional unions. The role of the unions is to supervise and enforce established standards of creative expression and to act as representatives for the members of their professions. A close relationship exists between the union leadership and the communist party, whose control of the unions and, thereby, of the members is exercised through the party leadership (see ch. 9).

Membership in the appropriate union is a prerequisite for effective artistic and intellectual activity. Only members can be employed in their professions and have their works published, performed, or exhibited. Deviation from established cultural policy results in expulsion from the union and consequent professional oblivion. Therefore, most artists and intellectuals exercise self-censorship rather than risk punishment, even if such censorship involves compromising principles and artistic standards.

ART, SCULPTURE, AND ARCHITECTURE

Folk Art

A long heritage of decorative folk art, expressed in wood carving, embroidery, weaving, pottery, and other forms, has been important as artistic expression for the peasants and has served as inspiration for the more sophisticated painters, sculptors, and architects. Regional differences in styles and materials reflect the way of life of the people as well as their needs and the resources available to them.

Some of the typical forms and motifs used through the ages have been found to date back to articles unearthed by archaeologists at Neolithic settlements. In common with the folk art of other countries of Eastern Europe, Romanian folk art uses mostly abstract and geometric designs. When floral or animal forms are used, they are usually stylized.

The carving of wood is a natural form of folk expression in the heavily forested areas of the Carpathians and Transylvania. Pillars and frames of houses and other buildings, farmyard gates, and furniture are decorated with carved geometric designs. Wooden household utensils are also decorated with carved designs, as are farm tools and other objects used in daily life.

Elaborate embroidery decorates the traditional costumes of

both men and women. Those used on festive occasions are particularly richly embellished. Designs and colors vary with the regions and make it possible to identify specific costumes with specific parts of the country. Similar embroidery is also used to decorate household linens.

Particularly well known outside the country are the woven rugs, tablecloths, and tapestries that decorate all rural homes and many urban ones. Designs are mostly geometric, and particular designs and color combinations are associated with particular regions. Well known for their unusual design and warm colors are Oltenian textiles in which a central animal, human, or floral design is surrounded by several frames of different colors. Muntenian textiles, on the other hand, have small geometric designs spread over the whole surface. Moldavian and Transylvanian textiles vary a great deal from one location to another and include both geometric and figurative designs. At one time, wool was used exclusively for weaving rugs and tapestries, but since the mid-nineteenth century cotton or hemp warp has been used in combination with wool. All-cotton and all-hemp rugs and wall hangings are also produced.

Pottery of various kinds is made both as decorative objects and as household utensils. Plates, pots, and jugs are used to serve and store food, but they are also displayed on shelves along the walls of peasant houses, making the interiors colorful and cheerful. The shapes, colors, and designs of the pottery show the many cultural influences from Neolithic to modern West European. Two distinct types of pottery are produced: a black pottery made by incomplete firing of clay with much smoke, and the more common red pottery. Black pottery, the origins of which date back to the Bronze Age or earlier, is made mostly in Moldavia and eastern Transylvania. It has a highly polished finish, which is achieved by the use of a special stone. The widely produced red pottery may be glazed or unglazed and is usually decorated in some fashion—by painting, scratching a design into the wet clay, or applying a design in relief.

Among the more unusual forms of folk art that continue to be practiced are the decoration of Easter eggs and painting on glass. Easter is a special time not only because of its religious significance but also because it heralds the beginning of the growing season, and Easter eggs as a symbol of fertility are an important element of the festivities. Eggs are decorated with highly ornamental patterns in various ways and often become respected works of art.

Painting on glass was introduced into Transylvania in the seventeenth century from Bohemia and was used for the production of religious icons. Icon painting formed an important bridge between folk art and the fine arts in the eighteenth and nineteenth centuries. It is no longer widely practiced.

A number of contemporary artists utilize the various forms of folk art as their medium of artistic expression. Their designs include not only the traditional but also elements of modern art styles, such as cubism and abstraction.

Fine Arts

The beginnings of fine art in Romania date back to the fourteenth century when frescoes and other paintings were created to decorate the churches of the period. All of the early art was created in connection with churches, although not all of it was religious in content. Portraits of those responsible for the building of churches or monasteries, and of their families, were often included among the pictures of saints and biblical scenes that decorate the interior and exterior walls of medieval religious buildings.

Romanian church art of the fourteenth and fifteenth centuries is recognized as some of the finest and most unusual of the later period of Byzantine art. It differs somewhat in style from other examples of Byzantine art of that period by reflecting the influence of folk art. Some of the finest examples are found at the Moldavian monasteries of Putna, Sucevita, and Voronet. They are unusual in that they were painted on the outside walls in order to educate the peasants in church history and in elements of their faith. The quality and imaginativeness of these frescoes has been termed one of the great contributions to European religious art. Their freshness after more than 400 years of exposure to the elements is remarkable.

In addition to paintings, religious art of the medieval period also included various objects, such as vestments, furniture, and vessels worked in wood, gold, or silver and richly decorated. Collections of these objects are preserved at the monasteries, the largest exhibits being at Sucevita and Putna.

During the seventeenth century a change in style took place in painting and other decorative arts, although the subject matter remained religious. Russian artists who had come to Moldavia and Walachia introduced the small, detailed painting of Russian iconography, which became evident in the murals and other painting of Romanian artists. At the same time, the simple, folk art decorative forms were replaced by a more elaborate style showing both Baroque and Oriental influences. A distinct Walachian style developed, and schools emerged in Bucharest and other cities. The most notable achievements of the Walachian school are the interior frescoes of the Hurez Monastery.

A secular trend was introduced into art in the eighteenth century with a greater involvement of merchants, craftsmen, and landowners as patrons. Not until the nineteenth century, however, did a completely secular art come into being, mostly through foreign influences. The earliest secular artists reflect in their styles the training they had received as religious artists.

In the early nineteenth century several foreign painters lived and worked in Romania and exerted a strong influence on young Romanian artists who, in turn, helped to train other artists of the nineteenth century. The spirit of nationalism and revolution that was sweeping Europe during that century involved Romanian artists as it did those in other countries under foreign rule. Art was a medium for expressing nationalist sentiments and the fight for self-determination. Most of the art of the period, therefore, represents historic and heroic subjects. Foremost among the revolutionary artists were Gheorghe Tattarescu and Theodor Aman, both extremely popular in their lifetime. Together, they exerted a great influence on the development of fine arts in Romania by founding the School of Fine Arts in Bucharest and by training young artists. Aman, in particular, is considered the country's first great modern painter.

By far the most outstanding artist of the nineteenth century was Nicolae Grigorescu. His work remains extremely popular among Romanians, and his lyrical landscapes and scenes of Romanian life are well known abroad.

The work of Stefan Luchian at the beginning of the twentieth century introduced to Romania some of the avant-garde styles that were appearing in European art elsewhere. Although he followed his predecessors in painting landscapes and rural subjects, he opposed their conservative style and introduced into his paintings a greater use of color than had been common. He also introduced social themes into his paintings by depicting the misery and poverty that were characteristic of the lives of most people. His best paintings, however, are flower studies, which bring out his love of color and of nature.

Luchian's break with tradition and his use of color were followed by a number of artists, the most celebrated of whom was Nicolae Tonitza. These and other artists of the interwar period were greatly influenced by the impressionist and postimpressionist painters in Paris and Munich, where they studied. Their landscapes, flower studies, and portraits show the effective use of bright colors, which is considered characteristic of Romanian art.

Because landscapes, floral studies, and other neutral subjects have traditionally been the main concern of Romanian painters, this form of artistic expression was the least affected by the strict controls of the first decade of communist rule. A number of interwar artists and several younger ones continued to produce their canvases in the precommunist tradition, but during the 1960s some young artists experimented with various avant-garde techniques and styles that were then current in Western Europe. Although the government disapproved of these works, it allowed the artists to exhibit them abroad and win considerable acclaim for Romanian art. In the late 1960s the PCR was disturbed by the extent to which abstract art had blossomed despite party disapproval. Artists had been introducing cubism and primitivism into their work under the guise of folk art, which is supposed to serve as their main inspiration.

Sculpture

Romanian sculpture has its origins in the tombstones and other grave markers dating back to the Middle Ages. As a fine art, sculpture began to develop in the mid-nineteenth century when the German sculptor Karl Storck arrived in Bucharest to teach at the School of Fine Arts. Among the earliest sculptors he trained were Ion Georgescu and his own son, Carol Storck, both known for their statuary and busts. Stefan Ionescu Valbudea, also in that group, was best known for his romantic statues and classical male figures in movement.

In the period between the two world wars, several sculptors produced large monumental works visible in public places. Dimitrie Paciurea was the first in this group. He was followed by his students Corneal Madrea, Ion Jalea, and Oscar Han. In addition to his monumental sculptures, Jalea is also known for his busts and bas-reliefs. Han is particularly known for his busts and statutes of famous Romanians.

Best known of all Romanian sculptors is Constantin Brancusi, who is considered one of the great sculptors of the world. Brancusi studied in Bucharest and in Paris. His earliest work, mostly busts, shows a strong influence of Auguste Rodin. Gradually he broke with tradition and developed a highly stylized and abstract style utilizing the simplest forms. His best known works are found in important collections throughout the world.

The work of contemporary sculptors included a wide range of styles and mediums. Modernistic works in stone, wood, and various metals, some of them completely abstract, can be seen in parks and other public places throughout the country. A number of contemporary sculptors have taken inspiration from folk art for their often massive works in wood.

Architecture

Architecture, more than any other form of artistic expression, reflects the many cultural influences that have been exerted on the people of Romania over the ages. The abundance of architectural styles found in the country has been a source of great pride for Romanians who have devoted much time and money to preserve them.

The simplest architectural forms are those of the peasant houses made of wood and clay. The style and building technique of many of these houses have been traced back to those used in Neolithic settlements.

Vestiges of Roman architecture can be found in Dobruja, Walachia, and Transylvania. The most important of these are the remains of the bridge built by Emperor Trajan across the Danube at Turnu Severin. A large amphitheater has been unearthed at the site of the Dacian-Roman capital of Sarmizegetusa at the southwestern tip of the Transylvanian plain. Other Roman remains include several monuments as well as sections of roads and aqueducts.

The period of greatest architectural creativity is usually referred to as the feudal period, dating from the tenth century to the beginning of the nineteenth century. The oldest structures of that period are the fully preserved Byzantine church at Densus, Transylvania, and the ruins of the Prince's Court at Curtea de Arges. Beginning in the fourteenth century, distinctive architectural styles developed in Walachia, Moldavia, and Transylvania.

The architecture of Walachia and Moldavia shows strong Byzantine influences and includes all the special forms and decorative styles of the several periods of Byzantine art. Specifically Romanian variations are the exterior frescoes and the massive protecting walls of some of the churches and monasteries.

Transylvanian architecture of the feudal period reflects Western European influences, including Romanesque, Gothic, Renaissance, and Baroque styles. The fortified churches and castles built by German and Hungarian settlers are reminiscent of similar structures in central Europe but distinguished by their massiveness and fortifications. The older architecture of several cities in central Transylvania is completely Germanic or Hungarian in character, contrasting sharply with that of Walachian and Moldavian cities. The typical Romanian architecture found throughout the Transylvanian countryside is particularly prominent in many rural wooden churches, which invariably feature fine pointed spires.

During the seventeenth century the Brancovan style of architecture was developed in Walachia, the name being derived from

99

that of the ruling Prince Constantin Brincoveanu. It is characterized by the use of open porches supported by large pillars. The pillars and door and window frames are usually elaborately carved with floral designs. The exterior of the building is usually ringed by a wide, carved wooden band. Outstanding examples of the Brancovan style are the Hurez Monastery and the Mogosoaia Palace in Bucharest. More recent adaptations of the style are seen in several public buildings and private villas built in Bucharest before World War I.

Starting in the nineteenth century, Byzantine influences began to disappear from architecture. Most building after that period followed contemporary European styles, although elements of Romanian folk art were often incorporated in the decorative details. Modern architecture began to develop in the period between the world wars and reached a high level of accomplishment in the 1950s and 1960s with the construction of the seaside resorts of Mangalia, Eforie Nord, and Mamaia. Most contemporary architecture, however, is oversized and utilitarian. The needs for rapid and cheap construction forced architects to disregard aesthetics and produce monotonous, dreary structures.

MUSIC

Romanians have the reputation of being a musical people. Song and dance play an important role in their daily lives, particularly among the peasants. A rich heritage of folk music, both vocal and instrumental, has been passed down from generation to generation and has formed the background for serious Romanian music that began to develop in the mid-nineteenth century.

Folk music can be broadly classified as dance music, ballads and laments, and pastoral music. Dance music is most frequently performed and is a major component of any festivity. Dance tunes are generally lively to accompany the fast and intricate steps of the dancers. Sometimes they are sung by the dancers, but more often they are played by one or more of the traditional instruments.

The basic instrument in folk music is the violin. It is often accompanied by the *cobza*, a large stringed instrument resembling the lute, or by a *tambal*, a zither-like instrument played with small hammers. A variety of flutes are also used both as solo intruments and in orchestras. The accordion is popular as a solo accompaniment for singing or dancing.

Folk musicians are known as *lautari* (lute players) and are often Gypsies. Small orchestras are found at weddings and other celebrations in every village and in the cities. Larger, specially formed folk ensembles perform on radio and television and give concerts.

Ballads and laments vary in style and subject matter from region to region. Over the years, ballads have lost most of their importance as a contemporary musical form, although they retain value as poetry. Laments, however, continue to play an important role in the musical life of the people. They reflect in song the hardships and problems of daily life and the trials and tribulations of love. Some laments have a distinctly Oriental quality.

Pastoral music was developed by the shepherds of the Carpathians as a diversion for their long, lonely days in the mountains and as a means of communication. The melodies are very simple, usually played on any of several types of alphorns or on flutes. With the changing way of life in the mountains, pastoral music has been disappearing as a musical form.

In the early nineteenth century folklorist Anton Pann began to collect Romanian folk music, to publish it, and to popularize it among educated Romanians, who were more familiar with the classical music of Germany, Italy, and France than with their own musical heritage. This resulted in the emergence of a group of Romanian composers who utilized folk melodies in the composition of operas, symphonies, and chamber music.

The period between the two world wars saw several composers adding to the repertoire of Romanian music. One who achieved international fame was Georghe Enescu. Dinu Lipatti became well known as a pianist, although he was also a composer.

The music of the interwar composers showed the influence of German romanticism and postromanticism and of modern French music. All of it, however, had a strongly Romanian character attained through the use of intonations and rhythms borrowed from folk music.

Several of the interwar composers were still active in 1970, together with new younger composers. Their music is regularly performed in Romania and in some of the other communist countries, but it is not well known elsewhere. Some of the young composers have experimented with avant-garde styles that have not been well received by the guardians of cultural policy. Composers are urged to use folklore as their source of inspiration and to write compositions reflecting the cultural policies of the PCR.

THEATER

Theater has always played a vital role in the life of the educated Romanian, and regular attendance at plays, operas, and ballets is considered an essential part of his cultural and intellectual life. The performing arts, therefore, have had a faithful and critical audience in all urban centers, which has stimulated playwrights and directors. In cities such as Cluj and Brasov, which have sizable minority populations, Hungarian and German theaters thrive beside the Romanian.

Since the end of the rigid restrictions of the 1950s, the performing arts have been flourishing with talented performers, directors, and writers. The government has been promoting the presentation of Romanian plays, and Romanian playwrights have striven to compete for audience favor with the best of contemporary and classical foreign plays, which are regularly presented.

Among contemporary playwrights who have achieved critical acclaim at home and abroad are Paul Everac, D. R. Popescu, Horia Lovinescu, Iosif Naghiu, and Paul Anghel. Eugene Ionesco, although Romanian by birth, is generally considered a French playwright since he writes in French. Romanians, however, proudly claim him as one of their own, even though his plays do not follow the desired standards of form and content.

Most contemporary plays have been categorized by critics as tribunal drama in that they pass judgment on ideas or actions and follow a format where one or more characters take the role of the accused and others act as prosecutors. Some plays are in the form of confessions of wrongdoings or wrongthinking. Both forms lend themselves well to imparting a message. Pure entertainment plays are usually boulevard comedies. Historic themes seem to be popular and safe topics, particularly if they promote Romanian nationalism. For the most part, plays are of local rather than universal interest, for they deal with matters limited in time and space. They usually arouse interest outside Romania for what they reveal of the Romanian character and society rather than for artistic merit.

The tightening of cultural reins in July 1971 seems to have had a greater effect on the theater than on any other form of artistic expression. The management of several major theaters was changed in late 1971 following admission by the replaced managers of having favored artistic merit over ideological value in the selection of plays for their repertory. The new managers pledged themselves to presenting plays that contain a clear-cut message conforming to high political, ideological, and educational standards. They also pledged themselves to encourage young playwrights to write such plays. In the meantime, the plays selected for the 1971–72 season were almost all true and tried classics, devoid of any political implications. Romanian directors, nevertheless, have shown themselves in the past to be able to impart to the audience a great deal of political meaning through their interpretation of such seemingly innocuous plays.

FILMS

The film industry has a long and venerable history dating back to 1912, when the first full-length feature was produced. The silent comedies of the 1920s compare favorably with those produced by the best film makers of the time. In the 1930s and 1940s, until the communist takeover, Romanian musicals and tales of suspense and of the supernatural were popular at home and abroad. Most of these films were produced with technical and financial assistance from France and other countries (see ch. 11).

Cultural restrictions in the 1950s and early 1960s prevented the Romanian film industry from taking part in the technical and artistic developments that were changing the film industry in France and other Western countries. As a result, films produced in Romania as late as 1970 were technically and artistically old-fashioned compared to those produced in noncommunist countries and even in Czechoslovakia. Most critics outside the country compare them to the good films produced by Hollywood in the 1940s. Nevertheless, several Romanian films in the 1960s have won prizes at lesser known international film festivals.

Two of the important directors in the late 1960s were Mircea Dragan and Ion Popescu-Gopo. Dragan specializes in historic adventure films of epic proportions, whereas Popescu-Gopo concentrates on fantasies, including science fiction. Popescu-Gopo is also well known for his animated films.

LITERATURE

Literature in the form of folk tales and poetry is of ancient origin. A vast collection of legends, tales, ballads, proverbs, and riddles has been preserved and is known to both rural and urban Romanians. Legends and tales deal with the daring exploits of a national hero, sometimes real and sometimes imaginary. In the oldest tales, the adversaries are monsters and inhabitants of the underworld; in later ones, they are the foreign conquerors and occupiers.

Ballads were originally intended to be sung but are now more often recited as poems. They deal with the same subjects as legends and tales, and many are of epic proportions. In the mountains of Transylvania and Moldavia separate groups of ballads developed dealing with the pastoral life of the people.

The earliest known texts written in Romania are chronicles in Old Church Slavonic. In the sixteenth century a number of religious texts were translated into Romanian, and the introductions to them are the first known original writings in the Romanian language.

Of significance in the seventeenth and eighteenth centuries were the chronicles written by a number of writers in Moldavia and in Walachia. Dimitrie Cantemir, ruler of Moldavia, wrote the *Description of Moldavia* and *History of the Rise and Fall of the Ottoman Empire* during the same period. A Transylvanian school of writing stressed the Latin origin of the Romanian people and their language and utilized a latinized Romanian in its writing. It was influential in awakening the national consciousness of Transylvanian Romanians.

Four members of the Vacarescu family wrote lyrical poetry in the eighteenth century. The best of them, Iancu Vacarescu, is regarded as the father of Romanian poetry. The lyric tradition was carried on in the early nineteenth century, and much of the poetry dealt with historic subjects and expressed the growing patriotism and nationalist sentiment of the time.

In the early nineteenth century the Latinist movement of Transylvania spread into Moldavia and Walachia and began to Romanianize the hitherto Hellenic culture of the Romanian upper class. The founding of the College of Saint Sava in Bucharest, using Romanian as the language of instruction, laid the foundation for the development of a reading public for Romanian literature. At the same time, the founding of a Romanian-language newspaper with a literary supplement gave writers a publication outlet. The newspaper was founded by Eliade Radulescu, who also founded the Philharmonic Society and the Romanian Academy, thus giving major impetus to the development of Romanian literature and culture.

In Moldavia, Gheorghe Asachi originated the historical short story, wrote verse, and also founded a newspaper. The literary supplement of Asachi's newspaper provided an outlet for Moldavian writers.

The nineteenth century was the romantic age of Romanian literature. Writers and poets wrote under the influence of Russian, French, and English romanticists whose works were widely translated. Outstanding among the poets was Grigore Alexandrescu, who also wrote fables and satires along the lines of Alphonse de Lamartine and Jean de LaFontaine. Many historical works were written by Nicolae Balcescu and Mihail Kogalniceanu, both of whom were political figures in the nationalist movement of their time as well as important writers. The founding in 1840 of the literary magazine *Dacia Literata* by Kogalniceanu marked the beginning of the traditionalist school, which was characterized by the use of specifically Romanian themes. An outstanding exponent of this school was the short story writer, Constantine Negruzzi.

The second half of the nineteenth century saw the development of modern literature through the impetus of serious criticism based on German and French philosophical thought and cultural trends. The period was dominated by Vasile Alecsandri and Mihail Eminescu. During Alecsandri's long career, he produced outstanding works in every form of literary expression—prose, poetry, drama, and nonfiction. Together with Negruzzi and Kogalniceanu, he was one of the early directors of the National Theatre in Iasi.

Eminescu is Romania's outstanding poet and holds his place among the important poets of the world. His lyrical poetry is influenced by Romanian folklore, Hindu thought, and German philosophy. His ballad *Luceafarul* (Evening Star) is a well-known classic. In addition to poetry, Eminescu wrote short stories and political and philosophical essays. He was one of the leaders of the Junimea, a literary circle for youth in Iasi, which was founded by the important critic Titu Mairescu. Other important members of the circle were Ion Luca Caragiale, a playwright who first introduced social comedy to Romania, and Ion Creanga, who wrote about the peasant life from which he stemmed.

Around the beginning of the twentieth century the growing popularity of peasant themes and descriptions of peasant life in the writing of such authors as Ion Slavici and Gheorghe Cosbuc led to the publication of a new literary periodical, *Samanatorul,* and the development of a literary school that took its name. The school stressed the national heritage of Romania, its folklore, and its rustic life as subjects for literary creation, in contrast to the cosmopolitan outlook of the Junimea circle.

Parallel to the Samanatorul school developed *poporanism* (of the people), which was similar to the then-current Russian populism in its social and political motivation. Its organ was *Viata Romaneasca,* which featured populist causes.

Several writers remained apart from any of the schools. Among them was Barbu Delavrancea, well-known for his trilogy about Stephen the Great and for stories of Walachian peasant life, and the poet Alexandru Macedonski, who introduced French symbolism to Romanian literature.

The period between the two world wars gave rise to the novel, which quickly took its place beside lyrical poetry as an important form of literary expression. An important contributor to the development of the novel was Liviu Rebreanu, whose *Forest of the Hanged* is a powerful description of the horrors of war. His other important novels are *Ion*, dealing with peasant life, and *Ciuleandra*, a psychological novel.

Mihail Sadoveanu, whose most important works were published in the 1920s and 1930s, is considered the foremost realist of the twentieth century. His writings deal mostly with history and with peasant life. In 1924 he won the national prize for literature, and in 1949, the Gold Peace Medal.

Outstanding interwar poets were Lucian Blaga, Ion Barbu, and Tudor Arghezi. Blaga's poetry was an exposition of his philosophy based on the traditional way of life interpreted as a cosmic mystery. Barbu's poems are of an abstract and esoteric nature. Arghezi is considered the greatest poet since Eminescu on the basis of his use of language and symbolism.

Immediately after World War II poetry again took the lead in literary expression. Although much prose was published, none of it was considered of particular importance. The poetry can be divided into three main schools: surrealist poetry, poetry of spiritual revolt, and a return-to-tradition balladry.

Several of the prewar writers and poets continued to produce after the communist takeover and subjected themselves to the constraints of Socialist Realism. Among them were Sadoveanu, Calinescu, Camil Petrescu, and Arghezi. Others were denounced for their previous writings and became silent. The literary output of the 1950s is generally regarded as second rate. Several notable novels, however, were published in the early 1960s. Among them were George Calinescu's *Bietul Ioanide* (Poor Ioanide), Ion Sadoveanu's *Ion Sintu* (Saint John), and Petru Dimitriu's *Cronica de Familie* (Family Chronicle). Of particularly outstanding merit and lasting quality are Marin Preda's peasant epic *Morometii* (The Moroments) and Eugen Barbu's naturalist novel *Groapa* (The Trench).

With the relaxing of cultural controls in the mid-1960s, many of those who had been silent resumed their writing, together with a new group of younger writers. The mid- and late-1960s saw an outpouring of literary creativity that had been pent up during the preceding decade. The variety of genres and styles was impressive; some continued the traditions of the past, others repudiated their literary traditions and ventured into new areas of expression. Lyricism dominated the poetry of Ion Alexandru, Adrian Paunescu, Marin Sorescu, and others. Their greatest appeal was among young people whose doubts, hopes, and restlessness they expressed.

Prose showed two trends: realism, which was now free to examine all aspects of human existence; and antirealism, which showed influences of some contemporary French writers.

Literary criticism, which had played an important role in the development of Romanian literature, was revived as a literary art and was removed from politics. Both old and new works were examined and evaluated, and Romanian literary traditions were studied and analyzed. The literary output of the 1950s was attacked for its lack of imagination and creativity.

The retightening of controls in 1971 reduced the volume of new works being published, and many writers retreated into a self-censorship, which restricted their creativity. Literary periodicals and other publication media were more selective in deciding what to publish, whereas some critics attacked the volume and quality of the recent literary output.

SCHOLARSHIP AND RESEARCH

A tradition of scholarship and research has in the past been limited to a small intellectual elite centered in Bucharest and Iasi. The group was oriented toward France and, to a lesser extent, Germany in terms of professional contacts and sources of inspiration. During the 1930s a number of sociologists at the University of Bucharest established a reputation for outstanding and original work in their field.

The great expansion of the educational system since the 1940s has provided a much broader base for scholarly activity but, in keeping with ideological dictates, scholarly activity must be socially useful, that is, directly applicable to the needs of the society. Therefore, great emphasis has been placed on applied research in the sciences and technology designed to improve the economy. All research is sponsored by the state and is directed and supervised by the National Council for Scientific Research.

The interest in sociology has continued, but work in this field, as in the other social sciences, has suffered from the restrictions imposed by communist ideology. The only accepted philosophy is that of Marxism-Leninism, and all scholarly work must be based on its precepts, which frequently leads to sterile research or preconceived results.

Two developments by Romanians in the field of medicine have caused considerable controversy among specialists in other parts of the world. One is a regeneration therapy for the aged based on the administration of procaine, which was developed by Anna Aslan of the Institute of Gerontology. The therapy, strongly backed by the government, is intended to free the elderly from the various chronic discomforts of advanced age and thereby make them more active. Many prominent gerontologists have questioned the efficacy of the treatments and the results claimed by the Institute of Gerontology, but others have reported it to be fully effective. A Romanian-developed drug used in the treatment is extensively sold in Europe. The other medical development acclaimed by Romania but questioned by many specialists in the field is the use of an extract obtained from cattle eyes for the treatment of many human eye diseases. The extract was developed by Professor Petre Vancea.

SECTION II. POLITICAL

CHAPTER 8

GOVERNMENTAL SYSTEM

As of early 1972 the structure of the government remained essentially the same as that established by the 1965 Constitution. Power is declared to belong to the working people united under the leadership of the Romanian Communist Party (Partidul Comunist Roman—PCR). That power is said to be expressed through their representatives to the Grand National Assembly, the nation's sole legislative body, and through the people's councils, the organs of government on county and local levels. Constitutionally, the Grand National Assembly, as the highest voice of the people, is asserted to be the supreme organ of state power, and all other government bodies are theoretically subordinate to it.

Actual political power, however, is monopolized by the PCR and particularly by the highest organs of the party under the leadership of Nicolae Ceausescu, who is simultaneously head of state. Although the system of government is, in theory, designed to emphasize participatory democracy, the government functions largely as the administrative structure through which the party exerts its will in all aspects of Romanian society (see ch. 9).

There is no separation of powers between the branches of the government, and it is difficult to draw distinctions between the executive and the legislative functions. The Council of State is closely tied to the structure and membership of the Grand National Assembly and functions as a permanent assembly presidium. The nation's highest administrative body, the Council of Ministers, is elected by the assembly and responsible to both the assembly and the Council of State. Although it is theoretically independent in its judicial decisions, the Supreme Court is also constitutionally responsible to the assembly.

The entire structure of the government, from national down to local levels, is organized on a principle of centralized control by which all lower bodies are subject to the authority and control of the next higher unit, the ultimate power resting in the central government. The governmental system consists of nominally representative bodies at community, town, and county levels, which are hierarchically subordinated to the authority of the central government. Throughout the entire system the predominant influence of the party is evident, the key positions at each level being held by party members.

THE CONSTITUTIONAL SYSTEM

Constitutional Development

Since coming under full communist control in December 1947, Romania has had three constitutions. The first, designating the country a "People's Republic," was adopted by the Grand National Assembly in April 1948, just four weeks after the assembly had been reorganized under new communist leadership. The second, officially adopted in September 1952, had first been made public the preceding July after Gheorghe Gheorghiu-Dej had assumed the post of prime minister in addition to his position as head of the party. A third constitution, incorporating the elements of Romania's changed social and ideological position, entered into force on August 20, 1965.

In many ways similar to the initial constitutions of the other Soviet-dominated states of Eastern Europe, the 1948 Constitution was designed to mark Romania's entry into the first stage of the transition from capitalism to socialism. As a people's democracy, state power was said to derive from the people as expressed through the Grand National Assembly, nominally, the supreme organ of state power. A nineteen-member Presidium was elected by and from the membership of the assembly to provide continuity of legislative authority when the assembly itself was not in session. The highest executive and administrative organ was the Council of Ministers, which functioned under the direction of the prime minister. Although it was not mentioned in the constitution, the Communist Party functioned as the supreme decisionmaking authority over and above that of the government.

The right of ownership of private property was guaranteed, although the constitution provided that privately held means of production, banks, and insurance companies could be nationalized when the "general interest" so required. Less than two months after the adoption of the constitution, the Grand National Assembly applied this "general interest" principle and nationalized all banking, industrial, insurance, mining, and transportation enterprises.

Described in the constitution in anticipation of their actual establishment, the organs of state power in the regions, counties, districts, and communes were designated "people's councils." Formally established by law in 1949, these bodies were organized into a centralized system in which the lower level councils were fully subordinated to the next higher council and all functioned under the direct control of the central organs of government.

Changes that were effected in the political, social, and economic structure of the country after 1948 were incorporated into a new constitution in 1952. Patterned largely after the 1936 Constitution of the Soviet Union, the 1952 document specifically designated the Romanian Workers' Party (title of the Communist Party between 1948 and 1965) as the representative of the working class and the country's leading political force. The nation's close ties with the Soviet Union were strongly emphasized. Several references to the Soviet Union glorified its role in the liberation of the country from fascism during World War II and described the Soviets as great friends of the Romanian people. Whereas the 1948 Constitution declared that "the Romanian People's Republic was born amid the struggle conducted by the people, under the leadership of the working class, against fascism, reaction, and imperialism," that of 1952 asserted the republic "was born and consolidated following the liberation of the country by the armed forces of the Soviet Union."

As did the 1948 Constitution, that of 1952 guaranteed full equality to the country's national minority groups, but the 1952 Constitution also established an autonomous administrative unit, the Hungarian Autonomous Region (Mures-Magyar), for the large Hungarian population. The region was given its own people's council and local authorities, although these were clearly subordinated to the organs of the central government. Including the Hungarian Autonomous Region, the country was administered through twenty regional units that, in turn, were subdivided into districts, towns, and rural localities.

Citizens were guaranteed the right to work for remuneration; the right to rest, assured by the establishment of the eight-hour workday and paid annual vacations for workers and office employees; the right to material security when old, ill, or disabled; and the right to education. Full equality in all aspects of economic, political, and cultural life was guaranteed to all working people regardless of nationality, race, or sex.

Freedom of speech, the press, assembly, and public demonstration were likewise assured, as was freedom of religion. Churches, however, were forbidden to operate schools except for the training of religious personnel. Other rights guaranteed the protection of the person from arbitrary arrest, the inviolability of the home, and the secrecy of the mail. The right of citizens to form public and private organizations was also assured, although associations having a "fascist or antidemocratic character" were prohibited.

Citizen duties to the state included the observance of the constitution and the laws of the republic and the obligation to preserve and develop socialist property, to practice discipline in regard to work, and to work in general for the strengthening of the "regime of people's democracy." Military service and the defense of the nation were described as duties of honor for all citizens.

In March 1961 the Grand National Assembly established a commission to prepare a new draft constitution. At the same time the 1952 Constitution was revised to transform the Presidium of the assembly into the Council of State. The new council, vested with supreme executive authority, consisted of a president, three vice presidents, and thirteen members. As was the case with the Presidium, the Council of State was elected by and from the assembly membership and was, in theory at least, responsible to it.

The authority of the council was threefold, consisting of permanent powers, powers to be exercised between assembly sessions, and special powers that could be exercised in exceptional circumstances. The permanent powers were exercised by the president, who was by virtue of his position the head of state, and focused primarily on the representation of the republic in international relations. Between sessions of the assembly the Council of State was empowered to oversee the activity of the Council of Ministers, appoint and recall members of the Supreme Court and the commander in chief of the armed forces, supervise the functioning of the Office of the Prosecutor General, and convene standing commissions of the assembly.

The council could also issue decrees having the force of law although, at least technically, these had to be submitted to the next assembly session for ratification. In the event of circumstances that might prevent the assembly from convening, the council was authorized to appoint the Council of Ministers, declare war, order mobilization, proclaim a state of emergency, approve the budget, and prepare economic plans: Gheorghe Gheorghiu-Dej, first secretary of the Romanian Workers' Party, was elected as president of the Council of State. Ion Gheorghe Maurer—who had been chairman of the assembly Presidium, and thus titular head of state, since 1958—became prime minister.

112

Although the draft constitution prepared by the commission appointed in 1961 was never adopted, it was used as the basis for the work of a second commission named in June 1965. Under the chairmanship of Ceausescu, the commission prepared a new draft and submitted it to the party congress and the Council of State. After being approved by these bodies the Constitution was adopted by the Grand National Assembly on August 20, 1965.

The Constitution of 1965

After the adoption of the first communist constitution in 1948 the country had officially borne the title of a people's republic. With the promulgation of the new Constitution in 1965 the name of the country was changed to the Socialist Republic of Romania (Republica Socialista Romania). In adopting this title, the Romanian leadership was asserting that the country had completed the transition from capitalism and had become a full-fledged socialist state.

Observers of Eastern European politics considered the emphasis placed on national sovereignty and independence in the new Constitution to be significant. Whereas the 1952 Constitution repeatedly stressed the country's close ties to the Soviet Union and the role of the Soviet army in the liberation of Romania during World War II, the 1965 Constitution omits all reference to the Soviet Union. Instead, it refers only to the policy of maintaining friendly and fraternal relations with all socialist states and, in addition, expresses the intention of promoting friendly relations with nonsocialist states.

There is also increased provision for civil liberties in the 1965 Constitution, including the right of petition, the right of individual recourse to the courts in the event of illegal acts of state agencies, and rights equivalent to habeas corpus. The extent of individual freedom is qualified, however, by the declaration that the "freedom of speech, of the press, reunion, meeting and demonstration cannot be used for aims hostile to the socialist system and to the interests of the working people." While proclaiming freedom of association and organization, the 1965 Constitution, as did that of 1952, prohibits associations of a "fascist or antidemocratic character."

Perhaps owing to the declared advancement to the stage of socialism, the 1965 Constitution contains no reference to the "private capitalist sector" of the economy, as had the 1952 document. Whereas the 1952 Constitution had recognized the private sector as one of three elements of the economic system, along with the socialist sector and the sector described as "small-scale commodity production," that of 1965 declares the basis of the economy to rest solely on the socialist ownership of the means of production. Cooperative farmers, however, are permitted the personal ownership of some livestock and tools, certain craftsmen are guaranteed ownership of their workshops, and peasants who are not in cooperatives are able to own small parcels of land and some farm implements.

Changes that had been made in the organizational structure of the government after 1952 were incorporated into the 1965 Constitution. The Council of State is described as the "supreme body of state power with a permanent activity," although it remains theoretically subordinate to the Grand National Assembly, which is designated as "the supreme body of state power." In contrast to the 1952 Constitution, which provided for representation to the Grand National Assembly on the basis of one deputy for every 40,000 persons, the 1965 document fixes the number of assembly deputies at 465 and requires the establishment of that number of constituencies of equal population.

Although the Hungarian Autonomous Region continued to exist, the 1952 provision guaranteeing "administrative and territorial autonomy" to the Hungarian population was omitted from the 1965 Constitution. All of the sixteen regional units were subsequently eliminated by a territorial reorganization of 1968, at which time a system of *judete* (counties) was established.

All power is ascribed to the people and exercised by their representatives in the people's councils and the Grand National Assembly. The Communist Party is described as the country's leading political force under whose leadership the working people have the expressed goal of building the socialist system to create "the conditions for transition to communism."

THE STRUCTURE AND FUNCTIONING OF THE GOVERNMENT

The Central Government

According to the 1965 Constitution the major institutions of the central government are the Grand National Assembly, the Council of State, and the Council of Ministers (see fig. 1). Although the Constitution declares the Grand National Assembly and the Council of State to be the supreme organs of state power, in practice the authority of both of these organs ranks after that of the PCR. The Constitution itself states unequivocally that "the leading political force of the whole society is the Romanian Communist Party." The basic national

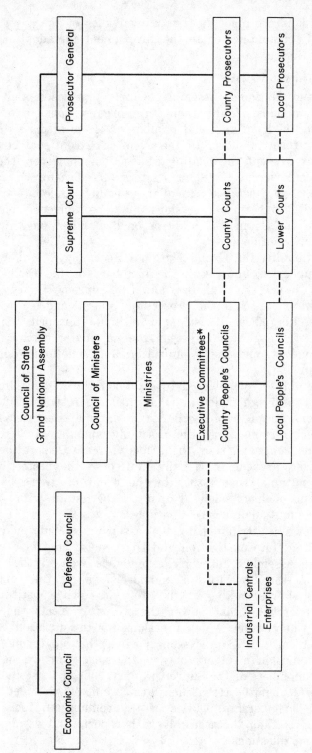

* Chairman of County People's Council is also secretary of the County Party Committee.

Figure 7. Structure of the Government of Romania, 1971.

115

policy decisions are made in the ruling bodies of the party and subsequently communicated to the government for adoption and implementation.

The Grand National Assembly

The Grand National Assembly, which supervises and controls the functions of all other state organs, consists of 465 deputies elected from an equal number of electoral districts for a four-year term of office. In the event of exceptional circumstances that prevent the holding of elections, however, the assembly is empowered to prolong its term of office for the duration of these circumstances. Regular assembly sessions are held, twice yearly, and special sessions may be convened on the initiative of the Council of State or on demand of one-third of the total number of deputies.

Constitutionally, the Grand National Assembly is empowered to elect, supervise, and recall the members of the Council of State, the Council of Ministers, and the Supreme Court. It is also empowered to name the prosecutor general and control the activity of his office. It is given ultimate authority in the regulation of the electoral system, the national economic plan, the state budget, and the organization and functioning of the people's councils.

The assembly is empowered to establish the general line of the country's foreign policy and has ultimate responsibility for the maintenance of public order and national defense. As a part of this responsibility the assembly appoints and recalls the supreme commander of the armed forces. Declarations of war, however, are constitutionally limited to the protection of Romanian national sovereignty in the event of aggression or in the event of aggression against another state with which Romania has mutual defense obligations.

Other powers attributed to the assembly include adopting and amending the Constitution and the general control over its application. Assembly authority extends as well to the interpretation of the Constitution and decisions on the constitutionality of laws, making it in effect its own constitutional court. In exercising that power the assembly elects the Constitutional Commission, which functions for the duration of the legislative term. The Constitution specifies that up to one-third of the commission members may be persons who are not deputies, but members of the Supreme Court, college and university teachers, and scientific researchers are specifically excluded from commission membership. Duties of the commission focus primarily on providing the assembly with reports and opinions on constitutional questions.

The Grand National Assembly functions under an elected chairman who presides over assembly sessions and is responsible for directing its activities. The chairman and four elected vice chairmen form the Bureau of the Grand National Assembly and are assisted in their duties by a panel of six executive secretaries. In addition to the Constitutional Commission, other standing commissions of the assembly include the Agriculture and Forestry Commission; Credentials Commission; Defense Commission; Economic and Financial Commission; Education, Science, and Culture Commission; Foreign Policy Commission; Health, Labor, and Social Welfare Commission; Industry, Construction, and Transportation Commission; Legal Commission; and the People's Councils and State Administration Commission. Any deputy may be elected to the standing commissions of the assembly or to temporary commissions created to perform specific functions. Reports, bills, or other legislative matters are submitted to the standing commissions by the assembly chairman for study and for recommendations on further action.

The assembly may function if one-half of the deputies plus one additional deputy are present. Laws and decisions are adopted by simple majority vote with the exception of an amendment to the Constitution, which requires a two-thirds majority of the total number of assembly deputies. Laws and decisions are signed by the presiding officer present at the time the decision is voted. Within ten days after adoption, laws are required to be signed by the president of the Council of State and published in the *Official Bulletin of the Socialist Republic of Romania.*

The Council of State

Described as the supreme body of state power with a permanent activity, the Council of State exercises certain permanent powers as well as special powers that fall to it when the Grand National Assembly is not in session. Formed of nineteen members, the Council of State is elected by the assembly, from its own membership, at the first assembly session as it begins a new term of office. The council's authority continues until the election of a new Council of State by the succeeding legislature. Although the president of the council is the head of state, the Constitution asserts that the functioning of the council is to be based on the principle of collective leadership. Almost all the members of the Council of State also hold leading party posts.

Among the most important permanent powers of the Council of State are the establishment of election dates; the appointment and recall of the heads of central government agencies, except for the Council of Ministers; and the ratification or denunciation of international treaties. The president of the council represents the republic in international relations. Other permanent powers include the granting of senior military ranks; the conferral of honors; the granting of citizenship, pardon, and refuge; and the appointment and recall of diplomatic representatives.

Grand National Assembly powers that devolve to the Council of State between assembly sessions, or in the event of exceptional circumstances that prevent the assembly from acting, include the authority to appoint and recall members of the Council of Ministers, members of the Supreme Court, and the prosecutor general. Also included in this category are powers to establish norms having the power of law, control over the application of laws and decisions passed by the assembly, and supervision of the Council of Ministers and other central administrative bodies as well as the activities of the people's councils.

Although the legal decisions passed by the council must be submitted for approval to the next session of the Grand National Assembly, they take effect as law immediately on passage by the council or on a date specified in the ruling itself. In the event of a national emergency the Council of State can also exercise the assembly's power to declare a state of war, subject to the same qualifications imposed upon the assembly— that is, in the event that Romania or one of its allies is the victim of external armed aggression.

In December 1967 PCR General Secretary Ceausescu was elected president of the Council of State by the Grand National Assembly and, by virtue of this position, became the head of state. The reason given for the concentration of the principal party and government positions in Ceausescu's hands was the desire to provide unitary leadership both as a means of efficiency and of ensuring full party control at the highest level of the government. The decision to unite the two posts, as well as to combine a number of party and government positions on lower administrative levels, had been taken at a national party conference a few days earlier and followed action taken by the PCR Central Committee in October. Outside observers saw the move as one of a series of steps designed to ensure the continued subordination of the state apparatus to the party.

In March 1970 the Grand National Assembly voted to establish the Defense Council, to be headed by Ceausescu and responsible to the Council of State. The formation of the Defense Council, which was given decisionmaking powers for high-level military

118

affairs, served to strengthen Council of State control over the armed forces and further enhance Ceausescu's personal authority. The same legislation that established the Defense Council also decreed that foreign troops could not enter Romania under any circumstances without the prior approval of the assembly. Coming in the aftermath of the Soviet-led invasion of Czechoslovakia, observers of Eastern European affairs interpreted this ruling as a means of preventing any dissident group from inviting foreign intervention on the pretext of preserving orthodox communist rule.

The membership of the Defense Council reflected the importance given it. Besides the head of state, other members of the council include the prime minister, the minister of the armed forces, the chairman of the Council of State Security, the minister of internal affairs, the minister of foreign affairs, the chairman of the State Planning Committee, and eight other members who also held leading government and party positions. The secretary of the council in 1971 was the chief of the general staff and a member of the PCR Central Committee.

Also connected to the Council of State and subordinate to it is the Economic Council. This body functions to advise on economic matters, coordinate planning, and make recommendations to the Council of State for the development of the national economy and the improvement of state enterprises. In late 1971 the chairman of the Economic Council was also a member of the PCR Secretariat.

The Council of Ministers

Defined in the Constitution as the supreme body of state administration, the Council of Ministers exercises control over the activities of all state agencies on both the national and local levels. The council is composed of a chairman (who is the prime minister), a first deputy chairman, an unspecified number of deputy chairmen, the ministers, and the heads of certain other important government agencies (see fig. 8). Unlike the 1952 Constitution, in which twenty-six specific ministries were listed, that of 1965 fixes neither the number of ministries nor their particular areas of competence, this being left to other laws.

In 1971 the Council of Ministers was composed of forty-four members, including the prime minister, first deputy, seven deputies, twenty-three ministers, and ten committee chiefs with ministerial rank. All but two of the members of the council were also members, or alternate members, of the PCR Central Committee, and the prime minister and his first deputy were members of the Standing Presidium of the party. These two, along with two

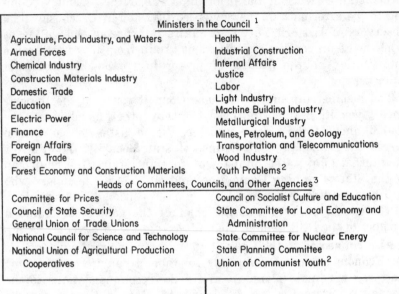

Chairman (Prime Minister)
First Deputy Chairman
Deputy Chairmen

Ministers in the Council [1]

Agriculture, Food Industry, and Waters
Armed Forces
Chemical Industry
Construction Materials Industry
Domestic Trade
Education
Electric Power
Finance
Foreign Affairs
Foreign Trade
Forest Economy and Construction Materials

Health
Industrial Construction
Internal Affairs
Justice
Labor
Light Industry
Machine Building Industry
Metallurgical Industry
Mines, Petroleum, and Geology
Transportation and Telecommunications
Wood Industry
Youth Problems[2]

Heads of Committees, Councils, and Other Agencies [3]

Committee for Prices
Council of State Security
General Union of Trade Unions
National Council for Science and Technology
National Union of Agricultural Production
   Cooperatives

Council on Socialist Culture and Education
State Committee for Local Economy and
   Administration
State Committee for Nuclear Energy
State Planning Committee
Union of Communist Youth[2]

General Secretariat of the Council of Ministers

Secretary General
Deputy Secretaries General

[1] There are twenty-three ministries.
[2] First secretary of the Union of Communist Youth is also the minister of youth problems.
[3] The heads of these bodies have ministerial rank.

Figure 8. Romania, Organization of the Council of Ministers, 1971.

other deputies, were also full members of the PCR Executive Committee.

The Constitution charges the Council of Ministers with responsibility for the general implementation of the nation's domestic and foreign policies, the application of laws, and the maintenance of public order. As the supreme administrative body of the government, the council coordinates and controls the activity of the ministries and other state organs at all levels. In economic matters the council administers the drafting of the overall state plan and the national budget and provides for their implementation. In addition, it directs the establishment of the economic enterprises and other industrial and commercial organizations (see ch. 14). The council's responsibilities also include the general ad-

120

ministration of relations with other states, the conclusion of international agreements, and the general organization of the armed forces.

Formally elected by the Grand National Assembly at the beginning of each new assembly session, the council's term of office continues until the election of a new council by the succeeding assembly. Both collectively and individually, the council members are responsible to the Grand National Assembly; and in the interval between assembly sessions, to the Council of State. The Constitution asserts that the Council of Ministers is to operate on the principle of collective leadership to ensure the unity of its political and administrative actions.

In late 1969 the Grand National Assembly enacted legislation aimed at strengthening the concept of collective leadership in the ministries and extending the principle to other national administrative agencies. In the case of the Council of Ministers, the measure provided for the establishment of a collegium in each ministry consisting of the minister, department heads, certain specialists, and representatives of labor unions or other organizations. Purposes of the collegium included collective decisionmaking, review of ministry activities, and recommendations on ministry programs and policies. The meetings of the collegium, at which decisions are made by majority vote, are also attended by representatives of the PCR appointed by the party Central Committee. In the event of serious disagreements within the collegium, the law provides for the matter to be referred to the Council of Ministers. No such disagreements have been reported, however.

Since the promulgation of the 1965 Constitution, the Council of Ministers has been reorganized several times. In late 1971 the importance of a number of the ministries and state commissions was emphasized by the prominence of the party position held by their ministers or chairmen: almost all of the members of the Council of Ministers were either full or alternate members of the PCR Central Committee; the chairmen of the General Union of Trade Unions, the National Union of Agricultural Production Cooperatives, and the State Planning Committee were full members of the party Executive Committee; the chairmen of the Council of State Security and the State Committee for Local Economy and Administration were alternate members of the Executive Committee, as was the head of the Ministry of the Armed Forces. The chairmen of the State Planning Committee and the Council of State Security and the ministers of internal affairs and the armed forces also were members of the Defense Council.

The general organization and functioning of the judiciary is established by the Constitution and by the 1968 Law on the Organization of the Court System. Overall responsibility for the functioning of the courts is vested in the Ministry of Justice, whereas the prosecutor general (attorney general) is charged with the general application of the law and the executing of criminal proceedings.

To fulfill its responsibility for the functioning of the courts and the supervision of state marshals, state notaries, and the national bar organization, the Ministry of Justice is divided into six directorates: civil courts, military courts, studies and legislation, personnel, administration, and planning and accounting. In addition, the ministry includes a corps of inspectors, an office of legal affairs, the State Notary Office, and a lawyer and legal expert service.

The court system includes the Supreme Court, *judet* courts, lower courts, military courts, and local judicial commissions. The Constitution places the judiciary under the authority of the Grand National Assembly; and between assembly sessions, under the authority of the Council of State. The Supreme Court, seated in Bucharest, exercises general control over the judiciary activities of all lower courts.

Members of the Supreme Court are professional judges appointed by the Grand National Assembly to four-year terms of office. The Supreme Court functions as an appeals court for sentences pronounced in lower tribunals and, in certain matters specified by law, may act as a court of first instance. It may also issue guidance, in the form of directives, on legal and constitutional questions for the judicial actions of lower courts and the administrative functions of government agencies. To fulfill its responsibilities, the Supreme Court is divided into three sections: civil, criminal, and military. Each of these sections is presided over by a panel of three judges, and plenary sessions of the entire court are held at least once every three months in the presence of the minister of justice for the purpose of issuing guidance directives.

With the territorial-administrative reorganization of February 1968, the jurisdictions of the former regional and district courts were restructured to correspond to the new administrative units. Accordingly, there are thirty-nine *judet* courts and the municipal court of Bucharest, which has *judet* court status. Each court on this level is presided over by a panel of two judges and three lay jurors, known as people's assessors, and decisions are made by majority vote. People's assessors were first introduced in December 1947 and given additional legal status in 1952 by the Grand National Assembly's Law on the Organization of Justice. The law required these lay assessors to be Romanian citizens and at least twenty-three years of age. Most of the people's assessors are appointed by the PCR or by one of the district bodies of the mass organizations (see ch. 9).

Below the *judet* courts, and subordinate to them, are the lower courts. In the city of Bucharest these consist of eight sectional courts, which function under the supervision of the municipal court. For the remainder of the country the number of these lower courts and the extent of their territorial jurisdiction are established by the Ministry of Justice. Courts on this level are presided over by a panel composed of one judge and two people's assessors; decisions are based on a majority vote.

Military courts are established on a territorial basis, subdivisions being determined by the Council of Ministers. The lower military tribunals have original jurisdiction over contraventions of the law committed by members of the armed forces; the territorial military tribunals exercise appellate jurisdiction for decisions of the lower units. In certain situations specified by law, cases involving civilians may be assigned to military courts. At each level, the military courts, when acting in the first instance, consist of two judges and three people's assessors. In appeals cases on the territorial level, the courts consist of three judges only. As in the civil courts, decisions are reached by majority vote.

In 1968 the Grand National Assembly enacted a law establishing a system of judicial commissions to function as courts of special jurisdiction in the state economic enterprises and in localities. These commissions were designed as "an expression of socialist democracy" to provide for the increased participation of working people in the settlement of problems involving minor local disputes and local economic issues. Functioning under the direction of enterprise management or municipal executive committees, the judicial commissions are assigned such matters as labor disputes, misdemeanors, property disputes, and violations of proper social conduct, a category that appears to provide broad latitude for prosecution. As a rule, the commissions consist of five members elected for a term of two years; however, in labor disputes two additional members are added to the commission, one representing the enterprise management and one representing the labor union committee.

General supervision over the application of the law and the initiation of criminal proceedings is exercised by the Office of the Prosecutor General. Headed by the prosecutor general, the office exercises supervisory powers that extend to all levels of the society, from the government ministries down to the ordinary citizen. Subunits of the Office of the Prosecutor General are hierarchically organized and include offices in each judicial district plus the prosecutor's military bureau. The prosecutor general is elected by the Grand National Assembly for a four-year term and is responsible to the assembly or, between assembly sessions, to the Council of State for the activities of his office. Three deputy prosecutors assist the prosecutor general in carrying out his official duties.

An important part of the prosecutor general's responsibilities consists of supervising the activities of the courts to ensure the uniform application of the law. Prosecutors on the *judet* level have a consultative vote in the meetings of local government agencies when important legal questions are being decided. The prosecutor general participates in those plenary sessions of the Supreme Court at which guidance decisions are made. In the event the prosecutor does not agree with a decision, he may appeal to the county people's council or to its executive committee for a review of the decision. On the national level, the Office of the Prosecutor General may appeal alleged violations of the law to the Council of Ministers.

Local Government

Local government bodies, known as people's councils, exist on the *judet*, town, and commune levels. The 1965 Constitution had also provided for subunits of state administration on regional and district levels, but a territorial-administrative reorganization voted by the Grand National Assembly in 1968 replaced the existing sixteen regions and 150 intermediate districts with a system of thirty-nine counties and forty-four independent municipal administrations. The expressed purpose of the change was the provision of more efficient administration.

In addition to the establishment of county and municipal people's councils, local councils were also set up in 142 smaller towns, and communal councils were formed in rural areas. A number of the smaller communes were combined in order to give them a larger population base. Boundaries of each of the new *judete* were drawn to include about fifty communes consisting of some 4,000 to 5,000 persons.

Along with the territorial reorganization, the decision was also made to combine party and government functions of the *judet* level so that the same person acted both as party committee first secretary and people's council chairman. In explaining this fusion of party and state authority, Ceausescu stated that there were many instances in which offices in both the party and the government dealt with the same areas of interest, a practice that resulted in inefficiency and the unnecessary duplication of party and state machinery. He asserted that the consolidation of these administrative positions would serve to eliminate this overlapping. At the same time, Ceausescu declared that, inasmuch as the government was responsible for the implementation of the PCR's economic decisions, there was no justification for the continued existence of the numerous economic sections of the party Central Committee and that future economic policy would be implemented within the structure of the government (see ch. 9).

According to the Constitution and the 1968 Grand National Assembly's Law on the Organization and Operation of People's Councils, the people's councils are responsible for the implementation of central government decisions and the economic, social, and cultural administration of their particular jurisdictions. Deputies to the people's councils are elected to four-year terms—except for the communes where the term is two years—from single-member constituencies of equal population. Based on population, the *judet* people's councils may have a maximum of 231, or a minimum of 141, deputies. The membership of the Bucharest People's Council is fixed at 369, and there are 151 deputies on the councils of each of its subdistricts. City people's councils range from eighty-one to 221 deputies, and those of the towns consist of from thirty-five to ninety-one deputies. Commune council memberships range from twenty-five to seventy-one persons.

Organized on the basis of highly centralized control, the people's councils function under the general supervision of the Grand National Assembly; and between assembly sessions the councils function under the direction of the Council of State. The Law on the Organization and Operation of People's Councils specifically places the people's councils under the overall leadership of the PCR as the leading political force of the society.

To expedite its work, each people's council established an executive committee as its chief administrative organ and a number of permanent committees to which it assigns specific responsibilities. The executive committee, consisting of a chairman, two or more deputy chairmen, and an unspecified number of other members, functions for the duration of the council's term of office. Each of the people's council executive committees also has a secretary, who is appointed with the approval of the next higher ranking council and is considered an employee of the central government rather than of the local executive committee itself. The chairman of executive committees in the cities, towns, and communes are officially considered the mayors of these units. The executive committees are responsible to the people's council that elected them as well as to the executive committee of the next higher council.

The executive committee meets whenever necessary and is required to convene at least once a month; full council sessions are held every two months on the city, town, and commune level and every three months on the county level. Responsibilities of the executive committees include the implementation of laws, decrees, and decisions of the central government, the carrying out of the decisions made by the people's councils, the working out of the local budget, and the drafting of the local economic plan. The executive committee is also charged with the direction and control of the economic enterprises within its area of jurisdiction and with the exercising of supervision over the executive committees of the councils inferior to it. The executive committees are also responsible for the organization and functioning of public services, educational institutions, medical programs, and the militia.

THE ELECTORAL SYSTEM

According to the 1965 Constitution, all power belongs to the working people joined in a worker-peasant alliance; power is exercised through the people's representative bodies—the Grand National Assembly and the several levels of people's councils. Theoretically, these bodies are elected by, controlled by, and responsible to the working people. Emphasis is placed on the direct participation of the citizens through their local people's councils, party units, and chapters of the mass organizations (see ch. 9).

Although the Constitution asserts the right of all citizens eighteen years of age and older to participate in the election of all representative bodies on the basis of a universal, direct, equal, and secret vote, it does not determine how elections are to be organized or specify who is responsible for conducting them. The Constitution does declare, however, that the right to nominate candidates belongs to the PCR, as well as to all labor unions, cooperatives, youth and women's leagues, cultural associations, and other mass organizations. Citizens who have reached the age of twenty-three are eligible to be candidates for elective office.

Separate legislation provides for general elections to be held every four years and local communal elections to be conducted every two years. Elections are organized under the direction of the Socialist Unity Front, the national entity that incorporates the country's numerous mass organizations under the leadership of the PCR (see ch. 9). All candidates for elective office must have the approval of the front in order to be placed on the ballot, a requirement that ensures that no candidate unacceptable to the front's leadership will be placed in nomination.

The Socialist Unity Front was officially established in November 1968 as a replacement for the People's Democratic Front, which had existed since the Communists began to organize effectively in the country during World War II. The Socialist Unity Front lists among its member organizations, in addition to the PCR, the labor unions; cooperative farm organizations; consumer cooperatives; professional, scientific, and cultural associations; student, youth, women's, and veterans' organizations; religious bodies; and representatives of the Hungarian, German, Serbian, and Ukrainian minorities. At the time of its formation, Ceausescu was elected as the front's chairman, and Ion Gheorghe Maurer, the prime minister, was named as first vice chairman. Both continued in these positions in early 1972.

General elections were conducted by the Socialist Unity Front in March 1969. Official results indicated that ballots were cast by 99.96 percent of the country's 13,582,249 eligible voters. Of the votes cast, a reported 99.75 percent were marked in favor of the single list of Socialist Unity Front candidates. Although the great majority of the candidates for the Grand National Assembly who were placed on the ballot belonged to the PCR, some nonmembers gained front approval and were elected. Nearly half of the candidates elected were newcomers to the assembly and included forty-one Hungarian, twelve German, and nine other minority representatives. The front has scheduled the next general elections for 1973.

CHAPTER 9

POLITICAL DYNAMICS AND VALUES

At the beginning of 1972 the country's political system continued to be based on the leading position of the Romanian Communist Party (Partidul Communist Roman—PCR). Within the party, political power was centralized in a small group of men who occupied the leading party and government offices. Political authority was particularly concentrated in the hands of the general secretary of the PCR, Nicolae Ceausescu, who was also the head of state.

Regarding itself as the leading force of the society, the PCR has made the government apparatus an instrument of party policy and, through a broad network of subordinate mass organizations, has mobilized all elements of the society in support of its programs and goals. Individual and group participation in the political process was limited to the forms and means permitted by the PCR.

The concentration of all political authority in the central bodies of the party has effectively precluded the emergence of any open opposition to the PCR leadership as well as the assertion of any particular group interests. Under Ceausescu's leadership the party has sought to strengthen its role in all spheres of social, economic, and political life and, at the same time, to broaden its base of support by taking steps to increase its membership. Although the party leaders have periodically demonstrated a cautious relaxation of the highly centralized system of control, the PCR has continued to be extremely sensitive to any potential threats or challenges to its position.

In attempting to build a broad base of popular support the party has drawn upon the symbols of nationalism and has made extensive use of Romanian history and tradition. Its independent stance in relation to Soviet domination has served to enhance its image among the general population; at the same time, the fact that membership in the party has been made relatively easy has helped the PCR become one of the largest communist parties of Eastern Europe.

In mid-1971 Ceausescu initiated a campaign to strengthen ideological and cultural orthodoxy and, for the first time in the six years since he had come to power, some political observers believed they were able to detect opposition to his proposals both within and outside the party. There was no indication, however, that the resistance was organized or was strong enough to affect Ceausescu's position. Throughout the period of Ceausescu's control there have never been any recognizable factions in the party in opposition to his leadership.

MAJOR POLITICAL DEVELOPMENTS, 1965 TO 1970

The leadership of the PCR changed hands in March 1965 when Nicolae Ceausescu became first secretary after the death of Gheorghe Gheorghiu-Dej, who had headed the party almost continually since 1944 (see ch. 2). Ceausescu's emergence as head of the party came in the midst of a period of growing Romanian nationalism that had begun in the early 1960s. Initiated by Gheorghiu-Dej, the policy of greater national autonomy was given additional form and substance by Ceausescu, who sought to cast himself in the role of the restorer of Romanian history and the country's national traditions.

As Gheorghiu-Dej's successor, Ceausescu was confronted with the necessity of consolidating his power. No member of the party Secretariat owed his position to Ceausescu, and he found particular challenges to his authority from three men who had been among Gheorghiu-Dej's closest associates: Chivu Stoica, a veteran party leader; Gheorghe Apostol, first deputy premier and a former PCR secretary; and Alexandru Draghici, minister of internal affairs and, as such, head of the powerful state security apparatus.

A temporary solution to the problem was found in a system of collective leadership by which Ceausescu became head of the party and Stoica took over Gheorghiu-Dej's other leading position as president of the Council of State and, as such, head of state. Apostol continued as first deputy prime minister, and Draghici remained as minister of internal affairs. Ion Gheorghe Maurer, who had served as prime minister under Gheorghiu-Dej, continued in that position. At the same time, changes were made in the party statutes to prevent one man from holding dual party and government offices as Gheorghiu-Dej had done.

In April, just one month after taking over as head of the PCR, Ceausescu announced that a party congress would be convened in July. During the month of June, while preparations were being made for the congress, he revealed plans to redefine the character and structure of the party and announced that its name would no longer be the Romanian Workers' Party, as it had been known since 1948, but would again be the Romanian Communist Party. Observers of East European political affairs saw the change of name as an assertion of the equality of Romanian communism with the communist parties of the Soviet Union and other communist states. During the same month the new PCR leaders also proclaimed that the official designation of the state would be the Socialist Republic of Romania rather than the Romanian People's Republic as it had previously been known (see ch. 8).

At the July party congress Ceausescu was successful in adding a number of his supporters to an enlarged PCR Central Committee and in having his own title changed to general secretary. At the same time the party structure was changed to add a new body, the Executive Committee, between the Standing Presidium (Politburo) and the Central Committee. Although he was not able to gain full control of the Executive Committee immediately, in time this new body provided Ceausescu with the means for including his supporters in the leading organs of the PCR and for implementing his own policies.

During the party congress Ceausescu was able to turn the PCR proscription against an individual's holding dual party and government positions to his own advantage by engineering the election of Draghici to the party Secretariat, a move that resulted in Draghici losing his power base as minister of internal affairs as well as his direct control over the state security forces. Later in the year the appointment of two additional "first deputy prime ministers" undermined the power of Apostol who had been, until that time, the only first deputy. Simultaneously, Ceausescu was making preparations for even more definitive actions against his rivals, preparations that took the form of an unpublicized decision of the PCR Central Committee, in November 1965, to establish a commission of inquiry to reexamine the political trials conducted by the Gheorghiu-Dej regime during the 1950s. The commission was particularly directed to investigate the 1954 trial and execution of Lucretiu Patrascanu, who had been the Romanian minister of justice from 1944 to 1948 and an important member of the party hierarchy. The formation of the commission of inquiry and its findings were not announced publicly until April 1968.

Political observers identified three principal factions within the PCR during the 1965–67 period: Ceausescu and his supporters; the veteran party men led by Stoica, Apostol, and Draghici; and the intellectuals, of whom Maurer was perhaps the nominal representative. Those allied with Ceausescu, who was forty-seven years old when he came to power, tended to be men of his own generation and outlook, and whenever possible he engineered their appointment or promotion into important party, government, and military positions.

One of Ceausescu's foremost concerns was what he termed the

revitalization of the PCR. To achieve this end, he not only brought his own younger men into the top party organs but also sought to broaden the professional skills represented in these bodies through the recruitment of technically trained men and academicians. At the same time, increased technical and scientific contacts were permitted with Western nations, and previously banned works of foreign writers and artists were allowed to be reintroduced—moves that helped Ceausescu gain additional support among the PCR's intellectuals.

Although the party encouraged a revival of nationalism and introduced several limited domestic reforms, it did not relax its tight political control and continued to direct the country's economy through a highly centralized system. The maintenance of strict party control was evidenced in the congresses of the youth and labor union organizations in mid-1966, when the delegates were informed that the PCR would begin to enforce the "patriotic education" of their members.

The 1967 National Party Conference

At a specially convened National Conference of the PCR in December 1967—the first such conference in twenty-two years—Ceausescu continued to strengthen his own position. The conference was attended by the members of the Central Committee as well as by 1,150 delegates from local party organizations. Ceausescu elected to employ the technique of the party conference rather than a special party congress in order to have his proposals approved by a larger body than the Central Committee. At the same time, he wanted to avoid the requirement of having to elect a new Central Committee, which would have been the case had a congress been held.

In his address to the conference, Ceausescu declared that in order to modernize Romania as a socialist state it was imperative to adopt new organizational and ideological forms. To achieve this end, he proposed a number of reforms in the structure and functioning of both the party and the government and defended the country's policy of independent development. Speaking of the relationship between party and government responsibilities, Ceausescu asserted the need to eliminate overlapping and duplication in party and government functions. As a remedy, he proposed that only one individual, whether in the party or in the government, should deal with a particular sector of activity. In addition, he called for a clearer delineation of the responsibilities of the government and the party. It was not necessary, he declared, for the Central Committee to decide all questions of economic affairs and continue to maintain a number of economic departments that duplicated the functions of the Council of Ministers and the economic ministries. He proposed that the Central Committee limit itself to basic decisions of economic policy and that the specific matters of implementation be left to the government ministries.

Political and ideological activity, Ceausescu proposed, would remain under the control of the Central Committee and would be given greater emphasis and direction through the creation of an ideological commission that would work to develop an intensified program of political education. A defense council, composed of the party's Standing Presidium and other members, would be established to deal with most military questions, but the basic questions of guidance for both the armed forces and the state security apparatus would continue to be the responsibility of the Central Committee. Major foreign policy questions would be decided by the Standing Presidium (see ch. 8).

Ceausescu also proposed reforms in the organization and responsibilities of governmental organs. In addition to proposing a reorganization of the state's territorial subdivisions, he asserted the need to broaden the activities of the Grand National Assembly and to increase the responsibilities of the assembly commissions in order to give that body a greater role in the government. Ministers and other high government officials were to be more aware of their responsibilities to keep the assembly informed of the activities of their departments. Ceausescu also declared the need to strengthen the role and organization of the Council of Ministers to enable it to provide for long-term economic planning. In addition, he suggested that the heads of three of the more important mass organizations—the General Union of Trade Unions, the Union of Communist Youth, and the National Union of Agricultural Production Cooperatives—be included in the government and be given ministerial ranking.

The party conference represented a major success for Ceausescu in his drive to gain undisputed political control. All of his proposals were unanimously adopted, and the party statutes were changed to enable him to become the head of state, as president of the Council of State, as well as head of the party, a reversal of the 1965 proscription against one individual simultaneously holding prominent posts in both the party and state. The nomination of Ceausescu was made by Stoica, the incumbent president of the Council of State, on the grounds that uniting the highest offices of the party and the state would eliminate the duplication of functions and increase efficiency. Stoica was given a position in the party Secretariat and later, in 1969, was named chairman of the Central Auditing Commission, a post he continued to hold in early 1972.

As a result of the approval of Ceausescu's recommendations, a number of changes were effected in local government and party organizations. Certain positions in the party and state organizations were fused, the county or city party first secretary also becoming chairman of the local people's council (see ch. 8). The secretaries of local party units and labor union representatives were included on the councils of the industrial enterprises.

Following the recommendations of the party conference, the day after the conference adjourned the Grand National Assembly convened to elect Ceausescu as president of the Council of State, and it approved legislation to implement most of the other conference decisions. At the same time, the assembly elected a new Council of State consisting of (in addition to Ceausescu) three vice presidents and fifteen other members. A new Council of Ministers was also elected, with Maurer again named as prime minister. Apostol was demoted from his position as a first deputy prime minister to his previously held post as chairman of the General Union of Trade Unions. Draghici was removed from the party Secretariat and given a position as a deputy prime minister under Maurer. With the successful demotion of his chief rivals, Ceausescu emerged at the close of 1967 as the undisputed leader of both the party and the state.

Rehabilitation and De-Stalinization

With his power base firmly established, Ceausescu acted to fully disassociate his regime from the Gheorghiu-Dej era. In April 1968, at a plenary session of the Central Committee, the report of the commission of inquiry, which had been secretly established in late 1965, was made public. The Gheorghiu-Dej regime was severely indicated for fraudulently conspiring to arrange the trial and execution of Patrascanu in 1954 and for violations of justice in the other political show trials of the 1950s. Patrascanu was exonerated of all charges, and several other of the trial victims were officially rehabilitated.

Because of this close association with Gheorghiu-Dej and his position as head of the internal affairs ministry during the period of the trials, the Central Committee dismissed Draghici from all his positions. Apostol and Stoica were censured but were allowed to remain in their posts, although their standing in the party was considerably weakened.

Throughout the 1968–70 period the Ceausescu regime continued a gradual and cautious policy of de-Stalinization in domestic affairs and continued, as well, to assert the country's independent stance in international relations. The domestic relaxation was limited, however, and, in an address to an association of artists in April 1968, Ceausescu cautioned both intellectuals and artists not to overstep the bounds established by the party.

The invasion of Czechoslovakia by Soviet-led forces of the Warsaw Treaty Organization (Warsaw Pact) in August 1968 posed a crisis to the Ceausescu regime and raised the possibility of Soviet intervention in Romania. Ceausescu's firm denunciation of the invasion, however, served to unify the population behind him. His call for national mobilization and the creation of a home guard for national defense elicited broad popular support and gained him stature as the defender of Romanian independence.

In late 1968 the PCR leadership acted to establish a new national political organization, the Socialist Unity Front, in order to bring representatives of the major mass organizations and other associations into a party-dominated framework for the political mobilization of the population (see ch. 8). As a replacement for the older and largely ineffective People's Democratic Front, the new front organization was structured around a national council and, theoretically, was given advisory powers on important policy matters.

In addition to the PCR, the Socialist Unity Front's National Council included representatives of: labor unions; cooperative farmers' organizations; consumers' cooperatives; professional, cultural, and scientific associations; women's youth, and veterans' organizations; religious bodies; and the councils of the Hungarian, German, Serbian, and Ukrainian minorities. Ceausescu was elected president of the front, and Maurer, the vice president.

The first major activity of the Socialist Unity Front was the conducting of national elections on March 2, 1969. As only the front was allowed to nominate candidates, just one candidate was named for each Grand National Assembly seat. The official results indicated that over 99 percent of the eligible voters cast their ballots and, of these, 99.75 percent endorsed the Socialist Unity Front slate. Elections to the newly organized bodies of local government took place at the same time (see ch. 8).

Convening ten days after the election, the new Grand National Assembly reelected Ceausescu as president of the Council of State and renamed Maurer as prime minister. At the same time, the assembly enacted legislation establishing the Defense Council that Ceausescu had earlier proposed. Observers of East

European political affairs considered the timing of this enactment, coming just three days before an important meeting of the Warsaw Treaty Organization, as a further assertion of Romania's independent course in international affairs (see ch. 10).

The Tenth Party Congress

Almost 2,000 delegates attended the Tenth Party Congress of the PCR held in Bucharest from August 6 to 12, 1969. In addition, delegations were present from sixty-six foreign communist parties (see ch. 10). The main features of the congress included Ceausescu's unanimous reelection as general secretary of the party for a five-year term, the enlargement of the Central Committee from 121 to 165 members, and the approval of revisions of the party statutes.

Among other things, the statute revisions provided for the election of the Central Committee by secret ballot and transferred the responsibility for electing the general secretary from the Central Committee to the party congress. It was also decided that party congresses would be convened every five years rather than every four so that each congress could discuss and adopt a five-year economic plan for the country. A unique feature of the congress was the division of the delegates into five working commissions, with their sessions open to foreign journalists.

When it came time for the congress to elect the Central Committee, nearly half of the remaining older members were replaced by younger men who were supporters of Ceausescu. Apostol and Stoica were conspicuously not reelected and, immediately after the congress, Apostol was discharged from his position as chairman of the General Union of Trade Unions after being charged with "serious breaches of Communist morality."

Although the modifications in the party statutes were designed to allow for more democratic procedures in party affairs, the principle of centralized control continued to be strongly maintained. Whereas all party members were encouraged to voice their opinions on any given issue, once a decision was adopted the minority was expected to yield to the majority and aid in implementation of policies. The congress resolved that party control and ideological guidance must reach into all aspects of the life of the people.

POLITICAL ORGANIZATIONS
The Romanian Communist Party

Originally founded in 1921, the Romanian Communist Party was declared illegal in 1924 and forced into a clandestine existence until the closing years of World War II. After the war, fully supported by the Soviet Union, the party gradually consolidated power and sought to extend its base of popular support through intensified propaganda activity. In early 1948 the PCR merged with one wing of the Social Democratic Party to form the Romanian Workers' Party. By the end of 1952, however, almost all of the former Social Democrats had been expelled from the leading party bodies and replaced by active Communists (see ch. 2).

Organization

Basic decisions concerning the organization, operation, and membership of the PCR are contained in the party statutes, the fundamental document of the party. Originally adopted in May 1948, the statutes have undergone several modifications, with more significant revisions being made in 1955, 1965, 1967, and 1969.

All organs of the party are closely interrelated and operate on the principle of democratic centralism. Derived from the Communist Party of the Soviet Union, the concept of democratic centralism provides for the election of party bodies at all levels but requires a firm hierarchical subordination of each party organ to the next higher unit. In practice, this means that party programs and policies are directed from a single center and that decisions of higher organs are unconditionally binding on all lower organs as well as on individual members. The statutes call for the free and open discussion of policy questions at congresses, conferences, local membership meetings, and in the party press; however, discipline requires that once a decision is made the minority fully submits to decisions of the majority.

According to the party statutes, the supreme organ of the PCR is the party congress consisting of delegates elected by the county (*judet*) conferences on the basis of one delegate for every 1,000 party members. As revised in 1969, the statutes call for the convening of a party congress every five years. Duties of the congress include the election of the PCR general secretary, election of the Central Committee and the Central Auditing Commission, and the discussion and adoption of programs and policies proposed by the central organs of the party.

Between congresses the leading party organ is the Central Committee. Consisting of 165 full members and 120 alternate members, the Central Committee is responsible for the overall direction of all party activities and the implementation of policies established by the party congress. In addition, the Central Committee screens nominations for the more important party and state positions. Party statutes require a plenary session of the Central Committee at least four times a year (see fig. 9).

After its election by the party congress, the Central Committee in turn elects, from among its own number, the members of the leading party bodies: the Standing Presidium, the Executive Committee, and the Secretariat. The election is large-

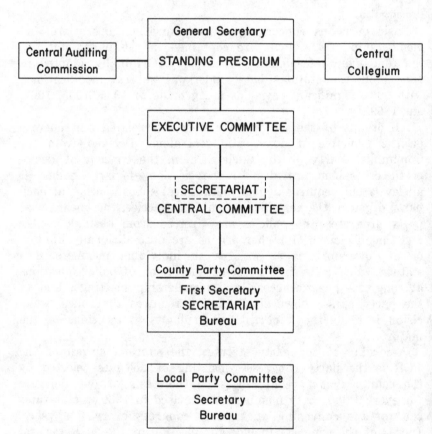

Note-- The Secretary of the County Party Committee is also chairman of the County People's Council.
Central Collegium was formerly known as the Party Control Commission.

Figure 9. Organization of the Romanian Communist Party, 1972.

138

ly a formality, however, for in practice the Standing · Presidium is the primary center of political power and is a self-perpetuating body. Any change in its membership or in that of the Secretariat is generated from within rather than through a democratic decision of the Central Committee. As general secretary of the party, Ceausescu heads both the Standing Presidium and the Secretariat and chairs the Executive Committee.

To accomplish its administrative tasks the Central Committee is provided with an extensive bureaucratic structure that in many instances parallels the organization of the government ministries. A chancellery office, headed by a chief and three deputies, coordinates the committee's overall administrative activities. Party work is organized under three directorates, each headed by a supervisory secretary, and a number of administrative sections and functional commissions. The directorates, designated as international affairs and propaganda, party organization, and press and cultural affairs, supervise and direct the work of the administrative sections. Not all of these sections are listed in the party statutes or by the party press. A partial listing includes sections for the economy, local administration, propaganda, press, international affairs, party organs and personnel, national minorities, and state security.

In addition to the directorates and administrative sections there were, in 1970, eight formally established commissions directly tied to the Central Committee. These were listed as the commissions for agriculture and forestry; economic problems; ideological and cultural-educational problems; international relations; organizational problems and internal party activity; training of cadres, education, and science; development of the social and state system; and social questions, public health, and living standards.

Two party training institutions, the Stefan Gheorghiu Academy of Social-Political Education and the Training of Leading Cadres and the Institute of Historical and Social-Political Studies, operate under the direct supervision of the Central Committee. Located in Bucharest, both of these institutions are designed to train and indoctrinate key bureaucratic personnel. The Central Committee also maintains a museum of party history in Bucharest.

In charge of all of the political machinery of the PCR, the Standing Presidium of the Central Committee is the party's center for decisionmaking and policy control and, as such, is the most powerful body in the country. There were, at the beginning of 1972, four party leaders who held positions concurrently on the Standing Presidium, the Executive Committee, and the Secretariat: Ceausescu, Manea Manescu, Paul Niculescu-Mizil, and Gheorghe Pana. Political observers considered these men to be the most powerful in the party and, hence, the nation. All of the nine members of the Standing Presidium are also members of the Executive Committee.

Little information is available on the responsibilities given the Executive Committee, although some observers have described it as providing an administrative link between the Standing Presidium and the Central Committee. In practice it has functioned as a rump Central Committee when the latter is not in session. The Secretariat serves as the continuing administrative unit of the party. It supervises the execution of policies decided upon by the Standing Presidium. Three members of the Secretariat serve as the supervising secretaries of the major directorates of the Central Committee.

Two other important party organs function under the supervision of the Standing Presidium and the Secretariat: the Central Auditing Commission and the Central Collegium, formerly known as the Party Control Commission. Consisting of forty-five members (none of whom may belong to the Central Committee), the Central Auditing Commission is empowered to exercise general control over party financial affairs and examine the management of finances by the various party organs. The nine-member Central Collegium deals with matters of party discipline and serves as a type of appeals court for penalties imposed on members by county or local party committees.

An interlocking of authority and functions at the highest level of the party and state is evidenced in the frequency with which the senior party officials also hold important government posts. All of the members of the Standing Presidium, the Executive Committee, and the Secretariat are also deputies to the Grand National Assembly, and most of them hold other prominent government positions in the Council of State, the Defense Council, or the Council of Ministers.

The party statutes describe the local cell, the basic party unit, as the foundation of the party. Cells exist in factories, offices, cooperatives, military and police units, social and cultural organizations, and residential areas. Some of these cell groups consist of as few as three members, whereas those in the larger enterprises may have as many as 300 members. In 1969 there were an estimated 69,000 of these local party units.

Functions of the local and occupational cell units include the implementation of party directives and programs, the recruit-

140

ment and indoctrination of new members, and the dissemination of propaganda directed at those outside the party. Members have the duty to participate in social, economic, and cultural activities, particularly in the direction of the economic enterprises, and to critically examine production and community life in the light of party ideology and goals. In all of its activities the local cell is required to uphold the discipline of the party and to adhere to the policies established by the ruling bodies of the PCR.

Between the local cell unit and the higher organs of the PCR stands a hierarchy of party committees organized on the county, town, and communal levels. Each of these units is directly subordinate to the next higher level of the party organization. In Bucharest a city party committee supervises the activities of the communal and enterprise cells. Each party committee sets up its own bureau and elects a secretariat. In most cases the secretariat consists of a first secretary, a first vice chairman, and three or more vice chairmen or secretaries.

The activity of the bureaus is conducted through several functional departments, which generally consist of sections on personnel, administration, agitation and propaganda, economic enterprises, youth, and women's affairs. The county and city committees also have their own control commissions and training programs. The first secretary of the county committee also serves as chairman of the county people's council, interlocking the party and government offices (see ch. 8).

The party leadership decided in late 1967 to require the active participation of the party secretaries in the administrative organs of the enterprises and other institutions in their respective areas. County committees are aided in their administrative duties by economic commissions that oversee the general economic development of the county and fix both current and long-range goals. In addition, the economic commissions are charged with the coordination of all economic activity, the conducting of studies and making of proposals for setting production goals, and the allocation of material and human resources in the county.

At each of these levels—county, city, town, and commune— the highest authoritative organ is the party conference, which fills a role on these lower levels similar to that of the party congress on the national level. The party statutes as revised in 1969 call for the convening of conferences every fourth year in the counties, in the city of Bucharest, and in the larger towns. In the communes and smaller towns the conference is required to be held once every two years. Although the conferences are held ostensibly to discuss problems and formulate policies, they serve in practice as transmission belts for the official party line set down by the central PCR authorities. County conferences and the Bucharest city conference elect delegates to the national party congress.

Membership

The PCR emerged at the close of World War II with only about 1,000 members. Four years later, just before it merger with the Social Democratic Party and after an intensive propanda campaign and a strong membership drive, the party reported over 700,000 members. When the PCR merged with the Social Democratic Party to form the Romanian Workers' Party in 1948, some 200,000 Social Democrats were added to the membership roll. A purge of so-called hostile and nominal members during 1950 resulted in the expulsion of 190,000 persons from the party, reducing the total membership to about 720,000 at the beginning of 1951.

During the early years of full communist control of Romania, the party considered itself the vanguard of the working class and made a sustained effort to recruit workers into party membership. By the end of 1950 the PCR reported that 64 percent of the leading party positions and 40 percent of the higher government posts were filled by members of the working class. The efforts to recruit workers into the party have consistently fallen short of the set goals, however, and from time to time throughout the period since 1950 party leaders have decried the fact that the social composition of the membership has not included an adequate proportion of workers.

By 1964 the party membership was reported at 1.2 million. This total was increased to 1.5 million by 1966, a figure that represented about 8 percent of the country's population. Membership composition, in 1966, was reported as 40 percent workers, 32 percent peasants, and 22 percent intelligentsia, with the remaining 6 percent not classified.

After Ceausescu's accession to power in 1965, he sought to increase the party's influence, broaden the base of popular support, and bring in new members. At a first step, he eliminated the probationary period, which had varied from one year for industrial workers to two years for peasants, white-collar workers, and intellectuals. Additional members were also sought by enticing those who had belonged to the old Social Democratic Party and the former Socialist Party by dating their membership from the time of their entry into those parties.

The result of the membership drive, announced at the 1967

party conference, was the addition of 230,000 new PCR members, bringing the total to 1,730,000. At the 1969 party congress it was announced that the PCR had 1,924,500 members, representing about one-seventh of the total adult population. In February 1971 the Central Committee reported that the membership had grown to 2.1 million, making the PCR one of the largest communist parties in Eastern Europe.

Statistics reported by the party press indicated the nationality composition of the PCR as consisting of 88.8 percent Romanians, 8.4 percent Hungarians, and slightly over 1 percent Germans, with the remainder encompassing other nationalities. As the 1966 census had shown that Hungarians represented 8.4 percent of the total population, the Germans 2 percent, and other nationalities about 2 percent, the nationality composition of the party compares favorably with that of the country as a whole.

Workers reportedly made up 44 percent of the party membership; peasants, 26 percent; and intellectuals and white-collar workers, 23 percent. Seven percent were unclassified as to status. Statistics indicating the age composition of the party were also published, revealing that 24 percent of the membership was under thirty years of age; persons between the ages of thirty and forty made up 36 percent of the membership, and 40 percent of the members were over forty years old.

The PCR membership campaign had been given particular emphasis in the major industries, such as the metal, machine-building, coal, petroleum, and chemical industries, where 27 to 36 percent of the workers were reported to belong to the party. Female membership was reported as 23 percent, up from 17 percent in 1960 and 21 percent in 1965. The report contained a recommendation that a larger number of women be assigned to responsible positions. Statistics for the army revealed that 90 percent of the officers and 55 percent of the noncommissioned officers were party members. The fact that over 926,000 members lived in rural areas was asserted by the PCR leaders to be proof of peasant support and a demonstration of the effectiveness of the party in organizing at the village level.

In 1970 the party press reported that an analysis of the leading national and local PCR bodies revealed that the greater proportion of their memberships consists of those drawn from the ranks of the working class. Of the 285 members and alternate members of the Central Committee, 197, or nearly 70 percent, were workers or persons who had come from the workers' ranks. Of the 4,698 members of county party committees, 2,144 or 45.6 percent were said to be workers or from the working class. Together, workers and peasants were reported to make up over 64 percent of the membership of county committees. As many as 81 percent of the activists of the county, municipal, and communal party committees were—according to their basic professions—workers, foremen, or technicians.

Party Training

In early 1970 the PCR carried out a major reorganization of its primary institution for the training of leading party workers, the Stefan Gheorghiu Party Academy. With the reorganization, the full name of the institution became the Stefan Gheorghiu Academy for Social-Political Education and the Training of Leading Cadres. Its tasks were defined as the training of party activists and the development of party leaders capable of resolving problems and "applying the science of political leadership to the party and society."

Ceausescu explained that the reorganization was necessary for upgrading the training of activists for the party as well as for various sectors of economic and state life. He also stated that the combination of party training with state and economic activity is based on the principle that the PCR is the leading force of the society and, as such, must ensure the proper training of the personnel needed to guide all sectors of activity.

As reorganized, the academy is divided into two departments, one for the training of cadres in the party and in mass organizations and a second for the training of personnel who work in the economy and state administration. Each department is subdivided into a number of institutes, sections, and training centers. Within the first department is the Institute for Training Cadres in Social-Political Management, which in turn is subdivided into sections for political-organizational activity, political-ideological activity, and political-economic activity. Also within the same department are the Journalism Faculty, the Center for the Education and Training of Party and Mass Organization Cadres, the Center for Improving the Political-Ideological Training of Teachers of Social-Political Sciences in State Schools, and the Center for Activist Training Courses. The Center for Activist Training Courses provided programs of study for activists in the party, the youth organization, labor unions, and workers in offices of foreign affairs. The last two centers are divided into several sections that specialize in the training of particular classes of activists.

The second department, that which provided training for state employees and for those working in economic activities,

144

consists of the Central Institute for the Education of Leading Cadres in the Economy and State Administration, a section for short-term courses, and a section for training in specialized management and organizational problems. The institute includes sections on the organization and management of industrial activity, of construction, of transport and telecommunications, of agriculture, of circulation of goods and services, of planning, and of state administration. In addition, the department organizes courses for chairmen of agricultural production cooperatives.

Admission to the academy programs is carefully controlled by the party. Courses in the first department last for four years, and candidates are selected from among the activists in the county and city party committees and the central PCR bodies and from loyal party workers in the mass organizations. Political activists in the Ministry of the Armed Forces, the Ministry of Internal Affairs, and the State Security Council are also eligible for training in the first department.

PCR regulations stipulate that candidates for training in the first department must have worked for at least three years in production and have had at least three years' experience in mass organizations. In addition, the candidate must have completed at least a five-month course in one of the lower level party schools, have a high school diploma or its equivalent, and be thirty-five years of age or younger.

Courses in the second department last for two years. Requirements for admission into this department include extensive experience in organization and management related to industry and labor, at least eight years of service, membership in the PCR, graduation from a higher education institute, and an age of forty years or younger.

In addition to the broad program of the academy, the PCR also maintains other ideological training institutions. These include the Institute of Historical and Social-Political Studies in Bucharest, which functions under the direct supervision of the Central Committee, and lower level training programs that operate under the county party committees.

During 1971 the PCR placed increased emphasis on both the political and general education of all party workers, and the Central Committee decreed that only those who can keep up to date in their fields of activity would be promoted. As a followup to the decree, the Central Committee initiated a series of twenty- to thirty-day training programs and required some 15,000 persons from party, state, and mass organizations to attend the sessions. The order included a warning that those who did not successfully complete the courses would lose their jobs.

Observers of Romanian politics stated that the decision to require this additional training of state and party workers stemmed from the fact that the majority of personnel on both the central and local levels had been named to their positions on the basis of faithful party activity rather than their professional qualifications. The stipulation that those who do not successfully complete the courses would lose their jobs enables the party to replace those who are not qualified to fill their positions.

The study programs, designed to include practical work, discussion of specific problems, and field trips, cover a number of subjects including "the basic Marxist-Leninist sciences of management and organization," automatic data processing, the utilization of electronic calculators, methods of socioeconomic analysis, and the projection of plans, as well as a number of special subjects related to the various fields of activity of the participants. To facilitate the training of larger numbers, branches of the Stefan Gheorghiu Party Academy's Center for the Education and Training of Party and Mass Organization Cadres were set up in Bucharest and in seven counties.

Mass Organizations

The PCR has fostered the development of a large number of mass organizations that function as its auxiliaries. Comprised of members of an interest group or a profession whose welfare they purport to serve, the mass organizations provide channels for the transmission of policy and doctrine from the party to the general population. PCR leaders have described the duties of mass organizations as the mobilization of the working people for the fulfillment of party policies and the provision for their participation in the economic, political, and cultural life of the country. Leaders of the mass organizations are always reliable PCR members.

Citizens are constitutionally guaranteed the right to join together in organizations. At the same time, the Constitution defines the leading role of the party in relation to the mass organizations, asserting that through such organizations the PCR "achieves an organized link with the working class, the peasantry, the intelligentsia, and the other categories of working people" and mobilizes them in "the struggle for the completion of the building of socialism."

Two broad classes of organizations are included under the rubric of mass organizations: those based on common interests or common categories or persons, such as youth and women's associations, and those based on professions, such as the General Union of Trade Unions. Several of the organizations belong to international organizations and associations, such as the World Federation of Trade Unions and the World Federation of Democratic Youth.

Among the more important of the mass organizations are the Union of Communist Youth, the General Union of Trade Unions, and the National Council of Women. The chairmen of the Union of Communist Youth and the General Union of Trade Unions sit on the Council of Ministers and have ministerial rank; the chairman of the youth union serves simultaneously as head of the Ministry of Youth Problems.

The Union of Communist Youth

At the time of its founding in early 1949 the Union of Communist Youth (Uniunea Tineretului Comunist—UTC) was looked upon as the youth branch of the PCR. It was set up with much the same organizational structure as the party and, in practice, functioned both as a youth political party and mass organization. Resulting from the party-decreed merger of all existing youth organizations, the UTC was given the task of educating the young in the spirit of Marxism-Leninism and mobilizing them, under the guidance of the party, for the building of socialism.

In early 1972 the UTC continued to be one of the most powerful of the mass organizations in the country, with an estimated membership of 2.5 million. Membership was open to young people between the ages of fifteen and twenty-six; those who have reached the age of eighteen could also become members of the PCR. The Tenth Party Congress, meeting in 1969, introduced the requirement that young people up to the age of twenty-six would be accepted into the party only if they were UTC members. Decisions on persons to fill the most important leadership positions in the UTC were made by the PCR Central Committee.

The structure of the UTC has undergone a number of changes since it was originally established. In early 1972 the organization functioned on the national level with an eight-member Secretariat, including the first secretary who is also the UTC chairman, and a bureau of twenty-one full and seven alternate members. In each of the thirty-nine countries and the city of Bucharest there exist UTC committees that are similarly organized with secretariats and bureaus. The UTC has its own publishing facilities and publishes its own propaganda organ, *The Spark of Youth* (Scinteia Tineretului).

Statistics on the composition of the youth organization, reported at the Ninth UTC Congress held in February 1971, indicated that the membership consisted of 30 percent workers, 39 percent students, and 17 percent peasants. The remainder consisted of those who were classified as intellectuals, clerks, and office workers.

Periodically throughout the 1960s PCR leaders demonstrated growing concern for what they termed as shortcomings in the political education of the nation's youth. In 1968 this concern led to the establishment of the Research Center for Youth Problems and an increased effort to instill in the young people a sense of "socialist patriotism." Ceausescu asserted the need for all levels of education to be permeated with Marxist-Leninist ideology and placed particular emphasis on ideological training in the universities.

Political education of young people, both members and nonmembers, and their mobilization in support of PCR policies is considered the primary duty of the UTC. It is charged with the organization of political and patriotic courses in schools, among peasant groups, and among workers and members of the armed forces. The UTC also guides and supervises the activities of the Union of Student Associations.

A second youth movement, the Pioneers Organization, was created for young people between the ages of nine and fourteen. In late 1971 the Pioneers Organization reported a total membership of 1.6 million. The organization's responsibilities toward those of its age group parallel those of the UTC and involve political and patriotic training. Until 1966 the Pioneers Organization functioned as an integral part of the UTC, but since that time it has been under the direct control of the party Central Committee.

The General Union of Trade Unions

As the official organization incorporating all blue-collar and white-collar workers, the General Union of Trade Unions (Uniunea Generala a Sindicatelr din Romania—UGSR) is the largest of the country's mass organizations, with a reported membership in early 1972 of 4.6 million. Headed by a general council, the UGSR consists of twelve component labor union federations and forty area councils, one for each county and the city of Bucharest. The Central Council is structured with a chairman, appointed by the PCR Central Committee, seven secretaries, and an executive committee of twenty-seven full and nine alternate members. There are an estimated 12,000 local union units.

The primary function of the labor unions is the transmission of party policies to the rank and file. The UGSR statutes specify that the organization will carry out all of its activities under the political leadership of the PCR, and a similar provision is also included in the statutes of the county UGSR committees. In addi-

148

tion, the statutes of the central body require the organization to work to mobilize labor union members to ensure the implementation of party policy. A 1969 resolution of the Central Council of the UGSR declared that all labor union activities would focus on the mobilization of the working people to fulfill the state economic plan.

In early 1971, after a period of increased labor discipline problems and following a time of severe labor unrest in Poland, the PCR took steps to reform the labor union organization. Announcing what he termed as the democratization of the UGSR and its component unions, Ceausescu promised the workers genuine protection of their interests and a voice in the appointment of industrial management. The goal of the PCR program was to improve the unions without losing party control, and Ceausescu defined democratization as meaning that the labor unions would serve the party as a framework for the organization of consultations with the masses and as a forum where workers can debate the country's economic and social development.

New UGSR statutes were introduced in mid-1971. Observers of Romanian political affairs asserted, however, that there were no major changes in the system and pointed out that the new statutes still did not give labor unions the right to take the initiative in matters concerning wages or the living standard. In this regard the unions could fill only a watchdog role to assure that the regulations approved by the appropriate party and management bodies were being correctly carried out.

PARTY POLICIES AND PROGRAMS

The major domestic programs that the party sought to promote centered on the country's economic development, the integration of national minorities, the extension of so-called socialist democracy, and the PCR's cultural-ideological campaign. As a means of strengthening its leading role, the party leaders acted to improve communication between the central PCR organs and the county, city, and commune organizations and, at the same time, took additional steps to win mass support.

The Economy

In the area of economics the PCR continued its primary emphasis on industrial development and was only secondarily concerned with agriculture and consumer goods. This emphasis was evidenced in the economic plan adopted for the 1971–75 period, approved by the 1969 party congress, which concentrates on heavy industry at the expense of consumer goods. Although Romania was primarily an agricultural country, the PCR leadership in the early 1960s, rejected the plan of the Council for Mutual Economic Assistance (COMECON) for a division of labor between the participating communist states that would have had Romania place the greatest emphasis on the development of agriculture. Instead, the PCR launched a drive to modernize the country through industrialization (see ch. 14; ch. 10).

The policies pursued by the PCR are designed to maintain firm party control of the economy. In the formulation of Romania's economic development plans, the will of the party is predominant, and the degree of party control was augmented by the territorial and administrative reorganization of 1968 when economic commissions were established in each of the new counties to function under the direct supervision of the county PCR committees. These comisssions made it possible for the party to have a direct hand in the local economic programs.

During 1970 and 1971 party leaders noted that, whereas the annual production increase envisaged by the Five-Year Plan (1971–75) had been fulfilled for industry, that for agriculture fell far short. Ceausescu called for a renewal of intensive efforts in both industry and agriculture to meet the requirements of the people and to enable the country to achieve the true socialist state of development.

National Minorities

The integration of the major non-Romanian national groups into the life of the country has posed periodic problems for the PCR throughout the post-World War II era. Each of the communist constitutions guaranteed equal rights to the national minorities, rights that included the opportunity to use their own language and to have representation on local bodies of government. The Hungarian Autonomous Region had been created by the 1952 Constitution but was not continued under the 1968 territorial reorganization (see ch. 8; ch. 4).

Party leaders explained the decision to abandon the concept of an autonomous region for the Hungarian population in terms of the need to integrate all of the minority groups fully into the Romanian political community. Spokesmen asserted that it is the policy of the PCR to respect the heritage of the various nationality groups and extend to them full political rights but at the same time to work to create conditions that will serve to unite all of the country under the leaderwhip of the party.

PCR leaders have feared the possibility of attempts by foreign elements to foster unrest among the country's larger minority groups. This was particularly true at the time of the Soviet-led invasion of Czechoslovakia, when Romanian leaders were apprehensive about the possibility of a similar intervention in their country. At that time PCR officials visited the areas where there were concentrations of Hungarian and German minorities, stressing national unity and equal rights for all national groups.

These efforts were followed in November 1968 by the establishment of nationality councils: the Council of Working People of Hungarian Nationality and the Council of Working People of German Nationality. Units of the Hungarian council were established in fifteen counties, and units of the German council were established in nine counties. In counties where there existed substantial Serbian or Ukrainian populations, similar local councils were established for these groups, although only the Hungarian and German minorities maintained councils on the national level. The nationality councils were affiliated with the Socialist Unity Front. A month after the establishment of the councils the Grand National Assembly, on the initiative of the party, passed legislation granting the minorities increased representation on local government bodies.

In explaining the purposes of the nationality councils, Ceausescu declared that they would "cultivate socialist patriotism, socialist internationalism, and devotion for our new order and for the common fatherland . . . against any backward nationalistic concepts and manifestations." Observers of Romanian political affairs pointed out, however, that the councils are closely tied to the party and, although they can serve as means of communication between the PCR and the minority groups, they function primarily as transmission belts for party policies and as instruments for PCR political and educational activities.

Social Democracy and Party Ideology

At the same time that the PCR has sought to present itself as a progressive force seeking the participation of the people in political affairs, it has also carried on a campaign to strengthen what it calls the Marxist character of all ideological, cultural, and educational activities. Within limits, Ceausescu has encouraged what he has termed as "socialist democracy"—open communication between the masses and the party leadership—and he has publicly called for the people to express their views on political issues.

Socialist democracy is defined by Ceausescu as a spirit of social responsibility by which the citizens are inspired to perform their duties in accordance with the needs and imperatives of the society as a whole. The goal of socialist democracy is to stimulate the masses to support the cause of socialism by involving them in the programs of the PCR to such an extent that the individual identifies his personal goals and values with those of the party.

In mid-1971 Ceausescu announced a new ideological program and the tightening of party controls over government, science, and cultural life. Observers gave various interpretations to the campaign. Some saw it as a move to respond to Soviet criticism of Romanian foreign policy by reminding Moscow that socialism was not endangered in Romania and that this pretext could not be used to justify Soviet interference; others considered it as an assertion of authority by Ceausescu at a time when he judged it necessary to combat ideological laxity at home. The action may also have been prompted by a concern that party authority and discipline were being undermined by Western cultural influences.

Partially directed at the youth of the nation, the campaign included curbs against alcohol in youth clubs and the screening of foreign television programs and music. Another objective of the campaign was increased party control over literature and cultural life; new ideological guidelines were issued for writers, publishers, and theaters. In speaking of the role of the arts, Ceausescu declared that they must serve the single purpose of socialist-communist education. At the same time, he called for increased guidance of the arts by all levels of the PCR and requested that works of art and literature be judged for their conformity with party standards and their service to the working class. Ceausescu ruled out repressive measures, however, and asserted that the party would rely on persuasion to implement the new ideological program (see ch. 7).

The campaign encountered some resistance, although more passive than overt. A number of writers boycotted the literary magazines in protest against the restrictions imposed on publishing and, despite the fact that the official writers' union circulated a statement in support of the party's stand, many of the more prominent writers refused to endorse it. In August 1971 the editor of a leading literary journal, who was also a member of the PCR Central Committee, resigned both positions as a protest against the stricter party controls.

Resistance was also evident in the party and state bureaucracy, where the ideological campaign was welcomed in principle but frequently ignored in practice. Many of the nation's youth also manifested disagreement with the restrictive content campaign. Assessing the progress of the program in late 1971, Ceausescu admitted that the new approach had not been generally adopted among the youth and asserted that the party organizations had not been diligent enough in the enforcement of the code. Particular criticism was directed at the Executive Committee and Secretariat for having failed to implement the decisions taken for the improvement of ideological activity.

Although it is difficult for outside political observers to detect differences within the top bodies of the party, in regard to the ideological campaign tensions have been more evident. For the first time since Ceausescu came to power in 1965, the Central Committee plenum, meeting in November 1971, did not report unanimous agreement on all issues. Some observers indicated that the effect of the campaign has stimulated opposition to some of Ceausescu's policies. There was no evidence, however, that such opposition is organized or that it provides any serious threat to Ceausescu's position, and no leading figure in either the government or the party has openly expressed views that differ from those of the general secretary.

POLITICAL VALUES AND ATTITUDES

The Regime and the People

Inasmuch as the PCR has proclaimed itself to be the only legitimate source of political power and, as well, the leading force in all aspects of economic and cultural life, the development of independent political and cultural values has been thoroughly circumscribed. Party control extends to all aspects of the society and embraces educational and professional opportunities. Although PCR leaders have promised changes in the manner of selection for advancement, promotions have been based more frequently on party activity and doctrinal reliability than on professional competence.

Because of the breadth of party control, accurate information on the attitudes of the people toward the regime and toward specific political issues is difficult to obtain. The Romanian press functions under the direct supervision of the PCR, and tight restrictions are placed on foreign correspondents reporting on events inside the country. Observers have indicated, however, that not all of the regime's domestic policies have been welcomed by all segments of the population and that some party policies have left a wake of latent resentments.

Some observers have pointed to the decrease in the number of peasants in the party (down 3 percent in the 1969–71 period) as an indication of peasant dissatisfaction with the poor living conditions in the rural areas and the low income of most of the agricultural cooperatives (see ch. 2). Frequently the party responds to signs of discontent by any segment of the population by increasing the ideological propaganda directed toward it, but the regime has also attempted various reforms to counter obvious inadequacies.

Among the more overt examples of discontent with party policy is the resistance to accepting job assignments in rural areas shown by technical school graduates. Other graduates have also refused to leave their home areas to work on collectives; all of these were criticized in the party press for giving priority to personal interests instead of considering the interests of the society as a whole. PCR officials declared that the graduates had been trained at state expense and that their refusal to fulfill their obligations as assigned by the party could not be tolerated. This resistance to party-decreed transfers was also evident among other groups during 1969 and 1970, including teachers, builders, and administrative workers.

Observers consider such situations as evidence that the party is having difficulty reconciling an essentially authoritarian system with a policy of socialist democracy that encourages public initiative and participation. The persistence with which Ceausescu pursued the new ideological campaign during 1971 gave some observers the impression that he had opted to put his weight down on the side of continued authoritarianism.

Romanian Nationalism

The regime scored a marked success in basing its appeal for popular support on nationalistic sentiments and in giving emphasis to Romanian history and cultural traditions. Ceausescu has attempted to broaden the communist movement to include the aspirations of the people as a whole. Whereas in the past the PCR leaders made reference only to communist achievements and attributed everything positive to the work of the party, Ceausescu has praised Romanian national heroes and has given positive emphasis to specifically Romanian contributions to socialist development.

To a significant degree the revival of nationalism has gone hand in hand with anti-Soviet attitudes. The image of the party was bolstered by the PCR leader's refusal to follow the Soviet line on a number of significant national and international issues (see ch. 10). At the time of the Soviet-led invasion of Czechoslovakia in August 1968, Ceausescu's denunciation of the action and his call for national mobilization in the face of the crisis served to unite the population and strengthen his position. Observers have pointed out, however, that this unity has appeared to wane with the ebbing of the crisis and with the return to the realities of everyday life in Romania.

154

CHAPTER 10

FOREIGN RELATIONS

Throughout the 1960s Romanian foreign policy increasingly diverged from that of the Soviet Union and its allies in Eastern Europe as the Romanian leaders asserted the country's national interests. In early 1972 the government continued to declare that its foreign policy was based on national independence, sovereignty, and the principle of noninterference in internal affairs. Government and party leaders asserted that Romania would continue to seek development of friendly and cooperative relations with all states without regard to differences in sociopolitical systems.

Foreign policy was formulated under the direct control of the Standing Presidium of the Romanian Communist Party (Partidul Communist Roman—PCR) and administered through the government ministries. Although the regime of PCR General Secretary Nicolae Ceausescu has steadfastly sought to maintain an independent stance in foreign affairs and to develop political and economic relations with both communist and noncommunist states, it has continued to assert the Marxist-Leninist character of both its domestic and foreign policies. PCR leaders have repeatedly affirmed the party's commitment to the international communist movement and to the solidarity of all socialist states.

In the development of an independent foreign policy position the PCR has sought to shift away from economic and political domination by the Soviet Union and to develop a form of communism geared to the country's national interests and in keeping with the regime's perspective on world affairs. Although such a course brought the Romanian party and government into frequent conflict with the Soviet Union, the Romanian leadership continued to insist on its own interpretation and adaptation of communism.

In early 1972 Romania maintained full diplomatic relations with more than ninety governments, over forty of which maintained embassies in Bucharest. In addition, trade and cultural relations were conducted with a number of other states with which formal relations had not been established. Romania is a member of the United Nations (UN) and a number of several UN specialized agencies. It is also a member of the communist military alliance known as the Warsaw Treaty Organization (Warsaw Pact) and the communist economic alliance called the Council for Mutual Economic Assistance (COMECON).

During 1970 and 1971 the regime made increased efforts to cultivate and strengthen the country's relations with the developing states of Asia and Africa and to extend its relations with the nations of Latin America. Personal diplomacy by Ceausescu and other ranking party and government leaders served as an important means for maintaining the country's international relations.

DETERMINANTS OF FOREIGN POLICY

Historical Factors

After coming under full communist control in the early post-World War II period, the country was closely aligned with the international policies and goals of the Communist Party of the Soviet Union. Romania's international and domestic policies generally supported the political and economic goals of the Soviet Union. Beneath the surface, however, an internal party struggle was being waged in Romania between certain communist leaders who were fully oriented toward the Soviet Union and others who sought an orientation that was less Soviet dominated (see ch. 2).

Although the internal struggle involved personal ambitions as much as political and ideological goals, the group surrounding party First Secretary Gheorghe Gheorghiu-Dej urged the attainment of national goals through cooperation with the Soviet Union rather than a position of complete integration and exclusive dependence on the Soviets. By mid-1952 Gheorghiu-Dej was able to gain full control of the party, purge his leading opponents, and assume the dual role of party chief and head of the government. Shortly after assuming the premiership, Gheorghiu-Dej began a slow and cautious disengagement from Soviet domination, being careful, however, not to advocate goals that were at variance with the policies of Soviet Premier Josef Stalin. Domestic politics, in fact, remained strongly Stalinist in orientation, and it was not until after Stalin's death in March 1953 that the first significant steps were taken to diminish Soviet control.

To a significant degree the country's foreign policy during the Gheorghiu-Dej era reflected the Romanian leader's struggle for his own political survival, particularly in the face of Soviet Premier Nikita Khrushchev's campaign to weaken the power of Stalinist-oriented Eastern European communist leaders. Important also was the growing Romanian determination to limit the influence of the Soviet Union in the country's internal affairs, especially in the realm of economic development. Political events within the communist world during the remainder of the 1950s and the early 1960s provided Gheorghiu-Dej the opportunity to assert an increasingly independent stance and to gain concessions from the Soviets.

Faced with Khrushchev's emphasis on de-Stalinization and his demands for communist unity under Soviet leadership, the Gheorghiu-Dej regime responded by giving lip service to Soviet policies while, at the same time, supporting moves aimed at weakening Soviet hegemony in the communist world. In early 1954 Gheorghiu-Dej sensed the political significance of Khrushchev's "peaceful coexistence" theme for Romania and began to exploit the situation to gain leverage for the extracting of concessions from the Soviet Union. The first significant achievement came later that same year when negotiations led to the dissolution of the joint Soviet-Romanian industrial enterprises that had been the primary instrument of Soviet economic exploitation during the postwar period.

The regime also sought to gain increased domestic support by emphasizing the country's historical traditions, by calling for "Romanian solutions to Romanian problems," and by cautiously exploiting the population's latent anti-Soviet sentiments. In August 1954, on the occasion of the tenth anniversary of the country's liberation from Nazi forces, Gheorghiu-Dej asserted that the primary credit for driving out the occupiers belonged to Romanian Communists rather than to the Soviet army, a view that was subsequently condemned by the Soviets and supported by the Communist Chinese.

Although the Gheorghiu-Dej regime formally supported the Soviet action in suppressing the 1956 Hungarian revolt, the Romanian leaders attempted to exploit the situation in order to obtain additional concessions from the Soviets and to gain recognition of the legitimacy of the so-called Romanian road to socialism. At that time, one of their primary aims was the removal of Soviet occupation forces that had remained in the country throughout the post-World War II period. Although the regime was not successful in obtaining formal Soviet recognition of a Romanian variant of communism, an agreement was reached placing a time limit on the presence of the Soviet troops, the forces finally being withdrawn in 1958.

Important problems were posed to the Gheorghiu-Dej regime by the reactivation of COMECON and the Soviet intentions to integrate the economies of the member states. Initially established in 1949 as the Soviet counterpart to the European Recovery Program (Marshall Plan), COMECON was largely dormant until 1955, when Khrushchev decided to revitalize the organization as an instrument of Soviet economic policy in Eastern Europe. CO-MECON plans called for the subordination of national economic plans to an overall planning body that would determine economic development for the member states as a whole. Romania was to be assigned the role of a supplier of raw materials and agricultural produce for the more industrially developed members (see ch. 2).

Gheorghiu-Dej rejected such a subservient role for Romania and proceeded with his own plans for the country's industrial development, asserting the right of each COMECON member state to develop its own economy in accord with national needs and interests, a position that was, in turn, rejected by the Soviets. As a reaction to Soviet pressures and the need to lessen Romanian dependence on COMECON, the regime initiated a gradual and cautious expansion of economic relations with noncommunist states.

In 1957 Ion Gheorghe Maurer became minister of foreign affairs and, under the direction of Gheorghiu-Dej, initiated programs that emphasized the national character of Romanian foreign policy. Included in these programs were plans for the attainment of self-sufficiency in the machine-tool industry and in the production of iron and steel. At the same time, additional steps were taken to increase trade with Western Europe and the United States.

The conflict with the Soviet Union became more acute in 1962 when Gheorghiu-Dej again rejected the COMECON plan for Romania and, later in the year, announced that a contract for the construction of a large steel mill at Galati had been concluded with a British-French consortium. Romanian statements in support of Albania further antagonized the Soviet leaders. During 1963 and 1964 Romanian-Soviet relations continued to deteriorate as the Gheorghiu-Dej regime sought to exploit the Sino-Soviet dispute and moved closer to the Communist Chinese position on the equality of communist states and the rejection of the leading role of the Soviet party. In November 1963 Maurer declared the readiness of Romania to mediate the Sino-Soviet dispute, a suggestion that Moscow considered arrogant and anti-Soviet.

A statement issued by the party Central Committee in April 1964 declared the right of Romania and all other nations to develop national policies in the light of their own interests and domestic requirements. During the remainder of that year the volume of economic and cultural contacts with Western nations increased significantly. The increased role of the United States in the Vietnam hostilities, however, served to curb the Gheorghiu-Dej regime's efforts to improve relations with the United States, and the sudden death of Gheorghiu-Dej in March 1965 raised questions as to the future direction of Romanian foreign policy.

Under Gheorghiu-Dej's successor, Nicolae Ceausescu, Romania's foreign policy continued to diverge from that of the Soviet Union and the other members of COMECON and the Warsaw Pact. Increasingly assertive of national interests, the Ceausescu regime antagonized the Soviet Union by its establishment of diplomatic relations with the Federal Republic of Germany (West Germany) in 1967 and by its refusal to follow the Soviet lead in breaking relations with Israel in the wake of the 1967 Arab-Israeli War.

The invasion of Czechoslovakia by Soviet-led forces of the Warsaw Pact in August 1968 posed a particular threat to Romania. Observers of Eastern European political affairs saw the invasion as a severe blow to the basic assumptions of Romanian foreign policy, which included the belief that the Soviet Union would not intervene militarily against another member of the Warsaw Pact as long as the system of communist party rule was firmly maintained and membership in the pact was continued.

From the outset of the Czechoslovak crisis the Ceausescu regime asserted that the only basis for relations between states was respect for national indepedence and sovereignty and a policy of noninterference in another state's internal affairs. The actual invasion, however, marked a reversal for Romanian foreign policy and, although the initial response was one of condemnation and defiance, Romania was put on the defensive.

The invasion of Czechoslovakia marked something of a turning point in Romania's relations with COMECON and the Warsaw Pact. The Soviet enunciation of the so-called Brezhnev Doctrine —the concept that the protection of socialism in any communist state is the legitimate concern of all communist states—was intended as a clear warning to the Ceausescu regime.

Pressures mounted on Romania to cooperate more fully in the Warsaw Pact and to agree to a supranational planning body within the framework of COMECON. Economic conditions as well as the political and military pressures pushed the Ceausescu regime toward closer cooperation with COMECON, although the Romanians continued to resist the Soviet efforts toward economic integration.

As a result of these pressures, the 1968–70 period was one of relative passivity for the Romanians in foreign affairs, although the period was marked by several important events, including the visit of President Richard M. Nixon to Romania in August 1969 and the long-delayed signing of the friendship treaty with the Soviet Union in July 1970. By early 1971 the Ceausescu regime again became more assertive of its independent line in foreign policy.

Principles of Foreign Policy

According to the 1965 Constitution, the foreign policy of the country is based on strict respect for the principles of national independence and sovereignty, equality of rights, noninterference in internal affairs, and interstate relations based on mutual advantage. The Constitution declares the nation's desire to maintain friendly and fraternal relations with all socialist states as well as to promote friendship and cooperation with states of other sociopolitical systems. Participation in international organizations is directed toward the furthering of peace and international understanding.

Spokesmen for the regime have repeatedly asserted these principles as the only acceptable basis for relations between states both within and outside the world communist movement. In contrast to the Soviet position that socialism can only be fully realized by transcending national forms, Romanian policy gives primary emphasis to the distinct requirements of the nation. At the same time, however, Romania recognizes the duties of each socialist state toward cooperative and mutually advantageous relations with all socialist nations and fraternal communist parties.

In keeping with these principles the PCR has rejected the so-called Brezhnev Doctrine of limited sovereignty of socialist states. Instead, regime spokesmen have asserted that within the socialist system all Marxist-Leninist parties are equal and have the exclusive right to determine appropriate solutions for their own problems and manage their own affairs. Romanian policy maintains that relations between socialist states must be based on equal rights, complete trust, mutual respect, and fraternal cooperation. In defending the country's policies, PCR leaders have repeatedly argued that, because the construction of communism is being carried out under a great variety of conditions, there will inevitably be different opinions regarding the forms and procedures employed as well as different points of view regarding international problems. Such differences, however, should not affect relations between socialist states or the unity of the socialist movement.

In response to Soviet calls for socialist solidarity, a ranking member of the PCR Standing Presidium declared, "it would be unrealistic to think that fourteen socialist countries spread over three continents, each with its specific characteristics, should show themselves strictly identical in the building of a new society." Additional party statements insisted that each country must be allowed to apply the principles of Marxism-Leninism to its own particular conditions and that no general line for all parties could be established. In adjusting Marxism-Leninism to national

160

needs each party must be able to make its own unique contribution to the enrichment of the entire communist movement.

During the negotiations for the renewal of the friendship treaties with the other Warsaw Pact countries, the Ceausescu government repeatedly stressed that its own formula for developing international relations with noncommunist nations was based on the same principles as those applied to socialist states and that Romania was open to the establishment of such relations "without regard for difference in the social order." A party spokesman asserted that the country's foreign relations are not determined by short-term circumstances that are vaild at one moment and superseded the next but by policies directed at long-term cooperation in all fields of common interests.

PCR policy has sought to support the country's independent political stance by increasing its economic independence. This has led to the rejection of COMECON attempts to integrate the economies of its member states and to establish a division of labor among them. Instead, the PCR has followed a policy aimed at the industrialization of the country, based on the proposition that an expanded industrial base is what is most needed for Romania's overall economic development.

In the same manner that the PCR has resisted complete integration into COMECON, the regime has also opposed Soviet plans for the fuller integration of military forces under the Warsaw Pact. Romanian objections to such integration stem from a concern for the preservation of the country's national sovereignty and a desire to limit Soviet hegemony in Eastern Europe. PCR leaders have described military blocs and the existence of foreign troops and military bases on the territory of other states as being incompatible with national independence and as the primary obstacles to cooperation among nations. On the other hand, party spokesmen have frequently stated that, as long as the North Atlantic Treaty Organization (NATO) is continued, the socialist countries will be forced to maintain the Warsaw Pact.

CONDUCT OF FOREIGN AFFAIRS

Policy Formation

The Constitution assigns to the Grand National Assembly the responsibility for establishing the general line of foreign policy and assigns its implementation to the Council of Ministers. It is the Council of State, however, that is given the overall executive functions of ratifying international treaties and establishing diplomatic relations with other states. As the head of state, the president of the Council of State is charged with representing the country in its international relations.

161

In practice, however, the basic foreign policy decisions are made by the Standing Presidium of the PCR rather than the Grand National Assembly. Owing to the fact that the same men occupy leading positions in both party and government, decisions reached in the Standing Presidium are promulgated as decisions of the Council of State. Party spokesmen have described the country's foreign policy as being the result of the "unitary thinking and action of the leading party bodies based on the principle of collective leadership" (see ch. 8; ch. 9).

Within the PCR, foreign policy decisions are channeled through the Central Committee's directorate for international affairs, which in turn transmits them in the form of directives to the appropriate government agencies and oversees their implementation. A commission on foreign policy in the Grand National Assembly functions largely to channel party decisions to the assembly for its official approval.

As head of the PCR and president of the Council of State, Ceausescu personally exercised the primary decisionmaking powers in matters of foreign policy just as he did in domestic affairs. Observers of Eastern European politics also ascribe influential roles in the determination of foreign policy to Prime Minister Maurer and Foreign Minister Corneliu Manescu.

Since coming to power in 1965 Ceausescu has been the dominant figure in the political life of the country and its principal spokesman in international affairs. Believing in the importance of personal diplomacy, Ceausescu has made frequent visits to other nations and cultivated personal relationships with other heads of state. The prime minister and the minister of foreign affairs have also made frequent visits to other states to foster international support for the country's foreign policy. Manescu had developed broad international contacts during his term as president of the twenty-second session of the UN General Assembly in 1967.

Administration of Foreign Affairs

The Council of Ministers is charged with the coordination and implementation of foreign policy and exercises these responsibilities through the Ministry of Foreign Affairs and the Ministry of Foreign Trade. Since decisionmaking powers rest in the top echelons of the party, the ministries function almost exclusively as administrative agencies. The Ministry of Foreign Affairs is responsible for the implementation of party directives in the country's foreign diplomatic relations and in the areas of educational, cultural, and scientific relations with other states and with international organizations. The Ministry of Foreign Trade functions as the central organ for the country's international trade and economic activities.

In early 1972 the organizational structure of the Ministry of Foreign Affairs remained essentially the same as it had been established after the adoption of the new Constitution of 1965. The ministry is organized into six geographical departments, twelve functional directorates, and three administrative offices. The geographical directorates are designated as: the Soviet Union, Poland, Czechoslovakia, and Hungary; the Balkans and the Near East; Western and Central Europe; North America and South America; Africa and the Middle East; and the Far East and Southeast and South Asia.

The functional directorates are: international organization; cultural relations; political synthesis; economic relations; legal and treaties; consular; press; protocol; personnel; finance, accounting, and work organization; technical and administrative; and secretariat. The three administrative offices are designated the Chancellery, the Office of Services to the Diplomatic Corps, and the Legal Office. The entire organization functioned under the direction of the minister of foreign affairs and five deputy ministers.

The Ministry of Foreign Trade is organized into nine bureaus, a legal office, and an office for protocol. Bureaus listed under the ministry in 1970, the latest year for which information was available in early 1972, included: economic relations with socialist countries; economic relations with developed capitalist countries; economic relations with emerging nations; currency and plan coordination; imports and exports; personnel and training; administration; budgets; and accounting. The ministry functions under the direction of the minister of foreign trade, four deputy ministers, and a secretary general.

INTERNATIONAL RELATIONS

In early 1972 diplomatic relations were maintained with ninety-six countries and the so-called Provisional Revolutionary Government of the Republic of South Vietnam (Viet Cong). Of these, forty-two governments maintained embassies in Bucharest. Nine other governments conducted relations through their embassies in Moscow; seven, through their embassies in Belgrade; two through their embassies in Prague; and one, through its embassy in Athens. The total includes Brazil, with which relations were maintained at the legation level, and Spain and San Marino, where Romania maintained consulates. Thirty-two of the states with which Romania maintained diplomatic relations had not established permanent embassies or legations in the country as of early 1972. Trade relations were conducted with several other states with which the government had not established formal diplomatic ties (see ch. 14).

Relations with Communist States and Communist Parties

The Soviet Union

Romania's pursuit of an independent foreign policy has resulted in frequent conflicts with the Soviet Union and tense relations between the two states. In general, the policy disagreements have centered on Romania's unwillingness to participate more fully in the Warsaw Pact, rejection of the concept of economic integration under COMECON, refusal to take sides in the Sino-Soviet dispute, and development of a foreign policy toward the West that runs contrary to Soviet desires. Soviet leaders have interpreted the Romanian policies as a direct challenge to the leading role of the Soviet party in the world communist movement and a rejection of the PCR's obligations to promote "socialist solidarity."

The general policy differences between the two countries were repeatedly demonstrated during the 1967–71 period in such instances as the Romanian establishment of diplomatic relations with West Germany, the refusal to follow the Soviet lead in regard to the Arab-Israeli conflict, the refusal to participate in the Warsaw Pact invasion of Czechoslovakia and Ceausescu's strong denunciation of the action, and the rejection of the Brezhnev Doctine of limited sovereignty.

Perhaps the most important element complicating relations with the Soviet Union has been Romania's refusal to take the Soviet side in the Sino-Soviet dispute. In keeping with its policy of maintaining friendly and fraternal relations with all socialist states, the Ceausescu regime has cultivated relations with the People's Republic of China and is thought by some observers to have played a role in the establishment of contacts between the Communist Chinese and the United States. In mid-1971 Romanian leaders also mediated the restoration of relations between the People's Republic of China and Yugoslavia. These actions led to charges in the Soviet press that Romania was organizing an anti-Soviet bloc in the Balkans under the patronage of the People's Republic of China.

Despite the ups and downs of Soviet-Romanian relations throughout the period of the Ceausescu regime, the two states signed a twenty-year treaty of friendship, cooperation, and mutual assistance in July 1970. This treaty replaced a similar 1948 accord that had been set to expire in 1968 but continued in force under an automatic five-year renewal clause. Negotiated before the Warsaw Pact invasion of Czechoslovakia, the actual signing of the treaty was delayed because of strained relations between the two states and Soviet attempts to insert a clause containing the essence of the Brezhnev Doctrine. The Ceausescu government refused to renegotiate the original agreement, however, and the treaty was finally signed at ceremonies in Bucharest.

Brezhnev did not attend the ceremonies and, in contrast to similar Soviet treaties with other Eastern European communist states, which were signed by both the party leaders and the prime ministers of each country, the Soviet-Romanian treaty was signed only by the prime ministers. Coming in the midst of serious disagreements between the two countries, the signing of the treaty was considered by some observers as a formality and something of a smokescreen intended to cover a widening split.

Other Communist States

In general, relations with Bulgaria, Czechoslovakia, the German Democratic Republic (East Germany), Hungary, and Poland mirrored Romania's relations with the Soviet Union. The communist leaders of these countries followed the Soviet lead in the policy differences with the Ceausescu regime and, although each state had friendship treaties that expired in 1968 and 1969, only the treaty with Czechoslovakia was renewed before the Soviet-Romanian treaty was signed. The Czechoslovakia treaty was concluded during the period of the government of Alexander Dubcek before the 1968 invasion.

In its relations with the Eastern European communist regimes Romania had adhered to the principle of cultivating fraternal relations with all socialist countries despite policy differences. Long-term bilateral trade agreements were concluded with Hungary and Bulgaria in late 1969, and the major portion of the country's foreign trade continued to be with COMECON states throughout 1970 and 1971. Visits on the ministerial level were regularly exchanged. Relations with the East German regime proved more difficult, however, the major obstacle being Romania's establishment of diplomatic ties with West Germany in early 1967. Despite the recognition of the West German government, however, the Ceausescu regime has continued to insist on the reality of two German states and has pressed for international recognition of East Germany.

Relations with Bulgaria had been generally cool throughout the latter period of the Gheorghiu-Dej regime but improved significantly after Ceausescu came to power in Romania in 1965. By the beginning of 1968, however, the policies pursued by the Ceausescu regime led to serious differences, although formal amenities continued to be observed. Relatons remained correct but not cordial until after the signing of the Soviet-Romanian treaty of friendship and alliance in July 1970. This action paved the way for improved relations with Bulgaria, and in September Ceausescu met with Bulgarian prime minister Todor Zhivkov, marking the first top-level bilateral contact between the two governments in three years. This meeting was followed by the exchange of a series of high-level delegations with the announced purpose of improving relations and increasing cooperation.

Friction with Hungary arose in mid-1971 over the Romanian region of Transylvania and the sizable Hungarian minority residing there. In the period of strained—Soviet-Romanian relations, the Budapest regime revived the Transylvanian minority question in order to put pressure on the Ceausescu government. Frequent visits of Soviet embassy personnel to Transylvania added to the concern of Romanian leaders, who initiated increased efforts to meet the needs and expectations of the country's minority groups (see ch. 4; ch. 9). By February 1972, tension between Hungary and Romania had eased and a friendship treaty was renewed.

Relations with Albania and Yugoslavia differed from those with the other Eastern European communist regimes, as neither participated in the Warsaw Pact and both had also pursued policies independent of the Soviet Union. In 1960 Albania sided with the Communist Chinese in the Sino-Soviet dispute and withdrew its ambassadors from all the Eastern European countries after Khrushchev denounced the Albanian regime at the Twenty-second Congress of the Communist Party of the Soviet Union in 1961. The Romanian position of neutrality in regard to the Sino-Soviet dispute opened the way for improved relations with Albania, and the Ceausescu government returned its ambassador to Tirana in 1964.

The Ceausescu regime has maintained that the policies of the Albanian Communists (the Albanian Workers' Party) are legitimate manifestations of socialism developed according to national needs. Common fears of Soviet designs against their countries after the Warsaw Pact invasion of Czechoslovakia brought about increased cooperation between the two governments.

Relations with Yugoslavia had progressed along lines of mutual interest throughout the period of the Ceausescu regime, and close cooperation had developed between the Romaian and Yugoslav heads of state as they sought each other's support for their independent foreign policies. The PCR was the only Eastern European party to send a delegation to the Ninth Congress of the League of Communists of Yugoslavia in 1969.

Although the two governments indicated almost identical views on all important international issues, they manifested widely divergent approaches to domestic affairs and, owing to the fact that their economies are not complementary, economic relations between the two countries have not kept pace with political relations. Efforts to increase economic relations resulted in a new five-year trade agreement in 1971 designed to increase the exchange of goods by 128 percent in the period covered. Cooperation between the two states was also demonstrated in the joint construction of the Iron Gate hydroelectric station on the Danube (see ch. 3).

During 1971 the PCR renewed efforts to promote cooperative relations among the Balkan states. The regime emphasized that the geographical isolation and the socialist systems of Albania, Bulgaria, Yugoslavia, and Romania make for common interest in increased economic, political, and cultural cooperation. Observers of Eastern European politics pointed out that Romania shares lengthy borders with Bulgaria, Hungary, and the Soviet Union and that improving relations with the other Balkan states would serve to overcome the country's relative physical isolation.

PCR leaders have also called for all of the Balkan area, including both the communist and the noncommunist states, to be designated a nuclear free zone and for the removal of United States military bases from the area. Observers pointed out that the Ceausescu regime believed that such actions would serve to reduce the strategic significance of Romania in the eyes of the Soviet leaders and possibly result in greater tolerance for Romanian deviation from the Soviet line. Political observers also attributed the growing willingness of Albania and Yugoslavia to increase cooperation and give support to Romania's initiatives for the Balkan area to the growth of Soviet naval power in the Eastern Mediterranean.

The Ceausescu regime successfully cultivated relations with the People's Republic of China and persisted in the development of these relations despite tremendous pressures from the Soviet Union and other Warsaw Pact states. An important byproduct of these relations has been increased economic exchanges between the two countries; in late 1970 the Communist Chinese extended Romania a long-term, interest-free credit amounting to the equivalent of US$244 million.

In June 1971 Ceausescu made a twenty-five day visit to Asia that included nine days in mainland China, the first such visit by a party leader of a Warsaw Pact state since the Sino-Soviet dispute became public. In a joint communiqué the Communist Chinese and Romanian leaders emphasized the necessity of sovereign and equal relations among all communist states and parties. Ceausescu reiterated his government's support for the admission of the People's Republic of China to the United Nations and asserted that the rightful sovereignty over Taiwan belonged to the Peking regime. In August 1971 a Communist Chinese military delegation attended the twenty-seventh anniversary celebrations of the liberation of Romania from Nazi occupation.

Maintenance of friendly relations with the People's Republic of China has also gained the Ceausescu regime support from other communist parties that have been critical of the Soviet Union in its conflict with the Communist Chinese, most notably the French and Italian parties. The PCR has taken special pains to cultivate relations with nonruling communist and workers' parties, efforts that were reflected in visits of top leaders from at least thirty of these parties to Romania during 1970. All of these visitors were received personally by Ceausescu. Observers pointed out that the cultivation of relations with the nonruling parties was an important means of gaining support for Romania's independent policies.

Relations With Noncommunist States

Romania has continued to improve relations with Western nations and has sought to cultivate ties with the developing countries of Africa and Asia. The expansion of relations beyond the Soviet alignment system was cautiously initiated in the mid-1950s by the Gheorghiu-Dej regime when pressures were building for Romania's full economic integration into COMECON. In addition to the desire to develop trade relations with Western nations, the government was interested in utilizing Western technology and in seeking an increased measure of detente in the cold war.

West Germany

In the period that followed the initiation of limited relations with noncommunist states, Romania's resistance to the Soviet Union contributed to a receptive attitude on the part of several Western states. Aside from the gradual development of trade relations, however, significant political relations with Western Europe did not materialize until January 1967, when the Ceausescu regime agreed to establish formal diplomatic relations with West Germany, becoming the first of the Warsaw Pact states, other than the Soviet Union, to do so.

Romanian leaders based the establishment of relations with West Germany on the so-called Bucharest Declaration issued by the leaders of the Warsaw Pact countries in 1966. The declaration affirmed that there were in West Germany "circles that oppose revanchism and militarism" and that seek the development of normal relations with countries of both the East and the West as well as a normalization of relations "between the two German states." Also included in the declaration was a statement affirming that a basic condition for European security was the establishment of normal relations between states "regardless of their social systems." The Ceausescu regime interpreted this as implying that bilateral relations could be developed between Eastern European states and West Germany.

Although the West German government made overtures to other Eastern European communist states, Romania was the only one to agree to the establishment of formal diplomatic ties at that time. Political observers saw the move as a means for Romania to dramatically demonstrate independence from the Soviet Union and, as well, a means of avoiding COMECON integration pressures by increasing trade and the possibility of obtaining economic aid from the West.

The establishment of diplomatic ties with West Germany did not alter the PCR position on the existence of two German states. Each country, at the time the diplomatic exchange was made public, simply reasserted its own positions: the West German government reiterated its right and obligation to speak for the entire German people, and the Bucharest government asserted that one of the fundamental realities of the post-World War II era "is the existence of two German states." Although Romania reaffirmed the existence of East Germany as a separate state, it did not make recognition of the East German regime by West Germany a precondition for the establishment of diplomatic relations with the West German government.

The East German regime was highly critical of the Romanian establishment of relations with West Germany, and there followed a serious decline in Romanian-East German relations. PCR leaders responded to East German criticisms by declaring that "the foreign policy of a socialist state is laid down by the party and the government of the country in question and they need render account only to their people."

In the period since 1967 relations with West Germany have continued without major difficulties. Although the Ceausescu regime has not hesitated to criticize elements of German policy with which it does not agree, the two governments have sought to minimize differences in ideology and in foreign and domestic policies in the interest of maintaining good relations. In economic exchanges between the two countries Romania has had a continuous balance of trade deficit, a situation that both countries were attempting to correct. In mid-1970 Prime Minister Maurer paid an official visit to Bonn, becoming the first Eastern European head of government to do so. In May 1971 the West German government reciprocated, President Gustav Heinemann making a state visit to Romania.

The United States

Relations with the United States were initiated on a limited scale in the early 1960s, and ambassadors were exchanged in 1964, but relations declined with the increasing United States role in the Republic of Vietnam (South Vietnam). After the opening of the Paris peace talks and particularly after the Warsaw Pact invasion of Czechoslovakia that same year, relations between the two states improved significantly. Trade relations remained minimal, however, partly because of United States legal restrictions on trade with Eastern European countries.

The improved relations between the two nations were demonstrated by the visit of President Nixon to Romania in August 1969, marking the first visit of a United States head of state to a communist country since the 1945 Yalta Conference. Press reports indicated that the president received an enthusiastic welcome from the Romanian people and that in meetings with Ceausescu a wide range of international problems were discussed.

At the close of the visit President Nixon reaffirmed that the United States "respects the sovereignty and equal rights of all countries, large and small, as well as their right to preserve their own national character." The two heads of state agreed upon the reciprocal establishment of libraries, the opening of negotiations for the conclusion of a consular convention, and the development and diversification of economic ties.

The presidential visit was reciprocated by Ceausescu in October 1970 when the Romanian leader traveled to New York to attend the twenty-fifth anniversary session of the UN General Assembly. Ceausescu followed the UN visit with a two-week coast-to-coast tour of the United States and talks at the White House with President Nixon. The Nixon administration moved to increase economic relations with Romania, and in early 1972 legislation was pending in the United States Congress to grant that country most-favored-nation status (see ch. 14).

Other States

As part of its campaign to improve relations among the Balkan states and in keeping with its policy of establishing relations with all states regardless of their political systems, the Ceausescu regime initiated efforts to ameliorate its relations with Greece and Turkey. The development of ties with Turkey has progressed without serious setback throughout the period of Ceausescu's rule, but Greco-Romanian relations have fluctuated. Although the regime has followed a policy of noninterference in the internal affairs of another state, it left the Romanian embassy in Athens without an ambassador for a year after the 1967 Greek military coup. In July 1968 the Romanian government returned an ambassador to Greece as a first step in improving relations between the two states. Increased trade and cultural exchanges followed, although the differing ideologies of the two regimes have kept official relations at a correct but cool level.

Although Turkey did not respond positively to the Romanian call for a nuclear free zone in the Balkans and the removal of foreign military bases from the area, asserting that such an agreement would have to be included in a wider accord between NATO and Warsaw Pact nations, relations between the two states have continued to improve. Ceausescu paid a state visit to Turkey in 1969, and the Turkish president visited Romania in April 1970. The satisfactory political ties have resulted in a number of cultural and economic agreements, Romania obtaining Turkish raw materials, particularly iron, chrome, and manganese, and exporting machinery to Turkey.

Political, economic, and cultural ties were expanded with a number of other Western countries during the 1965–70 period, particularly with Austria, France, Italy, and the United Kingdom. The Ceausescu regime placed primary emphasis on the cultivation of economic relations with these states, and several substantial trade agreements were concluded and high-level visits were exchanged during 1970 and 1971.

PCR policy statements have proclaimed that one of the principal guidelines of Romanian foreign policy is the steady cultivation and broadening of political and economic relations with the young independent states of Asia and Africa as well as with the countries of Latin America. The regime has also repeatedly affirmed its support for "the struggle of the peoples of Africa, Asia and other regions of the world for liberation and national independence against neocolonialism and the agressive actions of imperialism."

Policy statement have also consistently voiced support for the communist effort in South Vietnam. The communist Provisional Revolutionary Government of the Republic of South Vietnam (Viet Cong) is recognized as the legitimate government of South Vietnam and maintains an embassy in Bucharest.

The Middle East situation has posed a dilemma for the Ceausescu government, which has sought to maintain relations with both sides in the conflict. When, in August 1969, Romania and Israel announced an agreement to elevate their relations to the ambassadorial level, Syria and Sudan retaliated by breaking relations with Romania, and Iraq and the United Arab Republic reduced the level of their representation in Bucharest. Despite these actions by the Arab states, PCR leaders continued to voice support for "the struggle of the Arab people to defend their national independence and sovereignty" but called for a negotiated settlement of the conflict.

The Ceausescu regime systematically cultivated relations with the developing countries, and particular efforts were directed toward increasing relations with African nations during 1970 and 1971. Ceausescu made a state visit to Morocco, and other high Romanian officials visited Congo (Brazzaville), Congo (Kinshasa)—in late 1971 became the Republic of Zaire—Burundi, Kenya, the Malagasy Republic, Nigeria, Tanzania, and Zambia. Several prominent African leaders, among them President Jean Bedel Bokassa of the Central African Republic and President Joseph Mobutu of Zaire vistied Romania. Trade agreements were signed with a number of African nations, but little had been done to implement these agreements as of early 1972. As another means of increasing its influence in Africa and broadening relations there, the Ceausescu government established more than 400 scholarships for African students to study in Romania.

Relations With International Organizations

Romania became a member of the UN in 1955 and as of early 1972 also held membership in the following UN specialized agencies: the United Nations Educational, Scientific and Cultural Organization (UNESCO), the United Nations Food and Agriculture Organization (FAO), the United Nations Industrial Development Organization (UNIDO), and the International Atomic Energy Agency (IAEA). It also participates in the work of the United Nations Conference on Trade and Development (UNCTAD).

The two most important communist organizations to which the country belongs are the Warsaw Pact and COMECON. The Warsaw Pact was established in 1955 as a twenty-year mutual defense pact between the Soviet Union, Albania, Bulgaria, Czechoslovakia, East Germany, Hungary, Poland, and Romania. (Albania ceased its participation in the organization in 1961 and officially withdrew in 1968 as a symbol of protest against the invasion of Czechoslovakia). As an instrument of Soviet foreign policy, the Warsaw Pact has served to maintain Soviet hegemony in Eastern Europe and to provide the legal basis for the presence of Soviet troops on the territory of some of the participating states.

Romania has consistently refused to acquiesce in Soviet proposals for greater integration of the military forces of the Warsaw Pact states and did not participate in the invasion of Czechoslovakia. After the Czechoslovak invasion the Ceausescu government established a defense council and proclaimed that foreign troops were not to enter Romania for any purpose without prior approval of the Grand National Assembly. During the 1968-71 period the Romanians limited their participation in pact activities as much as possible. Rather than Romanian troops taking part in joint maneuvers of pact forces, participation has generally been limited to a small group of staff officers who attend the exercises as observers.

Official Romanian views on the integration of Eastern European communist forces under the pact were forcefully reiterated in early 1970 after the Soviet chief of staff spoke of "combined" or "unified" pact forces. Ceausescu responded by declaring that Romania's armed forces are not subordinated to any authority other than "the Romanian party, government, and Supreme National Command." Although he pledged continued cooperation with the pact and a fulfillment of his country's responsibilities, he asserted that no part of the party's and government's right to command and lead the armed forces would be ceded to any other body. In addition, Ceausescu gave emphasis to the defensive nature of the Warsaw Pact and reiterated the Romania position on noninterference in the internal affairs of another country.

Romanian policy toward COMECON has been cooperative in regard to mutually advantageous trade relations with the other member states but has consistently opposed pressures for the integration of their economies. The Soviet Union and the more industrialized of the Eastern European communist states have pressed for economic integration that would include a division of labor among COMECON members and a specialization of production. Romanian leaders, preferring to develop a diversified national economy, have refused the role of supplier of agricultural goods and raw materials that COMECON would have assigned to their country.

During the mid-1960s Romania successfully reoriented a substantial share of its trade toward the West and reduced its participation in COMECON. Trade with the West, however, produced sizable deficits and, along with other economic problems, including the disastrous floods of early 1970, forced the Ceausescu regime to again rely on its economic ties with the COMECON states. Despite these difficulties, the country has continued to develop its trade relations with noncommunist nations and has continued to resist COMECON integration pressures.

In 1970 a prominent Romanian economist proposed that COMECON become an open-ended organization in which all countries, socialist and nonsocialist, could participate on a voluntary basis. In mid-1971 an official PCR party spokesman declared that economic cooperation with COMECON must "in no way affect the national economic plans or the independence of the economic units in each country."

CHAPTER 11

PUBLIC INFORMATION

In the early 1970s the media of public information, under complete party and government control and supervision, were utilized primarily to propagandize and indoctrinate the population in support of the regime's domestic and foreign policy objectives. The system of control was highly centralized and involved an interlocking group of party and state organizations, supervising bodies, and operating agencies whose authority extended to all radio and television facilities, film studios, printing establishments, newspapers, book publishers, and the single news agency. In addition, this control apparatus also regulated the access of the public to foreign publications, films, newscasts, books, and radio and television programs.

Freedom of information, although never fully recognized in precommunist Romania, completely disappeared under the Communists after 1948. In late 1971, as a result of an ideological campaign launched by the regime, the communications media experienced measures that served further to reemphasize their assigned role as political tools in the indoctrination of the people. The effects of this campaign had not become fully evident in early 1972, but changes and modifications had begun to appear that tended to inhibit liberalizing trends, which had been incorporated gradually into the system during the 1960s.

GOVERNMENT AND FREEDOM OF INFORMATION

Although freedom of information was theoretically guaranteed by the early constitutions of precommunist Romania, censorship of the press was not unusual and commonly took the form of banning or confiscating newspapers and periodicals considered hostile to the ruling group. Newspapers had traditionally been published by political parties and special interest groups, only a few being uncontrolled and truly independent. In consequence, the public has long regarded the press as generally biased, tainted with propaganda, and not reliable as a source of objective news.

Under the dictatorship imposed by King Carol II in 1938 and during the wartime regime of Marshal Ion Antonescu, censorship was officially proclaimed and rigidly enforced. Since that time the communications media have enjoyed only one period of relative freedom, lasting only a few weeks following the coup d'etat of King Michael in August 1944. After Michael's deposition and during the struggle for power that followed, the Communists effectively controlled the press and radio through the unions serving these facilities, which they had heavily infiltrated. After their seizure of power in 1948, the Communists instituted a system of censorship and control that has continued without interruption.

The 1965 Constitution, the third promulgated by the Communists since their takeover of the government, is less moderate in tone than its predecessors in preserving the fiction of the right of citizens to individual freedoms. The document states that freedom of speech, of the press, and of assembly "cannot be used for aims hostile to the socialist system and to the interests of the working people." This same article also prohibits associations of a "fascist" or "anti-democratic" nature, as well as the participation of citizens in such associations. The Constitution names the Romanian Communist Party (Partidul Communist Roman—PCR) as the leading political force in the country; by virtue of its position, the party has become the ultimate authority in determining actions that are "fascist," "anti-democratic," or "hostile to the socialist system."

In 1972 the regime continued to utilize the conventional information media—newspapers, magazines, books, radio, television, and motion pictures—as an integrated, governmental system for the indoctrination of the population and the molding of public opinion in support of the state and its policies. In keeping with this overall objective, a campaign for the increased ideological and political indoctrination of the public was undertaken in July 1971 that brought about a reenforcement of party authority over the highest information control and policymaking bodies in the government (see ch. 7). The former State Committee for Culture and Art, established with ministerial rank under the Council of Ministers, was reconstitute⸱' as the Council on Socialist Culture and Education and was made directly subordinate to the Central Committee of the PCR. Similar changes were made in the Committee of Radio and Television, which became the Council of Romanian Radio and Television.

Under the direct guidance of the press and propaganda sections of the Central Committee, these two councils formulate policy guidelines and supervise all publication and dissemination procedures throughout the communications media. The

176

policies and directives, in turn, are implemented by other government-controlled operating agencies, such as the General Directorate for the Press and Printing, the Romanian press agency, and the individual publishing houses, printing establishments, book distribution centers, motion picture studios, and radio and television stations. To further assure a uniform collective effort consistent with the party line, and two national councils are also empowered to organize wherever necessary permanent commissions, temporary working groups, and local committees to assist the councils in "analyzing" the way decisions are applied and in "improving" local activities.

THE PRESS

Newspapers

According to the latest official statistics, there were a total of seventy-six "general information" newspapers published throughout the country in 1969. Of these, fifty-one were dailies, twenty-three were weeklies, and two appeared at infrequent intervals, from two to three times per week. Daily circulation estimates were available for very few newspapers. Together, these newspapers had to total annual circulation of more than 1.1 billion copies, a substantial increase over the 1950 level of 870 million copies that was achieved by the seventy-five newspapers then being published. The acceptance of high circulation figures as an indicator of reader appeal is of doubtfu' value, however, since many readers were required to subscribe to newspapers because of their party or work affiliation. Also, certain functionaries throughout the governmental apparatus and many supervisory workers had subscription costs automatically deducted from their salaries.

Newspapers traditionally have been published in the national minority languages, but since the mid-1960s the government has published no official statistics on them, apparently in keeping with its integrationist policy (see ch. 7). In 1964 it was estimated by Western observers that the ethnic minorities were served by approximately twenty newspapers, including eight dailies, with an annual circulation of slightly more than 103 million copies.

All newspapers are licensed by the General Directorate for the Press and Printing, the state agency that also controls the allocation of newsprint, the manufacture of ink and other printing supplies, and the distribution of all publications. Thus the government is in a position to prohibit the appearance of any newspaper or other publication either directly by revoking the license or indirectly by withholding essential supplies or services. Each newspaper is organized into a collective enterprise made up of the entire personnel of all departments. Chief responsibility for the content of the paper is vested in an "editorial collegium" headed by the chief editor. Meetings are held periodically between all chief editors and party representatives, which serve as an effective means of followup control in lieu of prepublication censorship.

Major mass organizations, government-sponsored groups, local government organs, and the PCR and its subsidiaries publish the most important and influential papers, both in Bucharest and in the larger cities of the various counties (see table 3). Little latitude is allowed in the presentation of news, and almost all papers follow a serious, monotonous format that has little popular appeal. Shortly after renewed emphasis was placed on the ideological and political education of the population in mid-1971, a Western journalist likened the nation to a huge classroom in which unpopular and trite subjects were being presented to an unreceptive class by an exhortative mass media.

The most authoritative and widely read newspaper is *Scinteia,* founded in 1931 as the official organ of the Central Committee of the party. It has, by far, the largest daily circulation and enjoys considerable prestige as the outlet for party policy pronouncements as well as for semiofficial government attitudes on both national and international issues. The eight-page newspaper appears seven days a week and is national in scope. Its editorials, feature sections, and chief articles are frequently reprinted, in whole or in part, by smaller newspapers in outlying areas. Quotations and summaries are also repeated regularly in shop bulletins and in information letters put on by many enterprises, plants, and factories.

The next most important dailies are *Romania Libera,* established by the Socialist Unity Front in 1942; *Munca,* founded in 1943 as the voice of the Central Council of the General Union of Trade Unions and *Scinteia Tineretului,* the organ of the Union of Communist Youth, which has been published since 1944. Each of these newspapers is much smaller than *Scinteia* and is directed at a particular group of readers of level of society. Although *Romania Libera* contains items of both national and international interest, it deals primarily with the problems associated with the "building of socialism" at the local level. Similarly, *Munca* directs its major effort at the labor force and stresses the cooperative relationship between workers and industry. *Scinteia Tineretului,* in like manner,

Table 3. Principal Romanian Daily Newspapers, 1971

Publication	Daily Circulation (in thousands)	Place	Publisher
Crisana	---	Oradea	Romanian Communist Party
Dobrogea Noua	---	Constanta	Do.
Drapelul Rosu	54	Timisoara	Do.
Drum Nou	---	Brasov	Do.
Drumul Socialismului	---	Deva	Do.
Elore [1]	---	Bucharest	Hungarian People's Council
Faclia	---	Cluj	Romanian Communist Party
Faklya [1]	---	Oradea	Hungarian People's Council
Flacara Iasului	---	Iasi	Romanian Communist Party
Flacara Rosie	---	Arad	Do.
Flamura Prahovei	---	Ploiesti	Do.
Igazsag	---	Cluj	Do.
Inainte	---	Craiova	Do.
Inainte	---	Braila	Do.
Informatia Bucurestiului	---	Bucharest	Do.
Munca	---	do	General Union of Trade Unions
Neuer Weg [2]	100	do	German People's Council
Romania Libera	200	do	Socialist Unity Front
Satul Socialist	---	do	Union of Agricultural Production Co-operatives
Scinteia	1,000	do	Romanian Communist Party
Scinteia Tineretului	300	do	Union of Communist Youth
Sportul Popular	---	do	Union of Culture and Sports
Steagul Rosu	---	do	Romanian Communist Party
Steau Rosie	---	Tirgu Mures	Do.
Szabad Szo [1]	---	Timisoara	Hungarian People's Council
Viata Noua	---	Galati	Romanian Communist Party
Voros Zaszlo [1]	---	Tirgu Mures	Hungarian People's Council

-- circulation unknown.
[1] Published in Hungarian.
[2] Published in German.

concentrates on the younger element of the population and stresses the ideological and political training of youth as the basis for a "sound socialist society."

The principal and most widely known minority-language newspapers are the Hungarian daily *Elore* and the German *Neuer Weg*, also a daily. Both of these newspapers contain generally the same news as Romanian newspapers with additional local items of minority interest, such as cultural developments and problems associated with minority language use in education and other fields.

Periodicals

The number of periodicals published throughout the country increased from a total of 387 in 1960 to 581 in 1969, according to the latest government statistics. The total annual circulation of periodicals almost doubled during this time, increasing from about 105 million copies to approximately 209 million. More than 340 of these magazines and journals were published either quarterly or annually, the remainder appearing either weekly, monthly, or at some other intervals. No indication was given within this general classification of the number of publications that were issued in the minority languages or were directed at special minority interest groups.

All periodicals are considered official publications of the various sponsoring organizations and are subject to the same licensing and supervising controls as newspapers. Virtually all magazines and journals are published by mass organizations and party or government-controlled activities, such as institutes, labor unions, cultural committees, and special interest groups. They cover a broad range of subjects and include technical and professional journals, among them magazines on literature, art, health, sports, medicine, statistics, politics, science, and economics. The technical and scientific journals are intended for scholars, engineers, and industrial technicians; cultural and political periodicals are aimed at writers, editors, journalists, artists, party workers, and enterprise managers; and general publications are intended to appeal to various segments of the population, such as youth, women, and both industrial and agricultural workers.

Two of the best known and most widely circulated magazines are *Lupta de Clasa* and *Contemporanul*. *Lupta de Clasa*, a monthly published by the Central Committee of the PCR, had an estimated circulation of about 70,000 in 1969 and was considered to be the foremost political review. It deals with the theory of socialism and is extensively quoted in the daily press as a semiofficial voice in domestic affairs. *Contemporanul,* the weekly organ of the Council on Socialist Culture and Education, had a circulation of approximately 65,000 and was a leading authority on political, cultural, and social affairs. Through its wide range of articles it serves as a primary vehicle for conveying party policy to writers, journalists, editors, and publishers in all fields. /

Other periodicals cover a broad spectrum and included *Femeia,* the monthly magazine of the National Council of Women; *Probleme Economice,* the monthly review of the Society of Economic Sciences; *Tinarul Leninist,* a monthly magazine for members of the Union of Communist Youth; *Luceafarul,* a semimonthly review of foreign policy matters published by the Union of Writers; *Romania Literara,* a literary, artistic, and sociopolitical weekly also published by the Union of Writers; *Urzica,* a humorous and satirical semimonthly review published by the PCR; *Volk und Kultur,* a monthly review published in German by the Council on Socialist Culture and Education; and *Korunk,* the monthly sociocultural review in Hungarian, published by the Hungarian Peoples' Council.

One of the magazines best known outside the country is *Romania Azi,* a richly illustrated social, economic, and cultural monthly magazine published by the Foreign Language Press. In addition to Romanian, it is also published in English, Chinese, French, German, Russian, and Spanish. The government also sponsors a series of scholarly reviews dealing with studies on southeastern Europe, the history of art, Romanian historical and artistic development, and linguistics. These reviews appear at infrequent intervals and, in addition to the Romanian edition, are offered on subscription in English, French, German, Russian, and Spanish.

News Agencies

The Romanian Press Agency (Agentia Romana de Presa—Agerpres) was established in 1949, with the exclusive right to the collection and distribution of all news, pictures, and other press items, both domestic and foreign. In recent years, however, it has concerned itself almost exclusively with news from foreign countries, leaving much of the domestic news coverage to the correspondents of the larger daily newspapers. Agerpres, in 1972, operated as an office of the central government under the direct supervision and control of the Central Committee of the party.

The headquarters for Agerpres is maintained in Bucharest, with some sixteen branch offices located in other major towns and cities throughout the country. In addition, it staffs on a full-time basis twenty-one bureaus abroad, principally in the larger capital cities of Europe, Africa, South America, and the Far East. Until 1960 its most important source of foreign news was the Soviet central news agency, through which it received the bulk of its foreign news releases and international news summaries. This arrangement was replaced by news exchange agreements with selected agencies of both the Western countries and the countries of Eastern Europe.

In addition to the Soviet agency, foreign news bureaus are maintained in Bucharest by the press agencies of Poland, Bulgaria, Yugoslavia, Hungary, Czechoslovakia, and the German Democratic Republic (East Germany). To service these bureaus and its own correspondents abroad Agerpres issues the daily Agerpres News of the Day and the weekly Agerpres Information Bulletin. For domestic consumption Agerpres distributes about 45,000 words of foreign news coverage daily to official government and party offices, to various newspapers and periodicals, and to radio and television broadcasting stations.

RADIO AND TELEVISION

Radio Broadcasting

In 1971 domestic radio broadcast service was provided by twenty AM (amplitude modulation) stations located in sixteen cities and by six FM (frequency modulation) stations located in Bucharest, Cluj, and Constanta. These stations are government owned and operate under the direct supervision of the Council of Romanian Radio and Television, an agency of the party's Central Committee. All broadcast stations are grouped into three major networks, known as Program I, Program II, and Program III. In addition, broadcast facilities are augmented by an extensive wired-broadcast network, which extended coverage into outlying areas where direct transmissions are subject to either geographic or atmospheric interference.

The most powerful stations are located in Brasov, Iasi, Boldur, Bucharest, and Timisoara. They range in power from 135 to 1200 kilowatts and transmit in the low- and medium-frequency bands. The FM stations operate exclusively in the very high frequency range and are all moderately powered at four kilowatts. The majority of the programs originate at studios in Bucharest and are rebroadcast by the network stations, which add short local news broadcasts and, from time to time, originate coverage of special events of local interest. In addition to government-provided subsidies, the industry also benefits from the license fees collected from the almost 3.1 million owners of radio receivers.

In 1971 scheduled regional programming was revised to include additional broadcast time for programs in the minority languages. These broadcasts were carried by four major stations including Radio Bucharest, with programs in Hungarian and German; Radio Cluj and Radio Tirgu Mures, with programs in Hungarian; and Radio Timisoara with programs in German and Serbo-Croatian. Most of these offerings are short and stress news, features, and talks by local personalities. These programs are also relayed over wire lines to local centers for distribution to public establishments, factories, and schools.

The programs offered on Programs I and II are generally of good quality but have a high ideological content and are lacking in diversity. In addition to news and weather reports, programs include special broadcasts for children and rural listeners, scientific, theatrical, cultural, and literary presentations, and a great variety of musical programs. Program III, which is limited principally to the Sunday evening hours, carries many of the regular concerts given by the various national orchestras and choirs. Despite its limited broadcast schedule, Program III also carries indoctrination programs in the form of interviews and panel discussions.

Foreign broadcasts in thirteen languages were beamed to Europe and overseas by Radio Bucharest on one mediumwave and six shortwave transmitters in early 1972. These programs were on the air for a combined total of approximately 200 hours per week, averaged one-half hour in length, and generally carried domestic news and comments on international developments. In addition to Romanian, the broadcasts to European listeners were presented in English, German, French, Greek, Italian, Portuguese, Serbo-Croatian, and Spanish. Overseas programs were beamed to North Africa and the Near East in Arabic, English, French, and Turkish; to Asia, in English and Persian; to the Pacific area, in English; to North America, in English, Romanian, and Yiddish; and to Latin America, in Portuguese and Spanish.

Radio Audience

The communist regime has long recognized the importance of radio broadcasting as a medium for both informing the people and for molding a favorable public attitude toward the government. As a result, the construction of broadcast facilities and the production of receiving sets have been steadily increased since 1960. Also, during this same period the number of radio receivers increased more than 50 percent, from 2 million in 1960 to almost 3.1 million in 1970. The number of licensed receiving sets included approximately 870,000 wired receivers and amplifiers that usually reached group audiences in public areas.

By early 1972 the government had given no indication as to the results achieved by the radio in the intensified ideological campaign launched in mid-1971. Press reports revealed that, whereas radio programs continued to be criticized as to content and purpose, changes more favorable to the socialist concept of culture and political thought have not yet been extensive. Western programs, though fewer, were still being offered, and certain musical programs were being revised to favor the light and popular music of native composers over the modern Western style. Listener resistance to changes intended to improve the "communist education of the masses" was revealed by official statements that called for the need of radio editors and program coordinators "to improve their skill" in arousing and focusing the interest of the radio audience on "up-to-date" programs.

Television Broadcasting

Since its inception in 1956, television broadcasting has been closely linked with radio, by the regime, as an increasingly important instrument of "propaganda and socialist education of the masses." Like radio, television operated under supervision of the Council of Romanian Radio and Television, whose policy guidelines were received directly from the party apparatus. Also, as in the case of radio, television came under close scrutiny and criticism in mid-1971 in the intensified ideological campaign initiated by President Nicolae Ceausescu. By early 1972 changes in television network programming resulting from this campaign had not been revealed, but the press indicated that most of them were intended to limit foreign influence in literary, theatrical, film, and artistic broadcasts and to stress the Marxist-Leninist interpretation in presenting current events.

Although only recently developed as a new medium in mass communications, television has expanded more rapidly than radio. From the six stations that were operational in 1960, the industry had increased to a total of eighty-five in 1971. Of these, sixteen were principal transmitting stations located in various parts of the country, and sixty-nine were repeater stations. The number of television sets also increased significantly during this period, from 55,000 to almost 1.3 million. It was estimated by government authorities that programs aired over the 1.3 million licensed sets covered more than 80 percent of the country and could be seen by between 5 million snd 6 million viewers.

The television network operates the Central European System of 625-line definition and broadcasts over two systems, Program I and Program II. Program I was on the air daily during the evening hours for a total of thirty-eight hours per week. Program II broadcast weekday mornings and evenings for a total of eighteen hours. Most presentations originate on Program I and include, in addition to political, literary, and cultural programs, sports, news, documentaries, and special programs for children and workers. Program II usually repeats most of the programs shown on Program I or summarizes certain telecasts for combined showings with other short features.

Foreign programs, chiefly from neighboring communist countries, are also available to Romanian televiewers. Most of this material is procured on a mutual exchange basis through Intervision (Eastern European Television), an organization to which Romania belongs. A substantial number of foreign telecasts, however, are also available to residents in border areas, by direct transmission.

BOOK PUBLISHING

Before World War II Romania was one of the leading Balkan nations in the publishing field. Annually, some 2,500 titles were commonly published in editions of 2,000 to 5,000 copies, with a high percentage representing original works of Romanian authors. After the communist takeover in 1948 all publishing facilities were nationalized, and the entire industry was converted to serve as a major propaganda and indoctrination instrument in support of the new regime. Between 1949 and 1953 the revamped publishing concerns turned out more than 13,500 separate titles, with a total of almost 250 million copies. This record amount of officially approved and censored material represented a whole new series of communist-oriented material needed to operate the highly centralized government, to re-educate the people, and to regulate their activities.

By 1955 the number of titles issued annually had decreased to a little more than 5,000, but total circulation remained relatively high at more than 48 million copies. From 1955 to 1966 the number of titles gradually increased and reached a plateau of about 9,000, where it remained through 1969. Annual circulation figures over the same periods of time fluctuated in a fairly regular pattern showing a controlled average number of copies issued per title each year also to be about 9,000. Thus, the planned publishing requirements as set by the government apparently were achieved in 1966 and have varied very little since them.

Publication

Government and party control of all printing and publishing activities is centered in the Council on Socialist Culture and Education. This party-state organization formulates policy guidelines for the publishing industry and utilizes other government-controlled or government-owned agencies, such as the General Directorate for the Press and Printing, the various publishing houses, and book distribution centers to supervise and coordinate day-to-day operations. Within this control machinery all short- and long-range publication plans are approved, and the distribution of all printed material is specified. This central authority also allocates paper quotas, determines the number of books to be printed, and sets the prices at which all publications are to be sold.

In 1972 about twenty-five publishing houses were in operation; of these, twenty-three were located in Bucharest, and one each was in Cluj and Iasi. Each of these enterprises produced books, pamphlets, periodicals, and other printed material within its own specialized field and was responsible, through its director, for the political acceptability and quality of its work. In 1969 some decentralization in publishing took place with the opening of branch offices of the larger houses in a few of the more heavily populated districts. Although this program was ostensibly initiated for the purpose of securing "a broader scope of reader preference" in the number and type of books to be published, press reports published in late 1971 indicated very little popular support for this experiment.

Of the 9,399 titles published in 1969, the greatest numbers were in the fields of technology, industry, agriculture, and medicine. Also included in this group were books, treatises, studies, and reports in the general economic field as well as translations from foreign sources. This category of titles, although representing about 33 percent of those published, had an average circulation of only about 3,500 copies per title—well below the overall average of approximately 9,000.

The second largest group of published titles was in the field of social sciences and represented approximately 22 percent of the total. This classification included all books dealing with political science and socioeconomic theory as well as all textbooks and materials used in the educational system. A particularly large segment of books in this area were documents and manuals used for party training, Marxist-Leninist classics, and party-directed studies and monographs dealing with the hisotrical, philosophical, or sociological development of the communist movement.

The material published in the fields of art, games, sports, and music dominated the third largest group and ranged from children's entertainment to musical scores. The fourth largest group, representing about 15 percent of the national publishing effort, related to general literature. This field covered novels, essays, short stories, and poetry written by recognized authors as well as by less well established modern writers, both domestic and foreign. The books selected from foreign sources were carefully scrutinized, and very few were published that dealt with contemporary Western subjects. Also banned, as a matter of general principle, was all material that (in the judgment of chief editors) "did not contribute actively to the socialist education of the new man" within the communist society.

Distribution and Foreign Exchange

The distribution and sale of books, both domestic and foreign, are vested in the Book Central, a state-owned organization that is also responsible for the coordination of all book production. The Book Central, with headquarters in Bucharest, operates directly under the Council on Socialist Culture and Education and maintains a network of bookshops throughout the country in district centers and other major towns. In addition to supplying major outlets such as libraries and schools with publications, the local bookshops also set up and operate bookstalls and book departments in rural areas, usually at industrial enterprises and farm collectives. Traveling bookmobiles are also used to serve factories, mines, or other isolated activities in outlying areas. Discount book clubs were reportedly established as early as 1952, but recent information was lacking as to their continued existence, size, and method of operation.

After receiving approval of their individual publishing plans, the publishing houses distribute catalogs, bulletins, and other informational material to the Book Central for distribution to major purchasing outlets. In addition, the local bookshops issue periodic lists of all books in stock as well as those scheduled to be printed during specific periods. Official statistics concerning the wholesale and retail sale of books are not habitually published, but recurrent articles in the press criticize the lack of enthusiasm and general ineptness of booksellers as major factors in lagging book sales to individual buyers.

The Book Central in Bucharest conducts all transactions involving the foreign exchange of publications. This agency issues annual lists of available Romanian publications, together with short bibliographic annotations or summaries as well as subscription details. Also, the sale of books is fostered at the various international book fairs in which Romania participates.

LIBRARIES

The Romanian library network consists of two broad categories—general libraries, administered by the central government and its territorial organs, and the various libraries administered by mass organizations, institutes, and enterprises. Those in the latter category are generally referred to as documentary libraries since most of them specialize in scientific and technical holdings. The number of general libraries declined appreciably from a total of almost 35,000 in 1960 to slightly more than 18,000 in 1971, due principlally to the consolidation of facilities. Over the same period the number of documentary libraries remained fairly constant, averaging slightly more than 4,000, the total number existing in 1971.

The greatest proportion of general libraries, by far, are those associated with primary and secondary schools and those that serve the general public. In addition, the state operates two national libraries, and forty-three others function as part of university and other higher level institutions. The total holdings of all these facilities exceeded 95 million volumes, and the number of registered readers in the public libraries was reported to have reached almost 5 million in 1971. No information was available as to the total annual circulation of books on personal and interlibrary loan in the general library system, but the two national libraries were reported to have circulated 55,000 volumes in 1968, and the combined circulation of the forty-three university-level libraries approximated 178,000 volumes in the same year.

The two national libraries, the Library of the Academy of the Socialist Republic of Romania and the Central State Library, together maintain stocks in excess of 10 million volumes, and both function as central book depositories. The Library of the Academy of the Socialist Republic of Romania, a precommunist institution founded in 1867, holds special collections of Romanian, Greek, Slavonic, Oriental, and Latin manuscripts, maps, and engravings as well as rare collections of documents, medals, and coins. The Central State Library, founded in 1955, also has important collections of books, periodicals, musical works, maps, and photographs and, in addition, acts as the Central Stationery Office and the National Exchange for books. It also issues the National Bibliography and annual catalogs, which list all books printed in Romania and the holdings of all foreign books in the state library system.

The largest libraries among the universities, each of which holds more than 1.5 million volumes, are those at Bucharest, Iasi, and Cluj. These holdings include the book stocks maintained in the libraries of the various faculties, hostels, and institutes associated with the universities as well as the central university library itself. The largest documentary library, the Library of the Medical-Pharmaceutical Institute, operates ninety-nine branch facilities, and its annual book inventory has been in excess of 1.2 million volumes.

FILMS

As in the case of other elements of the mass media, the small motion picture industry has also been affected by the intensified ideological campaign of mid-1971. In general, the regime has attempted to further limit the importation of foreign films, particularly those from the West, which are considered violent and decadent. There has also been a move to stimulate the production of more native films with a truly "profound ideological content which will express our Marxist-Leninist world outlook, convey the message of our own society in highly artistic terms, and reflect the life of the new man." Until more Romanian films of the appropriate type can be offered, the industry has been advised to utilize additional films from the National Film Library and to emphasize foreign presentations that are based on socialist concepts.

Production

Film production, distribution, and exhibition were controlled by the National Center of Cinematography, a state agency that operates under the supervision of the Council on Socialist Culture and Education. The national center operates two production studios: the Alexandru Sahia Film Studio in Bucharest, which produces documentaries, newsreels, cartoons, and puppet films, and the Bucharest Film Studio, which produces feature films at Buftea, a suburb about fifteen miles northwest of the capital.

In 1970 cinema production consisted of thirty-nine feature and short pictures, about 1960 documentary films (including animated cartoons), and seventy-six newsreels. This output reflected a twofold increase since 1960 in both feature and documentary films but a decrease of about 15 percent in the number of newsreels. The largest growth in the motion picture industry occurred between 1923 and 1930, when production rose from about seven motion pictures per year to about twenty-five. This increased output was a combination of native films and features coproduced with France, Germany, and Hungary. After the communist takeover of the government in 1948, film production fell drastically and did not again reach its pre-World War II level until 1955.

Romanian films, until 1968, continued to reflect much of the earlier French influence. Both the native and coproduced pictures of this period were of high quality, and several won awards at film festivals in Cannes, Trieste, and Chicago. Subjects treated were well diversified and included historical adventure, strong dramas, and both satirical and classical comedies. Beginning in 1968, the regime launched widespread criticism of the industry, and the quality of production decreased appreciably. The 1971 ideological campaign forced film making into a further regression. Western observers characterized post-1968 films as being totally lacking in originality.

Because of the relatively low number of Romanian films produced, the industry has generally depended on the importation of sizable numbers of foreign films to meet its needs. The government no longer publishes official statistics dealing with film imports, but in 1960 the regime reported that 188 feature films and 150 documenaries from foreign countries were shown. Approximately 40 percent of these films came from the Soviet Union; the remainder came from France, East Germany, England, Italy, Czechoslovakia, and the United States.

Distribution

Despite the emphasis placed by the government on motion pictures as both a propaganda and an entertainment medium, the number of theaters and attendance at film showings has decreased steadily since 1965. This trend was due principally to the competition offered by the expanding television industry, but the falling off in the quality of films was also a contributing factor.

Film theaters are of two types, those which show pictures regularly in designated movie houses or, periodically, in multipurpose recreation centers, and mobile film units, which exhibit documentary and educational films in schools or other local facilities in outlying areas. Motion picture houses of both types decreased in number from 6,499 in 1965 to 6,275 in 1970, and in the same period annual attendance dropped more than 6 million from the 1965 high of almost 205 million.

INFORMAL INFORMATION MEDIA

Lectures, public and organizational meetings, exhibits, and demonstrations also serve as means of communication between the government and the population at large. Although less significant than the formal mass media, these events are fostered by officials of the regime as highly effective elements in the indoctrination process because they offer direct personal confrontations at the lower levels. Word-of-mouth communication is also an important and effective medium, particularly as a means of spreading news heard from Western radio transmissions, which were no longer subject to government jamming as a matter of policy.

SECTION III. NATIONAL SECURITY

CHAPTER 12

PUBLIC ORDER AND INTERNAL SECURITY

By 1972 the internal security situation in Romania had changed a great deal from that of the post-World War II period and the first few years of the communist regime. In those days the regime had feared for its existence and for that of the system it was attempting to establish. It had feared interference from outside the country and active opposition from a large segment of the local population and had also doubted the reliability of a considerable number of those within its own ranks.

In the police state atmosphere of that time a good portion of the people had also, and frequently with good reason, feared the regime. People whose greatest crime might have been lack of enthusiasm feared that they might be suspected of deviant political beliefs. Because of the brief time then being spent on investigaton of a crime and seeking out an individual's possible innocence, such persons could easily emerge from hasty trails as political prisoners.

By 1972 the security troops—successors to the secret police that had held the population in dread and terror twenty years before—still existed in considerable force. They had receded into the background, however, and only infrequently had any contact with the average citizen as he went about his daily routine.

The population was undoubtedly not altogether content in 1972 and often chafed at bureaucratic redtape, at lackluster performance on the part of minor officials, and at other irritations. The youth, in particular, was showing reluctance to be molded into the uncompromising pattern of socialist society, and some of its resistance took on characteristics considered intolerable by the regime. On the other hand, there was little, if any, sign of organized opposition to the system or the leadership. The dominant attitude throughout the country was cooperative to the degree that, if the system was seen to be in need of change, it was preferable to attempt reform from within the system itself and along accepted guidelines.

Reflecting the easing of internal tensions, the formal framework of the judicial system—the penal code, the code of criminal procedure, and the courts—was extensively changed in 1968. Although the new code emphasized protection of the state and society more than individual rights, the code it replaced had been one of the most severe and inflexible in Europe. The new codes clearly specified that there was no crime unless it was so defined in law and that there was to be no punishment unless it had been authorized by law.

Procedures for criminal prosecution were set down in readily understandable language that, if adhered to, guaranteed equitable treatment during investigation, trial, and sentencing to a degree hitherto unknown in the court system. There were also provisions for appeal of lower and intermediate court sentences.

Petty cases were disposed of by judicial commissions that did not have court status. Such commissions were set up in villages, institutions, collectives, or enterprises comprising as few as 200 people. Although authorized to administer only small fines or penalties, they were established in a fashion designed to involve large numbers of people in the judicial process and to exert local pressures on those appearing before them.

INTERNAL SECURITY

During the mid-1950s the militia (civil police force) and security troops were busily engaged in apprehending alleged spies, traitors, saboteurs, and those who persisted in voicing beliefs considered dangerous to the regime and the socialist system. In the early 1970s directives for security agencies still identified the 1950 threats to the regime and exhorted the agencies to continue to combat the same old enemies of the people. The emphasis has been altered, however, and national authorities appeared generally satisfied with the improved internal security situation in 1972.

The regime had by then become seriously concerned much less over mass violence or organized subversion than over levels of unrest or passive resistance that are evidenced by widespread laxity, carelessness, indolence, or an obvious lack of popular support. The militia blamed a rash of railroad accidents in 1970 on laxity when investigation determined that the equipment had, in nearly all cases, operated properly and the people had received sufficient training to make the system work safely. It also blamed an excessive number of fires on carelessness and negligence. Classified political and economic data were found on several occasions during routine checks of unoccupied and unsecured automobiles. New laws were published in 1970 to deal with vagrancy, begging, prostitution, and persons not seeking employment or living what the authorities termed "useless lives."

194

Although they have been relaxed, controls over the population remain strict by Western standards. A 1971 decree on the establishment of private residence placed rigid limitations on movement to the cities, allowing only those who get employment and are allocated housing to move. For example, military personnel must have had previous residence in a city in order to establish residence there after retiring from the service.

All persons over fourteen years of age must carry identification cards. The cards are issued by the militia and are usually valid for ten-year periods to age forty-four, after which they have no expiration date. They are reissued, however, if the photograph no longer matches the appearance of the bearer or when a name change—such as that following marriage—affects the identity. In addition to the photograph and other data for identification, the card contains blood type and residence information. Identification cards of prisoners or persons held in preventive detention are withheld from them.

Ministry of Internal Affairs

The minister of internal affairs is one of the three members of the Council of Ministers who head governmental agencies charged with defense of the country and security of the regime and the social system. His ministry is responsible for the various police and related organizations that, although controlled from national headquarters, perform most of their functions at the local level in the defense of law, order, and property. It cooperates with the Ministry of the Armed Forces and with the State Security Council, a watchdog committee that oversees police activities, but neither of those agencies does a large share of its work with local government or party agencies (see ch. 8).

Two-thirds of the ministry's major directorates deal with the militia. They include the militia's general inspectorate; its political council; and directorates relating to firefighting, special guard units, the Bucharest militia, and Bucharest traffic control. Other directorates of the ministry deal with prisons and labor settlements, reeducation of minors, and state archives.

Militia

The militia is organized at the national level under the Ministry of Internal Affairs and is probably also responsible to the State Security Council. The chain of command between the ministry and local police units appears to work from inspectorate general offices in the ministry through the thirty-nine *judet* (county) inspectorates and one for the city of Bucharest. Local police units and local inspectorates, in addition to being subordinate to their counterparts at the next higher level, are also responsible to the locally elected people's councils. This dual subordination probably works because of the overriding influence of the Romanian Communist Party at all levels.

Most of the police work is done, and by far the greatest part of the organization is situated, in the many local police offices. These are located any place in which there are sufficient numbers of people or enough valuable property to justify them—in towns, communes, enterprises, or cities, where there may be several. The ministry may also establish other individual police jurisdictions at railroad stations, ports, airfields, and large construction sites and in other special situations on a temporary or permanent basis.

The militia is charged with defense of the regime and the society, with maintenance of public order, and with enforcement of laws. To accomplish the more general tasks, it is directed to detect criminal activities and to apprehend criminals. The militia is also given responsibility for preventing crime and for guiding, assisting, or directing other organizations involved in protection of the regime, the citizens, and state or private property. An increasing portion of routine police work is required in the control of highway traffic. The militia may also be called upon to assist in emergencies or in disaster situations.

Militia regulations require the police to respect individual rights and the inviolability of homes and personal property in normal circumstances. Restrictions are removed, however, if circumstances warrant. Police may commandeer any vehicle or means of communication, private or otherwise, if the situation demands. During chase or during investigation of flagrant crimes, they may enter private homes without permission or search them without warrant.

Citizens are directed to assist the militia when called upon or to act as police—to apprehend and hold violators—if no police are at the scene when a crime is committed. Provisions authorizing the formation of auxiliary police groups are established in law. Such auxiliaries would ordinarily be organized by the militia but, whatever their sponsorship, they would be expected to cooperate with local police authorities.

According to the law defining the militia's organization, its personnel consist of military and civilian employees on the staff of the Ministry of Internal Affairs. Officers, military experts, and noncommissioned officers are recruited from the graduates of schools operated within the regular military establishment. Policemen may be drawn from those selected annually for compulsory military service. The armed forces' personnel regulations apply to militiamen acquired from the draft process or from military schools. Graduates of civilian schools are employed in the police force to meet its requirements for specialists who are not trained in the armed forces. These individuals and others who have had no association with the armed forces retain civilian status and are subject to the provisions of the labor code and other regulations applicable to civilian employees.

The militia's personnel strength of 500,000 in 1972 means that about one person in every forty of the country's population is in, or employed by, the force. The reason for this high ratio is that the militia organization has branches at all government levels, from the national ministry down to the village. Also, its working groups include nearly all of the country's guard, regulatory, investigative, and paramilitary organizations, as well as those performing police and firefighting functions.

Security Troops

Security forces organized at the national level to protect the regime from subversive activities, whether locally or externally generated, were created in the late 1940s and are still maintained. The force in 1972 numbered roughly 20,000 men. It is organized along military lines, and most, if not all, of its men have military rank. It receives its administrative and logistic support from the Ministry of Internal Affairs but is supervised by the State Security Council.

According to pronouncements made during anniversary ceremonies held in August of 1968, during their twenty years of service the security troops had been a consistently reliable force. Their mission was described as identifying and apprehending foreign espionage agents and combating local spies, saboteurs, agitators, and terrorists. It was declared that the forces operated under the leadership and direct guidance of the party and governmental leadership and that local security forces were controlled by the party authorities in districts and cities.

Pronouncements by the leadership about their local subordination notwithstanding, the security troops, which are the direct descendants of the old secret police, are still controlled at the national level. Because of their declining mission in counterespionage and countersubversion, they undoubtedly cooperate wherever possible in usual militia functions, but they appear to have only nominal responsibilities to local government agencies.

The diminishing role of the security troops is evident in several areas. Their personnel strength in 1971 was a fraction of that of the militia. The country's efforts against external threat have been increasingly relegated to the regular armed forces. Also, although the chairman of the State Security Council—which was

197

newly established in 1968—is a member of the Council of Ministers, in 1970 he was the only man on the security council who was a ranking party member, and he was no more than an alternate member of the Executive Committee of the Central Committee of the Romanian Communist Party. His vice chairmen were military officers, and only one of them was prominent enough in the party to have been a member of the Central Committee. It is evident that the State Security Council in Romania does not have the status of the high-level groups that in some countries have the responsibility for coordinating party and governmental activities relating to national security and for providing basic guidance to all of the various military, paramilitary, and police agencies.

PUBLIC ORDER

As is the case in the other communist countries that pattern their systems after that of the Soviet Union, Romania's leadership relies on the party and several mass organizations to foster a climate in which the people will actively support and cooperate with the regime. These organizations involve as large a segment of the population as possible in a broad spectrum of programs and functions. The efforts they elicit from their members may consist of activities within the organizations themselves or in local governments, judicial systems, and security groups. Mass popular involvement provides an influence that is generally subtle but that may become direct pressure.

Mass Organizations

The party attempts to attract the most competent and elite element of the people, to ensure that its members adhere to basic socialist ideology, and to maintain the power to direct and control all other groups involved in major social and governmental activities. The mass organizations support the party and carry its programs to special interest groups. They keep the party informed of the concerns of their members and may also, within certain limitations, have an influence upon the party's actions (see ch. 9).

There are about a dozen mass organizations. The Socialist Unity Front is not typical of the group, as in theory it encompasses all of the others as well as the party—although it supports and serves the party. It functions as a coordinating agency in such things as running the national elections.

The largest typical groups are the General Union of Trade Unions and the youth groups. There are three of the latter: the Union of Communist Youth (Uniunea Tineretului Comunist—UTC), the Pioneers Organization, and the Union of Student Associations. The UTC is a general group whose members are between fifteen and twenty-six years of age, although members in leadership positions may retain their affiliation beyond the upper age limit. The pioneers are the younger children, seven through fourteen years old; their program is designed so that they move naturally into the UTC when they become fifteen. The student groups are organized in universities or in schools beyond the secondary level. They have experienced difficulties in attracting members and in persuading those they have attracted to accept all of the principles set down for them (see ch. 9).

The other organizations are a miscellaneous aggregation, including a women's organization, the Red Cross, a sports and physical education group, one that involves the various ethnic nationalities, another that is a Jewish federation only, one that is designed to foster ties of friendship with the Soviet Union, and one designed for the defense of peace. Although they are highly dissimilar and vary widely in importance, all are designed to attract groups with special fields of interest and to guide such groups into activities that promote harmony and order.

The labor and youth groups, in addition to being the largest, are also those most actively charged with supporting the regime. Labor union members are active in auxiliaries of the militia and in the military reserves. The UTC membership spans most of the age group that is drafted into the regular armed services and the security forces. Within the services it forms units throughout the organizational structures that either direct or actively assist in political indoctrination programs and manage sports and recreational activities. Where a party cell exists, the UTC is guided by it; where the military unit is too small to have a party cell, the UTC functions in its place.

Youth Programs

Although the economy has improved and the internal security situation has stabilized, youth problems have increased, and much effort is being expended on their solution. Officials point out that the percentage of young people that have become criminals or whose antisocial conduct gets most of the publicity is very small. They complain, however, that the number of those who will not associate with the UTC and who display other negative behavior is far too great. Negative behavior on the part of young people reportedly involves their manner of speech and dress, which "offends common decency," their creation of public disturbances, their apathy toward work, and the fact that many of them have become cynical and infatuated with "wrong beliefs."

Authorities understand the youthful tendency to be nonconformist and accept the fact that a certain amount of the behavior they deplore is an attempt to affirm new and differing youth attitudes. Attitudes and conduct considered to have exceeded permissible bounds, however, are dealt with firmly. Leaders blame the inadequacies of some educational facilities; the ignorance, injustice, or excessive indulgence on the part of some parents and educators; and the overlenient courts.

Solutions that have been proposed since the late 1960s have run the gamut from advice to parents to the creation of powerful governmental agencies. Parents are admonished to take a firm attitude toward their children. The first secretary of the Central Committee of the UTC was made a member of the Council of Ministers, as minister for youth problems. University student associations have been given much new attention, as have the other youth organizations and their programs. The militia, armed forces, and security troops have been required to undertake programs to cooperate with youth organizations.

During 1969 the minister for youth problems was provided a research center by the Council of Ministers. Its purpose was to investigate the problems experienced by schools, universities, youth mass organizations, the militia, and the courts. As case studies are documented, the center is directed to evaluate the problems and the solutions found for them locally at the time they occurred and to disseminate the information, with additional comments and recommendations, as widely as possible.

In early 1971 a considerably invigorated program was unveiled for the UTC. Wherever possible, all programs were to become more mature and more stimulating. Military exercises would involve field trips and more realistic maneuvers. Aerial sports would include parachuting, gliding, and powered flight. Hobbies, such as model ship building, amateur radio, and the study of topography, were to be given more adequate supervision. Better equipment and facilities would be supplied for touring, motorcycling, mountaineering, skiing, and hiking. More youths were to be scheduled for summer camps. No informaton concerning the effectiveness of the new programs had been made available by early 1972.

Many university students held their party-sponsored associations in low regard during the middle and late 1960s, and eventually the then-existing student unions were dissolved or consolidated into the new Union of Student Associations. The incentives and pressures that were applied, in addition to revamping the union's programs, had succeeded by 1970 in re-animating the association to the point that it was active in all of the country's universities and institutes of higher learning. It was authorized to make recommendations applicable to extracurricular sports and tourist programs, political education, and the entire academic area of the educational establishment.

Programs for the young pioneer groups have probably not been the object of the same degree of reform effort that has been applied to the UTC and the student associations. A party spokesman stated in late 1971, however, that the 1.6 million pioneers were not too young to develop a socialist consciousness and to be given a communist education. He stated that their major programs should feature direct involvement in work of educational and civic value.

To give young people a sense of accomplishment, as well as to keep them occupied in meaningful and productive work, large numbers of them are organized into youth construction groups. In typical situations temporary housing or camps are built near the project, and all necessary facilities are provided at the site. During the spring of 1970, for example, five such groups were scattered throughout the country, operating concurrently. A majority of the projects have involved land reclamation, irrigation, or drainage. Many of them are major undertakings, and thousands of young people take part in the program.

CRIME AND THE PENAL SYSTEM

During a 1971 discussion on the judiciary's philosophy with regard to the general subjects of law and freedom, the chairman of the Supreme Court stated that the penal code and criminal procedures adopted in 1968 assign to the law the role of regulator of social behavior. The law has become, he said, not simply an instrument stipulating the rights and obligations of the citizen; its important social role provides a firm foundation for society's behavior. Other spokesmen have amplified this theme. They emphasize that, once an individual understands the law and its objectives, he appreciates the fact that individual freedom is related to the freedom of others and that a free individual is bound to respect accepted ideological concepts and accepted moral and judicial standards.

Public prosecutors have a broad range of responsibility in the judicial and penal systems. Their duties are not confined to handling the prosecution of indicted individuals who have been brought to trail. As the appointed protectors of the civil liberties of the people, their duties extend from crime prevention to rehabilitation of criminals serving prison sentences. They are responsible for seeing that crimes are detected and investigated and that penal action is taken against the criminal. They also see to it that the criminal is held in preventive detention, if necessary, before trial. After sentencing, the prosecutors have access to any place in which the criminal might be detained and pass on the legalities of the detention and the conditions within the penal institution. If a sentence either does not involve imprisonment (but is, for example, in the form of a fine, restriction, or extra work) or is suspended, the prosecutors ensure that the terms of the sentence are carried out.

Public prosecutors are monitored by the Office of the Prosecutor General at the national level. The prosecutor general (attorney general) assures that the work of local public prosecutors is consistent throughout the country, both in the choice of cases to pursue and in the diligence with which the prosecution is undertaken (see ch. 8).

Crime

Statistics released to the public do not include crime rates. Reliable data that would include petty crime would, in any event, be difficult to obtain because many minor infractions of law and all but the more serious of personal disputes are not termed crimes and are tried before the hundreds of local judicial commissions.

A rough assessment of the overall crime situation can, however, be made from the concern expressed in the many speeches and articles published by government and party spokesmen. It is apparent that certain types of crime are considered to be adequately under control and occur infrequently enough to be statistically tolerable. There are, for example, few trials in the political category, such as those where dissidents are accused of attempting to undermine the authority of the regime or to subvert the population from the approved ideology. In an exceptional case (apparently at least his second serious offense) an engineer found guilty of passing economic information to a foreigner received a twenty-five-year sentence in March 1971 for espionage. Similar trials were a frequent occurrence during the early 1950s, but much of the publicity they have received since the mid-1960s has occurred because they have become so infrequent as to be noteworthy.

Furthermore, to emphasize the more moderate and strictly legal procedures adhered to by police forces and the judiciary, some of the 1950 political trials are being reexamined. Most of those sentenced to imprisonment from such trials have been amnestied, the largest group in 1964. A few of those who were executed are still being posthumously rehabilitated.

On the other hand, there is a greater percentage of crimes in the categories that are sometimes attributed to an improvement in the standard of living but that reflect dissatisfaction with the rate of the improvement. These include economic crimes—theft and embezzlement—misuse or abuse of property, and antisocial crimes and crimes of violence, which are committed most frequently by younger people. Party officials also deplore the prevalence of laxity in the use of state property and in the safeguarding of official information and documents.

Measures taken to combat crime have had varying degrees of success. Speculation is illegal, but efforts to prevent private sales of new and used cars at excessive profit have been ineffective. Cars two to five years old sell for more than their original cost. Crimes such as vagrancy, begging, and prostitution were, as of late 1970, defying the best efforts of the militia and the courts. This type of crime had been prevalent during the early post-World War II period but declined after about 1950. During the late 1960s it again began to increase. The militia has also encountered a problem in the amount of popular cooperation it is able to count upon. Individuals who have identified persons as having committed criminal acts have been subjected to reprisals. The militia has, however, been able to show good results against vandalism, pilfering, and petty theft. By mid-1971 crimes of that category had been reduced to pre-1969 levels.

The 1968 Warsaw Treaty Organization (Warsaw Pact) invasion of Czechoslovakia generated a certain amount of disillusion that probably contributed to the increase, during the late 1960s, in attempts to emigrate illegally. An émigré reported that about 40 percent of the prison populations at Arad and Timisoara, or some 500 inmates, had failed in attempts to cross the border into Hungary. Most of them were reportedly twenty to thirty years old and were serving sentences of from one to five years.

Modern crime-fighting facilities have been introduced more slowly than has been the case in the more prosperous European countries. During 1970 the Ministry of Justice established the Central Crime Laboratory and two branch, or interdistrict, laboratories. All of them serve the militia, the security and armed forces, the courts, and the public prosecutors. They are equipped to assist in the investigation of all aspects of crimes except those where medical and legal services are required. They include facilities for handwriting, fingerprint, and ballistic analyses and analysis of documents (for counterfeiting or alteration) and for performing a number of other physical and chemical tests.

Traffic Control

Traffic control demands a sizable portion of police energies, although by 1972 highway use remained low in comparison to the rest of the continent. There had been few motor vehicles before World War II, and numbers for personal use or for motor transport increased slowly during the immediate postwar years. Since about 1955, however, both categories have become available at an accelerated rate.

In 1963 traffic was up over 200 percent (and in 1965 approximately 300 percent) from 1955 levels. Total numbers of vehicles increased at about 10 percent a year during the late 1960s, and the number of those that were privately licensed doubled during the two-year period 1968 and 1969. Encouraged by the government during approximately the same period, tourist traffic tripled.

Irresponsible driving, lack of traffic controls, and lack of concern for their danger on the part of pedestrians, bicyclists, and wagon drivers contributed to an acceleration in the number of accidents and casualties that paralleled the increase in traffic. In 1969 there were 2,070 deaths resulting from about 5,300 reported accidents. Only about 40 percent of the victims were occupants of the vehicles involved and, of them, a considerably larger number of passengers than drivers were killed. Nearly 50 percent of the total fatalities were pedestrians; the remainder were on bicycles or wagons.

Considering accident statistics higher than warranted by the rising volume of traffic, the regime had enacted a series of stricter control measures, the bulk of them in 1968. Officials analyzing the problem attributed most of the poor record to disregard for driving regulations and inadequate traffic controls. Excessive speed had accounted for about 40 percent of the accidents. Driving under the influence of alcohol, failure to pay attention, and failure to yield the right of way accounted, in that order, for most of the others. Drivers were blamed for about 65 percent of accidents, pedestrians for 31 percent, and malfunction of vehicles for 4 percent. Accidents in which alcohol was a factor tended to be the most serious. One in every 2.3 alcohol-related accidents resulted in a fatality.

After 1968 the more stringent regulations and measures to enforce them began to yield results. By 1970, although both the numbers of local automobiles and tourist traffic had continued to increase steadily, accidents had decreased by 8 percent; and deaths and injuries from them were down by 7 and 8 percent, respectively. Officials gave credit to an educational program in secondary schools, the beginnings of a vehicle inspection program, and positive actions taken to reduce driving after drinking, as well as to the new regulations and enforcement efforts. During 1970 the militia suspended about 20,000 operators' licenses, canceling a number of them.

Penal Code and Code of Criminal Procedure

The penal code in effect before 1968 was one of the most severe in Europe. The penal code and the code of criminal procedure that have replaced it attempt to ensure that criminals are not able to evade the penalties provided for in the law but, at the same time, there is a stated guarantee against the arrest, trial, or conviction of innocent persons. Protective measures for accused persons are to be respected by all law enforcement and judicial agencies.

It is emphasized that an individual is found guilty according to the relevant evidence in his case. Courts are instructed to base sentences on the crime, rather than on an individual's reputation or extenuating circumstances. A Romanian assumes legal responsibility and is subject to the codes at age fourteen; he is considered an adult before the courts at age sixteen.

If the possible sentence for an alleged crime is five years or more, the accused is guaranteed counsel during any part of the in-investigation that involves his presence after he has been taken into custody, in the preparation of his defense, and throughout his trial. Minors and enlisted military personnel are authorized counsel without regard to the possible sentence. The defense counsel has access to all findings that are uncovered by the prosecutor or other investigators during the investigation of the case. Except in special cases specified in the law, trials are public. Decisions as to guilt or innocence and the sentence handed down are concurred in by a majority vote of the judges and people's assessors on the court.

The maximum prison sentence for a first offense is twenty years; for a repeated serious offense, it may be twenty-five years. The death sentence is also authorized, but it may be commuted to life imprisonment. The most severe sentences are still authorized for crimes in the political category—those endangering the state, the regime, or the society. Serious crimes against property and crimes of violence against a person are also considered grave but, unless they are exceptional, are not punishable by death. A person receiving the death penalty has five days in which to request a pardon. If the sentence is carried out, execution is by a firing squad.

The new codes attempt to reduce court time spent on minor offenses. Those that constitute no significant danger to society and should be prevented from recurring by social pressures have been removed from the list of crimes and have been relegated to the judicial commissions. In other cases, where an act is still classified as a crime, an offender may elect to plead guilty without a trial. If he does, he is charged one-half the minimum fine for the offense, and the case is closed.

Pretrial preventive detention is authorized to protect the individual, to assure that he will not elude trial, or to prevent his committing further criminal acts. Detention is ordinarily limited to five days for investigation of a crime or to thirty days if the person has been arrested and is awaiting trial. Extensions up to ninety days are authorized if requested by the prosecutor in the case. Longer extensions may be granted by the court.

According to the Romanian press, which has commented on the way that the new codes have served the people, examples of poor performance are usually attributable to the inertia of the bureaucracy. When citizens' rights are withheld, redtape or overworked personnel are most frequently to blame. Occasionally, however, officials are unresponsive to individuals' requests and provide services grudgingly without an adequate justification for delay.

Courts

The Constitution charges the judiciary with the defense of socialist order and the rights of citizens in the spirit of respect for the law. It also gives the courts responsibility for correcting and educating citizens who appear before them, to prevent further violations of the law. Party leader Nicolae Ceausescu, in a 1970 pronouncement, indicated that the party leadership may feel that the law should stress to an even greater extent the defense of the state and society rather than the rights of the individual. According to his statement, the first obligation of the courts is to collaborate with the militia and security forces and apply lawful punishment to those who disregard order and the laws of the country. He went on to say that he considered that the concepts of "solicitude for man" and "extenuating circumstances" were poorly understood and were abused by overlenient courts. In his view the courts had not shown sufficient firmness in cases involving trivial infractions, such as rowdiness or minor infractions of the norms of social relationships, or in cases dealing with persons who wish to live without working (see ch. 8).

Nonetheless, the court organization, as it was redesigned in 1968, is required to operate within a framework that is compatible with the penal codes and is thoroughly described and established in the law. Of greater significance, there has been an effort to make sure that the system is run by adequately qualified personnel. People's assessors, who need have no legal education, may outnumber the judges on the lower courts. Decisions of these courts may, however, be appealed and, if higher court panels are not made up exclusively of professional judges, the judges always outnumber the people's assessors. Judges must be lawyers and are preferably doctors of law.

The court system under the Ministry of Justice consists of the Supreme Court, *judet* courts, and lower courts. The lower courts, which might be considered lower municipal courts, are usually referred to only as "the courts." Bucharest has a court that is an equivalent of a *judet* court, and it has several of the lower courts (see ch. 8).

The lower courts are courts of first instance in all cases they hear. This could include cases that had previously been heard by judicial commissions. Such cases would not be considered to have been legally tried and would require reinvestigation and altogether new prosecutions, making sure that rights of the accused and all legal procedures were properly observed.

Appeals from the lower courts are heard by *judet* courts, which are also courts of first instance in more serious cases. Final appeal is to the Supreme Court. There is no appeal from its decisions, but it is not totally free and independent. It is within one of the government's ministries and is also responsive to the party leadership.

Judicial commissions function at a level below the formal court system. Each such commission is composed of several members (usually five), handles a wide variety of cases, and attempts to hear as many of them as possible in public. Because the judicial commissions are not a part of the court system, their cases are not included among criminal statistics. Unless appealed, however, their sentences are binding. Official documents describe the commissions as public organs for exerting influence and legal control, organized so as to bring about broad participation of the masses, providing them with a socialist education in legality and promoting a correct attitude toward work and good social behavior. The educational benefits are intended both for those serving on the commissions and for those who are judged by them.

The commissions handle small damage or personal disagreement suits between individuals—small first offense cases involving public property, petty thefts, misuse of property when no willful abuse is involved, negligence cases, and traffic violations. Judicial commissions set up in enterprises or collectives handle minor labor disputes and work-grievance cases. In all situations the commissions attempt to exert the influence of public opinion and, in personal disputes, to achieve reconciliations.

Penal Institutions

Depending upon the seriousness of a crime, its category, and the age and occupation of the individual, until the mid-1960s a convicted person was confined in a correction camp, a labor colony, a prison or, if subject to military law, a military disciplinary unit. Prisons included penitentiaries, prison factories, town jails, and detention facilities of the security troops.

A majority of labor colony inmates were political prisoners and, if there were a few of them that had not completed their sentences or were not released in amnesties by the mid-1960s, they were probably transferred to penitentiaries. Increased use of judicial commissions for petty crimes and an accompanying change minimizing confinement in lesser cases have further reduced prison populations and eliminated the need for separate categories of correction institutions. As a result, the 1970 law on the execution of court sentences treats all places of confinement as prisons or penitentiaries (under the authority of the Ministry of Internal Affairs) or as military disciplinary units (under the Ministry of the Armed Forces).

Place of detention vary, nonetheless. Maximum security prisons are provided for those convicted of crimes against the state's security, serious economic crimes, homicides or other violent crimes, and recidivists. All convicted persons are obliged to perform useful work, and an effort must be made to educate and rehabilitiate the inmates. Consequently, all but town jails and those facilities designed to hold persons for short stays have labor and educational facilities.

A convict is paid according to the country's standard wage scales. He receives 10 percent of his wages; the remainder goes to the penitentiary administration as state income. The maximum working day is twelve hours. If work norms are regularly exceeded, sentences are shortened accordingly.

Inmates are segregated for various reasons. Women are separated from men; minors, from adults; and recidivists and those convicted of serious crimes, from those serving short terms. Drug addicts and alcoholics are isolated whenever possible. Persons held in preventive arrest, not yet convicted of a crime, are separated when possible from convicted persons. Unless their conduct is considered intolerably uncooperative, they are not denied the ordinary prison privileges.

Usual convict privileges include some visits, packages, and correspondence. Privileges allowed vary with the severity of the original sentence and may be increased, reduced, or done away with altogether, depending upon the inmate's attitude and behavior. Consistently good conduct may also earn parole. An inmate who performs an exceptional service may be pardoned altogether; many were freed for their work in combating the great floods during the spring of 1970.

Other disciplinary measures include reprimand, simple isolation, severe isolation, or transfer to an institution with a more severe regimen. All convict mail is censored, and correspondence whose content is considered unsuitable is withheld. Conversation during visits is limited to Romanian or to a language familiar to someone available to monitor what is said.

Amnesties are granted periodically. Some, such as those that freed political prisoners in 1964 and the one in late 1970, reduce prison populations considerably. They may, as in 1964, free a particular category of prisoner or, as in the December 30, 1970, amnesty, serve to reduce sentences of all types but on a basis of the amount of the term unserved. At that time full pardon was granted all who had less than a year of their sentences to serve, even if an individual had been sentenced but had not yet begun to serve the term. Full pardon was also granted to pregnant women, women with children under five years of age who had up to three years of their sentences remaining, and to all women over the age of sixty. The amnesty even applied to cases in court. Trials were to continue, but the amnesty would take effect if it were applicable to the sentence. If, however, an amnestied person committed another crime within three years, he would be confined for the unserved portion of his commuted sentence in addition to the new one.

CHAPTER 13

ARMED FORCES

In 1971 Romania was a member of the Warsaw Treaty Organization (Warsaw Pact), but it was not fully cooperating in its activities nor in total agreement with the Soviet Union's interpretation of the organization's mission. Romania saw little threat to its territorial boundaries or to its ideology from the West. On the other hand, since the invasion of Czechoslovakia in 1968 by other pact members, various Romanian leaders have expressed concern about the danger to individual sovereignty from within the pact itself.

Much of the nation's military history has been that of an alliance partner. It has not fought a major battle in any other capacity. How well it has fared at peace tables has depended in large part on the fate of its allies or how the peacemakers believed that the Balkan area of the continent should be divided. In this tradition Romania aligns itself without significant reservation with the Warsaw Pact.

The military establishment consists of ground, naval, air and air defense, and frontier forces. They are administered by a defense ministry, which in turn is responsible to the chief of state. At topmost policy levels, party leaders are interwoven into the controlling group. Political education throughout the forces is supervised by a directorate of the ministry, but the directorate is responsible to the Romanian Communist Party.

Military service has become a national tradition, although the tradition is based largely on the continuing existence of sizable armed forces. The people accept the military establishment willingly enough even though conscription removes a great part of the young male population from the labor force for periods of from sixteen to twenty-four months. The military services are not an overwhelming financial burden and, in local terms, the forces undoubtedly have value to the regime. They support it and give it an appearance of power. Also, the discipline and political indoctrination given the conscripts during their military service is considered beneficial to them and to the country.

HISTORICAL BACKGROUND

The armed forces have been dependent on some major power for arms supply during most of the country's independent history. Equipment and assistance were furnished by Germany between 1870 and 1916. During that time, although the country's population was hardly more than 10 million, with German help it was able to support a large army. It fielded about 500,000 men against Bulgaria in 1913 during the Second Balkan War, for example. In 1916 Romania joined the World War I Allies, but its forces were defeated within a few months and were idled until a few days before the armistice in November 1918. From then until just before World War II they were assisted by France and, to a lesser degree by Great Britain (see ch. 2).

Because of the political situation at the time, Romania was unable to offer resistance when the Soviet Union, by terms of its agreement with Germany in 1939, annexed Bessarabia and northern Bukovina. In June 1941, however when Germany invaded the Soviet Union, Romania joined the Germans. Its forces fought the Soviets until 1944 but, after the battle for Stalingrad in 1943, they became too war weary to perform at their best. In 1944, as the Germans were being pushed westward, Romania was overrun by Soviet armies and joined them against Germany.

Nearly all of the military tradition cited by communist regimes since World War II starts at this point. On occasions honoring the forces they are reminded that they mobilized more than 500,000 men for this campaign, suffered 170,000 casualties, and liberated 3,800 localities while helping to push the German armies about 600 miles from central Romania.

A postwar buildup of Romania's forces began in 1947. Since then all major weapons and heavy equipment have been of Soviet design, and organization and training largely followed the Soviet model.

When the Warsaw Pact was formed in 1955 its members were given alliance responsibilities, and new procedures were introduced to enable them to perform as an integrated force. More modern equipment was furnished, basic units were brought closer to authorized combat strengths, and training was undertaken on a larger and more exacting scale. Romania's forces were expanded to nearly the maximum that could be readily sustained by universal conscription. Strengths were greatest before 1964, especially during the Berlin and Cuban crises of the early 1960s. Reduction of the tour of duty in 1964 to sixteen months for most conscripts necessitated a slight reduction in the overall size of the forces.

GOVERNMENTAL AND PARTY CONTROL OVER THE ARMED FORCES

The Ministry of the Armed Forces is the governmental agency that administers the military forces, but policymaking is a prerogative of the party hierarchy. Top ministry officials are always party members and often concurrently hold important party posts. In 1971 Nicolae Ceausescu—as president and chief of state, supreme commander of the armed forces, and chairman of the Defense Council—was, in each case, the immediate superior of the minister of the armed forces. At the same time, the minister of the armed forces was an alternate member of the executive committee of the party and, as such, not only was an important party leader but was again responsible to Ceausescu, this time in the latter's capacity as the party's general secretary.

One of the deputy ministers of the armed forces is secretary of the Higher Political Council. Although administered within the ministry, this council is responsible to the party's Central Committee. It is in charge of political education in the military establishment and has an organization paralleling, and collocated with, that of the regular services. It penetrates into the lower service units to monitor the content and effectiveness of political training in troop units.

The Union of Communist Youth (Uniunea Tineretului Comunist—UTC), the junior affiliate of the Romanian Communist Party, has responsibility for premilitary training and for active political work among the troops in their duty organizations. The UTC's premilitary programs prepare youth for military duty by introducing them to basic training and technical skills in addition to political indoctrination. Within the military organization, UTC work includes political educational programs conducted on duty and sports, cultural, and recreational activities conducted off duty (see ch. 12).

ORGANIZATION AND MISSION

The regular forces, which include the frontier troops, are under administrative and tactical control of the Ministry of the Armed Forces. The minister has a number of deputies, including the chiefs of the main directorates for training, political affairs, and rear services (logistics) and the chief of the general staff. The heads of operatioral or major tactical commands are also immediately subordinate to the minister. The highest level of the tactical organization includes the headquarters of the naval and air forces, the frontier troops, and the military regions (see fig. 10).

Area organization includes two military regions, with headquarters at Cluj and Iasi, and the Bucharest garrison. Regional headquarters, which are simultaneously corps headquarters of the ground forces, control support facilities for all services.

All commanders and force personnel subordinate to the minis-

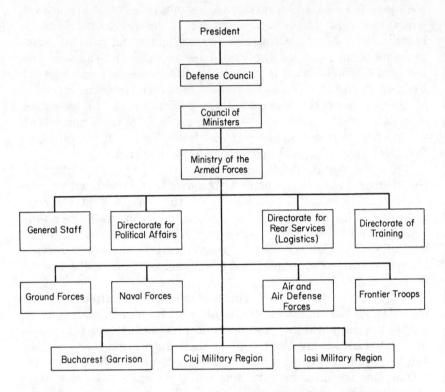

Figure 10. Romania, Organization of the Armed Forces, 1972.

ter are part of the regular military establishment, although appointments to the higher commands may be determined in varying degrees by political considerations. The minister is a political appointee but, whether or not he has had a military background, he assumes a senior military rank. The Romanian practice deviates from the usual in such situations, however, where the minister is expected to have an actual or honorary rank superior to any officer in his forces. The minister of the armed forces in 1971, for example, was appointed in 1966. He was promoted from colonel general to army general after about four years in his position and, during the early period, was technically subordinate in rank to an army general who commanded the General Military Academy in Bucharest.

In 1972 there were about 200,000 men in the regular forces. About 75 percent were in ground force or in support units common to all services. About 5 percent were naval; 10 percent, air force; and the remainder, frontier troops. The air force percentage included air defense forces.

When the mission of the armed forces is being described in relation to the Warsaw Pact, it is pointed out that the forces are structured and trained for major operations in concert with their allies against a common enemy. Because organized Romanian forces have not been involved in a major conflict except as junior partners in an alliance force, this experience makes the concept of participation in the Warsaw Pact mission easy to accept. Since about 1960, however, leaders have expressed ambitions to act somewhat independently of the Warsaw Pact. In this context the pact mission is occasionally downgraded or passed over in nonspecific terms. The forces' mission is then described as defense of the country only, and their use is said to be allowable only to resist aggression against Romania.

Ground Forces

The ground forces are commonly referred to as the army, although the Romanian People's Army comprises all of the regular armed forces administered by the Ministry of the Armed Forces. The ground forces proper have two tank and seven motorized-rifle divisions and a few other smaller combat units, including mountain, airborne, and artillery outfits of varying sizes. Combat units are thought to be kept at about 90 percent of their full authorized strengths. Most of the support agencies that provide services needed by all service organizations are manned by ground force personnel. Strength of the ground forces in 1972 was estimated at between 130,000 and 170,000.

Divisions are organized on the same pattern as those in the other Warsaw Pact countries. Tank divisions have one artillery, one motorized-rifle, and three tank regiments. Motorized-rifle divisions have one tank, one artillery, and three motorized-rifle regiments.

The division is the basic combat unit, and all of them have their own essential service and support outfits. They are, however, subordinate to corps headquarters of the military regions rather than directly to the Ministry of the Armed Forces.

Air and Air Defense Forces

The commander of the air and air defense forces occupies a position parallel to that of the commanders of the military districts and the naval and frontier forces. His immediate superior is the minister of the armed forces. His tactical units include about twenty fighter-bomber and fighter-interceptor squadrons and a squadron each of transports, reconnaissance aircraft, and helicopters. These units have a total of about 250 aircraft; there are about the same number of trainers and light utility planes.

Of the combat aircraft, MiG–17s would be used in the ground support role; MiG–19s and MiG–21s are interceptors that would be used in air-to-air combat. The reconnaissance squadron has Il-28 twin jet-engine light bombers. These airplanes are obsolescent, if not obsolete, and their crews are trained for reconnaissance only. A limited transport capability is provided by about a dozen twin-engine, piston-type transports. They are old and slow but are adequate for the short-distance work required of them. The helicopter squadron is equipped for air evacuation, for delivery of supplies to inaccessible areas, and for short-range reconnaissance.

Interceptor squadrons are presumably integrated into the Warsaw Pact air defense network, which is designed to function as a unit over all of Eastern Europe. The small numbers of fighter-bombers are probably capable of providing no more than marginal support for Romania's own ground forces.

Air defenses include surface-to-air missiles, antiaircraft artillery, and early warning and aircraft control sites. Surface-to-air missiles and their launching equipment, larger antiaircraft guns, radars, and most of the complex communication equipment are furnished by the Soviet Union.

Air defenses in all of the Warsaw Pact countries are integrated into a common network. Romania's are important because the southwestern border with Yugoslavia is the point at which an attack from the western Mediterranean Sea could be first detected. Within the country, Bucharest and Ploiesti have point missile defenses.

Naval Forces

The naval organization includes headquarters, schools, a major base at Mangalia, a minor base at Constanta, and stations on the Danube River. Mangalia is a Black Sea port about twenty-five miles south of Constanta and just north of the Bulgarian border. Naval personnel in 1972 numbered somewhat fewer than 10,000. The force has almost 200 vessels, but they are an assortment of old and miscellaneous ships that have little capability outside their local environment. None of them is designed to operate more than a few miles from the coast line and definitely not beyond the Black Sea.

Ships include minesweepers, escort vessels, patrol and torpedo boats, and a large assortment of small miscellaneous craft. Five of the patrol boats are of the modern Soviet Osa class and carry a short-range surface-to-surface missile. A few of the torpedo boats are fast, although they are not the latest models. Minesweepers have limited offshore capability but, if protected, could clear the Danube River and essential parts of its delta.

Frontier Troops

Borders with Bulgaria and Yugoslavia have defenses and are guarded, and there is some effort to patrol the Black Sea coastline. Borders with the Soviet Union and Hungary are not controlled except at highway and rail crossing points. Because the Danube River forms the greater share of the controlled borders, much of the patrolling is done by boat.

During the 1950s and early 1960s frontier or border troops were subordinate to the Ministry of Internal Affairs and were difficult to distinguish, except in their deployment, from that ministry's security troops. During the latter part of the 1960s authority over the border forces passed to the Ministry of the Armed Forces, but the move was apparently accomplished over a period of time, and the decree formalizing the transfer was not published until September 1971. The commander of the frontier troops is one of the major operational commanders under the minister of the armed forces and is on a level with the chiefs of the military regions, the air and air defense force, and naval forces.

Regulations defining border areas to be controlled and describing the authority of the forces were amended in late 1969. The border strip is a prohibited area, which is fenced in some places and often patrolled. On level, dry ground, it is sixty-five-feet wide but, where the borderline crosses marshy or rugged terrain, it may be widened enough to afford the troops easier access and control.

A border zone varies in width but extends into the country from the strip and includes towns and communes. Frontier troops have overall control within the zone. They are instructed not to interfere more than necessary with usual human activities in it and to cooperate with the local police, whom they do not supplant. Although they are paramount in the zone, they are not restricted to it and may work fifteen or twenty miles into the interior if necessary.

Troops are charged with controlling people, goods, and communications at the border and preventing unauthorized passage and smuggling. The major port city of Constanta, on the Black Sea coast, is listed as an exception to most of the border control regulations. Its city territory does not have a border strip, nor is it within a border zone. The regulation is presumably intended to facilitate port and shipping operations and to keep the more stringent controls inland from the port so that they do not interfere with international trade or tourist traffic.

217

FOREIGN MILITARY RELATIONS

Romania is a member of the Warsaw Pact, having joined when the pact was created in 1955. It also has bilateral treaties of friendship, cooperation, and mutual assistance with each of the other pact nations. Since each pact member has signed one of these treaties with all other members, all are bound to come to the assistance of any other that is attacked. In practical terms all are bound to the defense of any pact member in any conflict in which it might become involved since, no matter how it started, the other country would be branded the aggressor.

Pact members commit a substantial portion, or all, of their fully trained and equipped units to the pact's use. Committed units are considered to be part of an integral force. Romanian forces have a role in pact plans but, because they have failed to participate in several recent pact maneuvers, Western observers have expressed doubt that the organization would depend upon effective Romanian cooperation during the first phase of a major conflict or for any participation in an action such as the Czechoslovak invasion of 1968.

At the time of the pact's inception, leaders of the various member states were preoccupied with the security of their countries and their regimes. A threat from the new North Atlantic Treaty Organization (NATO) was real to them, as was danger from dissident elements within their own borders. It is doubtful whether in 1955 any one of the leadership groups seriously considered that its regime might—by itself or in deference to the wishes of its people—undertake economic or social practices or deviate from the ideology in ways that could be considered dangerous to the solidarity of the alliance. By 1965, however, Romania had embarked upon an independent course, to the extent that it, like Czechoslovakia, had reason to fear that it could be the object of retaliatory pact action.

In his Bucharest Declaration of July 1966, Nicolae Ceausescu—who at that time was head of the party but had not yet taken over as chief of state—announced that he considered the Warsaw Pact a temporary alliance and that it would lose its validity if NATO were to cease functioning. Then, in 1968, Romania openly supported the Czechoslovak government, denounced the pact's invasion of that country, and did not participate in it. Since that time Romania has not permitted other Warsaw Pact forces either to hold exercises on its soil or to cross it for maneuvers in another country. As a result, Bulgaria can send forces to other Eastern European countries only by air or by way of the Black Sea and the Soviet Union. Pact exercises held in Bulgaria during the summer of 1971 were performed by Bulgarian troops; other countries, including Romania, sent observers.

In addition to holding its military relations with the Warsaw Pact to a minimum, Romania's armed forces have attempted to make contacts with the military establishments in other countries. A military delegation visited Yugoslavia in 1971, and feelers have been put out to arrange other such conferences. A ranking military spokesman has stated that the army was developing friendly relations with its counterparts in all the countries of the socialist system in Europe, Asia, and Latin America. He added that Romania is increasing its relations of cooperation and collaboration with the nonsocialist states, as a contribution to the development of mutual trust.

MANPOWER, TRAINING, AND SUPPORT

Manpower

There are approximately 4.86 million men in the military age group, that is, the male population between the ages of eighteen and forty-nine. About 3.4 million—70 percent—are considered physically and otherwise fit for military service (see ch. 3).

A somewhat larger percentage, however, of the 180,000 young men who reach the draft age annually are physically able to serve. The preponderance of armed forces and most security troop personnel are acquired during the annual draft calls. Because of the short duty tours required of conscripts, it was necessary in 1971 to call up most of the eligible group in order to maintain the forces' strengths.

Men released from active duty, whether they served voluntarily or involuntarily, remain subject to recall until the age of fifty. Although nearly 100,000 men have been released from the services each year since about 1950, only a small portion of them are considered trained reserves. Only those recently discharged could be mobilized quickly and go into action without extensive retraining. There is insufficient emphasis on periodic reserve training to keep many of the older men in satisfactory physical condition or up to date on new weapons and tactics.

Young men of draft age are potentially good soldier material. There is almost no illiteracy within the adult population under fifty–five years of age. A large percentage of conscripts have rural, village, or small city backgrounds and are in better physical condition than the average urban youth. On the minus side, because the country has a low standard of living, conscripts have little familiarity with mechanical and electronic equipment.

Based on the numbers of males in lower age groups, the size of the annual military manpower pool will remain at about 1971 levels throughout the 1970s. It will then drop by nearly 25 percent during the first half of the 1980s but will rise sharply—and again temporarily—in the latter half of that decade. With the exception of the high and low periods during the 1980s, governmental population experts expect little overall change in available manpower during the remainder of the century.

Training

Since about the mid-1960s little public attention has been focused on the armed forces. Their capabilities, reliability, and preparedness have been taken for granted or have not been the subject of undue concern. Unit training and small exercises have been given little coverage in local media. Training programs, however, are dictated in large degree by organization and equipment and have changed little since 1960.

With the standardization of units, weapons, and tactics accompanying the formation of the Warsaw Pact, training was accomplished in Romania as directed in translated Soviet manuals. In the Warsaw Pact system the training cycle starts when a conscript arrives at his duty organization for individual training. This includes strenuous physical conditioning, basic instruction in drill, care and use of personal weapons, and schooling in a variety of subjects ranging from basic military skills and tactics to political indoctrination.

Individual training develops into small group instruction, usually around the weapon or equipment the individual will be using. As groups became more proficient with their equipment, they use it in exercises with larger tactical units under increasingly realistic conditions. Romanian forces have not participated since the late 1960s in the Warsaw Pact exercises that are usually held at the conclusion of the training cycle.

During early individual training, men are selected for a variety of special schools. Short courses, in cooking and baking or shoe repairing, from which a man emerges ready to work, do not require volunteers and do not extend the mandatory duty tour. Longer courses may involve schooling for most of the conscript tour or require time on the job after the school is completed to develop a fully useful capability, leaving no time for the newly acquired skill to be of value to the service. In such cases, selections to a school are made from volunteers who are willing to extend their period of active duty.

The most capable and cooperative conscripts are offered the opportunity to attend noncommissioned officer schools. They must accept voluntarily and agree to a longer period of service.

Frontier troops receive much the same individual training as ground force conscripts. Their later instruction involves less large-unit tactics and more police training and special subjects dealing with order documents and regulations. Larger percentages of naval and air forces personnel are required in mechanical or electronic work. Most of those who attend technical schools are required to serve for two years.

Reserve training receives little publicity and probably has low priority. A few reserves are sometimes called to active outfits for short refresher training, but there is little, if any, formal reserve training in local all-reserve types of units. The militia (a paramilitary organization subordinate to the Ministry of Internal Affairs) would probably be drawn upon to augment the services in an emergency. It could be expected to provide better trained personnel, in better physical condition, than would be acquired calling up untrained reserves (see ch. 12).

The General Military Academy in Bucharest—usually called the Military Academy—is a four-year university-level school whose graduates receive regular officer commissions and who are expected to serve as career officers. It also offers mid-career command and staff types of courses. An advanced academy, the Military Technical Academy, requires that its applicants have a university degree; they may be military officers, but they are not required to have had military service or military education of any sort. The academy offers advanced degrees in military and aeronautical engineering and in a variety of other technical areas.

Morale and Conditions of Service

The mandatory tour of duty for basic ground and air force personnel was set at sixteen months in 1964. Naval conscripts and some air force personnel are required to serve two years. The length of extra service required of those who apply and are accepted for special training or who wish to become noncommissioned officers varies with the amount of training required, with the rank attained, or with the added responsibility of the new duty assignment; but it is accepted or rejected on a voluntary basis.

Officers and noncommissioned officers serve voluntarily, and morale is usually satisfactory within those groups. The service experience of the noncommissioned-officer applicants and the long training period required of officer candidates assure that both leadership groups understand and freely accept the conditions of service before they assume their duty responsibilities.

Conditions are reasonably good, and morale in the armed forces is not a source of unusual concern to the national leadership. There are few exhortations to put extra effort into political indoctrination; a large, heavily armed security force to counter a possibly unreliable army has not been created; and there are less elaborate ceremonial affairs involving the forces than is typical of the Eastern European countries.

Romania has had compulsory military service at all times within the memory of the draft age group, and it is accepted as a routine fact of life. Exemptions from the draft are few, and a large proportion of them reflect upon the man because he cannot meet the qualifications for service. The tour of duty is brief. The standard of living in the country is low, and service life may offer some of the back-country young men the best opportunities for travel and excitement that they have yet experienced.

Medicine

Physicians required in the armed forces are ordinarily recruited from medical schools but may be called from their practices or from hospital residence assignments. They then attend a military medical institute in Bucharest for specialized instruction in procedures and practices that are peculiar to military medical work.

Emergency treatment is given military personnel in the most convenient facility, whether or not it is a military clinic. The same is true for the civilian population. Inasmuch as military facilities are equipped to cope with wartime casualties, they are often better able to deal with emergencies or disasters than nonmilitary hospitals, although they are seldom kept at wartime strengths during peacetime. They were especially commended for their assistance during the great floods that occurred in the spring of 1970.

Military Justice

The national penal code enacted in 1968 applies both to military personnel and to the public at large. A special section of the code, however, deals with military crimes. These are crimes committed by military personnel or by nonmilitary personnel on military installations or infractions of military regulations. In theory, any court may pass judgment on a military crime, but the military court system employs specialists in military law who are better able to understand the seriousness of crimes committed in relation to the military establishment. Military courts seldom surrender cases over which they have jurisdiction to civil courts.

There are two types of military courts: military tribunals and territorial military tribunals. The former are the lesser of the two and are established at major installations or are attached to large tactical units. They are the courts of first instance in all cases that come before them. The chairman, or judge, must be a major or higher ranking officer and have a degree in law. The judge is assisted by two people's assessors who, on military courts, are active duty officers. People's assessors need have no legal training but, as is the case for civil courts, they must be twenty-three years of age, have been graduated from secondary school, have a good reputation, and have no criminal record. In all military trials the judge and people's assessors must hold the same rank as, or higher than, the accused.

The higher territorial military tribunals are the courts of first instance for very serious crimes or the courts to which sentences of lower courts are appealed. In cases in which they are the courts of first instance, the court panel consists of at least two judges and three people's assessors. When they are hearing an appealed case, the panel has a minimum of three judges.

The Supreme Court of the land has final appeal jurisdiction over any case it may decide to hear, and it may review any case it chooses or that is sent to it by higher governmental agencies. It has a special military section that is headed by an officer of major general or higher rank. It may be the court of first instance for cases involving the most serious crimes or in lesser situations when an important legal precedent may be established.

Logistics

Military leaders state that their forces have adequate quantities of excellent and modern equipment. As is the situation with all other Warsaw Pact countries, Romania has received its heavy weapons and more complex equipment from the Soviet Union. Initially the Soviets distributed surplus World War II stocks. As these wore out or became obsolete, nearly all items were eventually replaced by postwar models. More complex and expensive weapons sometimes were used by Soviet forces first and appeared in Eastern Europe only after they had been replaced in the Soviet Union. In most circumstances, whether they were newly manufactured or secondhand, items have been supplied to other forces considerably after they were first issued to Soviet troops.

Equipment that is in short supply has not been distributed to each of the pact allies on an equal priority basis. Distribution has depended upon the strategic importance of the recipient, capability for maintaining and using the equipment effectively, and probable reliability as an alliance partner. Romania is located where it would not be involved in first contacts with any potential enemy of the pact; its conscripts' tour, and the resulting time to train individual soldiers, is short; it is an underdeveloped country; and it has been probing for ways to assert its independence from Moscow. It has not therefore been the first to receive newer equipment. The distribution of tanks is illustrative. Romania has received adequate numbers to equip its combat units and has received all models that have been distributed among the pact allies. Romania, however, has been authorized a smaller ratio of armored, as compared with motorized-rifle, divisions than is average for pact members. Poland and Czechoslovakia have many more tanks, and larger percentages of them are modern.

Ground forces have Soviet-made artillery, antitank guns and antitank wire-guided missiles, and some short-range surface-to-surface missiles. Weapons manufactured locally for the ground forces include all types of hand-carried weapons, antitank and antipersonnel grenade launchers, and mortars. Ammunition and explosives for most weapons, whether or not the weapon is locally produced, are manufactured in the country, as are common varieties of communication equipment and spare parts.

All of the air forces' combat aircraft and nearly all of its training and miscellaneous types are received from the Soviet Union. Romania produces some small utility models. A new one, designed for spraying forests and crops, was introduced in 1970 and can be used for military liaison.

Approximately the same situation exists with regard to naval vessels. The larger vessels and more complex smaller craft are built in the Soviet Union or by other members of the pact. Romania produces river craft and some smaller types, probably including the inshore minesweepers that operate in the Black Sea.

Romania is attempting to reduce its dependence upon the Warsaw Pact by producing more military matériel within the country. The armed forces maintain the Military Achievements Exhibit, designed to show progress in local production capability. The exhibit is visited periodically by important party and government personalities. Much is made of these visits, attempting to show all possible encouragement to the various projects.

Ranks, Uniforms, and Decorations

Ranks conform to those in armies worldwide with a few minor exceptions. There are the usual four general officer ranks. Field grades are conventional and have the three most frequently used titles—major, lieutenant colonel, and colonel. Company grade ranks include captain and three lieutenant ranks. There are no warrant officers.

Enlisted ranks also have familiar titles when translated. Basic soldiers hold the ranks of private and private first class. Conscripts serve their entire tours as privates unless they acquire a speciality or are put in charge of a small group. Corporal is the lowest noncommissioned-officer rank. Senior noncommissioned-officer grades include the ordinarily used sergeant ranks, including one (and possibly more) that is seldom seen but is equivalent to sergeant major or senior master sergeant.

Rank insignia tends to be ornate. All uniforms except the work and combat types display it on shoulderboards. Those of general officers have intricate gold designs with large gold stars. Other officer ranks have smaller stars clustered at the outer ends and stripes running the length of the boards. Stripes and borders on any one board are the same color, but the various service branches have different colors to identify them. For example, armored troops have black; frontier troops have light green.

Enlisted men's shoulderboards have no borders, and the background color, like the stripes and borders of the officers', indicates the service branch. Rank is shown by stripes that run across the outer end of the board. Privates have no stripes, corporals and privates first class have yellow stripes, and sergeants have brass. Other devices that also identify the service branch appear on the inward end of the shoulderboard on all ranks except those of the general officers and privates.

Cap insignia is more easily distinguished than that on the shoulderboard. Enlisted men wear a large brass star. General officers wear a star with a round blue center and red points mounted on an ornate round background. Other officers wear the red and blue star but without background.

There is less variety in uniforms than is common in Western and most of the other Warsaw Pact forces. Other than for extreme weather and rough work, enlisted men have one type of uniform for winter and one for summer. Material for winter wear is olive-green wool; for summer it is cotton and may be olive green or khaki.

Officers have a field or service uniform, which is similar to the enlisted men's, and a blue uniform for dress. The dress blouse has no belt, and shoes are low cut. The service uniform blouse is sometimes worn with a Sam Browne belt. Overcoats, except for buttons and insignia, are plain and conventional.

Service and dress uniforms are generally well tailored and made from durable materials. Cloth in the officers' uniforms is more closely woven and of finer texture; that in enlisted men's uniforms is warmer and more durable, but it is bulkier and does not hold its shape as well. Combat and extreme-weather clothing is heavy and loose fitting, reminiscent of the Soviet World War II winter wear.

A variety of decorations may be awarded to service personnel; a number of them may be given in three classes, and at least one of them is given in five. About a dozen have been authorized by the communist regime since 1948. Romanians may wear on their uniforms medals awarded by other Warsaw Pact countries but not those of any other foreign country.

The highest decoration is the Hero of Socialist Labor—Golden Medal, Hammer and Sickle. This is considered a dual award, although the parts are always awarded together, and the medal itself is a single one. Other awards that may be given to both military personnel and civilians include the Order of the Star, Order of Labor, and a medal commemorating "Forty Years Since the Founding of the Communist Party of Romania." The third one of the group is given those who were active in the Communist Party between 1921 and 1961 or those who did party work between the two world wars or during the early days of the country's communist regime.

Decorations designed exclusively for the armed forces include the Order of Defense of the Fatherland, the Medal of Military Valor, and the Order of Military Merit. Others recognize service during specific events, such as the Liberation from the Fascist Yoke medal and the Order of 23 August, both of which commemorate World War II service against Germany.

Despite the number of decorations authorized and the many classes provided for in several of them, medals are awarded less profusely in Romania's forces than in many armies, especially those that are made up largely of conscripts or that serve in a largely internal security role. Ceremonies that occur most often involve awards from foreign delegations at the conclusion of their visits to the country or the retirement of older, senior-ranking officers.

THE MILITARY ESTABLISHMENT AND THE NATIONAL ECONOMY

Although the labor force is smaller than the national leadership considers adequate, almost all physically fit young men are conscripted. Only a few, those who are essential to the support of a family or who have other exceptional circumstances, are deferred or exempted. On the other hand, the approximately 4 percent of men in the military age group that serve in Romania's armed forces is about the European average and is lower than average for the Warsaw Pact nations.

Some Romanian officials have suggested that the burden on the economy may be greater than that indicated by a comparison of national statistics arguing that, because labor productivity is low, the loss of 4 percent of the labor force may diminish total production. On the other hand, some Western analysts have argued that, because most of the conscripts are unskilled and underemployed, the military's drain on the manpower pool entails no great loss to productive enterprise (see ch. 14).

In monetary terms the armed forces have been somewhat less of a burden. Between 1967 and 1970 their costs averaged approximately 3.1 percent of the gross national product (GNP), which is low when compared either with the average for Europe or with the average of the other Warsaw Pact members. Beginning in 1970, however, in an effort to reduce dependence upon the Soviet Union, Romania began to stimulate local production of military matériel and to purchase some items from other countries. This resulted in a sharp increase in defense spending in 1970. Unless the size of the armed forces is reduced, some continuing increase in expenses over pre-1970 levels will be necessary if Romania chooses to continue its policy of nondependence upon the Soviet Union.

The armed forces engage in construction projects on a scale that local leaders say is an important contribution to the economy. They are employed in industrial construction, roadbuilding, railroad maintenance, and important agricultural and irrigation projects. Large numbers of troops participated in the disaster relief efforts made necessary by the great floods during the spring of 1970.

SECTION IV. ECONOMIC

CHAPTER 14

CHARACTER AND STRUCTURE OF THE ECONOMY

In 1972 Romania entered the second year of a five-year economic plan that is intended by the leadership to advance the country on the road to industrialization and to increase its economic potential sufficiently to make the economy one of the most dynamic in the world. This goal is to be attained mainly through a continued high rate of investment, a significant improvement in productivity, and an expanded and more efficient foreign trade. Although significant strides in industrial development had been made in the past, this achievement entailed a neglect of agriculture, an indequate provision for consumer needs, and a balance of payments deficit with Western industrial nations that threatened to undermine the leadership's policy of political and economic independence from the Soviet Union (see ch. 10).

Rigidly controlled by the PCR (see Glossary), the economy suffers from the basic weakness common to all centrally controlled economies, that is, a lack of adequate incentives for managers and workers. Rapid industrialization since 1950, made possible by massive inputs of capital and labor and aided by heavy imports of advanced Western industrial plants and technology, has involved a waste of resources on a scale that may hamper economic progress at the present stage of development. In trying to evolve a system of incentives that would lead to a more economic use of resources, the PCR is facing a dilemma. Greater efficiency requires more flexibility, which, in turn, implies a greater freedom of initiative at lower economic levels than the PCR has been prepared to grant thus far. In the search for a solution numerous administrative changes have been made since 1968 without basically altering the nature of the system.

A major problem facing the economy is its heavy dependence on imports of raw materials and equipment and the failure, thus far, to develop a sufficient volume of exports salable in world markets. At the present stage of development, Romanian industrial products compete poorly with the output of advanced Western nations. Expansion of agricultural exports, which have a ready market in many areas, has been hampered by the slow development of the country's agricultural potential and by a growing domestic demand. Although greater attention is to be devoted to agriculture under the current Five-Year Plan (1971–75), the additional resources to be allocated to this sector are not commensurate with the magnitude of its needs. Instead, major emphasis is placed in the five-year period on the development of the chemical, electronic, and precision tool industries for domestic needs and export.

The state of the economy in the early 1970s was revealed by two Romanian economists in articles evaluating their country's economic progress. According to their calculations, the per capita national income in Romania in 1975, provided that the economic targets for that year are reached, will approach the level attained by Italy and Austria in 1968 and will be somewhat larger than half that in France and the Federal Republic of Germany (West Germany) in the same year. At the same time they estimated that, even with continued acceleration of the rates of industrial modernization and growth of labor productivity, it will require several more five-year periods to reach the 1971 economic level of the more developed nations.

ORGANIZATION

The economy is highly socialized. The state owns virtually all industry and shares with collective farms ownership of more than nine-tenths of the farmland. Private artisan shops contribute only a fraction of 1 percent to the industrial output, and private farmers' limited holdings are confined mainly to marginal lands. The state owns all natural resources other than the collective and private farmlands; maintains complete control over the country's physical resources, finances, and labor; and has a monopoly of foreign trade and foreign exchange. The functioning of the economy is directed by comprehensive long-term and annual state plans, which are binding for all economic entities.

Control over the economy is strongly centralized, despite half-hearted attempts since 1968 to grant more freedom of initiative to lower management levels in the interest of greater flexibility and efficiency. Supreme decisionmaking power rests with the Standing Presidium of the PCR and the Council of State, the memberships of which are almost identical (see ch. 9). Compliance with PCR decisions is enforced through an administrative hierarchy that consists of three distinct levels: the Council of Ministers, all of whose members hold high positions in the PCR;

economic ministries, which are responsible for specific sectors of the economy; and trusts and combines, which group enterprises along functional or territorial lines. Specialized committees with ministerial rank administer certain aspects of economic activity; chief among these are the State Planning Committee and the Committee for Prices (see ch. 8).

The organizational structure of the economy has undergone frequent changes in efforts to resolve economic problems by administrative means. Officially, the reorganizations have been declared necessary to keep economic management abreast of the requirements of socialist economic development. The frequency of the changes, however, and a lack of clarity in many of the directives have brought about a blurring of jurisdictional lines with consequent overlapping of functions and conflicts of authority. The organizational problem has been compounded by the contradictory nature of the motives that have prompted the reforms—to grant more discretionary power to enterprise managers and, at the same time, to strengthen central controls by enhancing the directing role of the compulsory economic plans. In 1971 economic officials considered important aspects of the economic organization to be still in an experimental stage.

STRUCTURE AND GROWTH

Data on gross output and national income in absolute terms have not been published. Official statistics on these social accounts have been limited to a few index series for overall, productive sector, and per capita values and a percentage breakdown of gross output and national income by productive sector. The arbitrary nature of the pricing system and differences in statistical treatment compared to Western practice preclude a direct comparison of the published growth rates of the economy and its components with similar rates in Western countries. The same holds true for comparisons of economic structure. Independent studies of the economy by Western scholars in Western statistical terms yielded significantly lower rates of growth and a different structure of economic activities from those officially announced.

According to official data, national income (net material product, which excludes private and government services not directly related to production) more than doubled between 1960 and 1970, and industrial output more than tripled. Agricultural production, by contrast, increased by less than one-third. The rates of economic and industrial growth, even when translated into Western terms, have been relatively high and among the highest in countries of Eastern Europe. Such high growth rates have usually been associated with early stages of industrial development. The high growth rates were made possible by an official policy that allocated more than 30 percent of national income to investment. Growth rates in the 1966–70 period were somewhat lower than in the preceding five years, with the exception of agriculture, the performance of which was slightly better.

The predominant growth of industry has been a direct consequence of the leadership's policy. This policy was reflected in a disproportionately large allocation of investment to industry at the expense of other economic sectors. In the 1966–70 period, for instance, industry received 55 percent of total investment—60 percent if the construction industry is included—compared to less than 13 percent granted to agriculture.

Within industry preponderant emphasis has been placed on the development of the capital goods sector at the expense of consumer goods. Whereas total industrial output increased at an average annual rate of 11.8 percent from 1966 to 1970, production of capital goods rose at a rate of 12.7 percent, and production of consumer goods grew by only 9.5 percent annually.

As a consequence of the uneven sectoral growth, the structure of the economy changed significantly between 1960 and 1970. According to official data the contribution of industry to the net material product rose from 44 to 61 percent, whereas that of agriculture declined from 33 to 20 percent (see table 4). The relative importance of construction and transport rose slightly, but that of trade declined by half. A strikingly different struc-

Table 4. National Income (Net Material Product) of Romania, by Economic Sector, 1960, 1967, and 1970
(in percent)

Economic Sector	1960	1967	1970
Industry and handicrafts	44.1	51.7	60.8
Construction	9.0	8.4	9.6
Agriculture	33.1	28.6	20.0
Transport and communications	3.8	4.2	4.2
Trade	6.5	4.6	3.2
Other sectors	3.5	2.5	2.2
Total	100.0	100.0	100.0

Source: Adapted from *Anuarul Statistic al Republicii Socialiste Romania, 1970* (Statistical Yearbook of the Socialist Republic of Romania, 1970), Bucharest, 1970; and U.S. Department of Commerce, Office of Technical Services, Joint Publications Research Service—JPRS Series (Washington), *Translations on Eastern Europe: Economic and Scientific Affairs*, "Development of National Income Discussed," *Probleme Economice*, Bucharest, April 1971, (JPRS 53,521, Series No. 491, 1971).

ture of the economy emerges in terms of the Western concept of gross national product (GNP), which includes housing and services and treats both taxes and subsidies in a different manner. The contribution of industry was less than that of agriculture in 1960, but by 1967 it had increased more rapidly than is indicated by the official data (see table 5). The role of agriculture, on the other hand, declined more rapidly.

Published labor statistics leave many serious gaps, and unofficially reported data do not always agree with official figures in the annual statistical yearbooks. Information released on the size of the economically active population is limited to percentage changes over the years.

The economically active population increased by only 3.5 percent from 1960 to 1967 and remained stationary thereafter to 1969. During the ten-year period the number of persons active in industry increased by half, whereas the number of those engaged in agriculture declined by 19 percent. Nevertheless, in 1970 about half the population was still engaged in agriculture, and only 22 percent were active in industry.

Although there is no officially recognized unemployment, a substantial amount of underemployment is reported to exist in industry and, even more so, in agriculture. The reasons advanced by Romanian economists for this situation are the duty and the right of every citizen to work and the inability to achieve quickly full and efficient employment in a country that inherited a backward and predominantly agrarian economy with a large peasant population. Efforts toward obtaining full and efficient employment have been handicapped by the rapidly rising volume of investment needed to create new nonagri-

Table 5. *Gross National Product of Romania, by Sector of Origin, 1960 and 1967*
(in percent)

Economic Sector	1960	1967
Industry and handicrafts	24.4	32.9
Agriculture and forestry	31.8	22.0
Construction	7.6	11.1
Transport and communications	7.6	8.8
Trade	6.5	5.4
Housing	9.2	7.0
Government and other services	12.9	12.8
Total	100.0	100.0

Source: Adapted from U.S. Congress, 91st, 2d Session, Joint Economic Committee, *Economic Developments in Countries of Eastern Europe*, Washington, GPO, 1970.

cultural jobs. The average investment per nonagricultural job increased almost fivefold to 324,000 lei (for value of leu, see Glossary) from the 1951–55 period to the 1966–70 period, and a further 40 percent rise in cost was projected for the 1971–75 period.

PLANNING

As in all communist states, comprehensive economic planning has been a basic element of the PCR's dogma. Planning is conceived of as an indispensable tool for economic development. Traditionally, five-year and annual plans for all segments and aspects of the economy have been formulated by a central planning agency with the participation of economic ministries, trusts, and enterprises. Planning has proceeded from broadly defined goals set by the PCR to minute instructions for all economic enterprises. In line with the established priorities, the main planning effort has been devoted to industry.

The major problem in planning has been posed by the need to balance supply and demand, not only with regard to the final consumers but also at all stages of the production process and for each individual enterprise. This task entails detailed decisions on the allocation of thousands of different materials, machinery and equipment items, specialized labor skills, energy, and investment funds. With the expansion and growing complexity of the economy and, more particularly, of industry, the balancing task has assumed dimensions that defy solution by traditional means.

At the same time, the imposition of detailed operational prescriptions deprived enterprises of the freedom to exercise constructive initiative and of the flexibility needed to meet unforeseen contingencies. A failure by an enterprise to fulfill its planned assignment necessarily produces a chain reaction involving the production programs of enterprises dependent upon the missing output. Failures of this nature have been frequent.

The breakdown of the planning mechanism brought about a disorganization of the material and technical supply for enterprises, with adverse effects on productivity and output. It has been responsible for a general lag in the economy's performance in relation to official plans.

The deficiency of the traditional system of central planning was officially recognized in 1967, when a decision was made by the National Party Conference to raise the quality of planning to the level demanded by the needs of a modern industrial state. This aim was to be achieved by granting a larger degree

234

of autonomy to individual enterprises while, at the same time, maintaining and even strengthening the directing role of the central plan. The prolonged and intensive discussion engendered by the PCR decision has brought to light many flaws and proposals for change but has not provided a clear insight into the current planning process.

Modifications of the traditional pattern have taken place as a result of organizational and administrative changes introduced after 1967. The intended adoption of a new system, however, that would take into account market relationships and give greater weight to the needs of consumers has been delayed by differences of views among economists and officials on essential elements of the system, by disagreement on the nature of such basic concepts as productivity, economic efficiency, and profit, and by the need for a prior reform of the price system. A draft of a new planning law was reported to be in preparation toward the end of 1971.

As a means of decentralizing planning and mastering the intractable supply problem, the task of coordinating requirements with supplies was delegated to the centrals (see Glossary), trusts, and other enterprise associations and, ultimately, to the enterprises themselves by a law on economic contracts enacted in December 1969. Under the law, industrial and trade enterprises must enter into contracts with suppliers for all products and services needed to fulfill the tasks of the next year's economic plan. In theory, the demands of final consumers for consumption and capital goods would determine the nature of the contracts through all stages of production down to the producers of raw materials. This has not been the case in practice.

Most contracts must be concluded at least six months before the beginning of the plan year because they are supposed to serve as the basis for developing the final version of the annual plan; they must take into account the economic tasks set for that year by the five-year plan. The central planning authorities formulate the ultimate annual plan by modifying individual contracts, where deemed necessary, in the light of official policies and anticipated availabilities of materials and other inputs. Correction of original contracts was reported to be essential because enterprises tended to exaggerate their true requirements as determined by official norms and standards. In 1970 initial orders exceeded available resources of materials by from 20 to 200 percent.

In 1970 and 1971 a large number of interenterprise contracts were not concluded on time and, despite legal provisions for financial and other sanctions, thousands of contracts were not adhered to. This entailed a disruption of supplies and production, nonfulfillment of export obligations, and insufficient deliveries to the domestic market. In an attempt to cope with the supply problem, the Ministry of Technical-Material Supply and Control of the Management of Fixed Assets was created in September 1971—yet another example of trying to solve economic problems by administrative means.

The final stage in the planning process, as in the past, continues to be the assignment to each enterprise of specific tasks bearing on all aspects of its operations. These tasks, generally known as plan indicators, spell out in minute detail such items as the production and investment program, the size of the labor force and the wage bill, costs of production, and profits. They also specify norms for the use of all materials, equipment, and labor and set goals for raising productivity. In the case of large enterprises the number of indicators runs into the thousands. The indicators are also used to evaluate the performance of enterprises in relation to the plan. The entire process has been said to represent the application of democratic centralism to planning.

The number and type of indicators to be assigned to enterprises and their associations and the nature of the system of indicators best suited to stimulate greater efficiency and technological innovation have been subjects of wide-ranging and intensive debates. No clarification of the underlying issues, however, much less a consensus on appropriate measures to be undertaken, had emerged by early 1972. Officials have ascribed the lack of any significant progress in the planning reform to general inertia, organizational confusion, bureaucratic interests, and a reluctance on the part of many enterprise directors to assume the added measure of responsibility that is inherent in a greater freedom to exercise initiative. Most of the officials are aware, nevertheless, that the basic problem lies in the absence of adequate incentives. The reconciliation of an obligatory central plan with enterprise autonomy has thus far proved elusive.

Planning in the field of collective agriculture has also been highly centralized, at least through 1971, despite measures introduced at the end of 1970 to reduce the number of plan indicators for individual farms. Detailed instructions on crop and livestock production and on the volume of farm products to be delivered to the state have been handed down to farms by higher authorities insufficiently familiar with their natural and economic conditions. This method of planning has entailed

236

significant losses through improper use of land and other resources. The relatively minor relaxation of central controls beginning in 1971 was intended to eliminate this waste. The extent to which central controls over farming operations were retained even after the announced decentralization of agricultural planning was illustrated by the Grand National Assembly's enactment of a law toward the end of 1971 concerning correct methods of producing and using livestock fodder. Information on the method of planning for state farms was not available.

PRICE SYSTEM

As in all centrally directed economies, prices are set by the government. In 1967 the National Party Conference called for a reform of the price system on the grounds that the prevailing prices failed to ensure the desired balance in economic development or to promote greater efficiency in production and foreign trade. After four years of intensive debate, a new price law was enacted in December 1971. Preliminary information on the provisions of the law indicated that prices would continue to be fixed by the government, although the method of calculating them had been modified. In contrast to the announced policy of decentralizing economic management, the law provided for strengthening central controls over prices.

Until March 1970 there was no unified control over prices. The State Planning Committee and the Ministry of Finance administered industrial wholesale prices, and the State Committee for Prices had jurisdiction over prices of consumer goods and government procurement prices for farm products. In 1970 the reorganized State Committee for Prices was given authority to control all prices. Representation on the committee has been provided for the State Planning Committee; the ministries of finance, domestic trade, and foreign trade; the Central Statistical Bureau; and the Central Council of the General Union of Trade Unions. Participation by delegates from economic ministries and other organs is to be ensured at all sessions in which problems of interest to them are brought up for discussion.

The basic criticism leveled against the price system concerned its tendency to undermine the government's drive for economic efficiency through the failure of prices to reflect production costs, improper relationships among prices, and price inflexibility. A comprehensive, unified approach to price reform was considered beyond the capability of the authorities; a piecemeal approach of dealing separately with different types of prices was therefore decided upon. Priority in this program was given to the improvement of industrial wholesale prices.

Wholesale prices for industrial products have been based on average costs for each product in the relevant industrial branch. Prices have therefore been profitable for enterprises having below-average costs, whereas enterprises with costs above the average have had to rely upon state subsidies for continued operation. Wholesale prices were last fixed in 1963, and subsequent changes in technology and other aspects of production magnified the dissociation of prices and costs. For political reasons and because of general shortages the closing of uneconomic enterprises was not considered feasible. Maintenance of fixed prices over long periods of time has been deemed essential for purposes of planning.

Under the prevailing price system, which assured high profits to many enterprises and provided subsidies for unprofitable ones, there was no incentive for enterprises to reduce costs. This tendency was reinforced by the methods used to calculate costs and prices. The fact that cost calculations did not include any charges for rent or capital induced waste in the use of land and equipment. Prices included an element of planned profit determined as a pecentage of cost. In the price-setting procedure it was therefore advantageous for enterprises to overstate actual costs. This practice has been widely prevalent in fixing prices for new products.

Prices for raw materials, including products of the extractive industries and agriculture, were generally set below the cost of production. This policy has been responsible for a wasteful use of many materials in manufacturing. A price discrepancy also served to negate the official fuel policy. Efforts to increase the use of coal in electric power production were frustrated by the relatively much lower price for natural gas. This led some economists to advocate that prices for fuels be based on their caloric content. The price system has also been reported to have produced various other inimical results, such as inhibiting innovation and rewarding the continued production of obsolete goods.

Procurement prices for farm products have been deliberately kept low in relation to industrial prices; prices for farm requisites and consumer goods, on the other hand, have been fixed far above cost through the medium of a turnover tax channeled into the budget. In this manner the price system has served to transfer resources from agriculture to indistry and to keep consumption low for the benefit of investment.

Pending the completion of price reform legislation, a provisional measure was adopted in 1970 to lower wholesale prices for export goods and to reduce excess profits through a so-called regularization tax on domestic sales of the main products manufactured by state industry. The measure involved a recalculation of wholesale prices, based on the average cost of products within an industrial branch and a profit allowance of only 10 percent of cost. The difference between the recalculated prices and those in effect at the time was to be channeled into the budget by the tax. In the case of high-cost producers who would suffer losses under this procedure, the profit margin included in the price could be raised to a maximum of 15 percent. The new price measure put pressure on enterprises to lower the cost of production.

The comprehensive new law on prices for goods and services that will come into effect in March 1972 will have no immediate inpact on prices. On the basis of criteria outlined in the law and upon approval by the State Committee for Prices, economic ministries, central government agencies, collectives, and other public organizations are supposed first to issue norms for establishing and correlating prices within the areas of their respective jurisdictions, in accordance with the specific conditions of each producing branch, subbranch, or group of enterprises and the specific features of each product and service.

The law makes provision for fixed and ceiling prices. Both types of prices may be either uniform or differentiated. Uniform prices will apply throughout the entire country and will be applicable to the main products and to services of major importance to the economy and the standard of living. Differentiated prices for a product may be set at various levels depending upon territorial or seasonal factors and the nature of the producers or buyers. These provisions will also apply to agricultural procurement prices.

As in the past, uniform wholesale prices will be based on precalculated average costs for each product at branch level. For the first time, however, cost will also include taxes on capital and land (interest and rent) and expenditures for the introduction of new technology. An important change will also be made in determining the profit element of the wholesale price. In the future the planned profit level for enterprises, differentiated by branch and subbranch, will be calculated in relation to the fixed and circulating capital employed rather than in relation to cost.

The new law also contains provisions for pricing imports and exports and for establishing retail prices of consumer goods. Retail prices will include a profit for the trade organization and a variable turnover tax applied to the wholesale price. The tax is to be relatively low on goods produced for children and high on those manfactured in small quantities and on luxury products.

Changes in retail prices may be made only in the light of planned provisions for the real income of the population.

Authority to set prices and control over the implementation of price policy will be shifted from the Council of Ministers to the Council of State and the Grand National Assembly. The Council of State will make decisions not only concerning general price levels and price changes but also about specific prices for products and services of particular importance to the economy and the standard of living and on prices of products earmarked exclusively for the defense sector. In an effort to ensure a uniform price policy under a decentralized process of price fixing, the law spells out the responsibilities of all entities concerned with pricing, from the Council of State down to the individual enterprise. Jurisdiction over prices for products and services is to be allocated among the various sectors and levels of the economy, and the State Committee for Prices will be responsible for the correct application of the law.

In order to prevent further abuses in the formulation and changing of prices, a state price control inspectorate is to be created within the State Committee for Prices with power to supervise price control agencies in each county. Penalties for infractions of trade regulations have been increased to 2,000 lei, and persons guilty of price irregularities will be subject to prosecution under sections of the penal code on profiteering and fraud, which provide for imprisonment of from six months to seven years.

The intricacy of price formulation, the complexity of the price law (which contains 157 paragraphs), and disagreement among officials about the efficacy of some of the law's provisions suggest that the new measure may not be the final answer to the country's price problems. The determination of the authorities to retain firm control over prices and not to allow market forces to play any significant role in price determination, however, was made clear in a statement by the chairman of the State Committee for Prices to the effect that the building of socialism cannot be directed by transferring the leadership and decisionmaking to some self-regulating mechanism or to instruments that cannot be controlled.

BUDGET

The annual state budgets are more comprehensive than budgets in Western countries because they also cover economic activities that are the province of private enterprise in the West. Information on the manner in which budgets are formulated is not available, except that they are closely related to the annual economic plans and are prepared under the direction of the Ministry of Finance. Budgets must be approved by the Council of Ministers, the PCR, and the Grand National Assembly. The consolidated budget is divided into a central and a local budget; the local budget is roughly one-fifth the size of the central budget.

Official statistics on the budget are deficient in that only summary data are published on the major elements of revenue and expenditures and the source of one-third or more of the revenue is not disclosed. The published data show a small budgetary surplus each year, regardless of the vicissitudes of the economy and unforeseen emergency outlays. Information is not available on budgetary performance in 1970, when the country suffered a disastrous flood. In the planned budgets for 1971 and 1972 revenues and expenditures were perfectly balanced.

Budgetary revenues increased steadily from about 58 billion lei in 1960 to 147 billion lei in 1969, and expenditures rose correspondingly from about 55 billion lei to 143 billion lei. The budgets for 1971 and 1972 were planned to balance at a little more than 138 billion lei and 152 billion lei, respectively. Reasons for the decline in the size of the 1971 budget, the only decline reported in at least a decade, are not known.

A turnover tax levied on consumer goods, farm products, and farm supplies and a profit on the income of economic enterprises and organizations constitute the main sources of budgetary revenue. The relative importance of the two levies changed after 1966; the yield from the profit tax approached that from the turnover tax in 1967 and grew relatively larger in 1968 and 1969. Together, these two levies accounted for from 50 to 56 percent of the annual revenues. Direct taxes on the population yielded close to 6 percent from 1960 to 1969, except that in the first and last years of that period their proportion approached 7 percent. The magnitude of direct taxes does not reflect the real tax burden borne by the population, because the population ultimately pays both the turnover and the profit tax through higher prices of consumer goods.

Financing the national economy absorbed an average of 64.6 percent of annual expenditure in the first half of the 1960s and 68.3 percent in the second half of the decade. At the same time the proportion of outlays for social and cultural purposes declined from an average of 24.9 percent to 23.2 percent, although the absolute amount of these outlays more than doubled. Expenditures for defense declined from 6.1 percent of total outlays in 1960 to 4.4 percent in 1969.

BANKING

The banking system operative in early 1972 was the end product of several institutional reorganizations, the last of which was completed in May 1971. The main purpose of the reorganizations was to make bank credit a more effective tool for promoting economic development and for controlling the operations of economic enterprises and organizations. Control through credit extension has been officially considered an important means for inducing enterprises and trusts to attain the targets of the economic plans. Little information is available on the banks' operations beyond the formal statement of their functions. Data relating to the money supply and foreign exchange reserves have also been kept secret.

Banking Institutions

The banking system consists of the National Bank of the Romanian Socialist Republic (referred to as the National Bank), the Investment Bank, the Romanian Foreign Trade Bank, the Bank for Agriculture and the Food Industry, and the Savings and Loan Bank. The functions of the Romanian Foreign Trade Bank and of the Bank for Agriculture and the Food Industry had been exercised to a more limited extent by the National Bank until 1968. The Economy and Consignment Fund, a department of the Savings and Loan Bank, makes credit available for the construction of privately owned housing—a function exercised by the Investment Bank until the end of 1969. Information on the interrelations between the specialized banks and the National Bank or between the banks and the Ministry of Finance was not available in early 1972.

The National Bank, as reconstituted in December 1970 with a capitalization of 1 billion lei, is the country's central bank of issue, but it also acts as a banker for the government, a bankers' banker for the specialized financial institutions, and a short-term credit and discount agency for economic organizations. The main functions of the National Bank in the field of domestic finance include: the issue of currency and control over its circulation; management of the budgetary cash resources; coordination of all short-term credit and discount activities; and participation in the formulation of annual and five-year credit and cash plans, jointly with the State Planning Committee and the Ministry of Finance.

The National Bank establishes official foreign exchange rates, engages in foreign exchange operations directly or through the Romanian Foreign Trade Bank and other authorized organizations, and participates in working out the balance of foreign payments and in following up on its execution. The National Bank also controls the production, processing, and use of precious metals and gems and, together with the State Planning Committee and the Ministry of Finance, develops plans for their acquisition and allocation at home and abroad. The bank has exclusive authority to purchase from individuals items made of precious metals or stones and items of artistic, historic, or documentary value.

The National Bank is managed by an administrative council, the members of which must be approved by the Council of Ministers upon the recommendation of the bank's governor, who is also chairman of the administrative council. In addition to the chairman, the administrative council includes several vice presidents of the bank; the directors of the bank's fourteen divisions; superintendents of some of the subordinated units; delegates of the management of the Investment Bank, the Bank for Agriculture and the Food Industry, and the Romanian Foreign Trade Bank; experienced specialists from the bank's professional staff and from the outside; and a delegate of the labor unions, designated by the General Union of Trade Unions. The council as a whole and each individual member are responsible to the Council of Ministers for the entire activity of the bank.

The Investment Bank, created in 1948 and last reorganized in September 1971 with a capitalization of 700 million lei, serves to finance, and exercise control over, investment projects of all state, collective, consumer-cooperative, and other public organizations, with the exception of collective farms and organizations subordinate to the Ministry of Agriculture, Food Industry, and Waters. The control powers of the bank extend not only to projects financed with its own resources but also to projects financed through budgetary allocations and out of enterprise profits. The bank's management is organized along the lines of the administrative council of the National Bank.

The Investment Bank must participate in the preparation of draft plans for the financing of all investment projects undertaken by central and local state organizations from the ministerial down to the enterprise level. During the formulation and implementation of these plans the bank must ensure the most economical use of available resources. The bank is also called upon to determine appropriate rates of depreciation for fixed assets and to ensure that the required amortization payments to the budget are made on time.

Two of the bank's main functions are the review of technical and economic investment criteria submitted to it for approval by ministries and other state agencies and the evaluation of the feasibility of proposed investment projects on the basis of accepted standards; the more important of these standards also require approval by the Council of Ministers. Approval may be granted by the bank only for investment projects that satisfy all legal requirements regarding need, suitability, and adherence to prescribed norms; have an adequate raw materials base and assured sales outlets; and serve to improve the economic performance of the organization that undertakes the investment. In the event of disagreement between the bank and the organization seeking investment approval, appeal may be made to higher authorities.

The Romanian Foreign Trade Bank was established in July 1968. Its principal functions are to facilitate exports and, through strict controls over exchange allocations, to encourage import substitution by domestic producers. In 1970 about 73 percent of the bank's credits were devoted to exports, and only 21 percent were granted for imports. The remaining 6 percent of the credits were used to finance internal transport.

In July 1971 the Romanian Foreign Trade Bank and a group of eight French financial institutions opened the Romanian-French Bank in Paris. This bank was organized as a private limited-liability company with a capital of 20 million French francs underwritten in equal parts by the Romanian Foreign Trade Bank and the French bankers. In the second half of 1971 the Romanian Foreign Trade Bank acquired affiliates in London and Rome.

The Bank for Agriculture and the Food Industry was created in May 1971 by expanding the functions and changing the name of the Agricultural Bank established three years earlier. This reorganization followed the consolidation of previously independent ministries into the Ministry of Agriculture, Food Industry, and Waters (referred to as the Ministry of Agriculture). The bank was capitalized at 500 million lei and was required to create a reserve out of profits equal to the amount of its capitalization. The bank's function is to provide investment and operating credits for enterprises under the jurisdiction of the Ministry of Agriculture, including collective farms, and to finance the distribution of their products within the country.

A few summary data on credits extended by the Bank for Agriculture and the Food Industry to collective farms have been released to the country's press in an obvious effort to publicize official concern for this important but neglected farm sector (see ch. 15). Information on other aspects of this bank's operations have not been disclosed.

The Savings and Loan Bank, an institution nationalized at an early stage of communist rule, had 1,560 branches and agencies in 1971, most of which were located in rural areas. The main function of the bank has been to mobilize the cash resources of the population for investment, through obligatory periodic transfers of deposited funds to the National Bank. In the 1966–70 period subsidiary functions of the bank gained in importance, including small-scale commercial bank transactions, personal loans, and tax collections. Receipts from personal savings deposits accounted for 70 percent of total cash receipts in 1970. Since the beginning of 1970 the bank has also made loans for private housing construction.

The schedule of payments to the National Bank has been sufficiently stringent to induce the Savings and Loan Bank to mount special educational programs for attracting savings, particularly in rural areas, and to seek ways of stimulating cash collections from its other activities. To this end the bank is giving special attention to finding more effective means for identifying cash reserves held by the population. One avenue the bank has been exploring is to gain greater knowledge of the timing of income receipts and of the uses to which incomes are put.

The volume of savings has been steadily mounting; it rose at an average annual rate of more than 20 percent in the 1966–70 period and was 2.5 times larger at the period's end than at its beginning. In 1970, 13.6 percent of the population's cash income was deposited in savings accounts, compared to 5.8 percent in 1960. More than 65 percent of the population's cash assets in 1970 were on deposit in savings accounts, as against 56.6 percent five years earlier. Under the economic plan for the 1971–75 period, savings deposits of the Savings and Loan Bank are scheduled to increase by 87 percent—the equivalent of an annual 13.4 percent growth rate. An important reason for the growth of savings has been a general shortage of consumer goods.

Loans granted by the Savings and Loan Bank for private housing construction in 1970 amounted to 2.1 billion lei. In 1971 the bank planned to provide construction loans totaling 2.9 billion lei. Information on other bank transactions has not been published.

Credit Policy

Interest rates do not reflect the scarcity of money or the element of risk. They are used by the government as one of the economic levers intended to motivate enterprises toward greater efficiency. In 1969 the average rate for short-term operating credits was 2.9 percent; actual rates ranged from less than 1 percent to a level far above the average. New regulations issued about mid-1970 raised the interest rates, established greater uniformity among them, and introduced a differentiation among penalty rates based on the length of time that repayments remain in arrears or credits in excess of those planned are used. As a result of these measures, National Bank officials expected the average rate of interest to rise to 3.8 percent.

A uniform interest rate of 5 percent was established on all operating credits for inventory and production purposes in economic sectors other than agriculture. Preferential rates for artisans' collectives were abolished on the grounds that the collectives had received enough state support in the past to place them on an equal footing with state enterprises with regard to credit. A rate of 3 percent was continued on credits used in the distribution of goods. Interest rates of 4 percent and 2 percent, respectively, were established for state and collective farms.

The government attaches great importance to the penalty feature of the credit system, which allows it to discriminate between efficient enterprises that find themselves in temporary difficulties and enterprises that are poorly managed. Enterprises that require operating funds in excess of those prescribed by officially determined norms or are unable to repay credits on time must pay progressively higher interest rates. Excess and overdue credits carry an interest rate of up to 10 percent for the first three months and up to 12 percent for the next three months. Enterprises in the second stage are subject to a searching examination by a committee of experts and may be denied further credits. Information is lacking on the procedures followed in the case of enterprises that would be declared bankrupt in a Western economy.

According to a National Bank official, the new credit regulations were to be rigorously applied in order to combat a rising trend in the volume of overdue credits that became apparent in the first half of 1970. The credit and interest policies were to be applied in a manner that would protect the economy from the bad effects of mismanagement and that would place the onus only on poorly run enterprises. This task was said to demand a high level of competence from those called upon to resolve the difficult problems of the enterprises.

CURRENCY

The currency unit of the country is the leu (plural, lei), divided into 100 bani. It is nonconvertible and usable only within the country. The leu is officially defined to contain 148.112 milligrams of fine gold, so that 5.53 lei are equivalent to US$1. This basic rate of exchange became effective on December 23, 1971, in the wake of the agreement reached by the United States with other major Western trading nations to devalue the American dollar; before that date the rate was 6 lei per US$1. The basic rate is used in foreign trade accounting and is also applicable to nonresident accounts created by a transfer of foreign currencies into Romania.

A wide range of official noncommercial or tourist exchange rates is in effect for residents of other communist countries. These rates vary from about one-third to more than double the basic rate. Tourist rates for noncommunist country currencies embody a bonus of 189 percent over the basic rate, making 16 lei equivalent to US$1. In addition to the official exchange rates there are at least thirty-seven semiofficial rates resulting from seven multilateral trade and payments agreements with members of the Council for Mutual Economic Assistance (COMECON) and thirty bilateral agreements with other communist and noncommunist states.

The state has a monopoly of foreign exchange. Control over currency and foreign exchange is vested in the National Bank and administered by the bank jointly with the Ministry of Finance and the Romanian Foreign Trade Bank. All foreign exchange realized by state agencies from exports and other foreign operations must be surrendered to the Romanian Foreign Trade Bank, which also controls all exchange expenditures abroad.

Transferability of funds by private individuals is strictly limited. Only 15 to 30 percent of inheritances, royalties, pensions, and support payments derived from abroad may be used or retransferred; from 70 to 85 percent of the sums received must be surrendered at the tourist rate of exchange. Residents may send small amounts and get travel allocations to COMECON and some Western countries. Most currency transactions by individuals with residents in Western states are prohibited. Residents may not own foreign currencies or securities or have bank balances abroad without official permission, nor may they import or export Romanian banknotes. They are forbidden to own or trade in gold, to export jewelry and diamonds, and to engage in foreign merchandise trade.

Controls over financial transactions by state agencies in domestic currency and foreign exchange were tightened by a decree issued in September 1971. A companion decree also provided for much stricter border controls over foreign exchange, precious metals, and jewelry carried by individuals entering or leaving the country. Violations were more precisely defined, and penalties were substantially increased to discourage illegal traffic.

FOREIGN TRADE

Foreign trade is of crucial importance to the country's industrial development because imports must be relied upon for a large part of the requirements for materials and equipment.

Trade has been expanding at a rapid rate, and imports have been growing faster than exports. In a bid for economic and political independence from the Soviet Union, the country's leadership succeeded in reorienting a substantial portion of its trade toward the industrial nations of Western Europe during the mid-1960s (see ch. 10). After 1967, however, the inability to generate enough exports salable in Western markets to balance imports forced the country to turn increasingly to the Soviet Union and other Eastern European countries for its import needs.

Foreign trade is a state monopoly. Trade policy is established by the PCR and the government, and its implementation is the responsibility of the Ministry of Foreign Trade. Authority to engage in foreign trade operations has been partially decentralized by a law enacted in March 1971, although initial steps in this direction were taken under administrative regulations in the beginning of 1970. The main purpose of the law has been to raise the efficiency of foreign trade and to help expand exports. These ends are to be attained through greater exposure of domestic producers to international competition and by providing incentives for them to meet it. The law was also intended to create favorable conditions in the country for the establishment of industrial enterprises with foreign participation.

Before the adoption of the trade reform law, only specialized foreign trade enterprises directly subordinated to the Ministry of Foreign Trade were empowered to carry on trade activities. Producing enterprises were completely divorced from foreign buyers. They delivered their export goods to the foreign trade enterprises at domestic prices, without knowing to whom or at what price the goods were sold abroad. Imports were also obtainable only through foreign trade enterprises at domestic prices, regardless of their acquisition cost. Foreign trade losses were covered out of the state budget, and enterprises assumed no risk whatever in foreign trade transactions. Producing enterprises had no interest in marketing their output abroad or in making their products competitive in world markets; neither were they interested in using domestic substitutes to avoid the need for imports.

Under the new law authority to engage in foreign trade has been granted to some of the industrial ministries, trusts, and enterprises. Others must continue to trade through foreign trade enterprises. The delegation of authority has not involved a transfer of basic decisionmaking powers, and the continuance of central control is therefore assured. All trade must be conducted in accordance with binding state plans and guidelines issued by the minister of foreign trade. Every transaction requires approval by the Ministry of Foreign Trade in the form of an import or export

248

license. Central controls have also been retained over foreign exchange and over export and import prices. The main advantage of the new regulation lies in the opportunity it provides for producers to develop direct customer relations, thus enabling them to learn at first hand the preferences of buyers and the nature of the competition they must face. It also encourages them to exercise initiative in seeking out potential customers.

Under the law production for export must be given priority. Failure by economic units to discharge their export obligations adversely affects their profits, even if they meet their total output target, because in these circumstances the production plan is considered underfulfilled by the value of the undelivered exports. This provision applies equally to suppliers and subcontractors of export manufacturers. A positive incentive to exceed export quotas has been provided in the form of export bonuses. Export manufacturers, however, have a greater interest than their suppliers in exceeding the export plan because they are entitled to keep for their own use a portion of the above-plan foreign exchange earnings, whereas their suppliers have no opportunity to do so. This difference of interests has been interpreted by foreign observers as a weakness in the law, in that it may hamper manufacturers' efforts to maximize export production because the requisite supplies and components may not be forthcoming.

The decentralization of foreign trade activities necessarily entails an increased need for well-qualified specialists in foreign trade and international finance, both at home and abroad. The shortage of experts in these fields is to be alleviated through an intensive personnel training program.

Western economists believe the new law to be a step in the right direction in that it promotes an orientation of the economy toward exports. They hold the view, however, also shared by some Romanian economists, that, as long as the country's currency remains nonconvertible and prices fail to reflect the relative scarcity of goods, it will not be possible properly to calculate the profitability of foreign trade nor to improve the structure of the trade on the basis of such a calculation.

In the 1960–70 period the annual trade turnover increased by 2.8 times to a volume of 22.8 billion lei. Exports rose at an average annual rate of 10 percent to 11.1 billion lei, and imports grew by 11.7 percent per year to 11.7 billion lei. From 1965 to 1970 the rise in trade was more rapid; the rates of growth were 11 percent for exports and 12.7 percent for imports.

Although trade relations were officially reported to have expanded from twenty-nine countries in 1960 to 110 countries in 1970, the bulk of the trade was carried on with members of CO-

MECON and the industrial countries of Western Europe (see table 6). Only 15 percent of the trade in 1970 involved countries outside these areas. Between 1960 and 1967 trade with COMECON members increased by little more than half, whereas trade with Western so-called capitalist countries rose almost fourfold. The difference was even more marked in the case of imports from the West, which increased ninefold, so that imports from this area in 1967 were larger than imports from COMECON. The trend was reversed after 1967, mainly because of increasing balance of payments difficulties with Western trade partners.

With a turnover of 5.5 billion lei in 1969, the Soviet Union has been by far the most important of Romania's trading partners. Czechoslovakia and the German Democratic Republic (East Germany) were next in importance within COMECON, with a trade volume of 1.5 billion and 1.2 billion lei, respectively, in 1969. Among trading partners in Western Europe, West Germany occupied first place, with a trade volume of almost 1.8 billion lei, followed by Italy with a volume of 1.2 billion lei and France with 0.9 billion lei. The People's Republic of China has been the main communist trading partner outside Europe, with an annual volume of about 0.5 billion lei in 1968 and 1969.

Table 6.   Foreign Trade of Romania, by Groups of Countries, 1960 and 1969
(in millions of lei)[1]

Country Group	1960 [2]			1969 [2]		
	Exports	Imports	Total	Exports	Imports	Total
Western industrial states	918	913	1,831	2,980	4,432	7,412
COMECON [3]	2,821	2,636	5,458	5,042	4,819	9,862
Other communist states	318	206	524	781	506	1,286
Developing countries	245	131	376	996	686	1,682
Total	4,302	3,887	8,189	9,799	10,443	20,242

[1] For value of leu, see Glossary.

[2] Totals may not add because of rounding.

[3] Council for Mutual Economic Assistance.

Source: Adapted from U.S. Department of Commerce, Office of Technical Services, Joint Publications Research Service—JPRS Series (Washington), *Translations on Eastern Europe: Economic and Scientific Affairs*, "Foreign Trade Reform Analyzed," *Vierteljahresshefte zur Wirtschaftsvorschung*, West Berlin, July–September 1971, (JPRS 54,691, Series No. 580, 1971):

Trade between Romania and the United States has been small because of legal restrictions in the United States against trade with communist countries. The trade volume doubled from about US$40 million in 1969 to US$80 million in 1970 but declined to about US$65 million in 1971. About 80 percent of the trade in 1969 and 1970 was accounted for by Romanian imports; in 1971 the trade was more nearly balanced. Comparable Romanian statistics are available only for 1969. They show a lower volume of trade and a smaller trade deficit. No explanation of this discrepancy is available.

Measures to exempt Romania from the restrictions directed against trade with communist countries have been taken in the United States. In November 1971 exports to Romania were made eligible for Export-Import Bank financing. With support from the administration, legislation has been introduced in both houses of the Congress of the United States to accord Romania most-favored-nation treatment. Sources in the United States, however, believe that Romania will not be able to balance its trade with that country even in the event that the proposed legislation is enacted into law.

Imports have been overwhelmingly weighted in favor of capital goods. Machinery and equipment, fuels, and raw and processed materials constituted about 90 percent of all imports in the 1960s. Manufactured consumer goods accounted for from 5 to 7 percent of imports. Raw and processed food products made up the small balance. Machinery and equipment, including plant installations, were the major single import category; the share of machinery and equipment in total imports rose from about 33 percent in 1960 to 49 percent in 1967 but declined to 44 percent in 1969 because of payments difficulties. Imported machinery and equipment covered about 30 percent of requirements in 1970.

Exports in the 1960s consisted mainly of raw and processed materials and foodstuffs, about equally divided between products of agricultural and industrial origin. As a result of progressive industrialization, the proportion of these products in total exports declined from about 78 percent in 1960 to 63 percent in 1969. During the same period the share of machinery and equipment rose from about 17 to 22 percent, and that of manufactured consumer goods increased from about 6 to 16 percent. Official foreign trade policy is directed toward increasing the proportion of processed goods in total exports.

In the 1960–70 period the annual balance of trade was negative, with the exception of the years 1960 and 1965. The cumulative trade deficit at the end of 1970 amounted to about 5.1 billion lei—the equivalent of about US$850 million. The overall deficit, however, obscured the severity of the foreign exchange problem facing the country. Trade with the communist and developing countries during the period produced an export surplus that offset, in part, the deficit with Western trading partners. This

251

surplus, however, could not be used to reduce foreign indebtedness because it did not generate hard currency earnings. The cumulative hard currency trade deficit with the West reached US$1.2 billion in 1969 and an estimated US$1.5 billion in 1970.

Information on the country's balance of payments has been kept secret, so that it is impossible to know how the trade deficit has been financed. Hard currency receipts from tourism, which could be applied toward repayment of the debt, equaled only a fraction of the annual trade deficit. Western sources estimated Romania's indebtedness to her Western industrial trading partners to have risen from about US$300 million in 1966 to US$800 million in 1968 and to have increased further by 1970.

CHAPTER 15

AGRICULTURE

As a result of the government's industrialization policy, the relative importance of agriculture in the economy has declined. During the decade of the 1960s the contribution of agriculture to national income, in terms of arbitrarily established official prices, dropped from about 30 to 20 percent, even though half the working population continued to be employed on farms and farm output was gradually rising. The growth in output, however, did not keep pace with official plans, mainly because of a lack of income incentives for farmers under the government's low farm-price policy and because of inadequate investment and fertilizer inputs. The farm problem has been exacerbated by the generally low qualifications of the farm labor force and by the prevalence of widespread underemployment.

Various revisions in agricultural organization and methods of compensation made from 1968 to 1971 did not produce any marked improvement by the end of that period. The failure of agricultural output, including livestock products, to advance according to plans created economic difficulties by depriving the country of potential exports urgenly needed to pay for industrial imports. It has also hampered the improvement of the population's protein-deficient diet. Substantial advances in all phases of agriculture are planned for the 1971–75 period. In the light of past experience, attainment of the established goals is uncertain. The full production potential of agriculture remains largely unexploited.

AGRICULTURAL REGIONS

Natural conditions are generally favorable for agricultural development. A varied topography has produced diversified regional weather and soil conditions. The climate is basically continental, with warm summers and cold winters, but the growing season is relatively long—from 180 to 210 days.

The amount of precipitation fluctuates from year to year, which results in recurrent droughts. Rainfall averages about twenty-five inches, ranging from only fifteen inches on the Dobruja plateau to forty inches in the mountainous regions. In the principal farming regions, annual precipitation averages about twenty-three inches in the fertile southern plain but dips below twenty inches in the hilly regions of Moldavia in the northeastern part of the country. Moisture is generally sufficient during the spring growing period (see ch. 3).

Soils vary from mountain-type soils to heavy, relatively infertile podzolic soils in the plateaus and rich chernozem (black earth) soils in the plains. About 20 percent of the agricultural land is of the chernozem type. Alluvial soils cover the flood plains of the Danube River.

Topography and climate divide the country into five agricultural zones, the most important of which is Walachia. Walachia includes the rich southern plains, where half the country's grain is grown. Almost half the vineyards and orchards are located in the foothills surrounding the plains. Vegetable production is also important in this area, especially near the city of Bucharest. Despite the fertility of this region's soils, production in Walachia fluctuates because of recurrent summer droughts.

Transylvania, the largely mountainous region in the central and northwestern parts of the country, receives substantial rainfall but has relatively infertile soils. Livestock production predominates on the mountain pastures and meadows. Grain and potatoes are the major crops in the central basin.

Moldavia in northeastern Romania has generally poor soils and receives scant rainfall. Corn is the main crop in this zone, followed by wheat and potatoes.

The Banat region on the country's western border has the most favorable natural conditions for agriculture. Chernozem soils predominate, and the seasonal distribution of rainfall is more propitious than in Walachia. Grain, primarily wheat, is the principal crop; fruits and vegetables are also important.

The Dobruja plateau in southwestern Romania is the country's least important farming area. Although soils are generally fertile, cultivation is limited by inadequate rainfall. Grain, sunflowers, and legumes are grown in this area.

To combat the destructive effects of recurrent droughts, a large-scale program of irrigation was undertaken by the government. Execution of the program, however, has consistently lagged behind the plans.

LAND USE

In 1970 agricultural land comprised almost 37 million acres (63 percent of the country), about two-thirds of which was arable. The balance was devoted to pastures, meadows, vineyards, and orchards. During the decade of the 1960s substantial additions to the agricultural area were made through various land improvement measures. At the same time, however, large acreages were diverted to industrial and residential uses, particularly of the more valuable arable land. The net result was an increase in the total farmland area, mainly in orchards and pastures, and a decline in the arable acreage (see table 7).

Table 7. Land Use in Romania, Selected Years, 1960–70*
(in thousands of acres)

	1960	1962	1969	1970
Agricultural Land				
Arable	24,268	24,515	24,146	24,050
Pasture	6,953	6,924	7,426	7,420
Meadow	3,427	3,447	3,506	3,499
Vineyard	768	744	857	857
Orchard	529	662	1,053	1,067
Total Agricultural Land	35,945	36,292	36,988	36,893
Forest Land	15,822	15,807	15,607	15,604

*Agricultural land by type of use and forest area.

Source: Adapted from *Anuarul Statistic al Republicii Socialiste Romania, 1970* (Statistical Yearbook of the Socialist Republic of Romania, 1970), Bucharest, 1970, pp. 246–247.

Forests occupied an area of 15,604,000 acres in 1970, the equivalent of about 27 percent of the country's land surface. The forest acreage declined slowly but steadily after 1961, for a total loss of almost 247,000 acres.

Slightly more than two-thirds of the more than 24 million acres of crop area in 1969 was under grains. Technical crops for industrial uses, consisting mainly of oilseeds and sugar beets, and fodder crops occupied almost one-fourth of the sown area. The remainder of less than 10 percent was devoted to legumes, potatoes, vegetables, and melons and to seed-producing and experimental plots. Half the grain acreage was devoted to corn, which is used for food and feed by the farmers; and more than two-fifths was under wheat, which is the staple food of the urban population.

The grain acreage declined in absolute and in relative terms after 1960, when it accounted for almost three-fourths of the sown area. All other major crop acreages, excluding that under sugar beets, increased during the 1960–69 peroid (see table 8). Romanian economists attributed the shift in the crop pattern to the government's emphasis on adapting crop production to the economic needs of the country and to the natural conditions of individual farms. A severe flood in the spring of 1970, the worst in the country's history, reduced the crop area by nearly 1.25 million acres below the level of 1969.

Crop	1960	1969
Grain		
Wheat	7,008	6,817
Corn	8,826	8,137
Other	1,626	1,263
Total	17,460	16,217
Legumes	381	474
Technical crops (for industrial uses)		
Oleaginous	1,396	1,576
Sugar beets	494	445
Other	252	341
Total	2,142	2,362
Potatoes	722	754
Vegetables and melons	516	591
Fodder crops	2,711	3,356
Seed-producing and experimental plots	119	235
Total Cultivated Acreage	24,051	23,989

Source: Adapted from *Anuarul Statistic al Republicii Socialiste Romania,
1970* (Statistical Yearbook of the Socialist Republic of Romania,
1970), Bucharest, 1970, pp. 306–307.

Encroachment by builders upon agricultural and, more particularly, arable land was facilitated by the government's policy, pursued until the spring of 1968, of treating land as a free good and
assigning no value to it in calculating the cost of industrial and
housing investment projects. Arable land was especially attractive to builders because it required no expenditure for leveling.

In an attempt to prevent further waste of valuable farmland, a
law for the protection and conservation of agricultural land was
passed in May 1968. The law prohibited the diversion of farm
acreages to nonagricultural uses, with the exception of special
cases which, depending upon the nature and location of the land
involved, required the approval of either the Council of State, the
Council of Ministers, or the Superior Council of Agriculture (a
government agency that functioned in lieu of a ministry for several years). Nonagricultural state organizations that held land
that they could not cultivate were obligated to surrender it without payment to neighboring state or collective farms.

The conservation law enjoined socialized (collective and state)
farms and private farmers to put all land to optimum use; called
for a review of the building code to reduce the land areas allowed
to individual construction projects; provided for the inclusion of

the value of land in construction costs; and spelled out various other measures to safeguard and improve agricultural land. The law also directed the establishment of a land register, excluding lands of the socialized farms, to facilitate stricter controls over the remaining private farmers, who held 9.2 percent of the agricultural land and 4.6 percent of the arable acreage.

Heavy fines and criminal penalties, including imprisonment up to one year, were provided for infringements of the conservation law by enterprises and individuals. During the first year of the law's operation, fines were also to be imposed upon holders of uncultivated arable land, of improperly maintained orchards and vineyards, and of meadows and pastures on which maintenance work did not comply with agrotechnical rules. Like the establishment of the land register, this provision was also aimed at private farmers. A further provision stated that lands on which the described conditions continued after the first year were to be assigned to socialized farms for cultivation. The transferred land could be subsequently restored to the original owners under conditions prescribed by the Superior Council of Agriculture. The effect of the punitive regulations on private farm property was not apparent from the official statistics for 1968 and 1969.

Shortly after the adoption of the conservation law, the deputy chairman of the State Committee for Construction, Architecture, and Systematization published an article in which he stated that mere administrative regulations by the committee and the Superior Council of Agriculture could not ensure the proper use of land, particularly on the collective farms. He called for the development of appropriate economic levers based on an adaptation of "the systems that limit land waste in some capitalistic markets." This official's concern about the efficacy of the new legislation was well based. By 1970 the arable acreage had declined by 158,000 acres, at an average annual rate more than half again as large as the annual losses during the 1962–68 period.

ORGANIZATION

Collective and state farms are the principal types of farm organization (see table 9). Substantial areas of state agricultural land are also operated as subsidiary farms by various industrial and other economic organizations. Small private farms survive mainly in the mountainous regions where collectivization is impractical. In 1970 the state owned 30 percent of the farmland, about half of which was cultivated by state farms. Almost 61 percent of the land belonged to collective farms, including 6.6 percent in plots for the personal use of their members. The collective farm population consisted of almost 3.5 million families, includ-

Table 9. *Agricultural Land in Romania, by Type of Ownership, 1969*
(in thousands of acres)

	Arable	Pasture	Meadow	Vineyard	Orchard	Total
State agricultural units	4,959	5,545	264	148	173	11,089
(State farms)	(4,129)	(638)	(170)	(133)	(148)	(5,218)
Collective farms	18,075	1,315	1,712	682	692	22,476
(Private plots)	(1,969)	(20)	(54)	(262)	(121)	(2,426)
Private farms	1,112	566	1,530	27	188	3,423
Total	24,146	7,426	3,506	857	1,053	36,988

Source: Adapted from *Anuarul Statistic al Republicii Socialiste Romania, 1970* (Statistical Yearbook of the Socialist Republic of Romania, 1970), Bucharest, 1970, p. 253.

ing more than 10 million collective members. About 9 percent of the farmland was in the possession of private farmers.

In order to raise agricultural productivity and output, the state and collective farm sectors underwent frequent organizational changes, the latest of which went into effect in February 1971. There was not sufficient evidence in early 1972 on the extent to which they had been put into practice and even less information on their economic effects.

Collective Farms

At the beginning of 1971 there were 4,626 collective farms, officially called agricultural production cooperatives, comprising more than 22 million acres of farmland, about 18 million acres of which were arable. Their number had declined by 1,800 through consolidation during the preceding decade. The farms had an average of about 750 families and 1,000 able-bodied members each.

The average acreage of collective farmland per family in 1970 amounted to 6.4 acres, including a private family plot of about 0.7 acres. Although the family plots constituted only 6.6 percent of the country's farmland and 8.2 percent of the arable acreage, they accounted for a substantially larger share in the output of various crops and livestock products.

Information on the organization of individual collective farms and of the collective farm sector as a whole is inadequate, particularly with regard to the range of responsibilities and authority of the various administrative entities. The organizational framework has been complicated by the proliferation of new measures and regulations since 1967. Farm operations are carried out in common, under the direction of an administrative and management body theoretically accountable to the general assembly, composed of all the members of a collective farm. Groups of workers are organized into so-called brigades for the performance of specialized tasks. The farm management includes a chairman, a director, a management council, brigade leaders, and trained technicians specialized in various aspects of farm operation.

Intercooperative councils are charged with responsibility for improving collective farm management by initiating and coordinating cooperation on various levels among neighboring farms for better use of their physical and human resources. Collective farms are subordinated to the National Union of Agricultural Production Cooperatives and are also subject to the direction of the Ministry of Agriculture, Food Industry, and Waters (referred to as the Ministry of Agriculture) and of county authorities. Collective farm associations are organized for various types of specialized production.

In theory and according to law, but not in actual practice, collective farms are jointly owned by their members. The ownership supposedly extends to the land, other productive resources, and the annual farm output. About 11 percent of the collective farm land, however, is allocated for the personal use of members, and almost half the livestock other than horses is individually owned. No information is available on the existence of any provision for the compensation of members who are authorized to leave the farms for employment in other sectors of the economy.

Regulations concerning the allocation of their income by collective farms among investment funds and various social and other obligatory funds and distribution to members were modified in late 1970 or early 1971 with a view to stimulating the members' interest in raising the efficiency of production. Under the old system, distribution to members was made from residual funds remaining after all statutory public and social obligations were met. The revised farm statutes authorize the farms' general assemblies to allocate net income in ratios ranging from 18 to 25 percent for investment and from 75 to 82 percent for consumption. In actual practice, however, income distribution is reported to follow a somewhat different pattern, which tends to reduce the share available for distribution to members. The new regulations have not altered the generally acknowledged fact that farm incomes remain very low, particularly on the poorer farms.

The system of remuneration for collective farmers was also modified in 1970 with a view to strengthening work incentives. The new method provides for monthly payments on account, in cash and in kind, based on the farms' planned annual receipts and for a share of profits in excess of those planned. Payment to individual members is to be based on centrally established work norms and rates of pay for various categories of operations, similar to the practice in industry and construction. The system is intended to relate individual remuneration more closely to the quantity and quality of the work performed and thereby to eliminate inequities of the earlier method. It is also meant to provide a steady and assured income to all members who contribute a specified minimum of workdays per month. If, for reasons beyond its control, a farm's receipts turn out to be lower than the amount legally distributed to its members during the year, the shortage may be covered by a long-term bank credit. As a further inducement for farmers to remain on the land, their social security benefits, generally much lower than those of industrial workers, were substantially liberalized.

The extent to which the new pay system has been put into practice is not known. Effective January 1, 1971, a minimum wage of 300 lei (for value of leu, see Glossary) per month was to be paid to all male farmers who worked regularly at least twenty days and to all women who worked fifteen days. A survey published by a collective farm organ in March of that year found that within a single county twenty-one out of twenty-two farms had not taken the trouble to forward the necessary documents to the Agricultural Bank and apply for the funds with which to pay their members. Various excuses were offered by the farm chairmen for their lack of action. The chairmen, farm directors, and brigade leaders, however, were reported to have taken appropriate steps to secure their own minimum pay.

The marketing of farm products by collective farms is based on officially fixed prices and monopoly-buying powers of state procurement agencies and the food-processing industry. Products move into government stocks through contracts between the farms and state agencies for quantities specified by the government; through payments in kind for services rendered by agricultural mechanization stations, flour mills, and other specialized government agencies; and, in the case of meat and wool, in the form of compulsory deliveries. Any products remaining after the obligations to the state have been met may be sold in open markets.

State Farms

Through consolidation of 370 previously existing state agricultural enterprises, the farm reorganization of February 1971 created 145 larger enterprises subordinated to the Department of State Agriculture in the Ministry of Agriculture. In addition, seventy-four state agricultural enterprises for fattening hogs, raising poultry, and producing feeds and hothouse vegetables were subordinated to four specialized trusts. The consolidation increased the average size of the state enterprises from 16,000 acres to 34,600 acres of farmland. The enterprises comprised about 3,000 state farms on an area of over 5 million acres. Romanian sources reported that the reorganization was intended to bring management closer to production, to ensure improvement in all aspects of farm operation, to intensify concentration and specialization of production, and gradually to attain agro-industrial integration.

In official terminology, state agricultural enterprises will operate on the principle of economic self-administration. The enterprises will be responsible for their subordinate farms and will supervise operations according to the principle of internal economic administration. Briefly, this means that the agricultural enterprises and the farms must be financially self-sustaining, that directors of enterprises and farms are accorded a certain measure of discretion in planning and organizing production and in the use of resources, and that financial rewards beyond the normal pay accrue to each farm's managerial personnel and workers in accordance with the farm's own performance, regardless of the results obtained by other farms within the enterprise or by the parent enterprise itself.

Individual state farms, nevertheless, have no juridical status or bank accounts, nor may they enter into direct relation with other economic entities outside the state agricultural enterprise of which they are a part. In large measure, they remain subject to the direction of the enterprise management. Information on the division of authority between the agricultural enterprises and the Department of State Agriculture in the ministry is not available. Complaints have been voiced in the Romanian press about unwarranted interference by higher authorities in the management of both the farms and the agricultural enterprises.

Workers on state farms and other state agricultural units are salaried employees of the state, entitled to paid annual vacations, social security and medical assistance, allocations for children, age or disability pensions, and various other benefits provided by law for employees of state enterprises. During slack periods, workers may be allowed up to 120 days of unpaid vacation per year, without losing seniority or other rights.

State farms are the best endowed agricultural units in the country. Although they included only about 17 percent of the arable land in 1969, they possessed almost 28 percent of the tractors, 24 percent of the grain combines, and similar proportions of other major types of farm machinery. Moreover, they received more than 37 percent of the chemical fertilizers delivered to agriculture and farmed almost 33 percent of the irrigated land. As a consequence, per-acre yields on state farms have been generally higher than yields on collective farms.

Agricultural Mechanization Enterprises

The bulk of the mechanized operations on collective farms has been performed for payment in cash and in kind by specialized state enterprises for the mechanization of agriculture, which control a large share of the country's farm machinery and tractors. This policy has provided the state with an added lever of control over the farms; it was used in the past to extract a substantial volume of farm produce for the state through payments in kind for services rendered. For political reasons, and also because of the weak financial position of many collective farms, the government has not followed the example of other Eastern European states that disbanded their machine-tractor stations and sold the equipment to the farms.

In 1969 the agricultural mechanization enterprises controlled 70 percent of the available farm tractor power and an even larger share of the tractor-drawn and self-propelled farm machinery. State farms owned virtually all the balance. Collective farms, which cultivated 75 percent of the arable land, possessed only 1.6 percent of the tractor power and a still smaller proportion of major farm machinery items.

As of January 1, 1971, the system of agricultural mechanization enterprises was reorganized with a view to improving the quality of their operations. Forty enterprises were established throughout the country—one in each of the thirty-nine counties and one in the Bucharest area—with 772 subordinate stations to service an equal number of farm associations and about 4,500 sections to work with individual collective farms. The main stated task of the mechanization sections is to introduce and expand the mechanization of plant and animal production on the farms.

To accomplish the task, each mechanization section is to coordinate the use of its own equipment with that belonging to the collective. Within the framework of this cooperation, the state mechanization enterprises were made increasingly responsible for the agricultural production process. The planning of mechanized farm operations, the allocation of equipment for specific purposes, and the timing and supervision of all operations are joint responsibilities of the section chief and the farm's chief engineer. Close cooperation and a smooth working relationship between them is therefore needed for effective performance.

Mechanized work on farms is carried on by permanent teams composed of agricultural mechanics and collective farm members. They take over assigned areas in all sectors of the farm and are in charge of all relevant operations until the crops have been stored. In slack period the mechanization sections work outside the cooperative farms in order to utilize more fully their manpower and equipment.

The reorganization of the agricultural mechanization enterprises was accompanied by a change in the system of pay for mechanics and maintenance men to provide for greater incentives. For work done on the farms, these workers receive 80 percent of their annual salary, and the remainder is paid at the end of the year, in whole or in part, depending upon the degree to which the production plans of the farm on which they work are fulfilled. Provision was also made for bonus payments in the event of overfulfillment of production plans. The shift in wage policy was accompanied by a raise in the rates of pay for mechanics, maintenance men, and personnel operating the equipment in the field on a piecework basis. This measure increases the burden on the already strained budgets of many collective farms.

FARM LABOR

The agricultural labor force presents a paradox of substantial underemployment associated with widespread labor shortages, particularly of more productive, skilled personnel; the shortages are especially prevalent during the planting and harvesting seasons. This phenomenon is an outgrowth primarily of a progressive qualitative deterioration of the agricultural manpower pool, owing to a continuing transfer of predominantly young male workers into nonagricultural occupations. Maldistribution of the labor force and poor management of the available manpower resources have been important contributing factors. The outmigration from agriculture has been spurred by a wide disparity in urban and rural incomes and by the relatively inferior living conditions on the farms. At the beginning of the 1970s the average income of farmworkers was only half as high as that of industrial workers.

Only fragmentary information relating to the farm labor force has been published in official statistics. Agricultural employment in 1969 constituted 51 percent of total employment, compared with 65.4 percent in 1960 and 74.1 percent in 1950. Published absolute figures bear only on employment by the state; in 1969 the state employed 431,200 persons, including 290,000 on state farms and 93,500 in agricultural mechanization enterprises. Data published in connection with a conference held by the Romanian Academy of Social and Political Sciences, however, implied that total agricultural employment in 1968 amounted to 5.2 million persons, including 4.3 million able-bodied collective farm members. The proportion of women in the collective farm labor force was reported to be 57.5 percent in 1966; the proportion was much larger in highly developed industrial zones. More than 70 percent of the collective farm workers, but only about 10 to 15 percent of the workers on state farms, were engaged in crop production.

Not all the collective farm members participate in the work of the collective. Some are permanently employed in nonagricultural branches of the economy. Others—as many as 25 percent of all farmers in 1969—work as day laborers in industry and construction, on state farms, and in other occupations. Housewives with small children and wives of salaried farm employees also take no part in the collective work. Members who do participate generally work only a portion of the year because there is not sufficient work for them to be fully occupied. In the years 1967 to 1969, these members, on the average, contributed only from 139 to 142 man-days per year. In 1968, for example, 22 percent of all collective farmers put in not more than forty man-days, and 55 percent of the farmers worked fewer than 120 days. Many farmers work only the minimum number of days required to keep their personal plots. There are wide variations in the degree of labor participation between geographic regions, between individual farms, and among production sectors of a single farm. At the beginning of the decade of the 1970s about 40 percent of the income of collective farm families was derived from nonagricultural pursuits.

Underemployment in agriculture is expected to continue at least throughout the 1970s. Industry, though growing very rapidly, will not be able to absorb any significant numbers of farmworkers because of the government's emphasis on mechanization and automation of production. In the 1971–75 period industrial manpower requirements will be met almost entirely through natural population increase. Relieving agricultural underemployment through an expansion of the services sector is not being given serious consideration on the grounds that "no further expansion of this sector can be undertaken at the expense of achieving a high level of productivity in the branches of material production and hence in agriculture, too."

Raising the low productivity level of collective farm labor through greater capital inputs, and thereby increasing the incomes of members, presents a difficult problem not only because of a shortage of investment funds but also because the magnitude of the collective farm labor cannot be adjusted to the needs of production, as in the case of state farms; it is determined by the number of families living on the farm. The collective farm cannot limit the number of members who may participate in the work. Each member has the right and, at the same time, the duty to participate in the work performed for the collective, and the collective has the duty to provide equal opportunities for all its members to work and to earn adequate incomes; yet modernization of production necessarily brings with it an ever smaller need for manpower.

A solution of the farm manpower problem was not in sight by late 1971. There was general agreement among Romanian economists concerned with the matter about a need to improve the utilization of the available labor resources, to increase farm incomes and, above all, to stop the migration of young people from villages to towns. No concrete program for attaining these ends, however, emerged from a national conference on farm labor held in mid-1970. Proposals advanced by a number of economists to expand industrial activities in the villages, particularly cottage industries and the processing of farm products, were questioned by others who feared that these activities would tend to drain some of the remaining productive elements from the collective farm labor force.

As expressed by one of the conferees, the search was on for a hybrid solution that would ensure full employment of the redundant labor force despite the process of farm modernization—a policy that inevitably leads to the maintenance of low earnings on many farms because the available work must be spread among an excessive number of members. In this context, foreign observers adopted a wait-and-see attitude toward the changes in collective farm organization and in the method of payment to farmers introduced in January 1971 (see Organization, this ch.). They nevertheless expressed doubt about the ultimate efficacy of these measures because the income of farmers would still remain far below that of industrial workers.

INVESTMENT AND CREDIT

Investment

Investment in agriculture has been rising steadily, reaching an annual volume of almost 13 billion lei in 1970. The share of agriculture in total investment, however, declined from 19.5 percent in the 1961–65 period to 15.8 percent in the years 1966 through 1969. In relation to industrial investment during the same periods, investment in agriculture declined from 40 to 30 percent. Under the Five-Year Plan (1971–75), agriculture is to receive investments of at least 100 billion lei—an amount that is twice as large as the actual investment in the years 1966 through 1970 and that represents a somewhat larger share of total investment than was allocated to agriculture in that period.

No information is readily available on the proportion of the total investment used for the replacement of wornout assets and for the expansion of productive facilities. In the 1966–69 period replacement capital constituted about 30 percent of investments; in 1969 alone the proportion was as high as 46 percent.

The largest part—and a rising proportion—of the agricultural investment has been financed by the state; collective farms supplied the balance out of their own income. The share of state funds in the total agricultural investment increased steadily from about 66 percent in 1963 to 80 percent in 1969; this proportion is to be maintained during the Five-Year Plan (1971–75). Investment in collective farms has also been increasingly financed by the state through long-term credits; the share of government credits rose from 13 percent in 1965 to 35 percent in 1969. Investment out of the collectives' own funds remained stable during this period, at from 2.2 billion lei to 2.4 billion lei per year.

State farms have received a disproportionate amount of investment—38 percent in the 1965–69 period, as against 34 percent for collective farms. The investment share of collective farms during this period declined from about 38 to 30 percent of the total. On the basis of farmland acreage, investment in collective farms in 1969 amounted to only 18 percent of the funds invested in state farms. If the state investment in agricultural mechanization enterprises is included as investment for the benefit of the collective farms, the ratio of collective to state farm investment per acre was still only 25 percent.

Collective farm statutes require the farms to devote from 18 to 25 percent of their annual gross income to investment. Some Romanian economists consider net income to be a more equitable base; under such a system more of the farms' income would remain for distribution to members. In calculating gross income, amortization of fixed assets is generally not included as an expense, which further raises the base used for the computation of the compulsory investment fund. An official of the Agricultural Bank reported that, in the last few years of the 1960s, one-fourth of all collective farms set aside for investment up to 10 percent more than the maximum legal requirement.

Only partial information is available on the use of investment funds. Roughly 40 percent of the investment in the 1962–69 period was devoted to construction and assembly work, and 33 percent was used to increase farm mechanization. It has not been made clear whether land improvement and irrigation are included in construction, but it seems likely that this is the case. Substantial funds were also invested in the expansion of orchards, vineyards, and livestock. Although significant advances were made in most of these areas, the level of farm mechanization and of irrigation remained low. In 1969 the equivalent of one fifteen-horsepower tractor was available for every 136 acres of arable land, and irrigated acreage constituted 6 percent of the arable area. The use of fertilizers lagged by comparison with other Eastern European countries.

Credit

Farm credit has been provided by the government through the Agricultural Bank, which was reconstituted as the Bank for Agriculture and the Food Industry in May 1971. Available information on the credit operations of the bank is limited to a few summary data on credits to collective farms. Information on the financing of state farms is lacking.

As expressed by the bank's president, long-term credits for investment and short-term credits for production needs have been used by the state as levers for the economic and organizational development and for the consolidation of collective farms. Long-term credits granted during the 1962–69 period amounted to 6.4 billion lei, or an average of 800 million lei per year. During the same period the farms received about 30 billion lei in short-term production credits, or about 3.75 billion lei per year. The annual volume of investment credits increased sharply after 1967; it was reported to have reached 1.8 billion lei in 1970 and to have been planned at more than 2 billion lei for 1971. A rise was also reported in the yearly volume of production credit.

Investment credits generally carry an annual 3-percent interest charge, but the interest rate may be reduced to 2 percent for economically weaker farms. Comparable information on production credit is not available, except for an official statement that a large part of it has been granted free of interest.

Postponement of scheduled long-term credit repayments may be authorized by the bank with the approval of the Ministry of Finance for periods of up to one year in the case of collective farms that are unable to meet the due date for reasons beyond their control, such as a crop failure. At the same time the bank may discontinue credits or demand repayment before the due date in the event that borrowed funds are improperly or inefficiently used. Penalties are also provided for short-term borrowers who fail to respect contractual obligations. As a measure of assistance to poor cooperatives, the repayment of loans in the amount of 1.15 billion lei, contracted before 1968 and due in 1972, was remitted by decision of the Central Committee of the Romanian Communist Party in December 1971.

The distribution of long-term credits to collective farms among different types of investment projects changed significantly during the 1960s. In 1962 and 1963 more than half the credits were granted for the expansion of livestock production, and one-fourth of the credits were devoted to the construction of farm buildings. In the last two years of the decade, however, only 5 percent and 3 percent of the credits, respectively, were earmarked for these purposes. Emphasis shifted in the mid-1960s to land improvement, the extension of orchards and vineyards, and vegetable production. In the 1967–69 period 83 percent of the investment credits were used for these projects. A lack of significant progress in the livestock production of collective farms, despite the heavy investment, was the main reason for the drastic reduction in credits to this farm sector.

In mid-1971 the bank was authorized to grant credits to private farmers and to individual members of collective farms for periods of up to five years at an annual interest rate of 3 percent. These credits may be used to purchase for breeding and production purposes a limited number of cattle, sheep, bee colonies with hives, and fruit tree seedlings for orchards up to 7.4 acres in size. Credits may be granted up to 70 percent of the purchase value of these items. To ensure repayment of the loans, recipients must conclude contracts with state procurement agencies or collective farms for the sale of their products.

Procedures for granting credits to collective farms were tightened in 1969 in a move to ensure a more effective use of borrowed funds and the timely repayment of outstanding debts. Under the new regulations, credits may be granted only for investment projects and production expenditures that guarantee the attainment of planned returns and unconditionally ensure loan repayment on the due date. The principal criteria for granting long-term credits are the need for, and the economic effectiveness of, the investment projects and the outlook for completing the projects within prescribed time limits. Economic effectiveness is analyzed in terms of production growth, increase in output per acre or per head of livestock, and rise in labor productivity and revenues.

Despite increasingly close supervision by the bank of its borrowers' activities, the effectiveness of investment credits in many instances has not measured up to expectations. Inadequate project analysis, construction delays, cost overruns, dissipation of funds, program changes that made partially or fully completed projects obsolete, and various other shortcomings have been cited by bank officials as the major reasons for this situation. As a means of resolving the problems, the officials have stressed the need for more profound project evaluation, greater stringency in granting loans, and increased firmness in the supervision of borrowers. They have also emphasized the criterion of ability to repay as being one of basic importance.

PRODUCTION

Total Farm Output

Official statistics on total farm output are limited to a percentage distribution of the output between crop and livestock production. In the 1965–69 period, for which comparable data are available, crop production accounted for 62 to 63 percent of output; and livestock production, for the remaining 37 to 38 percent. This ratio is reported to have prevailed throughout the 1950–70 period, even though the government has consistently sought to raise the contribution of the livestock sector to total output. An increase in the proportion of livestock products to 40.6 percent in 1970, reported by another source, was attributable mainly to the damage sustained by crops from the spring flood in that year.

Total gross agricultural output was unofficially reported to have reached 72.4 billion lei in 1969 and to have fallen to 68.7 billion lei in 1970 as a result of disastrous spring floods. The 1969 output volume, equal to that of 1967, represented the highest level attained through 1970. According to official index data, farm output in 1967 and in 1969 was 31 percent larger than it had been in 1960; the 1970 output was only 24 percent larger. These figures are equivalent to annual growth rates of 3.9 percent for the 1960–67 period and 2.2 percent for the years 1969 through 1970.

Net farm output increased much more slowly because the cost of material outlays per unit of output was steadily rising. In the 1963–68 period the increase in material costs amounted to 33 percent.

The growth of farm output during the 1960s was well below the planned levels of 70 to 80 percent for the yars 1960 through 1965 and 26 to 32 percent for the 1966–70 period. Instead of more than doubling, output increased by barely one-fourth. Unfavorable weather conditions during some of the years were only partly responsible for the nonfulfillment of the agricultural output plans. Other major factors included the government's failure to provide the planned volume of inputs and an apathetic attitude on the part of farmers owing to inadequate incentives.

The shortfall in fertilizer deliveries during the 1966–70 period alone amounted to 1.3 million tons of nutrients, or one-third of the planned tonnage. For the decade as a whole, the shortfall approached 2 million tons. Deliveries of tractors and farm machinery also lagged behind schedule. Although an area of almost 2 million acres was to be irrigated by 1965 and, under revised plans, an acreage of from 1.6 million to 1.7 million acres by 1970, only 550,000 acres had been actually irrigated by 1965 and 1.45 million acres by 1969. A careful and sympathetic Western student of Romanian economy concluded that the production targets for 1965 could not have been achieved even if all the planned inputs had been provided on schedule.

In the view of some Western observers, an attitude of indifference on the part of farmers, based on the inadequacy of returns from farming, particularly on the collective farms, was an important contributing cause for the failure of agriculture to realize its growth potential. The real income of farmers was scheduled to rise by 20 to 25 percent during the 1966–70 period; the official announcement of the plan results, however, merely noted an increase in income, without citing any figure—a clear indication that the target was missed by a wide margin.

The negative effects of the disparity in incomes on the collective farmers' sense of responsibility and, hence, on agricultural production were officially recognized. This recognition led to a revision of the system of compensation for collective farm work and to a reduction of farm taxes in early 1971 but did not significantly alter the position of agriculture within the economy (see Organization, this ch.). The possibility of alleviating the situation by raising farm incomes through a general increase in farm prices was rejected on the grounds that such an increase, without a corresponding rise in productivity per worker and per acre, would constitute a redistribution of national income incompatible with the best interests of the economy.

Crop Production and Yields

Production of major crops and of fruits was larger during the 1960s than it had been in the preceding decade. The greatest advances were made in the output of industrial and fodder crops, and the smallest were in potato and vegetable production (see table 10). In large measure, the rise in output was achieved through greater yields per acre, owing to an increased use of fertilizers; the introduction of improved varieties; and some improvement in crop production methods, particularly on state farms. Crop yields, nevertheless, remained among the lowest in Eastern Europe.

Livestock and Livestock Products

Livestock numbers increased slowly from 1961 to 1970 but, except for poultry, were generally lower at the end of that period than the peak levels reached for the different types between 1965 and 1968. From 1961 to 1965 the number of cows declined but increased steadily thereafter, without, however, fully regaining the level of 1961.

Development of the livestock economy has been hampered by an inadequate feed base, poor quality of livestock and livestock breeding, and inefficient production methods. Significant improvements in the livestock sector are planned for the 1971–75 period and beyond to 1980.

Although livestock production failed to increase as a proportion of the total farm output, the volume of livestock products, nevertheless, rose significantly during the 1960s (see table 11). Compared with the average annual outputs of individual products attained in the 1962–65 period, increases in average annual production for the years 1966 through 1969 ranged from 18 percent for wool to 24 percent for meat.

Data on the contribution of the different types of farms to the

Table 10. *Production of Major Crops in Romania, Selected Years, 1960–69*
(in thousand metric tons)

Crop	1960	1963	1966	1967	1968	1969
Grain [1]						
Wheat	3,450	3,799	5,065	5,820	4,848	4,349
Corn	5,531	6,023	8,022	6,858	7,105	7,676
Other	845	614	812	834	817	799
Total	9,826	10,436	13,899	13,512	12,770	12,824
Oilseeds						
Sunflower	522	506	671	720	730	747
Other	93	54	63	61	41	59
Total	615	560	734	781	771	806
Sugar beets	3,399	2,298	4,368	3,830	3,936	3,783
Tobacco	16	40	40	35	33	24
Potatoes	3,009	2,692	3,352	3,096	3,707	2,165
Vegetables	1,831	1,702	2,177	2,000	2,296	1,963
Fodder Crops						
Hay	2,105	1,872	3,182	3,223	2,472	3,268
Green feed	1,222	2,922	4,749	4,380	3,995	3,885
Silage [2]	4,601	5,296	3,538	2,830	3,728	3,491
Root crops	276	293	371	269	302	420
Total	8,204	10,383	11,840	10,702	10,497	11,064
Fruits	829	1,048	1,390	1,206	1,054	1,677
Grapes	874	937	954	910	1,167	1,189

[1] Grain production in 1971 was unofficially reported to have reached about 14.5 million metric tons.

[2] Roughly 90 percent corn.

Source: Adapted from *Anuarul Statistic al Republicii Socialiste Romania, 1970* (Statistical Yearbook of the Socialist Republic of Romania, 1970), Bucharest, 1970, pp. 312–315.

Table 11. *Output of Livestock Products in Romania, Selected Years 1960–69*

	Meat [1]	Milk [2]	Eggs [3]	Wool [4]
1960	969	856,472	2,355	21,850
1965	1,116	859,061	2,630	25,410
1966	1,265	987,531	2,814	26,072
1967	1,356	1,089,320	3,011	28,626
1968	1,297	1,012,628	3,113	30,583
1969	1,271	992,762	3,315	30,752

[1] Thousand metric tons live weight.
[2] Cow, goat, and buffalo in thousand gallons.
[3] In millions.
[4] In metric tons.

Source: Adapted from *Anuarul Statistic al Republicii Socialiste Romania, 1970* (Statistical Yearbook of the Socialist Republic of Romania, 1970), Bucharest, 1970, pp. 430–431.

total farm output are lacking, but detailed figures are available for individual products. The most noteworthy aspect of these data is the light that they shed on the importance of the collective farmers' personal plots and of the private sector in the production of the higher valued farm products. On their small personal plots, the collective farmers in 1969 produced roughly one-third of the wool, vegetables, and potatoes; two-fifths of the meat, milk, and fruit; and three-fifths of the eggs (see table 12). Together with the small number of private farms, they accounted for 35 to 80 percent of the output of these items. Foreign observers have interpreted this phenomenon as clear evidence of the inadequacy of incentives for work on state and collective farms.

Exports

Substantial quantities of farm products have been exported in raw and processed form. In the 1965–69 period exports of grain, fruits, vegetables, and eggs ranged from 10 to 13 percent of output. Exports of wool reached almost two-thirds of the total production volume. A wide range of other vegetable and livestock products were also exported, including pulses; sugar; sunflower seeds and oil; live cattle; fresh, frozen, and canned meat; butter; wine; and tobacco (see ch. 14).

Table 12. Crop Production and Livestock Products in Romania, by Type of Farm, 1969
(in percent)

Product	State Agricultural Units	State Farms [1]	Collective Farms	Personal Plots	Private Farms
Grains	24.5	23.6	63.4	9.0	3.1
Fiber plants	5.2	4.7	92.1	0.6	2.1 [2]
Oilseeds	29.2	28.9	70.8	-- [2]	-- [2]
Sugar beets	0.4	0.3	99.6	0	0
Tobacco	0.2	0	99.8	0	0
Potatoes	7.1	6.5	39.1	36.4	17.4
Vegetables	11.6	10.6	52.9	29.6	5.9
Perennials for hay	30.2	28.3	64.7	3.2	1.9
Annuals for hay	23.5	19.4	58.9	13.9	3.7
Annuals for green feed	38.0	35.6	60.1	1.6	0.3
Fodder roots	53.8	50.9	39.8	4.8	1.6
Silage crops	44.5	42.8	55.4	0.1	0
Fruits	11.7	9.9	19.3	40.9	28.1
Meat	27.0	24.2	21.2	39.3	12.5
Milk	16.7	16.0	28.2	38.2	16.9
Eggs	17.0	16.7	3.2	60.0	19.8
Wool	17.7	16.8	38.4	33.1	10.8

[1] Breakdown included within state agricultural units.
[2] Less than 0.1 percent.

Source: Adapted from *Anuarul Statistic al Republicii Socialiste Romania, 1970* (Statistical Yearbook of the Socialist Republic of Romania, 1970), Bucharest, 1970, pp. 329–345, 406, 430–431.

CHAPTER 16

INDUSTRY

Stimulated by a high rate of investment and an infusion of Western technology, industry has expanded at a rapid rate. A qualitatively inadequate labor force, poor organization, and insufficiently experienced management personnel, however, have not been able to attain levels of efficiency and quality acceptable to the Romanian Communist Party and the government. Lowering the cost of production and improving quality are considered to be essential prerequisites for expanding exports, which are needed to pay for imports of materials and equipment. Various measures introduced since 1967 have not achieved the government's objectives. Economic plans for the 1971–75 period call for raising productivity through greater specialization of production and better utilization of plants and materials. To this end, several new economic laws were passed in December 1971, the contents of which were not yet known in early 1972.

NATURAL RESOURCES

Though widely varied, the country's mineral and agricultural resources are generally inadequate to maintain the current and planned levels of industrial production and exports. Natural gas is a major exception. Formerly plentiful supplies of crude oil are falling off, and the likelihood of discovering new deposits is considered poor by oil industry officials. The heavy dependence on outside sources of raw materials led the government to provide economic and technical assistance to several developing countries for the exploitation of their mineral resources in return for shipments of mined products. This dependence has also been a major determinant of the country's political relations with other members of the Council for Mutual Economic Assistance (COMECON), particularly the Soviet Union, and with noncommunist industrial nations of the West (see ch. 10).

Minerals and Metals

Information on the extent of most mineral reserves is unavailable. A delegation of Western petroleum experts who surveyed the petroleum industry at the end of 1970 made a tentative estimate that oil reserves would be exhausted in roughly eleven years at the current annual production rate of about 13 million tons. With a view to ensuring long-term crude oil supplies for the planned expansion of the domestic petroleum refining and petrochemical industries, the government has entered into economic cooperation agreements with several small petroleum-producing countries. The government has also discussed the possibility for joint exploration of offshore petroleum deposits in the Black Sea and elsewhere in the world with oil interests of various countries. In the meantime the government has been importing crude oil from Iran, Saudi Arabia, and Libya in exchange for industrial machinery and equipment. Oil imports from these countries in 1970 amounted to 2.1 million tons.

The major natural gas deposits that were exploited in 1970 are located in the Transylvanian basin and outside the Carpathian arc (see ch. 3). According to Romanian officials, the annual addition to reserves has been double the volume of annual production. Gas output has expanded steadily from about 365 billion cubic feet in 1960 to 845 billion cubic feet in 1969. Natural gas has been used for electric power production in thermal plants, for space heating, and as a raw material for the chemical industry. Less than 1 percent has been exported through a pipeline to Hungary.

Western observers believe that imports of natural gas from the Soviet Union may be initiated in the early 1970s. This belief is based on information that a gas pipeline to be built from the Soviet Union to Bulgaria will pass through eastern Romania, fairly close to the major port of Constanta, which is far removed from domestic sources of gas. Negotiations to this effect are not known to have taken place.

Deposits of coal are small and, with few exceptions, low grade. Known reserves in 1970 were reported to include less than 1 billion tons of bituminous and anthracite coal and 3.5 billion tons of lignite. Fields at Petrosani in the Jiu Valley of the southern Transylvania Alps contain 98 percent of the bituminous coal reserves; 90 percent of the lignite reserves are located in Oltenia, in the southwestern part of the country. Open pit mining is possible in much of the lignite area.

In order to conserve crude oil and natural gas, production of coal and lignite has been substantially increased and is scheduled to rise rapidly in the 1971–75 period. From 1950 to 1970 total coal output increased at an annual rate of 9.2 percent, including a growth of more than 15 percent per year in lignite output. By 1975 coal output is to reach from 37 million to 38.5 million tons, which corresponds to a planned annual increase of about 10.6 percent from the level of 22.8 million tons mined in 1970. The production of lignite is scheduled to advance more rapidly than that of bituminous and anthracite coal.

Two-thirds of the mined coal tonnage with 56 percent of its caloric content was used in 1970 to fuel electric power plants. Only 1.3 million tons were usable in the manufacture of coke, in large part as an admixture to imported coking coals of superior quality. The severe and growing shortage of domestic coke supplies poses a major obstacle to the expansion of the iron and steel industry. In 1969 it was necessary to import 2.1 million tons of metallurgical coke and 633,000 tons of coking coal.

Workable deposits of iron ore are situated in the vicinity of Reșița and Hunedoara in the southwest. Other known deposits, particularly those at Ruschita and Lueta, have a low metal content and harmful radioactive admixtures. Suitable mining and processing methods to handle these ores have not been developed and are not believed to be economically feasible. Domestic mines provided about 32 percent of requirements in 1965 but only 17 percent in 1970; by 1975 the importance of native iron ores will have further declined. Imports of iron ores almost quadrupled in the 1960s and reached a volume of 3 million tons in 1969. Most of the imports came from the Soviet Union.

Information on basic nonferrous ore reserves is tenuous and, in part, conflicting. The tenor of published reports points to a scarcity of reserves, low metal content of ores, and difficulties in ore processing. The great majority of existing mines are said to have only enough reserves left for a few years' production. Consideration has been given to the recovery of nonferrous metals from industrial wastes, such as blast furnace slag and metallurgical dross. For the time being, domestic reserves appear adequate to cover the needs of lead and zinc production and a portion of the requirements for smelting copper and aluminum. The bulk of bauxite and alumina and a substantial quantity of copper must be imported.

Romania is reported to be extracting small amounts of gold and silver. It is also mining uranium ore, which has been exported to the Soviet Union in exchange for isotopes and enriched uranium for use in experimental nuclear installations.

Timber

The country's 6 million acres of forests constitute a valuable source of raw material. Information on the volume of the annual tree harvests has not been published. Substantial quantities of lumber and, increasingly, of lumber products and furniture have been exported, although at the expense of domestic consumption.

In a program to conserve and rebuild this important resource, which was severely overexploited during World War II, a strict limitation was placed in the early 1950s on the annual volume of timber cut. A further reduction in the amount of timber felling was decreed for the 1971–75 period. Through a more efficient utilization of the timber and the expansion of wood processing, including the manufacture of plywood, chipboard, and furniture, the value of the output, nevertheless, increased substantially. Exports of lumber and wood products accounted for 13.4 percent of total exports in 1970, but this ratio is scheduled to decline to 6 percent in 1975, not because of a reduction in the volume of these exports but as a result of a planned expansion of other industrial and food product exports.

ELECTRIC POWER

Electrical power development has proceeded at a rapid pace. The installed generating capacity of 7.3 million kilowatts in 1970 was four times larger than the capacity available a decade earlier. Eighty-four percent of the installed capacity in 1970 was in thermal power plants, and the remaining 16 percent, in hydroelectric stations. Hydroelectric capacity development had been relatively more rapid, with a sixfold increase during the decade.

The production of electrical energy increased even faster than installed capacity because newly built plants operated at greater efficiency. The output of 35 billion kilowatt-hours in 1970 was 4.6 times greater than output in 1960. Power output is scheduled to reach 58 billion to 60.8 billion kilowatt-hours in 1975. These figures imply an average annual increase in power production of 10.5 to 11.7 percent, compared with an average increase of 16.5 percent in the 1960–70 period. Thermal power plants accounted for 92 percent of the output in 1970, and hydroelectric stations, for only 8 percent. Output per unit of thermal capacity was more than double that of hydroelectric generators. The total hydroelectric power potential that could be economically developed has been estimated at 24 billion kilowatt-hours per year.

The Romanian power grid is connected to the power grids of Bulgaria, Czechoslovakia, and Yugoslavia. This tie-in makes possible a more efficient use of available power through mutual exchanges to equalize the load and provides some insurance in the event of regional power failures.

Almost two-thirds of the thermal energy output in 1970 was based on natural gas fuel, and one-third, on coal—mostly coal of very low quality. Less than 3 percent of the fuel used was accounted for by oil. The proportion of natural gas in the fuel balance was roughly the same as in 1960 but ten percentage points lower than in 1965. The share of coal, particularly of low-grade coal, has been rising, in line with the government's policy of conserving natural gas for use in the petrochemical industry.

In 1971 construction was virtually completed of a huge hydroelectric station at the Iron Gate on the Danube River, built jointly with Yugoslavia and equipped, in part, with turbines made in the Soviet Union. The station's twelve turbines have a total capacity of 2.1 million kilowatts and are planned to produce about 11 billion kilowatt-hours of electricity per year. The output is to be evenly divided between the two participating countries. Nine of the twelve turbines were reported to have been in operation in September, and six were reported to have been connected to the Romanian national power grid in November. Completion of the Romanian portion of the project almost doubled the country's hydroelectric capacity and increased its power output potential by about 15 percent.

A second, much smaller, hydroelectric station with a capacity of 400,000 kilowatts and a planned output of 1.5 billion kilowatt-hours per year is to be built jointly with Yugoslavia on the Danube River below the Iron Gate plant. Plans for this station were to be initialed by the negotiators before the end of 1971, but information on the dates for the start and completion of construction is not available. Plans for the construction of yet another power station on the Danube River, as a joint venture with Bulgaria in the Cernavoda-Silistra area, were announced in the fall of 1971. This station is to have a capacity of 760,000 kilowatts and an annual output of about 3.8 billion kilowatt-hours. Construction is apparently scheduled to begin in 1975.

An agreement with the Soviet Union to build a 440,000-kilowatt nuclear power station, using a Soviet reactor, was signed in May 1970. Construction of the plant is to begin in 1972, and completion is scheduled for 1978. The agreement culminated extensive negotiations with the Soviet Union and several noncommunist countries. The ultimate choice is believed by Western observers to have been dictated primarily by political considerations.

Initial plans for nuclear power plants called for an installed capacity of 1 million kilowatts by 1975 and 2.4 million kilowatts by 1980. Construction was to begin in the 1966–70 period, but this target was not met. A subsequently revised plan for the 1971–80 period envisaged the construction of nuclear plants with a total capacity of from 1.8 million to 2.4 million kilowatts. Construction of the plants was to begin between 1971 and 1975, and their commissioning was to take place in the 1976–80 period. No information has been made public on the contemplated source or sources of the equipment for these plants, other than the agreed-upon Soviet unit. Romania must rely on foreign technical assistance for its nuclear energy program.

ORGANIZATION

In 1969 industry, excluding construction and small private artisan shops, comprised 1,151 enterprises employing almost 2 million persons. Seventy percent of the enterprises, which included 92 percent of the employed persons, were owned and operated by the state, and the remaining were run by collectives, including collective farms. State industry produced 95.7 percent of the gross output; collective enterprises contributed 4.1 percent; and private establishments accounted for only 0.2 percent of total production.

Seventy percent of the state industrial enterprises, which included 89 percent of the persons employed by the state, were administered by central authorities; the remaining were subject to the jurisdiction of local government bodies. Collective enterprises are subject to governmental controls; their activities are covered by the annual and five-year economic plans, and many of the enterprises act as suppliers of tools, spare parts, and miscellaneous equipment to state enterprises on a contractual basis. Their main function, however, is to provide consumer goods and services for the population.

Centrally administered enterprises include the largest and most important industrial units. A consolidation of these enterprises in 1969 reduced their number by half and correspondingly increased their average size. Employment per enterprise in 1969 averaged 2,860 persons; it ranged from 800 persons in printing to more than 8,000 persons in the leather and footwear industry. Individual enterprises may be composed of more than one plant, which accounts, in part, for the large number of workers. Over 60 percent of the enterprises under central government administration had more than 1,000 workers each, and almost 27 percent employed more than 3,000 workers per enterprise.

Enterprises under local government jurisdiction were generally smaller—95 percent of these employed from 200 to 2,000 workers each—but even in this group there were som enterprises with more than 5,000 workers. Collective enterprises were still smaller—77 percent employed no more than 500 workers per unit. One collective enterprise, nevertheless, employed between 2,000 and 3,000 workers.

Employment in construction totaled 648,000 persons in 1969. Information on the number and organization of construction enterprises is not available.

The internal management structure of state enterprises has undergone a transformation. By decision of the party's Central Committee in April 1968, amplified by another decision in May 1970, the principle of collective management replaced that of one-man management in all enterprises and state economic organizations. Management committees are chaired by enterprise directors and consist of the following members: the managerial personnel, appointed by the ministry; the chairmen of the trade union, as legal representatives of the enterprise trade union committees; the secretaries of the party committees and of the communist youth organizations in the enterprises; and a number of employee representatives.

The secretaries of the two party organizations were given full membership in May 1970 in a move to strengthen the control by the party. Before that date the secretaries of the party committees merely participated in the discussions, and the secretaries of the communist youth organizations played no role at all. County and municipal party organs also provide direction for the management committees' work.

According to party decisions, the management committees are deliberative organs with powers to make decisions concerning the conduct of the technical, economic, and social activities of the enterprise. Two-thirds of the membership constitutes a quorum, and decisions can be adopted by a simple majority of those present. In cases of disagreement between the committee chairman (the enterprise director) and a majority of the management committee, the matter is submitted for resolution to the higher administrative body.

A lack of legislation to legalize the institution of the management committees and conflict of the new party directive with earlier legislation that established the principle of one-man management hampered the introduction of the new management system. No clear-cut guidelines were provided for the scope of the management committees' competence or the numerical strength of employee representation. The function of the management committees was also undermined by higher administrative echelons through continued imposition of detailed directives concerning the work of the enterprises—contrary to the announced party policy of loosening central controls. Confusion prevailed about the relationships between management, management committees, and higher economic bodies.

There is no evidence on the effectiveness of the supplemental party decision of May 1970 in resolving the problems besetting the functioning of the management committees. A new law on the organization and management of state enterprises and institutions was passed by the General Assembly toward the end of 1971, but information on the provisions of that law was not available in early 1972.

Another new element in the management of enterprises is the

general assembly of employees, introduced in 1968 along with the management committees in accordance with the principles of collective management and socialist democracy. Adequate legislation to formalize the new institution had not been passed by late 1971, but an appropriate provision may have been included in the new law on industrial organization.

As described by a high government official, the general assembly of employees or, in the case of large enterprises, of employee representatives is a forum that will assure effective participation by workers and specialists in the organization and management of the economy and in decisionmaking concerning the fulfillment of enterprise plans. General assemblies are supposed to exercise control over the activities of management committees. Their authority extends beyond the discussion of problems and evaluation of performance to recommending and adopting decisions.

General assemblies are convened twice a year. On these occasions the enterprise management committee must present to the assembly reports on the committee's activities, on the results of enterprise operations, and on the fulfillment by the enterprise of its economic and social obligations. Together with the trade union committee of the enterprise, the management committee must also present to the assembly for discussion and approval the draft of a new collective contract listing mutual obligations of the management committee and of the employees. Decisions reached by the general assembly are obligatory for the management committee. Decisions on measures that require action by higher authorities must be handled by the relevant bodies responsibly and expeditiously.

Representatives of superior economic organs, including the ministries, and of county and local party committees participate in the work of the general assemblies of employees. The reason given for this participation is the opportunity that it provides for the management to become more familiar with problems of interest to the enterprise.

Available evidence indicates a wide variation among enterprises in the degree of influence exercised by the general assemblies of employees. Toward the end of 1971 some management committees were still reported to be disregarding or downgrading general assembly proposals, but such instances were said to be growing progressively fewer.

Industrial enterprises are grouped into combines, trusts, and, since 1969, so-called industrial centrals. The centrals were created in an attempt to improve the organizational structure of industry, reduce control by the ministries and other central government agencies, and provide greater flexibility, in order to increase industrial efficiency. A major task assigned to the centrals is to introduce specialization of production.

Neither the organizational forms of the centrals nor their authority and responsibility vis-a-vis the enterprises and ministries have been clearly defined or legally established. The resultant uncertainty, experimentation, and bureaucratic disharmony have created considerable confusion in the administration of industry, which has been inimical to the attainment of the efficiency goal. At the same time, a variety of factors, including a shortage of investment funds, an inflexible price structure, and the method of evaluating enterprise performance, have militated against the expansion of specialization. Industry officials believe that it may require from three to five years to resolve the organizational problems posed by the creation of the centrals and that many other problems will have to be solved before specialization can become a reality.

Industrial combines, trusts, and centrals function under the jurisdiction of industrial ministries, of which there were eleven at the end of 1971 (see ch. 8). Industrial ministries have undergone an almost continuous process of reorganization. New ministries have been created; old ones, abolished; still others, amalgamated and split. Spheres of the ministries' activities have been reshuffled, and their internal structures have been modified—all in the interest of improving socialist industrial organization and raising the efficiency of production. One foreign observer remarked that, whenever something went wrong in the economy, reorganization in one form or another was undertaken in an effort to solve the problem through administrative means.

LABOR

The average number of persons employed in industry in 1969 was 1,980,000, or about 40 percent of total employment excluding those employed on collective farms. Industrial employment had increased by 725,000 persons in the 1960–69 period. Employment in construction grew more rapidly—from 372,000 persons in 1960 to almost 648,000 in 1969. At the end of 1969 women constituted 43 percent of employment in industry and less than 9 percent in construction. In industry, the proportion of women in blue-collar and white-collar jobs was about equal. In construction, however, women occupied one-third of the white-collar positions and only 5 percent of the blue-collar jobs.

A distribution of employment by industry branches is available only for enterprises under the direct jurisdiction of the central government. Of these, machine building and metalworking absorbed 27 percent of the employed; fuels and metallurgy, 15 percent; forestry and woodworking, 15 percent; textile production, 12 percent; and chemicals and food processing, 7 percent each. Several less important industry branches accounted for another 11 percent of industrial employment, and an unlisted residue of fifty enterprises employing almost 100,000 persons, presumably constituting the defense industry, made up the balance of 6 percent.

The growth of employment in the 1960–69 period varied widely among the different industry branches. Whereas the number of employed rose by 60 percent for centrally administered industry as a whole, it increased by almost 2.4 times in the chemical branch, somewhat more than doubled in the production of cellulose and paper, and grew by 80 percent in nonferrous metallurgy and in machine building and metalworking. The lowest increases in employment occurred in the production of fuels, in ferrous metallurgy, and in the manufacture of glass and china. The increases in employment did not necessarily correspond to the priority ratings of the individual branches; high priority branches received relatively much larger investment.

The labor force is numerically redundant but qualitatively inadequate for the needs of modern industry. Despite the existence of labor training programs, there is a shortage of skilled personnel at the intermediate level, such as technicians and foremen. Few workers have professional school training; most acquire their skills through short courses or on-the-job training. The number of skilled workers is too small to allow efficient two-shift operation of plants throughout most of industry. The lack of adequate skills and the associated inept handling and poor maintenance of imported sophisticated machinery have been responsible for frequent breakdowns. The resultant work stoppages and the underutilization of available capacity have had a deleterious effect on productivity.

Because of a high rate of investment and large-scale imports of advanced Western technology and equipment, productivity per worker nevertheless has been rising at a relatively rapid rate. According to official data, productivity in industry increased by an annual average of 7.5 percent in the 1960–69 period, but the increase in 1969 was less than 5 percent. Official plans for the 1971–75 period call for an annual growth in productivity of at least 7.3 percent. Western economists, however, estimated the rise in productivity to have been only 5.6 percent per year in the 1960–67 period, compared to an official figure of 8 percent. Despite the impressive gains, productivity in industry remains low, mainly because of the inadequate qualifications and work habits of the labor force and the shortcomings of industrial organization and management.

Industrial labor discipline has been a subject of continuing concern to party and government. Both labor turnover and absenteeism have been high. During the first nine months of 1969 almost 455,000 workers left their jobs in centrally administered enterprises, in many instances without the requisite official permission. During the same period worktime losses from absenteeism amounted to about 12 million man-hours. Abuse of the provision for leave without pay and loafing on the job have also contributed significantly to losses of worktime. For centrally administered industry as a whole, the loss of worktime from all causes, including stoppages caused by deficiencies of the supply and distribution system, amounted to almost 47 million man-hours in the third quarter of 1969–the equivalent of about 74,400 workers.

Poor labor discipline was officially blamed on the failure of the prevailing wage system to provide adequate work incentives. After some experimentation in the food-processing industry during 1968 and 1969 a new wage system was introduced throughout industry on March 1, 1970, still on an experimental basis. Some of the changes brought about by the highly complex new system included: a reduction in the spread between wage rates in different industry sectors and between the upper and lower limits within certain wage categories; the establishment of in-grade wage differentials depending upon the personal achievement of the worker; a rise in the proportion of basic wages to total pay (which also includes bonuses); and a tightening of the provisions concerning the payment of bonuses. Provision was also made for withholding a portion of the pay in the event that production targets are not fulfilled.

Downgrading the importance of bonuses was intended to stimulate the raising of skill levels by making higher earnings dependent primarily upon promotion to higher wage categories, based on qualification rather than on surpassing quantitative production norms. As a means of reducing labor turnover, a seniority system was introduced, with wage increases based on length of service in the same unit. The reform of the wage system was accompanied by a general rise in wages averaging 12.3 percent.

A further increase in wages is planned for the 1971–75 period. The minimum wage of 800 lei (for value of leu, see Glossary) is to be raised to 1,000 lei in September 1972 and to 1,100 lei in 1975. The average wage is scheduled to reach almost 1,500 lei in 1972 and 1,805 lei at the end of the five-year period. In accordance with past policy, the rise in wages will be kept well below the increase in productivity (see ch. 14).

Along with the modification of the wage system, legal measures were enacted to tighten labor discipline. These measures provide for the imposition of fines up to 10,000 lei for violations of economic contracts and fines of from 50 to 1,000 lei for negligence while on duty; they oblige employees to make good the full amount of any damage for which they are responsible; and they enable the enterprise management to reduce workers' wages when standards of social behavior are not met. Penalties may be imposed by the enterprise director or the management committee. The only recourse open to workers is an appeal to the higher administrative bodies.

The broad concept of standards of behavior offers a wide latitude for the exercise of individual judgment by management. No criteria have been provided for determining the conditions under which wages may be cut or the maximum permissible amount of the wage cuts. The new rules thus introduced an element of discretionary exercise of punitive authority. They also deprived the accused of recourse to the courts, which had been available to them under earlier legislation.

INVESTMENT AND CONSTRUCTION

Industry has consistently received more than half the total investment in the economy. In the 1966–70 period industrial investment out of the state budget (centralized investment) amounted to 162.1 billion lei—a volume almost as great as that invested during the preceding fifteen years. Additional investment out of enterprise resources was only about 1 percent of the total and had been even less in earier years. From 86 to 90 percent of the industrial investment was channeled into branches producing capital goods. Centralized investment in industry during the 1971–75 period is planned at 281.2 billion lei, or about 60 percent of the total planned investment.

Industries producing fuels and energy absorbed the largest share of investment, but their share declined from 51 percent in the 1951–55 period to 31 percent in the 1966–70 period. The high priority accorded to the development of the chemical industry was reflected in a doubling of that industry's investment share from less than 7 percent in the former period to 14 percent in the 1960s. Similarly, a drive for qualitative improvement in machine building and metalworking was accompanied by an increase in the proportion of investment devoted to that industry from a level of 7 to 8 percent in the 1951–65 period to 14 percent in the second half of the 1960s. Ferrous metallurgy absorbed about 10 percent of the investment in the fifteen-year period that ended in 1970. A need to expand exports of manufactured goods and to provide material incentives for the working population stimulated a rise of investment in the light and food industries to 13 percent of the total in the 1966–70 period, compared to a share ranging from 7.5 to 10 percent in earlier five-year periods.

About 48 percent of the industrial investment was absorbed by building construction and installation work, 37 percent was spent on machinery and equipment, and 15 percent was devoted to the increase of working capital. One-third of the investment in machinery and equipment from 1966 to 1969 was used for procurement abroad, that proportion having increased from about one-fifth in the 1956–60 period.

Although substantial progress has been made in the expansion of industrial capacity, construction of new industrial plants has been beset by many problems and has consistently lagged behind official plans. Inadequate planning, poor design, disregard of the limitations of the materials base and of potential markets, improper location, excessive size of projects, and long delays in project development and in construction have been among the difficulties most frequently discussed in the country's press. Completed plants often require years to attain the projected output level, and many plants have never reached it.

Large losses to the economy have also been caused by long delays in installing new equipment, much of it imported at a heavy cost in foreign exchange. At the end of 1969 the Grand National Assembly was officially informed that the volume of unused equipment amounted to 3.5 billion lei; some of the equipment had been lying idle for from ten to twelve years. Government officials realize the urgent need to improve investment performance, particularly in view of the large investment program planned for the 1971–75 period.

PRODUCTION

Industrial production in 1970 was 3.8 times larger than it had been ten years earlier, according to official data. This increase is equivalent to an average annual growth rate of 12.8 percent. A rise of 11.2 percent in industrial output was unofficially reported for 1971. In terms of Western statistical concepts and methods, the annual increase in industrial output was estimated at 11.5 percent for the 1960–68 period, compared to an officially reported growth rate of 13.2 percent. Industrial growth in Romania has been among the highest in countries of Eastern Europe.

In line with the government's priorities, production of capital goods increased at an annual (official) rate of 14.2 percent, and that of consumer goods advanced by 10.2 percent. The proportion of capital goods in the total output therefore increased from 62.9 percent in 1960 to 70.6 percent in 1970; it is scheduled to reach 72.8 percent by 1975. Although the output of consumer goods increased 2.6 times during the ten-year period, the availability of goods to consumers did not rise proportionately because an increasing volume was exported to pay for imports of machinery and raw materials. Shortages of consumer goods, including foodstuffs, were not eliminated by 1971. The output of newly introduced products, such as chemicals and television sets, increased more rapidly in the 1960s than did the output of traditional items (see table 13).

Improving the quality of manufactured products has been a major concern of the party and government, particularly from the point of view of competitiveness in foreign markets. With some exceptions, such as men's and women's knitwear, a lack of competitiveness was clearly demonstrated in mid-1971 by the results of a giant Romanian trade exhibition in Duesseldorf, West Germany. This exhibit was reported to have achieved just the reverse of what was intended and to have demonstrated the inferiority of Romanian goods compared to Western European and Japanese products.

By decrees issued in 1970 and 1971 the State Inspectorate General for Product Quality was established as an organ of the Council of State with wide powers to establish and enforce quality

Table 13. Output of Selected Industrial Products in Romania, 1960 and 1969

Product	Unit of Measure	1960	1969
Pig Iron	thousand metric tons	1,014	3,477
Steel	.... do	1,806	5,540
Coal and lignite	.... do	6,768	16,976
Crude oil	.... do	11,500	12,346
Natural gas	billion cubic feet	365	850
Electricity	million kilowatt-hours	7,650	31,509
Fertilizers*	thousand metric tons	71	720
Artificial fibers	.... do	4	56
Plastics	.... do	12	137
Synthetic rubber	.... do	0	55
Tires	thousand units	743	3,166
Paper	thousand metric tons	140	398
Tractors	units	17,102	24,895
Motor vehicles	.... do	12,123	56,998
Cement	thousand metric tons	3,054	7,515
Timber	million cubic feet	139	186
Textiles	million square yards	393	672
Footwear	million pairs	30	63
Radios	thousand units	167	428
Television sets	.... do	15	221
Sugar	thousand metric tons	391	428

*In terms of plant nutrients

Source: Adapted from *Anuarul Statistic al Republicii Socialiste Romania, 1970* (Statistical Yearbook of the Socialist Republic of Romania, 1970), Bucharest, 1970, pp. 186–195.

standards, including the imposition of economic and criminal sanctions. At the same time, the decrees provided that extra payments be made to individuals and groups of workers who turn out products of superior quality. In announcing the creation of the new agency, Romanian commentators remarked that an administrative approach to the solution of the quality problem was made necessary by the failure of other measures.

BIBLIOGRAPHY

Section I. SOCIAL

Andrews, Colman Robert. "The Rumanian Film Today," *East Europe*, XVIII, Nos. 8–9, August–September 1969, 21–24.

Appleton, Ted. *Your Guide to Romania*. London: Alvin Redman, 1965.

Baldwin, Godfrey (ed.). *International Population Reports*. (U.S. Department of Commerce, Series P–91, No. 18.) Washington: GPO, 1969.

Basdevant, Denise. *Against Tide and Tempest: The Story of Romania*. (Trans., F. Danham and J. Carroll.) New York: Speller and Sons, 1965.

Bass, Robert. "East European Communist Elites: Their Character and History," *Journal of International Affairs*, XX, No. 1, 1966, 106–117.

Blumenfeld, Yorick. *Seesaw: Cultural Life in Eastern Europe*. New York: Harcourt, Brace & World, 1968.

Cloranescu, George B. "Romania After Czechoslovakia: Ceausescu Walks a Tightrope," *East Europe*, XVIII, No. 6, June 1969, 2–7.

Constantinescu, and Curticapeanu. "The Contribution of Culture to the Union of Transylvania with Romania," *Romania Today* [Bucharest], No. 168, December 1968, 10–13.

Cretzianu, Alexandre. (ed.). *Captive Romania*. New York: Praeger, 1956.

Dimancescu, Dan. "Americans Afoot in Rumania," *National Geographic*, CXXXV, No. 6, June 1969, 810–845.

Ergang, R. *Europe Since Waterloo*. Boston: Heath, 1967.

Fejto, Francois. *A History of the People's Democracies*. New York: Praeger, 1971.

Fischer-Galati, Stephen. *Man, State, and Society in East European History*. New York: Praeger, 1970.

―――. *The New Rumania*. Cambridge: Massachusetts Institute of Technology Press, 1967.

―――. *The Socialist Republic of Rumania*. Baltimore: Johns Hopkins Press, 1969.

―――. *Twentieth Century Rumania*. New York: Columbia University Press, 1970.

Fisher-Galati, Stephen. (ed.). *Romania*. New York: Prager, 1957.

Floyd, David. *Rumania, Russia's Dissident Ally.* New York: Praeger, 1965.

Forwood, William. *Romanian Invitation.* London: Garnstone Press, 1968.

Friendly, Alfred, Jr. "Rumanians Calm About Minipurge," *New York Times,* July 25, 1971, 11.

A Handbook of Romania. (Prepared by the Geographical Section of the Naval Intelligence Division, Naval Staff, Admiralty— Royal Navy.) London: His Majesty's Stationery Office, 1920.

Heltai, G.G. "Changes in the Social Structure of East Central European Countries," *Journal of International Affairs,* XX, No. 1, 1966, 165–171.

Hielscher, Kurt. *Rumania: Landscape, Buildings, National Life.* Leipzig: F.A. Brockhaus, 1933.

International Yearbook of Education, XXVIII. Geneva: United Nations Educational, Scientific and Cultural Organization, 1967.

International Yearbook of Education, XXX. Geneva: United Nations Educational, Scientific and Cultural Organization, 1969.

Ionescu-Bujor, C. *Higher Education in Rumania.* Bucharest: Meridiane Publishing House, 1964.

Ionescu, Ghita. *The Break-Up of the Soviet Empire in Eastern Europe.* Baltimore: Penguin Books, 1969.

———. *Communism in Rumania 1944–1962.* London: Oxford University Press, 1964.

Ionescu, Grigore. "The Road of Romanian Architecture," *Romania Today* [Bucharest], No. 151, July 1967, 12–15.

Langer, W.L. (ed.) *An Encyclopedia of World History.* Boston: Houghton Mifflin, 1968.

Lendvai, P. *Eagles in Cobwebs.* Garden City: Doubleday, 1969.

Liber, Benzion, M.D. *The New Rumania: Communist Country Revisited After Sixty Years.* New York: Rational Living, 1958.

Lindsay, Jack. *Romanian Summer.* London: Lawrence and Wishart, 1953.

Lovinescu, Monica. "The Wave of Rumanian Writers," *East Europe,* XVI, No. 12, December 1967, 9–1'.

Mackintosh, May. *Rumania.* London: Robert Hale, 1963.

Manolache, Anghel. *General Education in Rumania.* Bucharest: Meridiane Publishing House, 1965.

Matley, Ian M. *Romania: A Profile.* New York: Praeger, 1970.

Mellor, R.E. *COMECON: Challenge to the West.* New York: Van Nostrand, Reinhold, 1971.

Osborne, R.H. *East-Central Europe.* New York: Praeger, 1967.

Parkin, Frank. *Class Inequality and Political Order.* New York: Praeger, 1971.

Pounds, Norman J.G. *Eastern Europe*. Chicago: Aldine, 1969.

Roberts, Henry L. *Eastern Europe: Politics, Revolution, and Diplomacy*. New York: Knopf, 1970.

"Romania." Pages 1068–1092 in *Europa Yearbook, 1971*, I. London: Europa Publications, 1971.

"Romania." Pages 241–250 in M. Sachs (ed.), *Worldmark Encyclopedia of the Nations*, V: Europe. New York: Harper and Row, 1967.

Roucek, J., and Lottich, K. *Behind the Iron Curtain*. Caldwell, Idaho: Caxton Printers, 1964.

"Rumania." Pages 726–746 in *Encyclopaedia Britannica*, XIX. Chicago: William Benton, 1969.

"Rumania." Pages 965–975 in *World Survey of Education*, IV. New York: United Nations Educational, Scientific and Cultural Organization, 1966.

"Rumanian Literature." Pages 749–750 in *Encyclopaedia Britannica*, XIX. Chicago: William Benton, 1969.

Sbarces, George. "Jora at the Peak of His Creative Power," *Romania Today* [Bucharest], No. 151, July 1967, 25.

Schöpflin, George (ed.). *The Soviet Union and Eastern Europe*. New York: Praeger, 1970.

Seton-Watson, Hugh. *The East European Revolution*. New York: Praeger, 1968.

Seton-Watson, Robert W. *A History of the Roumanians from Roman Times to the Completion of Unity*. New York: Archon Books, 1963.

Singleton, F.B. *Background to Eastern Europe*. New York: Pergamon Press, 1965.

Statistical Pocket Book of the Socialist Republic of Romania, 1970. Bucharest: Central Statistical Board, 1970.

Stavrianos, L.S. *The Balkans, 1815–1914*. New York: Holt, Rinehart and Winston, 1963.

Steele, Jonathan. "The Maverick of Eastern Europe," *Manchester Guardian Weekly* [Manchester, England], CVI, No. 1, January 1, 1972, 6.

————. "Problems of an Old-Style Pedagogue," *Manchester Guardian Weekly* [Manchester, England], CVI, No. 1, January 1, 1972, 6.

Steinberg, Jacob (ed.). *Introduction to Rumanian Literature*. New York: Twayne Publishers, 1966.

Thompson, Juliet. *Old Romania*. New York: Scribner's, 1939.

Toland, John. *The Last 100 Days*. New York: Random House, 1966.

United Nations Educational, Scientific and Cultural Organization.

International Conference on Public Education: Summary Report (XXXI Session.) Geneva: 1968, 110–112.

U.S. Department of Commerce. Office of Technical Services. Joint Publications Research Service—JPRS (Washington). The following items are from the JPRS series *Translations on Eastern Europe: Political, Sociological, and Military Affairs.*

"Adult Education Program Examined," *Lupta de Clasa,* Bucharest, August 1970. (JPRS: 51,572, Series No. 272, 1970.)

"Adult Education Program, Examined, Praised," *Munca,* Bucharest, September 3, 1970. (JPRS: 51,745, Series No. 283, 1970.)

"Better Coordination Between Specialized Schools and Production," *Scinteia,* Bucharest, April 20, 1971. (JPRS: 53,539, Series No. 377, 1971.)

"Care in Criticism of Past Culture Urged," *Scinteia,* Bucharest, December 1, 1968. (JPRS: 47,202, Series No. 59, 1969.)

"Center for Education Information and Documentation," *Buletinul Oficial al Republicii Socialiste Romania,* Bucharest, April 15, 1971. (JPRS: 53,289, Series No. 364, 1971.)

"Changes in the Social Structure, 1960–1969," *Viata Economica,* XVI, Bucharest, April 16, 1971. (JPRS: 53,159, Series No. 356, 1971.)

"Changes Urged in Policy of Admitting Students to Higher Education," *Scinteia,* Bucharest, January 12, 1971. (JPRS: 52,452, Series No. 317, 1971.)

"Decree Governing Assignment of Graduates," *Buletinul Oficial al Republicii Socialiste Romania,* Bucharest, June 8, 1970. (JPRS: 51,399, Series No. 261, 1970.)

"Delays in Providing Modern School Equipment Cited," *Scinteia,* Bucharest, January 8, 1969. (JPRS: 47,598, Series No. 76, 1969.)

"Development of School System Discussed," *Scinteia,* Bucharest, January 12, 1969. (JPRS: 47,411, Series No. 68, 1969.)

"Economy Modernization Discussed in Relation to Socioprofessional Mobility," *Lupta de Clasa,* V, Bucharest, May 1970. (JPRS: 50,830, Series No. 308, 1970.)

"Equality at Law for National Minorities," *Scinteia,* Bucharest, April 11, 1971. (JPRS: 53,155, Series No. 355, 1971.)

"Government Revises Setup of Education," *Buletinul Oficial al Republicii Socialiste Romania,* Bucharest, December 29, 1968. (JPRS: 47,447, Series No. 68, 1969.)

"Harmful Influence of Religion Stressed," *Romania Libera,*

Bucharest, May 9, 1969. (JPRS: 48,249, Series No. 105, 1969.)

"Law on Education in Rumania," *Romania Libera,* Bucharest, May 15, 1968. (JPRS: 45,795, Series No. 8, 1968.)

"New Secondary School Class Program Discussed," *Gazeta Invatamintului,* Bucharest, August 28, 1968. (JPRS: 46,589, Series No. 32, 1968.)

"New Stage in General Education Discussed," *Revista de Pedagogu,* Bucharest, September 1969. (JPRS: 49,412, Series No. 162, 1969.)

"Organization, Operation of the Department of Cults," *Buletinul Oficial al Republicii Socialiste Romania,* Bucharest, August 15, 1970. (JPRS: 51,850, Series No. 289, 1970.)

"Political Education at Universities, Examined," *Scinteia,* Bucharest, January 29, 1969. (JPRS: 47,585, Series No. 75, 1969.)

"Position of First Deputy Minister of Education Established," *Buletinul Oficial al Republicii Socialiste Romania,* Bucharest, August 4, 1971. (JPRS: 54,004, Series No. 409, 1971.)

"Program for the Advanced Training of Teachers Explained," *Scinteia Tineretului,* Bucharest, January 11, 1971. (JPRS: 52,487, Series No 318, 1971.)

"Proper Training of Teachers Stressed," *Scinteia,* Bucharest, January 24, 1969. (JPRS: 47,598, Series No. 76, 1969.)

"Reorganization of Ministry of Education," *Buletinul Oficial al Republicii Socialiste Romania,* Bucharest, January 14, 1969. (JPRS: 47,598, Series No. 76, 1969.)

"Role of Intelligentsia in Socialist Society," *Lupta de Clasa,* Bucharest, April 1971. (JPRS: 53,730, Series No. 393, 1971.)

"Role of Science Education in Economic Development," *Probleme Economice,* Bucharest, April 1971. (JPRS: 53,289, Series No. 364, 1971.)

"Role of Technical Schools in Preparing Labor Force," *Invatamintul Professional si Technic,* Bucharest, June 1970. (JPRS: 52,243, Series No. 249, 1970.)

"Romania Starts 10-Year Compulsory Education," *Scinteia,* Bucharest, June 4, 1969. (JPRS: 48,448, Series No. 115, 1969.)

"Rumanian Education Growth, Improvement Noted," *Scinteia,* Bucharest, September 16, 1968. (JPRS: 46,737, Series No. 37, 1968.)

"School-Workshops Planned for General and Secondary Education," *Scinteia*, Bucharest, August 10, 1971. (JPRS: 53,970, Series No. 408, 1971.)

"Shortcomings in Workers' Universities Examined," *Scinteia*, Bucharest, September 17, 1968. (JPRS: 46,697, Series No. 36, 1968.)

"Social Mobility, Stratification, Examined," *Lupta de Clasa*, Bucharest, October 1970. (JPRS: 52,070, Series No. 298, 1970.)

"Social Responsibility of Schools Stressed," *Scinteia Tineretului*, Bucharest, January 11, 1971. (JPRS: 52,487, Series No. 318, 1971.)

"Special Secondary Schools Train for Jobs," *Lupta de Clasa*, Bucharest, February 1971. (JPRS: 50,552, Series No. 216, 1970.)

"A Study of Rumanian Family Life, I, II," *Munca*, Bucharest, August 29, 1967. (JPRS: 42,826, Series No. 427, 1967.)

"A Study of Rumanian Family Life, III, IV, V," *Munca*, Bucharest, September 9, 1967. (JPRS: 42,881, Series No. 473, 1967.)

"Training of Labor Force, Vocational Guidance of Youth," *Lupta de Clasa*, Bucharest, December 1970. (JPRS: 52,420, Series No. 315, 1971.)

"Unity of Rumanians and Ethnic Minorities Stressed," *Scinteia*, Bucharest, November 6, 1968. (JPRS: 47,118, Series No. 51, 1968.)

"Working Class Role in Modern Romania Sketched," *Probleme Economice*, Bucharest, December 1969. (JPRS: 49,942, Series No. 188, 1970.)

U.S. Department of Health, Education, and Welfare. Office of Education. *Education in the Rumanian People's Republic* by Randolph L. Braham. (Bulletin OE–14087, I, pp 1–229.) Washington: GPO, 1964.

U.S. Department of State. Bureau of Public Affairs. *Background Notes: Socialist Republic of Romania.* (Department of State Publication 7890.) Washington: GPO, 1970.

Vali, F.A. "Transylvania and the Hungarian Minority," *Journal of International Affairs*, XX, No. 1, 1966, 32–44.

Wardle, Irving. "Rumanian Theatre Plays Vital Part in Daily Life," *New York Times*, June 12, 1971, 18.

Warnstrom, Bennett. "With TV Camera Through Rumania," *East Europe*, XVIII, No. 10, October 1969, 11–16.

"Wheeling and Dealing in Rumania," *Newsweek*, LXXVII, No. 14, April 5, 1971, 39.

Wolff, Robert L. *The Balkans in Our Time*. Cambridge: Harvard University Press, 1956.

World Population Data Sheet, 1970. Washington: Population Reference Bureau, 1970.

"Writer's Block," *Newsweek*, March 2, 1970, 38–43.

Section II. POLITICAL

Andrews, Colman Robert. "The Rumanian Film Today," *East Europe*, XVIII, Nos. 8–9, August–September 1969, 21–24.

Anuarul Statistic al Republicii Socialiste Romania, 1970 (Statistical Yearbook of the Socialist Republic of Romania, 1970). Bucharest: Directia Centrala de Statistica, 1970.

Bromke, Adam (ed.). *The Communist States at the Crossroads*. New York: Praeger, 1965.

Brown, J.F. "Rumania Today I: Towards Integration," *Problems of Communism*, XVIII, No. 1, January–February 1969, 8–17.

———. "Rumania Today II: The Strategy of Defiance," *Problems of Communism*, XVIII, No. 2, March-April 1969, 32–38.

Brzezinski, Zbigniew K. "Communist State Relations: The Effect on Ideology," *East Europe*, XVI, No. 3, March 1967, 1–5.

Byrnes, Robert F. (ed.) *The United States and Eastern Europe*. Englewood Cliffs: Prentice-Hall, 1967.

Ceausescu, Nicolae. "Romania's Foreign Policy," *East Europe*, XX, No. 1, January 1971, 28–34.

Cretzianu, Alexandre (ed.). *Captive Romania*. New York: Praeger, 1956.

Davis, Fitzroy. "East Europe's Film Makers Look West," *East Europe*, XVII, No. 5, May 1968, 27–31.

Editor & Publisher International Yearbook, 1970. New York: Editor & Publisher, 1970.

Farlow, Robert L. "Romanian Foreign Policy: A Case of Partial Alignment," *Problems of Communism*, XX, No. 6, November-December 1971, 54–63.

Farrell, R. Barry. *Political Leadership in Eastern Europe and the Soviet Union*. Chicago: Aldine, 1970.

Fischer-Galati, Stephen. *The Socialist Republic of Rumania*. Baltimore: Johns Hopkins Press, 1969.

———. *Twentieth Century Rumania*. New York: Columbia University Press, 1970.

Fischer-Galati, Stephen (ed.). *Romania*. New York: Praeger, 1957.

Griffith, William E. (ed.) *Communism in Europe*, I and II. Cambridge: Massachusetts Institute of Technology Press, 1967.

Ionescu, Ghita. *Communism in Rumania 1944–1962*. London: Oxford University Press, 1964.

Jowitt, Kenneth. "The Romanian Communist Party and the World Socialist System: A Redefinition of Unity," *World Politics*, XXIII, No. 1, October 1970, 38–60.

Matley, Ian M. *Romania: A Profile*. New York: Praeger, 1970.

Olson, Kenneth E. *The History Makers*. Baton Rouge: Louisiana State University Press, 1966.

"Romania." Pages 1068–1092 in *Europa Yearbook, 1971*, I. London: Europa Publications, 1971.

"Romania." Pages 241–250 in M. Sachs (ed.), *Worldmark Encyclopedia of the Nations*, V: Europe. New York: Harper and Row, 1967.

Schöpflin, George (ed.). *The Soviet Union and Eastern Europe*. New York: Praeger, 1970.

Special Operations Research Office. The American University. Pages 1–69 in *Mass Communications in Eastern Europe-Romania*, VII. Washington: GPO, 1958.

Stanley, Timothy W., and Whitt, Darnell M. *Detente Diplomacy: United States and European Security in the 1970s*. Cambridge: Harvard University Press, 1970.

The Stateman's Year Book, 1971–1972. (Ed., J. Paxton.) New York: Saint Martin's Press, 1971.

Statistical Pocket Book of the Socialist Republic of Romania, 1970. Bucharest: Central Statistical Board, 1970.

Stebbins, R., and Amoia, A. *Political Handbook and Atlas of the World*. New York: Simon and Schuster, 1970.

Steele, Jonathan. "The Maverick of Eastern Europe," *Manchester Guardian Weekly* [Manchester, England], CVI, No. 1, January 1, 1972, 6.

————. "Problems of an Old-Style Pedagogue," *Manchester Guardian Weekly* [Manchester, England], CVI, No. 1, January 1, 1972, 6.

"Television in Eastern Europe," *East Europe*, XV, No. 4, April 1966, 12–16.

Triska, Jan F. (ed.) *Constitutions of the Communist Party-States*. Stanford: Hoover Institution Press, 1968.

United Nations Educational, Scientific and Cultural Organization. *World Communications*. New York: 1970.

United Nations Statistical Yearbook. New York: United Nations Statistical Office, 1970.

U.S. Congress. 80th, 2d Session. Senate. Committee on Foreign Relations. *The Warsaw Pact: Its Role in Soviet Bloc Affairs*. Washington: GPO, 1966.

U.S. Congress, 91st, 2d Session. Committee on the Judiciary. *World Communism, 1967–1969: Soviet Efforts to Re-establish Control.* Washington: GPO, 1970.

U.S. Department of Commerce. Office of Technical Services. Joint Publications Research Service—JPRS (Washington). The following items are from the JPRS Series *Translations on Eastern Europe: Political, Sociological, and Military Affairs.*

"Ceausescu on Film Industry Shortcomings," *Scinteia,* Bucharest, March 7, 1970. (JPRS: 52,712, Series No. 330, 1971.)

"Cultural Responsibility of Editors," *Scinteia,* Bucharest, August 18, 1971. (JPRS: 54, 448, Series No. 437, 1971.)

"Culture, Ideology and Current Events," *Luceafarul,* Bucharest, May 11, 1968. (JPRS: 45,815, Series No. 9, 1968.)

"Current Publishing System Described," *Carti Noi,* Bucharest, August 1971. (JPRS: 54,538, Series No. 443, 1971.)

"Democracy Equated with Worker Participation," *Lupta de Clasa,* Bucharest, May 1971. (JPRS: 53,722, Series No. 391, 1971.)

"Draft Law on Establishing Judicial Commissions," *Romania Libera,* Bucharest, November 3, 1968. (JPRS: 47,085, Series No. 54, 1968.)

"Favoritism Hampers Bucharest Film Enterprise," *Munca,* Bucharest, March 15, 1970. (JPRS: 50,335, Series No. 206, 1970.)

"Fight Against Immoral Foreign Films Urged," *Scinteia,* Bucharest, July 9, 1971. (JPRS: 53,927, Series No. 406, 1971.)

"Judicial Commissions Seen as Development," *Munca,* Bucharest, November 7, 1968. (JPRS: 47,118, Series No. 55, 1968.)

"Mass and Public Organizations Studied," *Revista Romana de Drept,* Bucharest, Vol. VI, June 1968. (JPRS: 46,478, Series No. 30, 1968.)

"Measure Related to Operative of State Committee for Culture and Art," *Buletinul Oficial al Republicii Socialiste Romania,* Bucharest, July 24, 1970. (JPRS: 51,561, Series No. 271, 1970.)

"Membership in State Committee for Culture and Art Presented," *Buletinul Oficial al Republicii Socialiste Romania,* Bucharest, July 25, 1970. (JPRS: 51,507, Series No. 269, 1970.)

"Membership of Romanian National Radio-Television Council," *Munca,* Bucharest, March 9, 1971. (JPRS: 53,052, Series No. 349, 1971.)

"National Sovereignty, Internationalism Discussed," *Lupta de Clasa*, Bucharest, Vol. 4, April 1970. (JPRS: 50,631, Series No. 221, 1970.)

"New Rules Govern State Radio-TV Committee," *Buletinul Oficial al Republicii Socialiste Romania*, Bucharest, September 21, 1971. (JPRS: 54,687, Series No. 453, 1971.)

"Organization of Planning Commissions," *Buletinul Oficial al Republicii Socialiste Romania*, Bucharest, Part I, No. 87, July 20, 1970. (JPRS: 51,690, Series No. 280, 1970.)

"Party Initiative in Perfecting Socialist Law," *Munca*, Bucharest, April 17, 1971. (JPRS: 53,499, Series No. 376, 1971.)

"Party-Minded Principles Govern Ideology," *Lupta de Clasa*, Bucharest, October 1971. (JPRS: 54,641, Series No. 450, 1971.)

"Popescu Speaks at Party Conference on TV Problems," *Presa Noastra*, Bucharest, April 1970. (JPRS: 50,854, Series No. 231, 1971.)

"Problems in Publishing Sociopolitical Literature," *Scinteia*, Bucharest, November 30, 1971. (JPRS: 54,835, Series No. 461, 1972.)

"Responsibilities of Editors Outlined," *Scinteia*, Bucharest, May 16, 1969. (JPRS: 48,291, Series No. 107, 1969.)

"Socialist Unity Front National Council Members," *Romania Libera*, Bucharest, November 20, 1968. (JPRS: 47,202, Series No. 59, 1969.)

"Textbook Publication Schedule Lags," *Scinteia*, Bucharest, January 16, 1971. (JPRS: 52,347, Series No. 311, 1971.)

"Training of Cadres in Local Administration and Economy," *Romania Libera*, Bucharest, April 17, 1971. (JPRS: 53,499, Series No. 376, 1971.)

"Trofin Attacks Radio-TV Producers for Indecent Attitudes," *Munca*, Bucharest, August 11, 1971. (JPRS: 53,958, Series No. 407, 1971.)

"Work of Association of Jurists in Developing Socialist Awareness," *Revista Romana de Drept*, Bucharest, May 1971. (JPRS: 53,722, Series No. 392, 1971.)

Urbanek, Lida. "Romania." Pages 714–727 in Richard F. Staar (ed.), *Yearbook on International Communist Affairs, 1969*. Stanford: Hoover Institution Press, 1970.

———. "Romania." Pages 75–84 in Richard F. Staar (ed.), *Yearbook on International Communist Affairs, 1970*. Stanford: Hoover Institution Press, 1971.

Wolfe, Thomas W. *Soviet Power and Europe 1965–1969*. Santa Monica: Rand Corporation, 1969.

World of Learning, 1970–1971. London: Europa Publications, 1970.

World Radio-TV Handbook, 1971. (Ed., J.M. Frost.) Hvidovre, Denmark: World Radio-TV Handbook, 1971.

(Various issues of the following periodicals were also used in the preparation of this section: *Current History* [Philadelphia], April 1967; *East Europe* [New York], January 1967–December 1971; *Economist-Foreign Report* [London], August-December 1971; *Manchester Guardian Weekly* [Manchester, England], January 1, 1972; *Newsweek* [New York], July 20, 1970, and August 9, 1971; *New York Times*, November 5, 1971–January 1972; *Washington Post*, October 19–December 27, 1971.)

Section III. NATIONAL SECURITY

Baldwin, Godfrey (ed.). *International Population Reports.* (U.S. Department of Commerce, Series P–91, No. 18.) Washington: GPO, 1969.

Blumenfeld, Yorick. *Seesaw: Cultural Life in Eastern Europe.* New York: Harcourt, Brace & World, 1968.

Bromke, Adam (ed.). *The Communist States at the Crossroads.* New York: Praeger, 1965.

Dupuy, T.N. *Almanac of World Military Power.* Dun Loring, Virginia: T.N. Dupuy Associates, 1970.

Fischer-Galati, Stephen. *The New Rumania.* Cambridge: Massachusetts Institute of Technology Press, 1967.

Liber, Benzion, M.D. *The New Rumania: Communist Country Revisited After Sixty Years.* New York: Rational Living, 1958.

Mackintosh, May. *Rumania.* London: Robert Hale, 1963.

The Military Balance, 1970–1971. London: Institute for Strategic Studies, 1970.

"Rumania." Pages 726–746 in *Encyclopaedia Britannica*, XIX. Chicago: William Benton, 1969.

Statistical Pocket Book of the Socialist Republic of Romania, 1970. Bucharest: Central Statistical Board, 1970.

U.S. Department of Commerce. Office of Technical Services. Joint Publications Research Service—JPRS Series (Washington). The following items are from the JPRS Series *Translations on Eastern Europe: Political, Sociological, and Military Affairs.*

"Border Guards Removed from Ministry of Internal Affairs," *Bulentinul Oficial al Republicii Socialiste Romania*, Bucharest, September 25, 1971. (JPRS: 54,397, Series No. 429, 1971.)

"Collaboration with Armies of All Socialist Countries

Stressed," *Scinteia*, May 9, 1971. (JPRS: 53,397, Series No. 370, 1971.)

"Decree on Border Protection System Passed," *Scinteia*, Bucharest, November 14, 1969. (JPRS: 49,241, Series No. 156, 1969.)

"Decree Organizes Office of Prosecutor General," *Scinteia*, Bucharest, Spetember 29, 1971. (JPRS: 54,361, Series No. 432, 1971.)

"Draft Law Established Judicial Commissions," *Romania Libera*, Bucharest, November 3, 1968. (JPRS: 47,085, Series No. 54, 1968.)

"Law Concerning Public Prosecutor's Office Passes," *Scinteia*, Bucharest, December 28, 1968. (JPRS: 47,551, Series No. 73, 1969.)

"Law on Execution of Penalties Adopted," *Buletinul Oficial al Republicii Socialiste Romania*, Bucharest, November 18, 1969. (JPRS: 49,760, Series No. 180, 1970.)

"Law on Police Organization, Functions Adopted," *Buletinul Oficial al Republicii Socialiste Romania*, Bucharest, November 18, 1969. (JPRS: 49,760, Series No. 180, 1970.)

"Law Passed on Organization of Court System," *Scinteia*, Bucharest, December 28, 1968. (JPRS: 47,551, Series No. 73, 1969.)

"Mass and Public Organizations Studied," *Revista Romana de Drept*, No. 6, Bucharest, June 1968. (JPRS: 46,478, Series No. 30, 1968.)

"New Law on Identification Cards, Moving, Residence," *Romania Libera*, Bucharest, March 19, 1971. (JPRS: 53,014, Series No. 347, 1971.)

"Provisions of the New Penal Code Explained." *Revista Romana de Drept*, Bucharest, December 1968. (JPRS: 47,525, Series No. 72, 1969.)

"Rumanian Code of Criminal Procedure," *Buletinul Oficial al Republicii Socialiste Romania*, Bucharest, November 12, 1968. (JPRS: 47,556, Series No. 74, 1969.)

"Statute of Union of Communist Youth," *Scinteia Tineretului*, Bucharest, February 27, 1971. (JPRS: 52,726, Series No. 331, 1971.)

"Supreme Court Chairman Discusses Laws, Freedom," *Scinteia Tineretului*, Bucharest, February 5, 1971. (JPRS: 52,726, Series No. 331, 1971.)

"Training Youth for Military Described," *Viata Militara*, Bucharest, July 1969. (JPRS: 48,913, Series No. 136, 1969.)

"Training Youth for National Defense," *Sport si Technica*,

Bucharest, February 1971. (JPRS: 52,888, Series No. 340, 1971.)

"Warsaw Pact Defends Against Imperialism," *Romania Libera,* Bucharest, May 7, 1971. (JPRS: 53,454, Series No. 374, 1971.)

Section IV. ECONOMIC

Anuarul Statistic al Republicii Socialiste Romania, 1970. (Statistical Yearbook of the Socialist Republic of Romania, 1970). Bucharest: Directia Centrala de Statistica, 1970.

Montias, John Michael. *Economic Development in Communist Romania.* Cambridge: Massachusetts Institute of Technology Press, 1967.

U.S. Congress. 91st, 2d Session. Joint Economic Committee. *Economic Developments in Countries of Eastern Europe.* Washington: GPO, 1970.

U.S. Department of Agriculture, Economic Research Service. *The Agricultural Economy and Trade of Romania.* (ERS-Foreign 320.) Washington: GPO, 1971.

U.S. Department of Commerce. Office of Technical Services. Joint Publications Research Service—JPRS Series (Washington). The following items are from the JPRS Series *Translations on Eastern Europe: Economic and Scientific Affairs.*

"Activities of Romanian Foreign Trade Banks Noted," *Finante si Credit,* Bucharest, August 1971. (JPRS: 54,541, Series No. 568, 1971.)

"Antiquated Methods Hinder Conclusion of Economic Contracts," *Scinteia,* Bucharest, June 13, 1971. (JPRS: 53,695, Series No. 506, 1971.)

"Better Use of Economic Potential," *Probleme Economice,* Bucharest, April 1971. (JPRS: 53,416, Series No. 485, 1971.)

"Development of National Income Discussed," *Probleme Economice,* Bucharest, April 1971. (JPRS: 53,521, Series No. 491, 1971.)

"Development of Trade with Socialist Countries Detailed," *Viata Economica,* Bucharest, March 12, 1971. (JPRS: 53,001, Series No. 459, 1971.)

"Economic Planning Process Described," *Lupta de Clasa,* Bucharest, July 1971. (JPRS: 53,945, Series No. 524, 1971.)

"Foreign Trade, 1966–1970 Reviewed," *Viata Economica,* Bucharest, February 12, 1971. (JPRS: 52,736, Series No. 441, 1971.)

"Foreign Trade Reform Analyzed," *Vierteljahresshefte zur Wirtschaftsvorschung*, West Berlin, July–September 1971. (JPRS: 54,691, Series No. 580, 1971.)

"Improvement of Wholesale Prices Discussed by Specialists," *Viata Economica*, Bucharest, September 11, 1970. (JPRS: 51,680, Series No. 368, 1970.)

"Improvement of Wholesale Price System," *Viata Economica*, Bucharest, September 18 and 25, 1970; October 2 and 16, 1970. (JPRS: 52,117, Series No. 398, 1970.)

"Interest Rates in New Credit System," *Viata Economica*, Bucharest, October 9, 1970. (JPRS: 52,001, Series No. 389, 1970.)

"Local Budgetary Problems, Proposed Measures Cited," *Finante si Credit*, September 1971. (JPRS: 54,748, Series No. 584, 1971.)

"Manpower Distribution Analyzed," *Revista de Statistica*, Bucharest, November 1970. (JPRS: 52,236, Series No. 407, 1970.)

"Measures for Increasing Foreign Trade Efficiency," *Gazeta Finantelor*, Bucharest, December 22, 1970. (JPRS: 52,510, Series No. 426, 1970.)

"Modernization of Planning Advocated," *Probleme Economice*, Bucharest, December 1970. (JPRS: 52,614, Series No. 434, 1970.)

"National Income in 1966–1970, 1971–1975," *Probleme Economice*, Bucharest, May 1971. (JPRS: 53,755, Series No. 510, 1971.)

"New Methods for Planning Agriculture Discussed," *Agricultura*, Bucharest, December 10, 1970. (JPRS: 52,324, Series No. 413, 1970.)

"Profits Termed Essential Indicator of Economic Efficiency," *Scinteia*, Bucharest, November 27, 1971. (JPRS: 54,748, Series No. 584, 1971.)

"Relationship of Domestic, Foreign Prices Influences Export Efficiency," *Finante si Credit*, Bucharest, June 1971. (JPRS: 54,056, Series No. 531, 1971.)

"Significance of Accumulation Rate Analyzed," *Probleme Economice*, Bucharest, October 1971. (JPRS: 54,558, Series No. 570, 1971.)

"Socialist Planning in Light of World Planning," *Probleme Economice*, Bucharest, April 1971. (JPRS: 53,392, Series No. 484, 1971.)

"Structural Changes in Manpower Distribution in 1966–1970," *Viata Economica*, Bucharest, March 12, 1971. (JPRS: 52,942, Series No. 454, 1971.)

GLOSSARY

centrals—Industrial associations that group enterprises engaged in the same or similar lines of production or enterprises at successive stages of production as, for example, iron mines and steel mills.

COMECON—Council for Mutual Economic Assistance. Founded in 1949; headquartered in Moscow. Members are Bulgaria, Czechoslovakia, East Germany, Hungary, Mongolia, Poland, Romania, and the Soviet Union. Purpose is to further economic cooperation among members.

judet (pl., *judete*)—Local administrative division corresponding to county or district. There are thirty-nine such counties plus the municipality of Bucharest, which is administered as a *judet*. There is no intermediate level between the central government and the *judet* government.

leu (pl., lei)—Standard unit of currency. Officially rated at the level of 1 leu to US$0.18, the actual exchange rate varies according to specific transactions, such as tourist exchange, foreign trade exchange, hard currency purchase, or black-market transaction.

PCR—Partidul Comunist Roman (Romanian Communist Party). Founded in 1921. Declared illegal in 1924; operated underground until 1944. Known as Romanian Workers' Party from 1948 until 1965.

UGSR—Uniunea Generala a Sindicatelr din Romania (General Union of Trade Unions). Official organization incorporating all labor unions of blue- and white-collar workers. Estimated membership in 1972 was 4.6 million.

UTC—Uniunea Tineretului Comunist (Union of Communist Youth). Official organization that functions as the youth branch of the PCR (*q.v.*). Membership open to young people between ages fifteen and twenty-six. Membership estimated in early 1972 at 2.5 million.

Warsaw Treaty Organization—Formal name for Warsaw Pact. Military alliance of communist countries founded in 1955, with headquarters in Moscow. The Soviet minister of defense is traditionally the supreme commander of Warsaw Pact forces. Members are Bulgaria, Czechoslovakia, East Germany, Hungary, Poland, Romania, and the Soviet Union.

INDEX

consumer goods: 149, 229, 232, 235, 237, 239, 241, 251, 287–288; export, viii; production, 8, 30, 42

cooperatives: 82, 85, 114, 126, 127; agricultural, 59, 153

Council of Ministers: 109, 110, 112, 114, 115, 116, 118, 119–121, 123, 124, 133, 140, 147, 161, 162, 176, 195, 198, 200, 214, 230, 240, 241, 243, 244, 256

Council for Mutual Economic Assistance (COMECON): iv, 1, 2, 8, 26, 27, 150, 156, 157–158, 159, 161, 164, 168, 169, 172, 173, 174, 247, 249–250, 275

Council of Romanian Radio and Television: 182, 184

Council on Socialist Culture and Education: 94, 120, 176, 181, 186, 189

Council of State: vii, 109, 112, 114, 115, 116, 117–119, 121, 122, 124, 125, 133, 140, 161, 162, 230, 240, 256, 289

Council of State Security: 119, 120, 121

counter-subversion: ix, 194, 202, 205

county. See judet

courts: viii, 115, 122–124, 194, 200, 205, 206–207; military, 223

credit policies: 242, 245–246, 260, 266, 267–269

crime (see also penal system): 193, 194, 196, 199, 201–203, 205, 206, 223, 257

Crimean War: 16

Crisana: 10, 32, 179

cultural activity (see also architecture; arts and the artists; folk culture; literature; music; painting; sculpture): 4, 7, 12, 14, 41, 52, 53, 54, 85, 87, 91, 92, 152

cultural influences: 4, 7, 12, 14–15, 50, 51, 62, 63, 69, 76, 93, 95, 96, 97, 98, 99, 100, 101, 104, 105, 106; nationalism, 7, 92, 97, 102, 104

currency (see also exchange): 246–247

Cuza, Alexander: 16

Cyrillic alphabet: 14

Czechoslovakia: xiv, 20, 21, 30, 46, 163, 165, 172, 182, 190, 218, 224, 250, 278; invasion of, 7, 9, 28, 119, 135, 150, 154, 159, 164, 165, 166, 170, 172, 211, 218

Dacia (see also Dacians): 3, 11, 50, 67, 99

Dacia Literata: 104

Dacians (see also Dacia; Daco-Romans): 2, 10, 11, 14, 50

Daco-Romans: 3

Danube River: 29, 31, 32, 33, 34, 35, 36, 38, 41, 43, 45–46, 47, 48, 55, 167, 216, 217, 254, 279; history, 10, 11, 12, 99

death rate: 39

defense (see also armed forces; security): 116, 195, 241; Commission, 117

Defence Council: 115, 118, 121, 133, 135, 140, 173, 213, 214

Densus: 99

Department of Cults: 5, 66

Description of Moldavia: 104

divorce: 57, 58

Dobruja: vii, 31, 32, 33, 34, 72, 99, 253; history, 10, 20, 37; population, 41, 55

Dogmatic Period: 92, 93

Dragan, Mircea: 103

Draghici, Alexandru: 130, 131, 134

droughts: 254

Dubcek, Alexander: 165

Eastern Europe: v, 8, 68, 94, 110, 155, 156, 158, 165, 166, 169, 172, 173, 182, 216, 218, 262; economic relations, viii, 26, 170, 248

Eastern Orthodox Church (see also Romanian Orthodox Church): 11, 13, 14, 53, 67, 99

Economic Council: 115, 119

economic development (see also Five Year Plan): viii, 6, 8, 17, 61, 73, 119, 149–150, 156, 161, 242; plans, 234–237, 242

economy (see also agriculture; economic development; finance; industry): v, viii, 8, 24, 25, 26, 42, 112, 113, 116, 120, 132, 133, 149, 158, 174, 226–227, 229–237; Commission, 117 education (*see also* adult education; indoctrination; schools; technical/vocational education; universities): viii, 4, 6–7, 14, 15, 16, 60, 61, 62, 66, 73–83, 126, 200; Act (1964), 74; Commission, 117; curricula, viii, 7, 74, 75, 77, 78, 82; higher, 6, 59, 61, 73, 74, 76, 77, 80, 84, 85–86, 107–108; law (1948), 77; law (1968), 78, 87; traffic, 204

Eforie Nord: 100

elections: vii, 23, 116, 117, 126–127; (1937), 19; (1948), 24; (1969), 127, 135

electricity: ix, 277, 278–279, 288; hydro, 29, 36, 167, 278, 279

elite class: 6, 60

emigration: 40–41, 53, 71; illegal, 203; Jews, 4, 72

Eminescu, Mihail: 105, 106

employment (*see also* labor; wages): 41, 59, 84, 154, 195, 233–234, 253, 265, 266, 280, 284–286

Enescu, Georghe: 101

English language: 83, 181, 183

ethnic groups (*see also* individual groups; minority ethnic groups): vii, 3, 49–50, 55–56

European Recovery Program (Marshall Plan): 26, 157

Everac, Paul: 102

exchange, foreign: ix, 187, 230, 242, 244, 247

expenditure: 241

export: 236, 239, 244, 248–249, 251, 253, 286; agricultural, viii, 36, 230, 273

Export-Import Bank: 251

family: 49, 56–58, 226, 257, 259

fauna. *See* wildlife

Federal Republic of Germany: 28, 34, 43, 53, 159, 164, 165, 168–170, 190, 288

Ferdinand, King: 18, 19

films: 103, 175, 177, 189–190

finance (*see also* budget; foreign exchange; investment; taxation; trade): viii–ix

fishing and fisheries: 33

Five-Year Plan: viii, 8; (1960–65), 26; (1971–75), 8, 149–150, 229, 230, 245, 266, 275

floods: 43, 173, 208, 222, 227, 255, 270

folk culture: 65, 91, 94–96, 98, 100–101, 105

foodstuffs: 42–43; export, viii, 30

foreign exchange. *See* exchange

foreign relations: 1, 2, 7, 25, 27, 28, 63, 118, 134, 136, 139, 154, 155, 162–174; Commission, 117; diplomatic representation, 118, 155, 159, 162, 163, 164–172; economic. *See* trade; policy, 116, 120, 133, 152, 156–162, 175

forests and forestry: 29, 30, 32, 33, 35, 36, 85, 233, 255, 277–278, 284; Commission, 117

France: 16, 20, 103, 168, 171, 212, 250; cultural influence, 15, 62, 63, 76, 101, 104, 105, 106, 107, 190; language, 83, 181, 183

freedom of expression (*see also* press): 91–92, 111, 113, 175, 176

frontier troops: ix, 7, 211, 213, 214, 217, 221

fruit (*see also* orchards and vineyards): 254, 272

Galati: 44, 48

gems: 243, 247

General Military Academy, Bucharest: 214, 221

General Regulation for Religious Cults (1948): 66, 70

General Union of Trade Unions: 120, 121, 133, 134, 136, 147, 148–149, 178, 198, 237, 243

geology: 30–32

Georgescu, Ion: 98

German Democratic Republic: 165, 172, 182, 190, 250

German ethnic group (*see also* German language): vii, viii, 3, 4, 18, 49, 51, 53–54, 55, 56, 57, 69, 71, 102, 127, 135, 143, 151; history, 11, 99

German language: vii, 51, 53, 54, 69, 83, 89, 180, 181, 183

Germany (*see also* Federal Republic of Germany; German Democratic Republic; Nazis): 18, 71, 101, 107, 212

Gheorghiu-Dej, Gheorghe: 3, 22, 23, 24, 25, 27, 47, 110, 112, 130, 131, 134, 168; foreign relations, 156, 157, 158, 159, 165

Giurgiu: 43, 44
gold: 277
Goths: 50
government (see also Constitution; local government): vii, 17, 109–110, 115, central, 114–124, 126
Grand National Assembly: 88, 109, 110, 114, 115, 116, 117, 118, 121, 122, 123, 124, 125, 126, 133, 140, 151, 161, 162, 173, 237, 240, 241
Great Britain: 20, 23, 158, 171, 190, 212
Greater Romania: 18
Greece: 170–171
Grigorescu, Nicolae: 97
gross national product (GNP): 227, 233
ground force: 215, 224
Groza Petru: 23

Habsburgs (see also Austro-Hungarian Empire): 14
handcrafts: 94–96
health: 42, 126; Commission, 117; education, 85
Heinemann, Gustav, president of the federal Republic of Germany: 170
Higher Political Council: 213
History of the Rise and Fall of the Ottoman Empire: 104
Hitler, Adolf: 20
Holy See. See Vatican
housing: 40, 41, 42, 57, 58, 59, 61, 99, 195, 201, 233, 245, 256
Hungarian Autonomous Region (Mures-Magyar): 52, 111, 114, 150
Hungarian ethnic group (Magyars) (see also Hungarian language): vii, viii, 3, 4, 18, 49, 51, 52–53, 55, 56, 57, 69, 71, 72, 102, 111, 127, 135, 143, 151, 166; history, 3, 11, 13, 37, 52, 63, 99
Hungarian language: vii, 51, 53, 69, 83, 89, 180, 181, 183
Hungarian People's Union: 23
Hungary (see also Austro-Hungarian Empire): 37, 43, 46, 54, 163, 165, 166, 167, 172, 182; border, vii, xiv, 10, 29, 38, 52, 203, 217; history, 11, 19, 20, 21, 52, 53, 55, 67; revolt, 26, 157

Iasi: 15, 105, 182, 186, 189, 213
ideological campaign: 152, 153, 154, 175, 178, 184
imports: 229, 239, 248, 249, 251, 253, 277, 284, 287; substitute, 244
income: 40, 41, 59, 60, 61, 153, 240, 260, 264; church, 66; national, 231, 232, 253; per capita, 230
independence: 15–17, 113, 135, 160; 'declaration of', 1, 2, 27
indoctrination, political (see also propaganda): viii, ix, 132, 133, 139, 141, 144, 145, 146, 175, 176, 178, 183, 191, 201; armed forces, 211, 221–222; youth, 7, 73, 76, 77, 78–79, 80, 83, 84, 87, 132, 148, 180
industrialization (see also industry): v, 6, 8, 15, 17, 18, 26, 41, 43, 49, 77, 85, 150, 161, 229, 247, 251, 253
industry (see also construction; electricity; industrialization; investment; nationalization): viii, 25, 110, 149, 157, 229–230, 232, 233, 275–283, 287–289; commission, 117; labor, vii–viii, 61, 264, 275, 283–286
information (see also newspapers; periodicals; press; radio; television): ix, 65, 175–177, 190–191; foreign, 132, 152, 175, 181–182, 184, 185, 186, 189, 190
Institute of Historical and Social-Political Studies: 139, 145
intelligentsia (see also arts and the artists; professionals): 59, 60, 62, 142, 148
international commitments (see also individual pacts): v, ix, 121, 160, 172–174, 218–219
Intervision: 185
Investment Bank: 242, 243–244
investment, capital: 30, 42, 229, 233, 243, 268; in agriculture, viii, 266–267; foreign, 18; in industry, viii, 232, 275, 286–287
Ionescu, Eugene: 102
iron: 277, 288
Iron Gate: 31, 34, 55; hydroelectricity, 167, 279
Iron Guard: 19, 20, 21
irrigation: 201, 227, 254
Islam: 4, 72
Israel: 4, 28, 41, 72, 159, 164, 171
Italy: 20, 21, 101, 168, 171, 190, 250

312

party politics (*see also* individual parties): 14, 17, 20, 22, 175; single party, 2, 5
pasture: 32, 33, 36, 254, 255, 257
Patrascanu, Lucretiu: 131, 134
Pauker, Ana: 22, 24, 25
peasantry (*see also* folk culture, working class): 53, 58, 61, 62, 68, 74, 148, 153; history, 12, 13; revolt, 17
penal system: 201–202, 257; code, 194, 205–206, 222; institutions, 207–209
people's councils: 111, 114, 115, 116, 124, 125, 126, 196; Commission, 117
People's Democratic Front: 24, 127, 135
People's Republic of China (*see also* Sino-Soviet issue): 1, 27, 157, 158, 164, 167, 168, 250
periodicals: 53, 176, 180–181, 182; library, 105, 107, 152
Peter, tsar of Russia: 2
petroleum: ix, 17, 20, 29, 37, 47, 276, 278
Petrosani: 276
Phanariots: 12–13, 15
Pioneers Organization: 77, 80, 198, 199, 201
pipelines: ix, 29, 47
Ploiesti: 37, 41, 44, 47, 216
Plowmans Front: 22, 23
Poland: xiv, 165, 172, 182, 224
police (*see also* militia): ix, 24, 195, 196, 197, 198, 202, 203; secret, 3, 25, 193, 197
pope: 14, 67, 68, 70, 71
Popescu-Gopo: 103
population: vii, 3, 30, 35, 38–41, 74
ports (*see also* individual ports): ix, 17, 48, 196, 217
president, office and functions: 117, 118, 161, 214
Presidium: 110, 112
press: ix, 23, 93, 139, 176; freedom, 16, 113, 153, 176
prices: 237–240, 249, 283
prime minister, office and functions: 110, 119, 120
private sector: 113–114, 230, 258, 268–269, 273, 280
professionals (*see also* intelligentsia): 6; unions, 94

propaganda (*see also* indoctrination): v, 92, 139, 141, 153, 175, 176, 184, 190
Prosecutor General: 112, 115, 116, 118, 122, 123–124, 202
Protestants (*see also* religion): viii, 4, 5, 13, 53, 71–72
Provisional Revolutionary Government of the Republic of South Vietnam (VietCong): 163, 171
Prut River: 29, 30, 31, 33, 38, 46
publishing: 147, 175, 176, 177, 185–187
purges, political: 3, 24, 25, 77, 142, 156

Radescu, Nicolae, General: 22, 23
radio: ix, 54, 101, 175, 176, 177, 182–184, 191, 288
Radulescu, Ehade: 104
railways: ix, 16, 29, 43–45, 194, 196, 227
reform: 14, 16, 19, 132, 133, 153; economic, 8, 19, 231, 237, 248, 285; education, 73, 77–79; land, 16, 17, 18, 55, 58
religion (*see also* church-state relations; clergy; Protestants; Roman Catholicism; Romanian Orthodox Church): viii, 4, 5, 62, 65–66, 127; education, 4, 14, 66, 69, 72, 75, 76, 112; freedom of, viii, 5, 65, 68, 111; persecution of 4, 65, 68, 70
Republic of Vietnam (South Vietnam): 170, 171
research: 107–108
revenue (*see also* taxation): 241, 269
riparian rights: vii
rivers (*see also* individual rivers; riparian rights; waterways): ix, 29, 31, 33–34, 36
roads and highways: ix, 29, 43, 44, 99, 203, 227
Rodin, Auguste: 98
Roman Catholicism (*see also* church-state relations; religion): viii, 4, 13, 53, 67, 69–71
Romania Libera: 178, 179
Romanian Academy of Social and Political Sciences: 82
Romanian Air Transport (TAROM): ix, 46
Romanian Communist Party (Partidul Comunist Roman, PCR): vi,

ence over Romania, v, viii, 1, 5, 7, 9, 24, 76, 92, 110, 111, 137, 152, 156, 158, 198; trade, viii, 190, 250, 276, 277; World War II, 9, 20, 21

Stalin, Joseph (see also Stalinism): 2, 7, 9, 25, 156

Stalinism: 2, 25, 156; deStalinization, 7, 92, 134–136, 157

State Committee for Prices: 115, 120, 237, 239, 240

state enterprises: 80, 82, 87, 119, 120, 126, 141, 188, 194, 230, 231, 234–237, 238, 239, 242, 243, 246, 248, 281, 283; farms, 257, 258, 261–262, 267, 273; industry, 280, 283

State Inspectorate General for Product Quality: 289

State Planning Committee: 119, 120, 121, 237, 242, 243

State Security Council: 195, 197, 198

Stephan Gheorghiu Academy of Social-Political Education and the Training of Leading Cadres: 139, 144

Stephen the Great (1457-1504): 12

Stoica, Chivu: 130, 131, 133, 136

Storck, Carol: 98

Storck, Karl: 98

students (see also schools): 73, 80, 86, 87, 148; organizations, 77, 78, 80, 87, 199, 200

suffrage: 126

sugar beet: 255, 256, 272

Superior Council of Agriculture: 256, 257

Supreme Court: viii, 109, 112, 116, 118, 122, 124, 201, 223

Szeklers: 13, 52, 53

Szekelys. See Szeklers

tambal: 100

TARCM. See Romanian Air Transport

Tatars: 3, 4, 11, 12, 50, 51, 72

Tattarescu, Gheorghe: 97

taxation: 233, 239, 241, 245

teachers: 78, 79, 82, 83, 88, 154; training, 75, 76, 77, 82, 84, 85, 87–88, 89, 144

technical/vocational education: viii, 6, 7, 73, 74, 75, 76, 78, 80, 81, 84, 85, 87, 145, 284

television: ix, 54, 101, 152, 175, 176, 177, 182, 184–185, 288

text books: 2, 78, 80, 82

textiles: 95, 284, 288

theater: 53, 101–102, 105, 152

Thracians. See Dacians

timber: 277–278, 288

Timisoara: 44, 193

Tirgu Mures: 44, 52

Tisza River: 31, 33, 46

Tonitza, Nicolae: 97

topography (see also mountains; rivers): vii, 31, 253

tourists and tourism: 33, 217, 252; exchange rate, ix, 247

trade (see also export; import; individual countries): 232; balance, viii, 8, 169, 173, 229, 242–243, 248, 251–252; domestic, 236; foreign, viii, 27, 155, 162, 163, 164, 167, 168, 170, 171, 172, 173, 217, 229, 230, 237, 246, 247–252

traffic, vehicular: 203–204

Trajan, Column of: 14

Trajan, Emperor: 11, 50, 99

transport (see also air transport; pipelines; railways; roads and highways; traffic; waterways): 43–48, 110, 216, 232

Transylvania (see also Transylvanian Alps): vii, 3, 4, 32, 34, 35, 37, 47, 68, 99, 166, 254, 276; cultural, 94, 95, 99, 103; history, 3, 10, 11, 13–14, 16, 18, 20, 21, 37, 50, 55, 67, 70; population, 41, 52, 53, 54, 56; transport, 43, 47

Transylvanian Alps: vii, 30, 31–32, 33, 35, 47, 276

travel: 61

Treaty of Berlin (1878): 16

'Tudor Vladimirescu': 21

Turkey (see also Ottoman Empire and the Turks; Turks): vii, 15, 16, 170, 171

Turks (see also Ottoman Empire and the Turks): 3, 4, 15, 50, 53, 55

Turnu Severin: 44, 99

UTC. See Union of Communist Youth

underemployment: 233, 253, 264, 265

Uniate Church: 4, 13, 67, 68, 69

Union of Communist Youth (Uniunea Tineretului Comunist, UTC): 77, 78, 80, 87, 120, 133, 147–148, 178, 181, 198–199, 200, 201, 213

Union of Student Associations: 77, 80, 198, 200
Unitarians: 4, 5, 13, 53, 73
United Nations: ix, 155, 168, 170, 172
United Principalities: 16
United States: 23, 167, 170, 190; trade, 158, 246, 250–251
universities (see also University of Bucharest): 75, 76, 80, 81, 84, 85–86, 88, 199, 200, 221; foreign, 15; teachers, 116; workers, 87
University of Bucharest: 107
uranium: 277
urban society: 4, 15, 17, 38, 41, 49, 54, 57, 62, 75, 87, 102, 141, 255, 264, government, 124, 125, 126

Vacarescu, Iancu: 104
Valbudea, Stefan Ionescu: 98
values and traditions: political, 153–154; social, 49, 62–63, 65
Vatican (see also pope): 69, 71
vegetables: 254, 256, 261, 268, 270, 272, 273
vegetation (see also forests and forestry): 36
Vietnam (see also Provisional Revolutionary Government of South Vietnam; Republic of Vietnam): 158
villages: 38, 41, 91, 100; justice, 194
Vlachs: 11, 12, 50
Vyshinsky, Andrei: 23

wages (see also income): 88, 149, 260–261, 263-264, 285; prisoners, 208
Walachia: vii, 31, 32, 34, 35, 36, 43, 47, 254; cultural, 96, 97, 99, 103; history, 3, 10, 11, 12, 13, 15, 16, 37, 67, 74; population, 41, 54

Warsaw Pact. See Warsaw Treaty Organization
Warsaw Treaty Organization (see also Czechoslovakia): ix, 1, 2, 7, 8, 28, 46, 135, 136, 156, 159, 161, 164, 166, 167, 168, 171, 172, 203, 211, 212, 215, 216, 218, 219, 220, 223, 224, 225, 226, 227
waterways: ix, 29, 44, 45–46, 48
West Germany. See Federal Republic of Germany
Western nations (see also individual nations): 163, 164, 169, 171, 182; cultural influence (see also France), 91, 93, 95, 98, 99, 100, 101, 104, 105, 107, 132, 152, 168, 187, 189, 190, economic relations, 8, 25, 27, 158, 168, 229, 230, 246, 247, 248, 250, 251, 275
wildlife: 32–33
women: viii, 39, 40, 57, 79, 141, 143, 180, 181, 208, 209; labor, 56–57, 58, 264, 283; organizations, 5, 126, 127, 135, 147, 199
working class (see also peasantry): 6, 17, 58, 59-60, 61, 86, 92, 126, 142, 143, 148, 149, 152
World Council of Churches: 72
World War I: 3, 4, 9, 17–18, 32, 37, 40, 74, 212
World War II: 9, 20–21, 32, 33, 37, 40, 41, 54, 72, 113, 226, 277

youth (see also students; Union of Communist Youth): 7, 73, 76, 78, 82, 141, 152, 180, 193, 199–201, 203, 219; organizations, 5, 57, 77, 78, 105, 126, 127, 132, 135, 144, 147, 152, 198, 199, 200, 201, 281
Yugoslavia: 3, 33, 39, 46, 164, 166, 167, 182, 219, 278, 279; border, vii, xiv, 10, 29, 34, 37, 216, 217

Zhivkov, Todor: 166

317

PUBLISHED AREA HANDBOOKS

550–65	Afghanistan	550–154	Indian Ocean Territories
550–98	Albania	550–39	Indonesia
550–44	Algeria	550–68	Iran
550–59	Angola	550–31	Iraq
550–73	Argentina	550–25	Israel
550–169	Australia	550–182	Italy
550–176	Austria	550–69	Ivory Coast
550–175	Bangladesh	550–177	Jamaica
550–170	Belgium	550–30	Japan
550–66	Bolivia	550–34	Jordan
550–20	Brazil		
550–168	Bulgaria	550–56	Kenya
550–61	Burma	550–50	Khmer Republic (Cambodia)
550–83	Burundi	550–81	Korea, North
		550–41	Korea, Republic of
550–166	Cameroon		
550–96	Ceylon	550–58	Laos
550–159	Chad	550–24	Lebanon
550–77	Chile	550–38	Liberia
550–60	China, People's Republic of	550–85	Libya
550–63	China, Republic of		
550–26	Colombia	550–163	Malagasy Republic
550–67	Congo, Democratic Republic	550–172	Malawi
	of (Zaire)	550–45	Malaysia
550–91	Congo, People's Republic of	550–161	Mauritania
550–90	Costa Rica	550–79	Mexico
550–152	Cuba	550–76	Mongolia
550–22	Cyprus	550–49	Morocco
550–158	Czechoslovakia	550–64	Mozambique
550–54	Dominican Republic	550–35	Nepal, Bhutan and Sikkim
		550–88	Nicaragua
550–52	Ecuador	550–157	Nigeria
550–43	Egypt		
550–150	El Salvador	550–94	Oceania
550–28	Ethiopia		
		550–48	Pakistan
550–167	Finland	550–46	Panama
		550–156	Paraguay
550–29	Germany	550–92	Peripheral States of the
550–155	Germany, East		Arabian Peninsula
550–173	Germany, Federal	550–185	Persian Gulf States
	Republic of	550–42	Peru
550–153	Ghana	550–72	Philippines
550–87	Greece	550–162	Poland
550–78	Guatemala	550–181	Portugal
550–174	Guinea		
550–82	Guyana	550–160	Romania
		550–84	Rwanda
550–164	Haiti		
550–151	Honduras	550–51	Saudi Arabia
550–165	Hungary	550–70	Senegal
		550–180	Sierra Leone
550–21	India	550–184	Singapore

319

550–86	Somalia	550–80	Turkey
550–93	South Africa, Republic of		
550–171	Southern Rhodesia	550–74	Uganda
550–95	Soviet Union	550–97	Uruguay
550–179	Spain		
550–27	Sudan, Democratic	550–71	Venezuela
	Republic of	550–57	Vietnam, North
550–47	Syria	550–55	Vietnam, South
550–62	Tanzania	550–183	Yemens, The
550–53	Thailand	550–99	Yugoslavia
550–178	Trinidad and Tobago		
550–89	Tunisia, Republic of	550–75	Zambia

☆ U.S. GOVERNMENT PRINTING OFFICE : 1979—O-280-990 (104)